Portraits in Words

Portraits in Words

An Introduction to the
Study of Biography

Edited by **DONALD C. REHKOPF**

Oak Park and River Forest High School, Oak Park, Illinois

 THE ODYSSEY PRESS · *New York*

To the Teachers Who Will Use This Book

HIGH SCHOOL STUDENTS enjoy reading biography. They do not need to be convinced of the value of it—not, at least, in the same way that they must be taught how to appreciate poetry and plays. As Samuel Johnson wrote, "Biography is, of the various kinds of narrative writing, that which is most eagerly read, and most easily applied to the purposes of life." However, as eager as adolescent boys and girls are to read biography, it is nevertheless necessary to have an orderly process of teaching it in order to enable them to gain the full value of this type of literature and to help them apply these values to the "purposes of life." *Portraits in Words,* one of *The Odyssey Texts in Types of Literature,* provides this planned study.

To bring the students to an appreciation of the full value and pleasure of reading biography, two broad approaches are used in this text: Part One, selections illustrating specific benefits that the reading of biography offers; and Part Two, selections edited to show that the reading of biography can give a greater understanding of the sweep and meaning of life.

Of the specific benefits offered by the reading of biography, for Part One I have selected five. The first is the fact that biography introduces the reader to *interesting persons.* The second is that biography illuminates *history.* The third is that biography helps the reader to shed his prejudices and attain *wider sympathies.* The fourth is that biography is a source of *vocational guidance.* And the fifth is that biography is a source of inspiration to *higher ideals.*

But the fact that biography makes these particular contributions to the pupil's development is not the only reason—indeed, not the main reason—for reading this type of literature. Every good biography records the life story of some individual and

v

should make the reader aware of the important elements of which a life consists. Therefore for Part Two I have taken in order the elements which are common to all biographies—the important periods in the biographee's life, and, for that matter, the important stages in the life of every individual. Birth, marriage, and death are generally accepted as the three great events of a person's life. (Someone has facetiously called life a sequence of "yells, bells, and knells.") Shakespeare expanded these three into "seven ages." I have given Part Two a Shakespearean title, but because I have combined some of his stages, I have only five subdivisions: heredity, home, and family; schooldays and education; love and marriage; adult life; the close of life, retrospect.

The student studying this textbook realizes that he is in the second of these five stages—schooldays and education. Looking backward a very little way, he can compare his own heredity and home life with the ones presented in section one. In sections three, four, and five the student, looking forward to his uncertain future, can see how the persons he meets in biography faced the responsibilities and solved the problems which await him as he approaches love and marriage, adult life, and the close of life. It is in Part Two, then, that *Portraits in Words* becomes not just a study of "lives" but of life itself. This approach makes *Portraits in Words* a unique experience for the young student. In our complex and bewildering world, this little volume, by meeting the need of young people for contact with the springs of human action, may help some of them to find in biography a richer source of education than even their teachers have imagined it to be.

At the end of his study in this text, the pupil should have added to his natural enthusiasm for biography a clearer perception of its enjoyable, its practical, and its inspirational uses. He will also have gained a greater awareness of the power of this type of literature to deal satisfyingly with all areas of life. (I hope every pupil will be required to read at least one complete biography before this unit is ended.)

In addition to selections from complete biographies and autobiographies, I have included in *Portraits in Words* illustrations of other important types of biographical material: profiles, journals, diaries, and letters. Study questions, with occasional detailed explanations of some of the more common technical features of biography, accompany the selections throughout Parts One and Two. Suggestions for written assignments are frequent. The glossary should be useful for work on vocabulary. Lists for further reading are provided.

In editing this text I am deeply indebted to my colleagues, James Berkley and Edwin Rakow, for their continuing counsel and encouragement. And for his wise and generous guidance I owe a large debt of thanks to John Gehlmann, who is really a co-editor of this book.

D. C. R.

Contents

Portraits in Words

To the Students Who Will Use This Book

THE TEXT that you have in your hands is a book about biography. You quite likely have discovered, through your reading, that this type of literature can open up to your acquaintance many hundreds of real persons, with their wide range of experiences, adventures, and achievements. But perhaps you have not discovered all the good, all the values, all the pleasures, all the enrichment, which await the alert and educated reader of good biographies.

In what ways may the reading of biography enrich you? Part One of *Portraits in Words* names five ways. The first of these is simply introducing you to interesting persons. But biographies go beyond individuals: they throw both broad and intimate searchlights on the lives of nations and peoples; they illuminate history. Thirdly, biography widens your sympathies by taking you inside other persons' lives—letting you see from the inside lives that you may have seen only imperfectly from the outside. (Few other forces in the world can more easily break down barriers between persons distant from each other and thus remove foolish prejudices.) In the fourth section of Part One you will examine the way in which biography can direct you in the all-important task of settling upon a life work, because most of the subjects of biographies share with you their experiences in the choice and pursuit of a vocation. The fifth value of biography is that you learn from others their rules for triumphant living: by reading about a great life, or a good life, you are inspired to lift your own a little higher.

In Part Two you will learn how a biography presents an understanding of the meaning and sweep of life as a whole.

Throughout all parts of this text you will find that the selections, while they are for the most part chapters from full-length biogra-

2   *To the Students Who Will Use This Book*

phies, make room for the introduction of other materials that are biographical in nature—letters, diaries, and profiles.

You and I live in a country that values highly the worth of the individual. With increased interest in reading biography, you can add countless individuals to your circle of acquaintances, from an endless number of places and times.

PART ONE

Why We Read Biography

To Meet Interesting Persons

WHEN INTERESTING COMPANY comes to your home, your life takes on new flavor and excitement. Similarly, biography brings new interest into your life by introducing you to the great variety of fascinating persons whose portraits have been painted in words. Biography records the lives of individuals in any age of history, any country, any social status. Even persons to whom your home might be forbidden (the gangster, the traitor, the irresponsible playboy) may be met with safety and pleasure —and interest—on the pages of a good biography.

The biographer, moreover, usually has done considerable research to provide the reader with inside information that is not available even to those who are intimate acquaintances of the person written about. Like the baseball enthusiast who stays home from the ball park because he can see the game better on television, the reader of biography often learns more about interesting persons than he could ever hope to learn even from a real-life association with them.

My Aerial Marathon

BOB HOPE, AS TOLD TO PETE MARTIN

In the field of professional entertainers there is an abundance of biographical material available. But much of it is written for magazines which, for the purpose of achieving a sensational effect or notoriety for the subject, often present inaccurate or highly exaggerated accounts of some phase of the entertainer's personal life. What many young people may not know is that there are excellent full-length biographies written with good taste and vitality about the many interesting people who make their living in the entertainment world. It is in these books that you can become acquainted with people whose lives you already know enough about to suspect that they are very interesting.

Bob Hope is not a writer. (You may have noticed how often he makes jokes about the men who write his material.) *Have Tux Will Travel* is Bob Hope's reminiscences about his life as he told them to Pete Martin. The following excerpt tells of his experiences during World War II when he entertained many of our overseas fighting units.

MY AERIAL MARATHON to put on shows for servicemen during World War II began in 1942, when I was at the Goldwyn Studio. I'd played some shows at nearby camps and had gotten a taste of it, and when I heard that Joe E. Brown and Edgar Bergen had been to Alaska to entertain the troops, I said, "I'd like some of that."

Frances Langford, who was on my radio show, said, "I'd like some of it too."

There was a brief delay—but only a brief one—while her husband Jon Hall, told her, "You can't go. You have symptoms of acute appendicitis."

Frances said, "They have doctors in Alaska too."

End of argument.

So I got a unit together and off we went. The members of my unit promised each other that we wouldn't fly in Alaska at night, unless we had to. That way we'd have daylight on our side in case of a forced landing or if a storm came up. But the city of Anchorage, Alaska, was having a street dance and Lieutenant General Simon Bolívar Buckner, who was our No. 1 man up there, asked us to be on hand for it. We took off from Cordova, Alaska, for Anchorage at seven-thirty, thinking we'd make it before it got too dark. No sooner were we aloft than we ran into a combination lightning and rain storm and began to bounce around. We felt as if we were flopping back and forth between two giants who'd somehow gotten the notion that we were a badminton bird.

We buffeted along that way for forty-five minutes. We could hear the pilots having an argument in the cockpit. Then they slammed the door. That didn't help our peace of mind. The storm was bad enough, but to have our pilots arguing worried us even more. Our pilots were a twenty-one-year-old second lieutenant and a twenty-two-year-old first lieutenant. I'd nicknamed one of them Junior, the other Growing Pains. We liked them, but they did seem kind of young to be juggling our lives.

We flew in that mess for about twenty minutes more. Then we could tell we were circling. I asked the plane's staff sergeant, "What goes?"

"They're having trouble with the radio," he said.

Finally the flight mechanic came back, told Frances to stand up, and put a parachute on her. He put a Mae West [1] on her, too. Then he said, "That's in case we land in water."

"We might have to jump," he said to me. "You put on a parachute and a Mae West too."

I thought, *This is it.* I felt chilly. I looked out of a window, but I could see nothing. So I said my prayers. I knew that if you jumped in Alaska—especially in a storm—the odds against you were fantastic. I'd heard that the water was so cold you lived only forty-five seconds in it.

[1] *Mae West:* An inflatable life-saving jacket, worn by fliers in flights over water.

"What do you think?" Frances asked.

"I guess when we land this time the station wagon won't be there either," I said.

In our show I told a joke about how my brother had gotten into the paratroopers, and his first day in, some joker in his outfit told him, "When you're up there, count ten; then pull the ring. When you land, the station wagon will be there to pick you up and bring you back to camp."

The way I told it, the chute didn't open when my brother pulled the parachute ring, and he looked down and said in an annoyed voice, "And I'll bet that station wagon won't be there either."

In saying that to Langford, I was trying to be funny. But my teeth were chattering and my delivery was bad. It was as unhappy a moment as I've had. Then a light broke through the clouds and we followed it down. We came into the runway crosswise instead of parallel, but we landed. This was what had happened: General Buckner, who was waiting for us down there, had been told that we were in trouble by the pilot of a United Airlines ferrying plane. This pilot had landed and had reported that he'd felt our backwash—he'd come that close to us!—and that we were off the beam and were lost. We'd gone off the beam when our radio conked out. Since then, our pilots had been trying to keep us from losing altitude because the mountains around us were thirteen thousand feet high.

General Buckner had ordered every anti-aircraft searchlight in the place to throw up its finger of light—there were thirty of them. One of those fingers had broken through the cloud blanket. We saw it and dived for it. With our radio out, they couldn't have "talked" us down. Anyway, it was too early for Ground Controlled Approach, the device which was afterward developed to enable those at a landing field to lead a fog-bound pilot in by the hand.

People have told me, "I couldn't have gotten on another plane after an experience like that. From then on I'd have done my traveling underground by mole team." It didn't affect me like that. I've flown a million and a half miles since. It's like falling off a horse (and I don't mean a studio prop horse). If you get right back on you're all right. However, I admit that I didn't sleep much that night.

Not all of the things that happened to me while I was flapping around the world were scary. At times we got more laughs than we gave. Also, things happened that were interesting because they were so revealing. In this last category is a story that's never been told, so far as I know. I want to tell it myself before someone else gets it fouled up. Our entertainment group went into Palermo [Italy] three days after our boys took it. We played for the 1st Division, the 82nd Airborne, and other outfits.

Then we paid a courtesy call on General Patton, whose divisions had gone snorting across Sicily like a herd of fire-breathing mountain goats. We shook hands with him and left to do more shows. That night we were scheduled to do an outdoor performance. But before we took off we arranged to have a late supper of spaghetti and meat balls at the Excelsior Hotel, where we were staying. Tony Romano had worked the whole thing out. He'd done the ordering and was to supervise the meal, and visions of spaghetti and meat balls danced through our heads.

While we were doing our show, a captain came up to me and said, "I'm from General Patton's headquarters. The General wants you to have dinner with him after the show."

"Tell the General that's very nice," I said, "but we've arranged to have spaghetti and meat balls at the hotel."

"I think you'd better go to General Patton's," the captain said.

"I'm afraid we can't," I said.

"Look," he said, "if you don't show up at the General's it'll be your scalp and mine too."

A lot of my hair had been scared off by German air raids and I didn't have any to spare. "That's different," I said. "We'll go."

"No spaghetti and meat balls," I told the others. "We *have* to dine with General Patton."

When we left the field, the soldiers were standing behind ropes and a little fellow in the mob yelled, "Hi ya, Bob!"

I hollered back, "Nice to see you."

He could tell from my voice that I didn't recognize him, for he said, "Ernie Pyle." [2]

I rushed over and asked, "How long have you been here?"

"Ever since the invasion," he said. "Where are you staying?"

[2] *Ernie Pyle:* famous American journalist, killed in World War II.

"The Excelsior," I said.

"I'm at the Excelsior, too," he told me. "Let's have dinner there."

"Can't," I said. "I have to go to General Patton's for dinner."

"See you after," he said.

The General served us pot roast, and we sat around while he told us stories about the Sicilian campaign. To us it was thrilling, being that close to a great American military hero.

I said to our group, "Why don't we do a little show for the General?"

When we finished, the General put his arm around me and said, "I want to ask you a favor."

"Certainly, General," I said.

"You can do me lots of good when you go back home," he said. I was puzzled. Why should he need a helping hand? I didn't get it.

"Tell all the people who listen to you on the radio that I'm crazy about my men," he said. "That I think they're great; that I'm very proud of them."

"You don't have to worry about that, General," I said. "The whole country gets a wallop out of you."

"I know," he said, "but there're press people here who are out to get me." *What this man needs is rest,* I thought. *He's been going so hard he's beginning to snap his cap.*

So I said to the others, "Let's let the General have a little sleep." When I got back to the Excelsior, Ernie Pyle was sitting in the lobby, and I asked, "How've you been, Ernie?"

Instead of answering, he said, "How'd you enjoy your visit with the General?"

"It was wonderful," I said.

"How do you like that heel?" he asked.

It rocked me back on my own heels. "Don't you know what happened in the hospital?" Ernie said. "He slapped a wounded soldier." Then he told me the story and for the first time I understood the reason for the General's request.

But for every serious thing that happened to me, like being around when a General lost his head, there were ten comical things. When we reached Tarawa in 1944, we did a few shows.

They had a wire stretched across the stage—an electrical wire—because they used this amphitheatre for pictures. During the show while I was on, a mouse started across the wire. He stole my audience. Three or four thousand marines stopped looking at me and watched this little mouse walk across that wire. I stopped trying to get them back and watched it myself. When the mouse finally made it across, we went on with the show.

In 1949 I did a personal appearance tour with Doris Day and Les Brown. When we hit Little Rock, Arkansas, one of my advance publicity men was waiting for us. "I've arranged a show for you at a hospital up on the hill," he told us. So Doris Day and I went up there. We didn't find out until we reached it that it was a mental hospital. The patients were very moody, very sunk in depression. You've got to lift such an audience, and to lift them you have to do something broad. Usually physical comedy will get through the shell they live in. Edgar Bergen and Charlie McCarthy are wonderful in such a situation. A ventriloquist's dummy intrigues a P.N.[3] audience. It's a little out of this world, a little fantastic, and they buy that.

I started by saying to these boys, "Who won the ball game today between Cleveland and New York?" I got a couple of 'em yelling answers at me. Then I started to ad lib and I opened them up pretty good. But I thought, "I'd better not stay here too long. I'd better bring out Doris Day because a girl may open these fellows up even more."

Doris came out and they liked her. She did a couple of songs, without a piano, then I went back on and said, "I'd like to sing a little song for you, but I need music. Is there anybody in the audience who can play 'Buttons and Bows'?"

"Yes," the crowd said. "Charlie can do it."

They yelled for Charlie and he came up and I shook hands with him. He sat down at the piano and played "Buttons and Bows" with one finger. Also he lagged behind me, following me with the notes instead of keeping up with me. This made it difficult, but I went through with it. When I finished, the crowd applauded, I thanked Charlie and shook his hand again.

[3] *P.N.:* psycho-neurotic.

A month later, when we were back in Hollywood, a Paramount publicity man brought me a letter from a doctor at that hospital. The letter said, "I thought you'd like to know that the fellow you brought up on the stage to play piano was one of the worst cases we've ever had in this hospital. But from the day you brought him up on the stage and made him smile, he has improved. We think now that he'll eventually lead a normal life."

SUGGESTIONS FOR STUDY

1. What is the meaning of the phrase "by Bob Hope, as told to Pete Martin"? What is a "ghost writer"? What advantages does such an arrangement have?

2. What does Bob Hope say was his reason for going abroad to entertain the servicemen? What other reasons do you think there might have been?

3. Of what value was Bob Hope's sense of humor during the airplane crisis over Alaska? When the plane was in real danger, what did Bob do that proves he could be serious?

4. How much truth do you think there is in the advice about "getting back on the horse"? Cite experiences which you or your friends have had which support the truth of this idea.

5. Why did Bob Hope finally consent to go to General Patton's dinner party? What trait of character does this reveal? What was General Patton's great worry? Give evidence to prove that there were good reasons why General Patton should have been worried.

6. What was Bob Hope's technique for warming up to his audience in the mental institution? In your opinion why is it that Charlie would eventually lead a normal life?

7. Point out passages in this chapter which remind you of the kind of banter Bob Hope engages in on radio and television programs. Which of the jokes would you say have the Hope stamp on them? From what you know about the way *Have Tux Will Travel* was written, how can you account for the similarity between the pages of this book and a Bob Hope television script?

8. Would you like to have Bob Hope as a friend? Why, or why not?

9. Try your hand at writing a little monologue for Bob Hope. As a start you might write a joke that he could have told while the mouse was walking across the wire.

I Become City Editor

MARK TWAIN

Among American writers, few can match Mark Twain as an interesting personality. This greatest of American humorists reveals himself in his *Autobiography* and in a number of other autobiographical books: *Innocents Abroad, Roughing It,* and *Life on the Mississippi.*

In *Roughing It* you can read the adventures of this rambling Missourian in the mining camps of the West with his partner, Cal Higbee. These two prospectors located a "blind lead" (a ledge of gold ore that does not "crop out" above the surface), celebrated their good fortune in extravagant exultation ("Let's burn the house—or kill somebody! Let's go out where there's room to hurrah!"), and then discovered that the mine belonged to another! Riches to rags! What to do next? Read on.

WHAT TO DO NEXT?

It was a momentous question. I had gone out into the world to shift for myself, at the age of thirteen (for my father had indorsed [1] for friends; and although he left us a sumptuous legacy of pride in his fine Virginian stock and its national distinction, I presently found that I could not live on that alone without occasional bread to wash it down with). I had gained a livelihood in various vocations, but had not dazzled anybody with my successes; still the list was before me, and the amplest liberty in the matter of choosing, provided I wanted to work—which I did not, after being so wealthy. I had once been a grocery clerk, for one day, but had consumed so much sugar in that time that I was relieved from further duty by the proprietor; said he wanted me outside, so that he could have my custom. I had studied law an entire week, and

"I Become City Editor" from ROUGHING IT, Vol. II, by Mark Twain. Reprinted by permission of Harper & Brothers.
[1] *indorsed:* guaranteed loans, evidently not paid back by the friends.

then given it up because it was so prosy and tiresome. I had engaged briefly in the study of blacksmithing, but wasted so much time trying to fix the bellows so that it would blow itself, that the master turned me adrift in disgrace, and told me I would come to no good. I had been a bookseller's clerk for a while, but the customers bothered me so much I could not read with any comfort, and so the proprietor gave me a furlough and forgot to put a limit to it. I had clerked in a drug store part of a summer, but my prescriptions were unlucky, and we appeared to sell more stomach-pumps than soda-water. So I had to go. I had made of myself a tolerable printer, under the impression that I would be another Franklin some day, but somehow had missed the connection thus far. There was no berth open in the Esmeralda *Union*, and besides I had always been such a slow compositor that I looked with envy upon the achievements of apprentices of two years' standing; and when I took a "take," [2] foremen were in the habit of suggesting that it would be wanted "some time during the year." I was a good average St. Louis and New Orleans pilot and by no means ashamed of my abilities in that line; wages were two hundred and fifty dollars a month and no board to pay, and I did long to stand behind a wheel again and never roam any more—but I had been making such an ass of myself lately in grandiloquent letters home about my blind lead and my European excursion that I did what many and many a poor disappointed miner had done before; said, "It is all over with me now, and I will never go back home to be pitied—and snubbed." I had been a private secretary, a silver-miner and a silver-mill operative, and amounted to less than nothing in each, and now—

What to do next?

I yielded to Higbie's appeals and consented to try the mining once more. We climbed far up on the mountainside and went to work on a little rubbishy claim of ours that had a shaft on it eight feet deep. Higbie descended into it and worked bravely with his pick till he had loosened up a deal of rock and dirt, and then I went down with a long-handled shovel (the most awkward invention yet contrived by man) to throw it out. You must brace the

[2] *"take"*: the portion of copy or composition a compositor has at one time.

shovel forward with the side of your knee till it is full, and then, with a skilful toss, throw it backward over your left shoulder. I made the toss, and landed the mess just on the edge of the shaft and it all came back on my head and down the back of my neck. I never said a word, but climbed out and walked home. I inwardly resolved that I would starve before I would make a target of myself and shoot rubbish at it with a long-handled shovel. I sat down, in the cabin, and gave myself up to solid misery—so to speak. Now, in pleasanter days I had amused myself with writing letters to the chief paper of the territory, the Virginia *Daily Territorial Enterprise,* and had always been surprised when they appeared in print. My good opinion of the editors had steadily declined; for it seemed to me that they might have found something better to fill up with than my literature. I had found a letter in the post-office as I came home from the hillside, and finally I opened it. Eureka! (I never did know what Eureka meant, but it seems to be as proper a word to heave in as any when no other that sounds pretty offers.) It was a deliberate offer to me of Twenty-five Dollars a week to come up to Virginia and be city editor of the *Enterprise.*

I would have challenged the publisher in the "blind lead" days —I wanted to fall down and worship him, now. Twenty-five Dollars a week—it looked like bloated luxury—a fortune, a sinful and lavish waste of money. But my transports cooled when I thought of my inexperience and consequent unfitness for the position— and straightway, on top of this, my long array of failures rose up before me. Yet if I refused this place I must presently become dependent upon somebody for my bread, a thing necessarily distasteful to a man who had never experienced such a humiliation since he was thirteen years old. Not much to be proud of, since it is so common—but then it was all I had to *be* proud of. So I was scared into being a city editor. I would have declined, otherwise. Necessity is the mother of "taking chances." I do not doubt that if, at that time, I had been offered a salary to translate the Talmud from the original Hebrew, I would have accepted—albeit with diffidence and some misgivings—and thrown as much variety into it as I could for the money.

I went up to Virginia and entered upon my new vocation. I was

a rusty-looking city editor, I am free to confess—coatless, slouch
hat, blue woolen shirt, pantaloons stuffed into boot-tops, whisk-
ered half down to the waist, and the universal navy revolver slung
to my belt. But I secured a more Christian costume and discarded
the revolver. I had never had occasion to kill anybody, nor ever
felt a desire to do so, but had worn the thing in deference to popular sentiment, and in order that I might not, by its absence, be
offensively conspicuous, and a subject of remark. But the other
editors, and all the printers, carried revolvers. I asked the chief
editor and proprietor (Mr. Goodman, I will call him, since it
describes him as well as any name could do) for some instructions
with regard to my duties, and he told me to go all over town and
ask all sorts of people all sorts of questions, make notes of the
information gained, and write them out for publication. And he
added:

"Never say 'We learn' so-and-so, or 'It is reported,' or 'It is ru-
mored,' or 'We understand' so-and-so, but go to headquarters and
get the absolute facts, and then speak out and say 'It *is* so-and-so.'
Otherwise, people will not put confidence in your news. Unas-
sailable certainty is the thing that gives a newspaper the firmest
and most valuable reputation."

It was the whole thing in a nutshell; and to this day, when I
find a reporter commencing his article with "We understand," I
gather a suspicion that he has not taken as much pains to inform
himself as he ought to have done. I moralize well, but I did not
always practise well when I was city editor; I let fancy get the
upper hand of fact too often when there was a dearth of news. I
can never forget my first day's experience as a reporter. I wandered about town questioning everybody, boring everybody, and
finding out that nobody knew anything. At the end of five hours
my note-book was still barren. I spoke to Mr. Goodman. He said:

"Dan used to make a good thing out of the haywagons in a dry
time when there were no fires or inquests. Are there no haywagons in from the farms? If there are, you might speak of the
renewed activity and all that sort of thing, in the hay business, you
know. It isn't sensational or exciting, but it fills up and looks busi-
ness-like."

I canvassed the city again and found one wretched old hay-truck dragging in from the country. But I made affluent use of it. I multiplied it by sixteen, brought it into town from sixteen different directions, made sixteen separate items of it, and got up such another sweat about hay as Virginia City had never seen in the world before.

This was encouraging. Two nonpareil columns had to be filled, and I was getting along. Presently, when things began to look dismal again, a desperado killed a man in a saloon and joy returned once more. I never was so glad over any mere trifle before in my life. I said to the murderer:

"Sir, you are a stranger to me, but you have done me a kindness this day which I can never forget. If whole years of gratitude can be to you any slight compensation, they shall be yours. I was in trouble and you have relieved me nobly and at a time when all seemed dark and drear. Count me your friend from this time forth, for I am not a man to forget a favor."

If I did not really say that to him I at least felt a sort of itching desire to do it. I wrote up the murder with a hungry attention to details, and when it was finished experienced but one regret— namely, that they had not hanged my benefactor on the spot, so that I could work him up too.

Next I discovered some emigrant-wagons going into camp on the plaza and found that they had lately come through the hostile Indian country and had fared rather roughly. I made the best of the item that the circumstances permitted, and felt that if I were not confined within rigid limits by the presence of the reporters of the other papers I could add particulars that would make the article much more interesting. However, I found one wagon that was going on to California, and made some judicious inquiries of the proprietor. When I learned, through his short and surly answers to my cross-questioning, that he was certainly going on and would not be in the city next day to make trouble, I got ahead of the other papers, for I took down his list of names and added his party to the killed and wounded. Having more scope here, I put this wagon through an Indian fight that to this day has no parallel in history.

My two columns were filled. When I read them over in the morning I felt that I had found my legitimate occupation at last. I reasoned within myself that news, and stirring news, too, was what a paper needed, and I felt that I was peculiarly endowed with the ability to furnish it. Mr. Goodman said that I was as good a reporter as Dan. I desired no higher commendation. With encouragement like that, I felt that I could take my pen and murder all the immigrants on the plains if need be, and the interests of the paper demanded it.

However, as I grew better acquainted with the business and learned the run of the sources of information I ceased to require the aid of fancy to any large extent, and became able to fill my columns without diverging noticeably from the domain of fact.

SUGGESTIONS FOR STUDY

1. What in this selection made you feel that Mark Twain would have been interesting to know? What other interesting persons of the past have you met by reading biographies of them?

2. Read to the class sentences or short passages which illustrate Mark Twain's humor. Which ones are humorous exaggerations?

3. What opinions expressed by Mark Twain indicate that he possessed humility?

4. *Mark Twain* was the pen name of Samuel Langhorne Clemens. He found this pseudonym in the calls of the men on the steamboat who measured the depth of the water. What other famous pseudonyms do you know? Why do authors and actors often prefer pseudonyms to their real names?

5. Write an account of an experience in job-hunting, or in starting out on a new kind of work.

FOR FURTHER READING

Other autobiographical writings of Mark Twain: *Autobiography; Innocents Abroad;* and *Life on the Mississippi.*

Knowing Walt Whitman

LOGAN PEARSALL SMITH

Logan Pearsall Smith, one of the most delightful of American essayists, wrote a brief autobiography called *Unforgotten Years,* notable for its recollections of his association with other men of letters.

One of the most entertaining chapters in this autobiography tells how the Smith family made friends with Walt Whitman. By reading Mr. Smith's account of this friendship you too can make friends with the "Good Gray Poet," one of the great Americans of all time.

By reading this selection you may also be inspired with the courage necessary to promote acquaintance with persons who can add variety to your own circle of friends.

IN 1882, returning home again for the Easter holidays, I was told important news by my sister, when she too arrived for her holidays from Smith College, for the ban on college education for girls was now removed. There was a poet, she informed me and the rest of our family, a great American poet and prophet—though most Americans were not at all aware of his greatness—now living in poverty and neglect among us in America, living actually not far from our neighborhood, and it was her purpose, she informed us, to go without delay and offer him a due tribute of praise and admiration. How had she heard of this poet, her anxious and perturbed relatives inquired. A lady lecturer, she replied, had come from Boston to Smith College, and had praised his works, which she herself had immediately ordered from Boston, and which had revealed to her a message of tremendous import, and the purpose of her intended visit was to discuss this message. Consternation fell upon us all, and my father at once forbade it. He vaguely knew the name of the poet, which was by no means a name of good repute in Philadelphia; the district in which he lived was a district not visited by people who respected their own position. No daughter of his, my father declared, should, while she lived under his roof, be allowed to take so unseemly a step.

My father's refusal to permit this indecorum, though impressive as the poor man could make it, had no effect whatsoever upon my sister. She thought of going, she said, on the following Thursday; and my father, being in his heart well aware of the powerlessness of American parents in their dealings with their daughters, and convinced, as he was, that if my sister meant to go on Thursday, on Thursday she would go, wisely, if unheroically, decided that the best thing under the circumstances was for him to accompany her and thus lend an air of propriety to this visit. I was invited to join the party, and so off on Thursday afternoon we started from our home in Germantown, behind the pair of my father's fine horses. We flashed along through Fairmount Park, we drove across Philadelphia, we embarked in the ferry and crossed the Delaware, and dashed up before the little two-story wooden house in Camden to which we had been directed. The poet's elderly sister, who answered the doorbell, ushered us into a little parlor, and shouted upstairs, "Walt, here's some carriage folk come to see you." We heard a stirring above us as of a slow and unwieldy person, and soon through the open door we saw two large feet in carpet slippers slowly descending the stairs, and then the bulky form of the old man appeared before us. Walt Whitman greeted us with friendly simplicity; he had no notion who we were, and we had no introduction to him, but the unannounced appearance of these "carriage folk" from across the river—this portly and opulent-looking gentleman with his tall son and beautiful tall daughter— did not seem to surprise him in the least. My sister informed him that our name was Smith, that she had read his *Leaves of Grass,* and had come to express her immense admiration for that volume, and this explanation was received with great complacency; we were all invited to follow him upstairs to his den, where we sat down on what chairs could be hastily provided, and were soon engaged in lively talk.

My father, who at first held himself aloof in the most disapproving manner, soon, to the surprise of my sister and myself, began to join in this friendly conversation, and we were still more surprised, when we got up to take our departure, to hear our impulsive parent invite the object of his grave disapprobation to drive back with us to Germantown and spend the night. The afternoon was, he urged, a fine one, the drive across the Park would be pleasant, and it would be a pity to bring to a premature end so agreeable a confabulation. "No, Mr. Smith, I think I won't come," the poet answered; but when he had hobbled to the window and seen, waiting in the street outside, my father's equipage, he said that he thought he might as well come after all, and, hastily putting a nightshirt and a few other objects in a little bag, he hobbled downstairs and we all drove off together. It was, as my father had said, a pleasant afternoon; we crossed again the ferry, we drove through Philadelphia and through the Park to our home in Germantown, where Walt Whitman remained with us for a month, and whither he would often afterward return. He became indeed a familiar and friendly inmate of the house, whose genial presence, even when we did not see him, could hardly pass unnoticed, for he had the habit of singing "Old Jim Crow" when not occupied in conversation, and his loud and cheerful voice could be heard echoing every morning from the bathroom. His arrivals were always unannounced; he would appear when he liked, stay as long as he liked; and then one morning we would find at breakfast a penciled note to say that he had departed early, having had for the present enough of our society.

The reputation which the author of the *Leaves of Grass* had acquired by that daring and not decent publication was but a dubious one in America at that time; this reputation had reached our Quaker suburb, and our neighbors and relations would avoid our house and forbid their children to visit it when it was known that Walt Whitman was staying with us. Our friendship with him shocked them gravely; but no one who met him could retain this prejudice for long. His manners were grand and primeval, like those of old patriarchs or bards; he treated all human beings with the same politeness, and only on one occasion did we notice in him any sense of times and occasions and the demands of social etiquette. He had arrived on a visit in a knitted jacket, and, when told that a number of people were coming that evening to dinner, the thought occurred to him that probably he ought to put on a coat for the occasion, and after some meditation he appeared at dinnertime a consummate man of the world in his overcoat, thus sacrificing his comfort, for the night was hot, to the demands of the occasion.

Almost every afternoon my father would take Walt Whitman driving in the Park; it was an unfailing interest to them to drive as close as they could behind buggies in which pairs of lovers were seated, and observe the degree of slope towards each other, or "buggy-angle," as they called it, of these couples; and if ever they saw this angle of approximation narrowed to an embrace, my father and Walt Whitman, who had ever honored that joy-giving power of nature which the pagans symbolized under the name of Venus, would return home with happy hearts.

My acquaintanceship with this great and famous poet—for Walt Whitman had already become famous in England, and his glory had flashed back across the Atlantic to Boston, and thence, as I have described, to where we sat in Germantown in darkness— the familiar presence of this poet in our house, must have had an influence upon me which was much greater than anything that I was aware of at the time. He was, as John Burroughs [1] has well described him, "large and picturesque of figure, slow of movement, tolerant, receptive, democratic and full of charity and good will toward all. His life was a poet's life from first to last—free, unworldly, unhurried, unconventional, unselfish, and was contentedly and joyously lived." He was already old and half-paralyzed when we made his acquaintance, but of the disabilities of age he never spoke, although their shadows are not absent from his poems of this period. In one of these, for instance, "Queries to My Seventieth Year," which was written just when we came to know him, he thus addresses the oncoming year:

> Approaching, nearing curious,
> Thou dim, uncertain specter—bring'st thou life or death?
> Strength, weakness, blindness, more paralysis and heavier?
> Or placid skies and sun? Wilt stir the waters yet?

[1] *John Burroughs:* famous American naturalist (1837–1921).

Or haply cut me short for good? Or leave me here as now,
Dull, parrot-like and old, with crack'd voice harping, screeching?

It was, however, the calm serenity of age, its placid skies and
sun, which diffused about him that atmosphere of peace and leisure which made his companionship so genial, and our endless
conversations with him so great a pleasure. He was fond of talking with young people, and would listen with the utmost good
nature to our crude notions; and when he was not with us, my
sister and I would often visit him in Camden, where on summer
days we would find him seated at his window, fanning himself
with a large palm-leaf fan, and gazing out on the lazy sunshine
that filled his little street. Not infrequently during our visits he
would recognize some workingman of his acquaintance as he
passed, and call out, "Come in, Bill, and meet some friends of
mine," and the workingman would come in, or the passing post-
man, or the driver of an express wagon, and we would all share an
improvised meal together.

The floor of the room upstairs in which he lived was covered to
the depth of a foot or so with a sea of papers, and now and then
he would stir this pool with his stick and fish up a letter from an
English admirer—perhaps some newspaper article about "the
Good Gray Poet." Walt Whitman, who had been himself so long
a newspaper writer, was curiously fond of newspaper publicity;
his floor was strewn with press cuttings in which his name was
mentioned, and he would even, I believe, now and then, write
anonymous articles about himself for insertion in the local papers.
Otherwise he was quite free from literary vanity, and never spoke
of his writings unless we questioned him. Then, however, he
would answer with great simplicity and frankness. . . .

My sister Mary (whom he called his "bright, particular star")
recalls how once, when she was on the Camden ferry, she saw an
Englishman also on the boat. He must, she rightly concluded, be
on a pilgrimage like herself to visit Walt Whitman, for how otherwise account for the presence of that Englishman? She, therefore,
accosted the correct and dapper figure, who confessed, with some
surprise, that this was in fact his purpose. My sister offered to

show him the way to Walt Whitman's house, and they proceeded thither, to find, however, that the door was locked and they could get no answer to their knockings. "I'm sure he's upstairs," my sister said; "he always is, so the best thing is for me to boost you up to the window, which you can open, and then come down and let me in." Edmund Gosse [2] (for the Englishman was Edmund Gosse) seemed considerably surprised, my sister says, by the unconventionality of this proposal, but as he had come a long way to visit Walt Whitman, and did not wish to be baffled in his object, he finally allowed my sister to boost him up; and then he descended to open the front door to her, and they found Walt Whitman as usual in his study, and their visit was a satisfactory one in every way. It is only fair, however, to add that when, thirty or forty years after, I arranged for my sister and Sir Edmund Gosse to meet at luncheon, the latter, though admitting that he had met my sister at Walt Whitman's, angrily denied the boosting and his informal entrance. Knowing both Gosse and my sister to be endowed with more picturesque than accurate memories, I have never been able to decide which of them was telling the truth.

I remember once speaking to Walt Whitman about his poem, "With Husky-Haughty Lips, O Sea!" which had just been published, and he told me, sitting one summer evening on our porch in Germantown, of the way he had come to write it; how always, from the days of his boyhood on the Long Island coasts, he had tried and tried again to seize the meaning which the voice of the ocean was always whispering in his ears; how often by day, and more often by night, he had sat or lain amid the sandhills on its margin, listening in a kind of torment of attention to that great voice—some voice—in what words could he best describe it?

Some voice, in huge monotonous rage, of freedom-lover pent,
Some vast heart, like a planet's, chain'd and chafing in those breakers.

This notion of receptivity to experience, and of a complete surrender to it, combined with a patient effort to grasp its deepest meaning and to embody that meaning in significant and reverberating words—this account of the old man's poetic method, as

[2] *Edmund Gosse:* English poet and critic (1849–1928).

he told it one summer evening, was deeply impressive to his boyish listener, although that listener had then no thought of attempting to coin his own experience into enduring metal. To melt material sand into salable glass bottles—this, he believed, was to be his destiny; and the idea that all such massy unmetaphorical gold might be gladly bartered, as Walt Whitman would gladly have bartered it, for the ability to embody in words some one of Nature's aspects—the sea's voice, for instance, or the breath of its salt fragrance, or even, as he himself had said, "the undulation of one wave"—the idea of so mad a preference would have seemed to his youthful listener at that date fantastic indeed.

Thus I listened to the impressive talk of the old poet, and though I had no notion of following his example, the effect upon me of his poems, as I read and reread that strange volume, the *Leaves of Grass*—how can I adequately describe it? There are books which come to us as revelations, which, as Emerson says, "take rank in our lives with parents, lovers, and passionate experiences," and to come on such a book to which one can yield oneself in absolute surrender—there is no intellectual enjoyment, I believe, no joy of the mind greater in youth than this. Books of this kind, for their most passionate acceptance, should be contemporary books, written by the living for the living; and should present us with a picture of life as we ourselves know it and feel it. And they should above all reveal us to ourselves, should hold up a looking glass before our eyes in which we see our own faces. Much that was suppressed in the young people of my generation found a frank avowal in the *Leaves of Grass;* feelings and affection for each other, which we had been ashamed of, thoughts which we had hidden as unutterable, we found printed in its pages, discovering that they were not, as we had believed, the thoughts and feelings of young, guilty, half-crazy goblins, but portions of the Kingdom of Truth and the sane experience of mankind.

It was above all Walt Whitman's rejoicing in his flesh and blood —"there is so much of me," he sang, "and all so luscious"—his delight in his own body, which seemed a revelation and gave the *Leaves of Grass* so strong a hold upon a generation born of puritans who had ignored, or treated as shameful, those habitations of the spirit. Then, too, Walt Whitman's affection for his fellow human beings—for he was one of those rare spirits who really love the human race—his feeling that all men and women, of whatever race or class and in whatever state of degradation, were all of them not worthless and of no account, but lovable and mysterious and divine—this seemed to fill for us the many-peopled world with innumerable creatures all dear and infinitely precious to us. These were the streams of life which flowed from that fountain; and catching also from its pages the fervor of his exultant pride in Democracy, in America and the age we lived in, and moved also by the splendid passages here and there of great poetry, we came to regard as a sacred book the vast printed chaos of the *Leaves of Grass.* It gave us ears, it gave us eyes, it revealed to us the miracle of our own existence, and for me, at least, with my meager ideals of borrowed culture, it seemed to open a great shining window in my narrow house of life.

SUGGESTIONS FOR STUDY

1. What is meant by the term "carriage folk"?
2. Which of the persons mentioned in this selection, including the author, did you find interesting? Which ones are you sure you would not care to have for friends? Tell why.
3. What are the characteristics which make persons interesting to you?
4. What can you do to make yourself the kind of person whom others will consider interesting and therefore worth cultivating?
5. From what the author says about the episode of his sister and the visiting Englishman, Edmund Gosse, state one of the difficulties that the biographer often encounters.
6. Reread John Burrough's description of "a poet's life." Which of these adjectives would you like to be able to apply to your own life?
7. Reread the paragraph beginning "This notion of receptivity to experience. . . ." What does it mean? Does it seem to you "fantastic indeed" or does "so mad a preference" appeal to you?
8. If you found Walt Whitman interesting, as did all the Smiths, find a good biography of him and read it. Or, better still, turn to *Leaves of Grass* for the poet's own "Song of Myself."

A Voice like a Banner Flying

THE EDITORS OF TIME

Are you the proud possessor of an opera or play program on which is written the autograph of some great performer? Have you ever waited in line to get a seat to hear and see a favorite actor or musician? Just to be in the audience when a famous artist comes out on the stage is a thrill unlike anything else in the world.

How much more exciting must it be to meet the artist personally! You can meet a great artist personally by reading the following biographical *profile*.

A profile is a short, timely sketch of a person's life, usually written for publication in a periodical. Reading a profile is a good way to meet personally the famous people who have captured the fancy and received the acclaim of the world. The following profile will introduce you to the famous Metropolitan Opera star, Leontyne Price.

BIG AUNTIE sits in the parlor listening to French art songs on the phonograph. They sound, she says, "a little like the cha cha cha."

Past the veranda of the one-story, frame house runs South Fifth Avenue. It is a narrow, rutted road of yellow clay shaded by oak trees. On the other side of town, beyond Magnolia Street and the county courthouse with its marbled Confederate soldier, runs the avenue known as North Fifth. There stand the great mansions with their porticoes and colonnades and carriage houses. Big Auntie has been there—as downstairs maid and cook on the cook's night out—in the big green house set back from the street by a lawn. Although their names might suggest otherwise, North and South Fifth—one a white street, the other Negro—converge at no point in the town of Laurel, Miss. But in the person of a local girl who "went over the water to sing," they converged this winter on the stage of the Metropolitan Opera House.

The voice in Big Auntie's phonograph belongs to one of the world's great singers: her niece, Leontyne Price. When Laurel-born Soprano Price, 34, made her Metropolitan debut, she faced, in the audience, a score of Laurel friends and relatives from both Fifth Avenues and from the sleepy streets in between. Her triumph monopolized the front page of the Laurel *Leader-Call* ("She reaches the pinnacle") and for a time, even crowded out the achievements of that other local Negro hero, Olympic Broad Jumper Ralph Boston. Laurel knew about Leontyne before Rudolf Bing of the Metropolitan Opera ever heard of her, and few of Laurel's 27,000 people are likely to forget it. The night of her debut, the local Western Union operator turned cranky under the weight of well-wishing wires. "I know where to reach her," she eventually snapped to callers; "just tell me what you want to say."

Biggest Moment. What critics and audiences have wanted to say of Leontyne's Met performances is that they surpassed even the expectations raised by an already glowing European reputation. For her first Met season, Leontyne Price contracted to sing five roles: Leonora in *Il Trovatore*, Aïda, Cio-Cio-San in *Butterfly*, Donna Anna in *Don Giovanni*, Liu in *Turandot*. Her Leonora proved to be a remarkable portrayal of a woman in whom dignity struggled with desperation and in whom grief somehow shone more movingly through a profound sense of repose. The amalgam of qualities made her fourth act aria *D'amor sull'ali rosee* a dramatic as well as a technical triumph. It was perhaps the most wildly applauded moment of the present Met season—a season made somewhat lackluster by several dull, slack productions but rendered memorable by what seemed like a new age of brilliant singers, most notably Birgit Nilsson, triumphant in *Turandot*, and Soprano Price herself.

The Butterfly she unveiled was, in contrast to her Leonora, a creature that lived on the surface of emotion—tentative, vulnerable but never mawkish. In the last act, when Soprano Price enacted the difficult suicide with a dignity that many a famed soprano is unable to muster, Cio-Cio-San ceased to be a quaintly pathetic figure and became what she rarely is—a truly tragic one.

But Soprano Price's triumph at the Met, as it often has been elsewhere, was her Aïda. Moving about the stage with feline grace, passing with a kind of visceral instinct through moods that were supplicating and menacing, aggressive and sweet, she achieved one of the great Aïdas of operatic history. Sustaining all of the performances was the voice, unfurling like a bright banner from the stage and through the opera house.

With Power to Spare. "Leontyne leads with that voice," says her accompanist, David Garvey. "It is her Rock of Gibraltar." Leontyne's Gibraltar is known technically as a lyric *spinto*—a high soprano voice with dramatic feeling. No singer today is better capable of straddling both the lyric and the dramatic moods than she is, and none possesses a voice that is more secure throughout its considerable range—the G below middle C to the D above high C. Says she: "I never try an F in public. I sometimes do it in the shower, but there I may just be intoxicated by the soap."

She can send her soprano flooding through a house the size of the Met without straining and with the marvelously reassuring suggestion that she has power to spare; but her singing also has all the agility and the feather-lightness of a much smaller voice. Her special glory is a legato line of floating, fine-spun phrases. A most demanding critic passed judgment on her voice when he heard it for the first time: it gave him goose pimples, said Conductor Herbert von Karajan.

What gives a voice goose-pimple potential? What makes a singer great? Obviously talent and training. Amply talented, Leontyne Price has never stinted the training, still works hard with her teacher, Florence Page Kimball, even takes phonograph records along on her tours to study other singers' versions of a role during the long hours in hotel rooms. Like many other singers, she did not really reach her peak until she passed 30, has developed remarkably in style and power during the last three or four years. Says Teacher Kimball: "It is not lessons that have done it. It's her life—that solid, secure feeling she gained from the people around her who love her and help her."

Earthy Presence. Others seeking to identify Leontyne Price's special quality also point not only to her voice but to her person. . . . Many sopranos and actresses have been called "the essential female," but Leontyne Price convinces most of her audiences that she really fits the description. Not beautiful but with almost translucent brown skin, high cheek-bones, and compelling eyes set in charcoal shadows, she has a memorable face; her figure—broad-hipped yet lithe, strong yet feminine, medium tall yet commanding—animates any costume she wears, and she can whip a train or thrust a sleeve with regal authority. . . .

Whipped, with Love. Much of the joy, according to Leontyne's mother Kate, derives from the fact that Kate was singing hymns in the choir of St. Paul's Methodist Church in Laurel, back in 1927, when she felt the first pangs signaling the impending birth of Mary Leontyne Violet Price—a first child after 13 years of barrenness. Her father James, an erect, dignified, sparrow-thin man, now 79, worked in the local sawmills (Laurel used to call itself the Yellow Pine Capital of the World before the woods gave out). Kate Price, an iron-willed woman with some of Leontyne's own incendiary temper, took to midwifery to bolster the family income. Working at first for a fee of $10 per baby—or sometimes for a side of bacon or a barrel of peas—Kate delivered about 900 children over the years and never, she boasts proudly, lost a mother. But she created some problems for Leontyne: "The neighbor kids would say, 'You didn't come the right way; your mamma carries babies in her black bag.'" Although Leontyne has "retired her," Kate Price delivered a child shortly before traveling to New York for the Met debut, returned promptly to Laurel because another child was on the way.

As Leontyne recalls it, she and her brother George—two years younger and now an Army captain—had the kind of childhood any kid might expect from old-fashioned, God-fearing and strict parents. If you disobeyed, "you got yourself whipped—with love, but you were torn up just the same." The color bar was as strong in Laurel as anywhere in the South, but the children were not aware of it at the time: "We were taught to judge people as individuals, not on the pigment of their skin," says George. . . .

The Other Family. On South Fifth Avenue, when Leontyne was growing up, few children owned two pairs of shoes, and some did not even have one pair. At a sacrifice, James and Kate Price

always saw that Leontyne had a pair for school as well as "patent
leathers for Sunday." Says Leontyne: "Mamma never wanted us
to go barefoot like the other kids; she wanted us to amount to
something." Leontyne's first memory of music is hearing her
mother sing in "a lovely lyric soprano voice" as she hung out the
clothes in the long, level Price backyard. Leontyne had a doll
piano when she was three, and, recalls Kate, "That child run me
crazy giving me concerts." At 3½ Leontyne took her first lessons
from Mrs. Hattie McInnis, the town's Negro music teacher, and if
Kate Price could not raise the fee of $2 a lesson, she would do Miss
Hattie's washing and ironing.

When Leontyne was five, Kate traded in the family Victrola as
down payment for a piano. "When she came home from school,"
says Kate, "that child had one-half of a fit."

On the other side of town, on North Fifth Avenue, lived the
Alexander Chisholms. Elizabeth Wisner Chisholm was the daughter of a lumber baron, and Alexander Chisholm a Vermonter who
met his wife while she was a music major at Smith. He returned
to Laurel with her, is now chairman of the board of the First National Bank. After school Leontyne would sometimes wander over
to the large green house to visit "Big Auntie" Everlina Greer, the
Chisholms' maid (before that, she had been the Wisners', served
the two families for 45 years before she retired four years ago). Leontyne would play with Jean and Peggy, the two older of the three
Chisholm daughters. They were, she recalls, her "other family,"
and she was their "chocolate sister."

Where She Came From. "Miss Elizabeth" Chisholm remembers
Leontyne in those days as the girl with the "high-glee eyes" who
was forever singing. She took to accompanying Leontyne at the
piano, and later she occasionally had her perform at informal
musicales. Between Leontyne and the Chisholms—who eventually
helped send her to the Juilliard School of Music in Manhattan—
grew an attachment that both sometimes feel has been misunderstood. Says Leontyne: "Everyone finds it so amazing that two
families should love each other in the middle of Mississippi, which
is, let's face it, a red-hot state where my ancestors were not so
high on the social scale. Well, that hasn't got a cotton-pickin' thing

to do with it. There wasn't anything in the world Mrs. Chisholm wouldn't have done for me. But she was my friend first and my benefactress second—whatever I turned out to be, and even if I didn't turn out to be much of anything." Says Mrs. Chisholm of Leontyne: "Don't call me her patron. I don't think I have ever 'patronized' Leontyne. I have only loved her. I'm just where she came from."

But where she came from remained in many respects a divided world. Leontyne entered the Chisholm mansion by the back door, as she does to this day. She is free to use the front door, Mrs. Chisholm explains, but it would make the help uncomfortable.

The First Leontyne. At Laurel's Oak Park High School, Leontyne seemed to specialize in everything. She was a high school cheerleader ("There would be Leontyne at half time," says Kate Price, "walking around the field on her hands") and a soloist on virtually every one of the Negro community's civic and church programs. She also appeared at funerals, until one group of mourners was so overcome by her expressive performance that she was asked to stop singing. She did but vowed angrily: "That's the last funeral I'll ever do."

At 17, "high on the hog, with my first piece of luggage and two coats," Leontyne left Laurel for the North. Impressed by her voice, an Army chaplain from nearby Camp Shelby had helped her win a scholarship to Wilberforce University, a mostly Negro school in Ohio. On her entrance application she wrote, under Plans for the Future: "I'm worried about the future because I want so much to be a success."

Because she wanted to help her Brother George through college, she signed up for a teacher's training course (he later went through South Carolina State on a full athletic scholarship). But she kept on singing—in the glee club, the choir, the dormitory shower. Even as a freshman she had what a friend remembers as "a star quality." Once she was stopped by hazing upperclassmen and ordered to sing: "Well, she just sang—the song was *Because*—and when she stopped, everyone just stood there. Her voice took them so much by surprise they stopped hazing her and didn't bother any of the others."

Leontyne finally abandoned her teaching plans in her senior year and set her sights on Juilliard and the Met. (No Negro had ever sung a solo role there at the time. The first: Marian Anderson, who in 1955—long past her vocal prime—appeared in the minor part of the fortune teller Ulrica in Verdi's *A Masked Ball.* Following Anderson, three Negroes have had lead roles at the Met: Baritone Robert McFerrin, Sopranos Mattiwilda Dobbs and Gloria Davy.)

At a concert at Antioch College Paul Robeson heard her, decided that she was marvelous, and agreed to sing at a benefit to help her musical education: the concert raised $1,000. At that point Elizabeth Chisholm went to James Price and asked permission to help Leontyne too. Says Leontyne: "I love her more for that—for asking—than for any check she ever gave me." Leontyne Price fiercely insists on distributing credit for her success—not just to "the wonderful Caucasian family" but to "the Omnipotent" for providing talent and "to my parents for having *birthed* me."

Crisis at Juilliard. Leontyne's greatest stroke of luck at Juilliard was being turned over for vocal coaching to Florence Page Kimball, herself a former concert singer. The Leontyne who came to her was a "gawky, very simple child—just another student to me." Miss Kimball realized that Leontyne was more than another student after hearing her sing Mistress Ford in a Juilliard production of *Falstaff.* Officially, Miss Kimball was her voice teacher; unofficially, she counseled her on how to dress and carry herself, how to handle the social perplexities of a Northern city. Says a Juilliard friend: "Lee used to go to Miss Kimball the way other people would take to a psychiatrist or a priest." Miss Kimball still coaches Leontyne, makes critical notes at her rehearsals, will travel almost anywhere—as will the Chisholms—to hear her perform.

For four years Leontyne labored at Juilliard, appearing in any student production she could get into, singing for anybody who cared to listen in the lobby of the International House where she lived, or at the customary candlelit Sunday night suppers. Says a pianist friend of the Juilliard days: "It never entered my mind that Leontyne would not make it." But Leontyne herself was far less sure. She fell in love with a Haitian ("He was no musician," says Leontyne now, "but he sure was an artist"), and when the episode ended abruptly, she began threatening suicide. One night at a Riverside Drive party during which she had been dancing in her stocking feet, she was suddenly overcome by melancholy and started out toward the Hudson. A friend calmly told her to put on her shoes first. She did, and after driving up and down the river most of the night, she shook off her gloom.

Enter a Goddess. Soon afterward, at a student performance, Soprano Price was heard by Producer Robert Breen, who was then signing a cast for a revival of *Porgy and Bess.* At Breen's request, Leontyne sang for Ira Gershwin—*I Loves You, Porgy* and *Summertime.* Before the audition, she stood despairingly with a friend on a Broadway street corner. "Nothing's going to happen," she said. "Nothing can happen." By nightfall she had the female lead.

For two years Leontyne Price sang "at least four Besses a week" —on Broadway, on the road and in Europe. She also married her Porgy, Baritone William Warfield, in Harlem's Abyssinian Baptist Church, with one of the Chisholm daughters attending and with six members of the cast as bridesmaids. Married for 8½ years, Leontyne and Warfield are kept apart most of the time by the demands of their careers.

In Leontyne's mind, *Porgy and Bess* was only an interlude: she still wanted a career in grand opera, and she started on that road by giving her first serious recital at Town Hall in the fall of 1954. The critics were enthusiastic, especially the *Herald Tribune's* Jay Harrison, who detected "a goddess performing among us." She has spent six seasons singing on the Community Concert circuit and in 1955 broke into opera as the lead in the NBC *Tosca.* Casting a Negro in the role, says Leontyne composedly, "created quite a rumpus, but it was a successful rumpus." At any rate, she feels that Bess was good preparation for Tosca: "Both were strumpets, only Tosca dressed better."

That same year she laid the foundation for her European career. A manager friend of hers had asked her to sing an audition at Carnegie Hall, without saying who was to hear her. As she started to sing, she noticed a "slim, good-looking man with salt-and-pepper hair eating a club sandwich." Midway through the audition, the slim man abandoned his sandwich, excitedly pushed the accompanist aside and rushed Leontyne through *Pace, pace mio Dio!* from *La Forza del Destino.* "I then learned," says she, "that it was Herbert von Karajan."

The Ultimate. Leontyne made her grand opera stage debut in 1957 at the San Francisco Opera in *Dialogues of the Carmelites* by Francis Poulenc, who had been impressed by her concert performance of his songs. Although she "enjoyed a real cold petrification," the debut was a major success. On the strength of it, she was invited to return to San Francisco that year to sing *Aïda* in place of Antonietta Stella, bedridden with an appendectomy. She had become familiar with the role when she sang it with the Philadelphia Orchestra. A year later at Covent Garden, when Anita Cerquetti was forced to withdraw from *Aïda* for the same reason, Leontyne again filled in. "My career," says she, "was launched on the appendectomies of Italian sopranos."

Remembering the Carnegie Hall audition, Herbert von Karajan invited her in 1958 to make her European debut with the Vienna State Opera in *Aïda.* Since that triumphant evening, Leontyne and Von Karajan have enjoyed a kind of mutual-admiration pact. After Vienna, the road went speedily upward. In 1960 she walked through the stage door of La Scala (she had vowed never to enter as a tourist) and made her debut, again in *Aïda,* without a single stage rehearsal. "After all," she says, "what's the problem? The Nile can only be upstage." The crowd shouted *"Brava Leonessa!"* Then, for the new opera house at the Salzburg Festival last summer, Von Karajan "had this big, fat, crackpot idea of my doing Donna Anna." Leontyne did it, and followed it by opening the Berlin Festival as soloist with the Berlin Philharmonic. By then the Met's Rudolf Bing had signed her, and that was "the ultimate." Says Leontyne, looking back: "It was all so fast. My mind was so wide open. It was like having growing pains before your time."

Makeup Savers. When Leontyne was departing for Juilliard, Big Auntie recalls, "Miz Chisholm called her and she say, 'Promise me you'll keep on bein' just Leontyne.' " Not many people know who "just Leontyne" is—perhaps not even Leontyne. . . .

Says Leontyne herself: "I am not a crusader in anything except

my career." Often when she talks about her race, it is in joking
fashion. The dusky Aïda she refers to as her "makeup-saver role."
Once a wardrobe mistress forgot and warned her about soiling her
light costume with the dark Aïda makeup. Leontyne pointed to
her skin and said, "Honey, you'd be surprised; that won't come
off."

Abroad she likes the relaxed atmosphere concerning "the matter
of pigmentation," nevertheless spends most of her time with her
accompanist, or secretary, or the professionals that cluster around
opera houses and recording companies. She was been taken in
warmly at the Met where she is known, according to a colleague,
as "not typical by singer standards—she's too nice."

Havin' a Ball. But Leontyne also has a fierce professional pride
and a temper to match. Told that a male singer was unable to
make a rehearsal, she raged: "I don't give a hoot about him or any
other singer. He's lucky to be in this with me, dear. That jerk—he
can't sing because he hasn't got any vocal technique, that's why!"
After such an outburst she is likely to shrug her shoulders, smile
and murmur, "I don't know why I get so excited."

Occasionally she expresses her professional grievances with a
gag. Once she overheard a tenor telling an admirer that his "lovely,
pure, full and beautiful" voice moved Miss Price to tears. "I hate to
bring this up," said Leontyne, "but it is *my* voice so warm, full and
beautiful that moves me to tears." Of a well-known soprano who
decided to get married and retire, Leontyne asked: "Retire from
what?" She has a great, saving capacity for laughing at herself,
too. Back home one Christmas, she made a joke of helping at table
at the Chisholms when the maids were away: "I'm keepin' my
hand in," she said. "The first flat C and I'll be back here."

Leontyne can sometimes play the grand diva sprinkling her
conversation with Italianisms, rolling her r's across the room. After
taking a college course in elementary French, Brother George recalls, she suddenly stopped spelling her name Leontine, replacing
the *i* with the *y* that she still uses. Says a friend: "Sometimes she
can be all mink and ermine, and the next minute she'll be plain
old southern Mississippi." But the southern Mississippi usually
pops out first. After her Met debut she encountered Metropolitan

General Manager Rudolf Bing backstage. He asked how she was. "Mr. Bing," said Leontyne, "I'm havin' a ball." Later that night, at a party in her honor, a guest asked her to sing something. "Nobody's gonna leave this party unhappy," said Leontyne. She broke into *Summertime*.

A Silver Shield. Leontyne rarely has taken a vacation, rarely sees her twelve-room house in Manhattan's Greenwich Village. With a six-figure income, the only luxury she finds time for is buying dresses (in Rome) and hats and suits (in Vienna). She has also completely refurnished the Price home in Laurel, built a room to accommodate Big Auntie. She now has a considerable entourage, including a personal manager, a concert manager, an accompanist, a pressagent, a male secretary and a housekeeper, all of whom, as Teacher Kimball once put it, "would like to put a silver shield around her to protect her."

But Leontyne Price usually knows how to take care of herself, and her preparation for each performance is a calm ritual. She likes to spend the day "with myself." At 4 p.m. she has a half-hour bath, during which, "if I'm a good girl, I study the score." She has a solid meal at 5 because, with all the energy a singer needs, she can't look like a *Bazaar* model. "I never worry about my weight— you're going to look smaller from the audience anyway." (Leontyne Price does not look particularly small.) She carries a thermos of hot bouillon with her to the theater for steadying swigs before particularly difficult scenes that might "tensify" her. She usually arrives in her dressing room an hour and a half before the performance. "I like time," says Leontyne, "to put out my trinkets on my dressing table—my pictures of my brother and his children and of my mother and father and of Mr. von Karajan and a little mascot dachshund to make me laugh."

Just Begun. Perhaps the key to her career, says Teacher Kimball, is that "she's never defeated by things that haven't gone right." Her *Thaïs* reviews in Chicago two years ago were not good, and Miss Kimball stayed over to read them with her, warning that they were disappointing. "What do they say about my voice?" asked Leontyne. "They say you have a great voice," said Miss Kimball. "All right, then," said Leontyne. "The rest I can learn, and I will."

Her determination is undergirded by a powerful religious faith (she is the granddaughter of two Methodist ministers). She talks about "the Omnipotent" as naturally as if he were her neighbor. "I never go onstage," says Leontyne, "without saying a prayer—sometimes an *extra* prayer before arias like *D'amor sull'ali rosee* in *Trovatore* or *O patria mia* in *Aïda.*" And the debut? "I just stood there in the wings and thought: 'Dear Jesus, you got me into this, now you get me out.' "

Six weeks later she said, "About once a day I still lie back on my little couch and close my eyes, and I just relive tidbits of that ovation. That's about the highest cloud I could ever float on." But to a friend who called to congratulate her she said grimly: "You realize that my work has only just begun." Wherever the work takes her, she knows that from time to time she must go home to Laurel again: it is the place where she feels she can be "just Leontyne." After the triumphs at Salzburg and Milan, she recalls, she made a flying visit and encountered a deacon of St. Paul's Methodist Church walking up South Fifth Avenue. "Hi, Leontyne," said the deacon. "Still singin'?"

She was—and is.

SUGGESTIONS FOR STUDY

1. According to this profile, what are the two things which make a singer great? What other things does Leontyne Price possess which make her especially great?

2. Present evidence from the selection to show that Miss Price owes much to her family in getting her started on a musical career. What part did the Chisholm family play in her professional career? What position do the Chisholms occupy in her personal life?

3. What have you learned about Leontyne Price from this selection which shows that she knows how to use criticism constructively? That she knows how to control her emotions?

4. What is meant by a *temperamental* artist? Give reasons for believing that Leontyne Price is, or is not, temperamental.

5. What quotations here lead you to believe that Leontyne Price has a lively sense of humor? What things that she has said tell you of her constructive religious faith?

6. How did Leontyne Price prepare herself for an important musical appearance? What do the details of this preparation tell you about her personality?

7. Elizabeth Chisholm went to Leontyne's father to ask permission to help Leontyne in her career. Leontyne said of this: "I love her more for that—for asking—than for any check she ever gave me." Considered in the light of the great hope of the world for racial equality, what is the true significance of this statement?

8. Leontyne Price, we are told, "did not really reach her peak until she passed thirty." Contrast this fact with what you know about popular jazz singers. What does this contrast tell you about the two art forms: jazz and opera?

9. If someone were to write a full-length biography of Leontyne Price instead of this profile, what additional information would you like to see included in it?

10. In which way would you learn more about Leontyne Price: by talking to her for an hour, or by reading this profile? What does your answer to this question tell you about the values to be gained from reading biography?

FOR FURTHER READING

Some more interesting persons to meet: *Come North with Me*, Bernt Balchen; *High, Wide and Lonesome*, Hal Borland; *The Roosevelt Family of Sagamore Hill*, Hermann Hagedorn; *Act One*, Moss Hart; *Albert Einstein*, Elma Levinger; *Little Britches*, Ralph Moody; *Anything Can Happen*, George Papashvily and Helen Waite; *Tiger of the Snows*, James Ullman; *Jim Bridger*, Stanley Vestal; *How Do I Love Thee?*, Helen E. Waite.

To Illuminate History

BIOGRAPHY MAKES three special contributions to the reader's knowledge of history.

In the first place, biography tells the thoughts and attitudes, the reactions, the fears, the joys, the misgivings of important persons at the time they were engaged in affairs of historical moment. History books tell you that King Edward VIII of England read a proclamation in which he abdicated his throne; they also tell the effects of this act upon his nation and upon the world. Biography, in addition to relating these events, makes you realize that Edward VIII was not only a king but also a person and shows the effect of his act upon him as a person and upon his family—his mother, and his brother forced into the kingship much against his desire.

In the second place, biography tells what historically significant men and women did while they were *not* engaged in shaping history. You may happen to know that Frederick the Great played the flute; but do you know how his association with great composers and with music generally helped to shape his life? Biography tells you this and all the extra-curricular facets of great men's lives. And when you know all the activities of a man, you understand better his part in the historical events with which he is associated.

And last and perhaps most importantly, biography illuminates history by enabling you to develop a "feeling for the times." Since a biography is limited to just one lifetime, the biographer, unlike the writer of history textbooks, has time to present a word picture of the daily life of an historical period. In biography you are taken into Franklin's print shop, into Paul Revere's silversmith's shop, into the President's mansion when Dolley Madison was First Lady, into Richmond, Virginia, when the Lees came home to live after

the War between the States, into a British army camp where Bene-
dict Arnold was being received. In these encounters with people,
you get from biography not just the events of history, but also the
atmosphere of the cities, villages, and countryside in which these
events took place. And when *feeling* is added to *knowledge* your
appreciation of a period of history is greatly enlarged.

As you read the following four selections, note how the pages of
history are opened up to you in a fresh and illuminating way. And
bear in mind that if these short selections illuminate history for
you, a reading of the complete biographies would be much more
rewarding.

Two if by Sea

ESTHER FORBES

By April of 1775, General Gage, who was in command of
the British troops stationed in Boston, had learned from his spies
that cannon and other military supplies were being collected and
hidden in small towns in and around Boston—at Worcester and
Concord specifically. King George III had already ordered that all
such stores be seized and was becoming impatient to have his orders
carried out. General Gage also knew that John Hancock and Samuel
Adams, two of the leaders of the growing rebellion, were hiding out
in or near Lexington, Massachusetts. With the coming of spring, Gage
determined to send his troops to Concord to confiscate or destroy the
military stores and to arrest Hancock and Adams.

Meanwhile, the American patriots were busy making plans to protect their supplies from seizure and to warn their leaders about the
British plans.

In the following selection from *Paul Revere and the World He
Lived in*, Esther Forbes tells what happened on Monday and Tuesday,
April 17 and 18, as one of these patriots, a man named Paul Revere,
prepared to make his famous ride.

MONDAY CAME taut and overstrung. At the Province House General Gage was constantly in conference with his officers. Colonel Smith was to command the eight hundred men. Pitcairn himself was to go as second in command, serving as a volunteer. Lord Percy was to bring up reserves if necessary. General Gage "did not think the damned rebels would . . . take up arms against his Majesty's Troops." He was confident the sortie could be made, the stores destroyed, and his men brought back to Boston before any alarm roused the "countrymen" to action. Only two people were told the destination of the regulars—Lord Percy and Gage's own wife.

Tuesday was even tenser. The grenadiers and light infantry companies of the various regiments were ordered to prepare to march that night. Some of these men were billeted in private houses, or their women worked as servants. It was impossible to keep it a secret that they were to report for active duty. For instance, a Mrs. Stedman had hired as a housemaid the wife of one of the soldiers. As the sergeant went about rounding up his men, he could not find the husband, Gibson. He went to Mrs. Stedman and asked her to tell the man, if he turned up at her house, "he was to report himself at eight o'clock at the bottom of the Common, equipped for an expedition." Mrs. Stedman immediately sent word to Doctor Church. When Gibson arrived, she told him to prepare for the march, and "Oh, Gibson," she said, "what are you going to do?"

"Ah, Madam, I know as little as you do. I only know that I must go."

So in one way or another it might be guessed that the British were about to march. But where? Somehow Gage's secret was betrayed.

On Tuesday afternoon Gage sent out a group of picked officers. It was for them to block the roads leading towards Concord so no rebel express could ride through and warn the town. They were to pretend to be merely a pleasure party riding out to Cambridge for a dinner in the country. Their arms would be hidden by their cloaks. If questioned closely, they could admit that they were out after their own deserters. At Cambridge some of these men would turn towards Charlestown and after dark hide in the bushes to waylay any messenger who might cross the river and try to reach Concord by that route. The other officers were to do their intercepting closer to Concord. This latter is the most famous of the two groups. They were under Major Edward Mitchell. With him were Captain Lumm, Captain Cochrane, Lieutenant Grant, and one other officer—or perhaps the "sarjant" that Revere noticed. The British accounts say that all these men were officers, the Yankees call them sometimes officers and sometimes officers and their servants. These men knew Paul Revere's name, but not his face. Of these two nets spread out to catch him or any other man who attempted to go through that night, Paul Revere knew nothing. Of the third precaution all Boston knew. The man-of-war *Somerset* was moved into the very mouth of the Charles River, commanding the expanse of water any boat headed for Charlestown must cross.

The officers must have known before they left Tuesday afternoon what was their destination. Hanging about the stable, making sure for themselves that their horses were properly saddled and in top condition, talking happily about "the hell to pay tomorrow," it is likely they are the ones who let slip Gage's plans. For a groom at the Province House is said to have overheard the officers' talk. He confided in a friend of his, a fellow hostler at a near-by stable. This second boy (who had pretended to be a supporter of the Crown) then ran to Paul Revere. There was hell to pay on Wednesday and Concord was the objective.

"You are the third person who has brought me the same information," Paul Revere said, and he cautioned the boy not to say anything to anyone else. But even as the web of Paul Revere's and Joseph Warren's spy system closed about Gage's secret, the British officers were, with a pretence at nonchalance, but causing much excitement wherever they went, preparing to take their stations along the country roads to ensnare Paul Revere.

At dusk, Lord Percy left General Gage at the Province House and went quietly to the Common, where the boats were drawn up and already troops lined up waiting to embark. The townspeople stood about watching these preparations. The Earl was not recognized and listened to their comments. He heard a voice say:

"The British troops have marched, but will miss their aim."

"What aim?" asked Percy.

"Why, the cannon at Concord."

Percy went back to Gage. In some way their secret was known. The story is that Gage believed it was his American wife who had betrayed him, she being, as an early historian has it, "unequally yoked in point of politics" to her famous husband. This version seems to be gossip started by Gage's own officers, who did not like him and wanted to throw suspicion upon him and his wife.

At Joseph Warren's, the plans were perfected. As soon as it was definitely known whether the British went by land or sea, Robert Newman would be notified and the lanterns in Christ's [1] hung. This he had already agreed to do. He was twenty-three at the time. His older brother was organist at Christ's and he was sexton. He did not like the work, but had taken the job "because," as he said, "times are so hard." Not only did he have the keys to the church, but lived just across the street from it. The only drawback was that his mother's house was full of British officers billeted on the family.

These lanterns would give the warning, but no detail, of the expedition. Farther up stream the British boats would be ferrying over the troops. There was a chance Paul Revere could get past the *Somerset*—but only a chance. He was ready to take it.

William Dawes, the young cordwainer, would attempt to ride out through the British sentries on the Neck. He lived near North Square and his father was a silversmith. Undoubtedly Revere knew him well. He had played no conspicuous part in the brewing revolution, as had Revere, and was not a marked man, although he had recently knocked down a soldier for insulting his pretty wife. In previous years he had carried letters for the Salisbury family. "Billy" Dawes was a born actor. Later, during the siege of Boston, he used to go in and out almost at will, disguised as a drunken farmer, thoroughly enjoying himself and the risks he took. In the portrait painted of him in middle age, when he could write Major in front of his name and the proud word "merchant" after it, he is still a comical-looking fellow, with his close-set eyes,

[1] *Christ's:* in later years called "Old North Church."

long nose, and humorous mouth. If anyone could allay suspicion
of the sentries, act the part of an inebriated farmer or a half-witted
bumpkin, it would be Billy Dawes. Paul Revere looked as clever
as he was. Billy Dawes did not. He would have farther to go than
Revere and about an equally poor chance of getting through. He
passed the gates by pretending great innocence and with the connivance of a British soldier.

Now that the troops were actually at the bottom of the Common,
Joseph Warren started Billy Dawes over the Neck and sent for
Paul Revere. The time had come.

"About ten o'clock Dr. Warren sent in great haste for me, and
begged that I would immediately set off for Lexington, where
Messrs. Hancock and Adams were, and acquaint them of the
movement, and that it was thought they were the objects. When
I got to Dr. Warren's house, I found he had sent an express by land
to Lexington—a Mr. William Dawes." As is often pointed out,
Paul Revere never got to Concord; it is noteworthy that it was only
Lexington he originally started out to warn. Yet he definitely had
Concord in mind as well.

The two friends parted. When, if ever, they would meet again
they could not know. Joseph Warren would chance staying inside
the lines a little longer for the sake of the information he might
pick up. But any moment he might hear the rap on his door and
see a corporal's guard, an officer with the warrant for his arrest in
his hand—wanted in London for treason. Paul Revere also risked
all he had and life as well. General Gage had handled the insurrection thus far with kid gloves, but no country has ever hesitated
to drop with a bullet, if necessary, a man caught exciting to armed
revolt.

First Paul sought out Robert Newman, who, knowing that it
might be awkward for a prominent Son of Liberty and express
rider to rap at his mother's door and call him out, had pretended
to go to bed early, leaving the officers in the living-rooms, then
slipped out an upper window, over a roof, and was already in the
dark street waiting for any orders. One of the vestrymen at
Christ's, John Pulling, went with Newman, as probably did Revere's neighbor, Thomas Barnard. The door was locked after him

and the guard stood in the street as the young fellow took the lanterns from the closet and softly mounted the wooden stairs Paul Revere's feet had once known so well. Higher and higher, feeling his way in the darkness, he climbed, past the eight great bells, silent in the bell loft, until he came to the highest window of the belfry. To the north he could see, over the shoulder of Copp's Hill, the mouth of the Charles, the black hull of the *Somerset,* the glimmer of her riding lights. Beyond was Charlestown, and there he knew men were waiting, watching for his signal. He lit the lanterns, hung them, and felt his way back to the floor of the church. Probably Newman displayed his lanterns for a moment only. He certainly could not wish to warn the *Somerset.* They were out by the time Paul Revere had crossed into Charlestown. In spite of the poem, they were not a signal to Paul Revere, but from him. The Sunday before he had told Colonal Conant to watch for them. When the men in Charlestown saw 'a glimmer and then a gleam of light,' Paul Revere was still in Boston.

Something must have happened in the street while Newman was inside, for he dared not leave by the way he had come. Instead he climbed out of a window at the rear of the church, circled about, and entered his mother's house by the roofs and the upper window. Lying awake, he might hear below him the laughter of the officers over their cards. That much of the deed was done.

Having started Robert Newman on his ascent to fame, Paul Revere went to his own house in North Square. In all directions, marching in full battle gear, small groups of redcoats were leaving their barracks and billets, heading for the Common. Troops were lined up in North Square. No one was allowed to enter it or leave. Somehow Paul Revere got through them. He put on his short surtout and heavy riding boots. Perhaps Rachel tried to argue him out of this dangerous ride, for he seems to have been curiously absent-minded for so competent a man. He forgot two things. His spurs and some cloth with which to muffle the oars of his rowboat. So he left the house, and his dog followed him.

Joshua Bentley, a boatbuilder, and Thomas Richardson were ready to row him across. He picked them up at some prearranged place and the three started for the part of North Boston where that winter Paul Revere had kept his boat hidden. Then the matter of muffling the oars came up. None of them wished to return to his own house, but one of them had a girl friend. He gave a peculiar whistle outside her window, at the corner of North and North Centre Streets. The window went up. There was a whispered conversation and a flannel petticoat was tossed down. Revere told his children that it was still warm when they got it. Then Revere remembered his spurs. He wrote a note to Rachel, tied it to his dog's collar. Soon the dog was back again with the spurs. This story he also told his children, but perhaps only to amuse them. So at last he was booted and spurred, but a long way yet from being ready to ride.

The *Somerset* blocked the shortest route, forcing them to keep rather well out to sea. She was a great frigate of sixty-four guns and was stationed there for but one purpose—to keep men like Paul Revere in Boston. A cry to heave to or even a spatter of shot was expected. Beyond her, upstream, the British boats were going back and forth already, carrying the regulars to Cambridge.

All winter it had been abnormally warm and spring had come almost a month ahead of itself. Fruit trees were in blossom; the fields already ploughed. That night, however, was chill, and "it was young flood, the ship was winding and the moon was rising," as Paul Revere noticed. The muffled oars softly eased his little rowboat closer and closer to the Charlestown side. There had been neither hail nor shot from the *Somerset*. So he leaped to dry land close to the old Battery. Richardson and Bentley had done their work. Revere went on alone.

At Colonel Conant's he found a group waiting for him. Had they seen his signals? They had. He told them "what was acting" and learned to his surprise that the roads towards Cambridge and on to Concord were already patrolled by British officers who had left Boston in the afternoon.

Richard Devens, of the Committee of Safety, said he had left Menotomy in his chaise around sunset. And he had seen "a great number of B.O. (British officers) and their servants on horseback." As they were behaving in a suspiciously nonchalant manner and had asked where "Clark's tavern was," Devens had sent word to the Clark parsonage. It might be they were out to arrest the two rebel chiefs housed there. He knew this messenger might be

picked up, as he was. Paul Revere himself might have better luck.
He would need a good horse to slip through the cordon. Probably
he had as fine a mount as the luxurious town of Charlestown could
produce. John Larkin was one of the wealthiest citizens. It was
his best horse that was now turned over to Revere. Twenty-three
years later, he gratefully remembered how good, how "very good,"
was this Larkin horse. It would be slender and nervous in the
Yankee manner, small by modern standards, surefooted, tireless.
Now for the remainder of the night Revere's success, perhaps his
life and the lives of others, would depend upon this horse. He
would adjust the stirrups carefully to his own length, test with a
forefinger the snugness of the girths. They must be tight, but not
binding. The bit must hang exactly right. In that unhurried moment before mounting, he could measure the courage and stamina
of his companion, catch the flash of white in the wild, soft eye,
note the impatient stamp of the small hooves, feel under his hand
the swelling of muscle along the neck, the strength in withers and
loin, his touch and voice assuring the sensitive animal that he was
his friend.

And now it was eleven o'clock. Only an hour before, he had
stood in Joseph Warren's parlor knowing that the time had come.
Then, by the bright cold moonlight everyone noticed that night,
he swung to the saddle. Colonel Conant, Richard Devens, the light
from the open door, were left behind. He eventually rode about
twelve miles to get to Lexington and Concord was six miles farther
on. Probably he would set a pace which he believed would last
him through. With the hundreds of miles he had ridden the last
few years, he would be able to judge well. Nor would he wish to
fling himself headlong into any trap set for him by that advance
guard of officers Devens had warned him of, with a jaded mount.
For such an emergency his horse must have an extra spurt of speed
left in him. That he rode the Larkin horse with more care than he
does on sugar boxes, American Legion posters, copper advertisements, and all known pictures and statutes is proved by the excellent condition the animal was in five hours later.

So away, down the moonlit road, goes Paul Revere and the
Larkin horse, galloping into history, art, editorials, folklore, poetry;

the beat of those hooves never to be forgotten. The man, his bold, dark face bent, his hands light on the reins, his body giving to the flowing rhythm beneath him, becoming, as it were, something greater than himself—not merely one man riding one horse on a certain lonely night of long ago, but a symbol to which his countrymen can yet turn.

Paul Revere had started on a ride, which, in a way, has never ended.

SUGGESTIONS FOR STUDY

1. What part did each of these persons play in making Paul Revere's mission a success: Joseph Warren, Robert Newman, William Dawes, John Pulling, Thomas Barnard, Joshua Bentley, Thomas Richardson, Colonel Conant, John Larkin?

2. What are "muffled oars"?

3. When Paul Revere told his children the story about the part his dog played in the events of this chapter, do you think Revere did so because the incident was true, or did he make it up simply to amuse the children?

4. In what way is General Gage's predicament with respect to his superiors in the British government made clear in this chapter?

5. Find a copy of Longfellow's poem, "Paul Revere's Ride." In what way is the poem historically inaccurate? For instance, what is there in the Longfellow poem which gives you the impression that Paul Revere was the only patriot out riding on that fateful night? List the misconceptions or misunderstandings you had about Paul Revere before reading this portion of his biography. In what way has Esther Forbes's biography presented you with a more exciting telling of the events than you found even in the Longfellow poem?

6. In connection with the elaborate preparations to cross the Charles River, what details are given by the author which add suspense to the account? What detail adds a touch of humor? How would you describe the ascent to the tower of Christ's Church? What atmosphere prevailed there as the lanterns were being carried to their place?

7. You may be interested in reading a short story, "A Tooth for Paul Revere," by Stephen Vincent Benet, an excellent example of historical fiction. (For a discussion of the use of historical facts in the writing of fiction, see *The Short Story Reader*, p. 189.)

8. Using a good reference book, find out how Patriots' Day is celebrated in Massachusetts today.

A Flogging at Sea

RICHARD HENRY DANA, JR.

Without biographies to remind us of cruelties and sufferings that existed in the past, we would be more inclined to forget the unpleasant pages of history. To help you see the ordeals and indignities that were the life of the American seaman in the early 1800's, you can turn to *Two Years before the Mast*, by Richard Henry Dana, Jr. Having served in the lowly position of ordinary seaman, Dana felt keenly the rigors of that life. He was an educated person, and his straightforward, well-written journal of his own personal grievances, when published, aroused the general public, who ultimately—and with success—pressed for reform.

As you read "A Flogging at Sea," think not only of the grim realities of the situation in which Dana found himself, but also of the effect his account had on the people of his day.

FOR SEVERAL DAYS the captain seemed very much out of humor. Nothing went right or fast enough for him. He quarreled with the cook, and threatened to flog him for throwing wood on deck, and had a dispute with the mate about reeving a Spanish burton; the mate saying that he was right, and had been taught how to do it by a man *who was a sailor!* This the captain took in dudgeon and they were at swords' points at once. But his displeasure was chiefly turned against a large, heavy-moulded fellow from the Middle States, who was called Sam. This man hesitated in his speech, was rather slow in his motions, and was only a tolerably good sailor, but usually seemed to do his best; yet the captain took a dislike to him, thought he was surly and lazy, and "if you once give a dog a bad name"—as the sailor-phrase is—"he may as well jump overboard." The captain found fault with everything this man did, and hazed him for dropping a marline-spike from the main yard, where he was at work. This, of course, was an accident, but it was set down against him. The captain was on board all day Friday, and everything went on hard and disagreeably. "The more you drive a man, the less he will do," was as true with us as with any other people. We worked late Friday night, and were turned-to early Saturday morning. About ten o'clock the captain ordered our new officer, Russell, who by this time had become thoroughly disliked by all the crew, to get the gig ready to take him ashore. John, the Swede, was sitting in the boat alongside, and Mr. Russell and I were standing by the main hatchway, waiting for the captain, who was down in the hold, where the crew were at work, when we heard his voice raised in violent dispute with somebody, whether it was with the mate or one of the crew I could not tell, and then came blows and scuffling. I ran to the side and beckoned to John, who came aboard, and we leaned down the hatchway, and though we could see no one, yet we knew that the captain had the advantage, for his voice was loud and clear—

"You see your condition! You see your condition! Will you ever give me any more of your *jaw?*" No answer; and then came wrestling and heaving, as though the man was trying to turn him. "You may as well keep still, for I have got you," said the captain. Then came the question, "Will you ever give me any more of your jaw?"

"I never gave you any, sir," said Sam; for it was his voice that we heard, though low and half choked.

"That's not what I ask you. Will you ever be impudent to me again?"

"I never have been, sir," said Sam.

"Answer my question, or I'll make a spread eagle of you! I'll flog you, by G—d."

"I'm no Negro slave," said Sam.

"Then I'll make you one," said the captain; and he came to the hatchway, and sprang on deck, threw off his coat, and, rolling up his sleeves, called out to the mate: "Seize that man up, Mr. Amerzene! Seize him up! Make a spread eagle of him! I'll teach you all who is master aboard!"

The crew and officers followed the captain up the hatchway; but it was not until after repeated orders that the mate laid hold of Sam, who made no resistance, and carried him to the gangway.

"What are you going to flog that man for, sir?" said John, the Swede, to the captain.

Upon hearing this, the captain turned upon John; but, knowing him to be quick and resolute, he ordered the steward to bring the irons, and, calling upon Russell to help him, went up to John.

"Let me alone," said John. "I'm willing to be put in irons. You need not use any force"; and, putting out his hands, the captain slipped the irons on, and sent him aft to the quarter-deck. Sam, by this time, was *seized up,* as it is called; that is, placed against the shrouds, with his wrists made fast to them, his jacket off, and his back exposed. The captain stood on the break of the deck, a few feet from him, and a little raised, so as to have a good swing at him, and held in his hand the end of a thick, strong rope. The officers stood round, and the crew grouped together in the waist. All these preparations made me feel sick and almost faint, angry and excited as I was. A man—a human being, made in God's likeness—fastened up and flogged like a beast! A man, too, whom I had lived with, eaten with, and stood watch with for months, and knew so well! If a thought of resistance crossed the minds of any of the men, what was to be done? Their time for it had gone by. Two men were fast, and there were left only two men besides Stimson and myself, and a small boy of ten or twelve years of age; and Stimson and I would not have joined the men in a mutiny, as they knew. And then, on the other side, there were (besides the captain) three officers, steward, agent, and clerk, and the cabin supplied with weapons. But besides the numbers, what is there for sailors to do? If they resist, it is mutiny; and if they succeed, and take the vessel, it is piracy. If they ever yield again, their punishment must come; and if they do not yield, what are they to be for the rest of their lives? If a sailor resist his commander, he resists the law, and piracy or submission is his only alternative. Bad as it was, they saw it must be borne. It is what a sailor ships for. Swinging the rope over his head, and bending his body so as to give it full force, the captain brought it down upon the poor fellow's back. One, twice,—six times. "Will you ever give me any more of your jaw?" The man writhed with pain, but said not a word. Three times more. This was too much, and he muttered something which

I could not hear; this brought as many more as the man could stand, when the captain ordered him to be cut down.

"Now for you," said the captain, making up to John, and taking his irons off. As soon as John was loose, he ran forward to the forecastle. "Bring that man aft!" shouted the captain. The second mate, who had been in the forecastle with these men the early part of the voyage, stood still in the waist, and the mate walked slowly forward; but our third officer, anxious to show his zeal, sprang forward over the windlass, and laid hold of John; but John soon threw him from him. The captain stood on the quarter-deck, bareheaded, his eyes flashing with rage, and his face as red as blood, swinging the rope, and calling out to his officers, "Drag him aft! Lay hold of him! I'll *sweeten* him!" etc., etc. The mate now went forward, and told John quietly to go aft; and he, seeing resistance vain, threw the blackguard third mate from him, said he would go aft of himself, that they should not drag him, and went up to the gangway and held out his hands; but as soon as the captain began to make him fast, the indignity was too much, and he struggled; but, the mate and Russell holding him, he was soon seized up. When he was made fast, he turned to the captain, who stood rolling up his sleeves, getting ready for the blow, and asked him what he was to be flogged for. "Have I ever refused my duty, sir? Have you ever known me to hang back or to be insolent, or not to know my work?"

"No," said the captain, "it is not that that I flog you for; I flog you for interference, for asking questions."

"Can't a man ask a question here without being flogged?"

"No," shouted the captain; "nobody shall open his mouth aboard this vessel but myself"; and he began laying the blows upon his back, swinging half round between each blow, to give it full effect. As he went on his passion increased, and he danced about the deck, calling out, as he swung the rope, "If you want to know what I flog you for, I'll tell you. It's because I like to do it! because I like to do it! It suits me! That's what I do it for!"

The man writhed under the pain until he could endure it no longer, when he called out, with an exclamation more common among foreigners than with us: "O Jesus Christ! O Jesus Christ!"

"Don't call on Jesus Christ," shouted the captain; *"He can't help you. Call on Frank Thompson!* He's the man! He can help you! Jesus Christ can't help you now!"

At these words, which I never shall forget, my blood ran cold. I could look on no longer. Disgusted, sick, I turned away, and leaned over the rail, and looked down into the water. A few rapid thoughts, I don't know what—our situation, a resolution to see the captain punished when we got home—crossed my mind; but the falling of the blows and the cries of the man called me back once more. At length they ceased, and, turning round, I found that the mate, at a signal from the captain, had cast him loose. Almost doubled up with pain, the man walked slowly forward, and went down into the forecastle. Every one else stood still at his post, while the captain, swelling with rage and with the importance of his achievement, walked the quarter-deck, and at each turn, as he came forward, calling out to us: "You see your condition! You see where I've got you all, and you know what to expect! You've been mistaken in me! You didn't know what I was! Now you know what I am! I'll make you toe the mark, every soul of you, or I'll flog you all, fore and aft, from the boy up! You've got a driver over you! Yes, a *slave-driver!* I'll see who'll tell me he isn't a slave!" With this and the like matter, equally calculated to quiet us, and to allay any apprehensions of future trouble, he entertained us for about ten minutes, when he went below. Soon after, John came aft, with his bare back covered with stripes and wales in every direction, and dreadfully swollen, and asked the steward to ask the captain to let him have some salve, or balsam, to put upon it. "No," said the captain, who heard him from below; "tell him to put his shirt on; that's the best thing for him, and pull me ashore in the boat. Nobody is going to lay-up on board this vessel." He then called to Mr. Russell to take those two men and two others in the boat, and pull him ashore. I went for one. The two men could hardly bend their backs, and the captain called to them to "give way!" but finding they did their best, he let them alone. The agent was in the stern sheets, but during the whole pull—a league or more—not a word was spoken. We landed; the captain, agent, and officer went up to the house, and left us with the boat. I and the man with me stayed near the boat, while John and Sam walked slowly away, and sat down on the rocks. They talked some time together, but at length separated, each sitting alone. I had some fears of John. He was a foreigner, and violently tempered, and under suffering; and he had his knife with him, and the captain was to come down alone to the boat. But nothing happened; and we went quietly on board. The captain was probably armed, and if either of them had lifted a hand against him, they would have had nothing before them but flight, and starvation in the woods of California, or capture by the soldiers and Indians, whom the offer of twenty dollars would have set upon them.

After the day's work was done we went down into the forecastle and ate our plain supper; but not a word was spoken. It was Saturday night; but, there was no song—no "sweethearts and wives." A gloom was over everything. The two men lay in their berths, groaning with pain, and we all turned in, but, for myself, not to sleep. A sound coming now and then from the berths of the two men showed that they were awake, as awake they must have been, for they could hardly lie in one posture long; the dim swinging lamp shed its light over the dark hole in which we lived, and many and various reflections and purposes coursed through my mind. I had no real apprehension that the captain would lay a hand on me; but I thought of our situation, living under a tyranny, with an ungoverned, swaggering fellow administering it; of the character of the country we were in; the length of the voyage; the uncertainty attending our return to America; and then, if we should return, the prospect of obtaining justice and satisfaction for these poor men; and I vowed that, if God should ever give me the means, I would do something to redress the grievances and relieve the sufferings of that class of beings with whom my lot had so long been cast.

SUGGESTIONS FOR STUDY

1. What is there in the opening lines of this selection which indicates that the captain is an incompetent seaman?

2. What is there in the action of the mate during the flogging of Sam which shows that the mate is unsympathetic with the captain?

3. What can be said in defense of the captain in his disagreement with the cook? With Sam? With John, the Swede?

4. Find the passage in which Dana most forcibly makes the case for reform.

5. Tell in your own words what Dana was thinking while Sam was being flogged. What, for instance, were his thoughts on the subject of piracy? What resolution did he make while lying in his berth that night?

6. If this selection makes you interested in the life on a sailing vessel in the 1830's, read the whole book and report to the class what you learn of such life, an important feature of that historical period.

7. *Two Years Before the Mast* not only illuminates history, it also made history. Two novels which also had an effect upon the course of history are *Uncle Tom's Cabin,* by Harriet Beecher Stowe, and *The Jungle,* by Upton Sinclair. Why are these books of historical or sociological importance?

8. Let some nautical enthusiast look up the following terms and make a report to the class on their meanings and significance in the selection: *reeving* a Spanish *burton,* dropping a *marline-spike, from the main yard, hatchway, aft, quarter-deck, waist, windlass, gangway, forecastle, toe the mark, stern sheets.*

The End of Lee's Battles

DOUGLAS SOUTHALL FREEMAN

As early as 1861 Robert E. Lee of Virginia was aware that the nation was threatened by anarchy and civil war. Only months later, Lee made a choice—he declined the President's offer to be commanding officer of all the Union forces and returned to his native state, in defense of which he regretfully decided that circumstances demanded him "to draw sword."

In this selection from Douglas Freeman's life of Lee intended for the young adult, you meet this man of "Christian fortitude" in further moments of decision. The year was 1865. A third of the Confederate Army had been captured in the Battle of Saylor's Creek. Lee's men had gone without rations for four days. The sad and pitiful state of things, as Lee knew, could not endure much longer. Must he, should he, surrender?

BY THE EVENING of the 7th of April, Lee had with him only the strongest and the most resolute of his soldiers. Many of the bravest had dropped from exhaustion. Other devoted men had dragged themselves along but reluctantly had thrown away the rifles they no longer could carry. The few cowards and some of the feeble of heart had crept away in the darkness to beg, to steal, or to surrender. Starved horses were breaking down along with the men. Everywhere on the highway that led to Lynchburg, vehicles and dying animals littered the road. When possible, the loaded wagons were set afire to keep their contents from falling into the hands of the enemy. Pale, staggering men looked like ghosts where their faces were lighted by the flames.

If General Lee knew by this time that the end had come, he told nobody. He was weary and burdened but outwardly he was calm and almost as confident in appearance as if he still felt sure the Army would escape and join Johnston in the successful continuance of the war. On the 8th of April, conditions made thousands think the General would pull them out of the trap the Federals were trying to spring. The march that morning was not interrupted by Union pursuit. Spring sunshine was bright. Scarcely a shot was heard. The cavalry reported that the blue infantry was behind them. Indications there were, also, that the Federals were moving westward parallel to the Confederates and south of them. Of course, if this parallel column marched faster than Lee's Army could, then the Unionists might cut off the retreat, just as they had at Jetersville. If the Federals did *not* head off the retreat, all still would come out all right as the boys so often had said when they had talked of General Lee's outwitting the enemy.

On the evening of the 8th, the Army halted on the nearer side of a little stream close to Appomattox Court House. It was a humble countryside, untroubled by war. The road was ugly and deeply washed, but the pines had the lustrous green of new life. The tall oaks were tasseling. If there had been rations, the men might have rested in hope. Even as it was, at sunset they were not wholly in despair.

After nightfall there was a difference for those soldiers on high ground. North of them the clouds shone gray. Eastward, there was a red reflection in the sky—Federal campfires! In the south, it was the same. Almost the whole of that arc of the horizon was red from the fires that far-extended Union Divisions had lighted. Eagerly, anxiously, heart in mouth, observers looked westward, up the road to Lynchburg. There, too, the Confederates saw the ominous glow of fires. They were not so numerous as in the south and in the west, but the red was there! Federals in unknown numbers were across the road. On three sides, the Army was surrounded. The only escape was northward, in the direction that would carry the Army into a land made barren by war.

At his camp in the woods, Lee met with his senior lieutenants to decide what should be done. The day before he had received under flag of truce a letter in which Grant had called for the surrender of the Army. Lee had shown this to no one except Long-

street, whose only comment had been, "Not yet." In an answer to
the Federal commander, Lee had inquired what terms would be
offered. Grant had said in a second letter that he would insist on
no terms except the surrender of the men and their pledge not to
fight again until they were exchanged. Lee's reply had carried his
refusal to surrender but had suggested a meeting for a general
consideration of peace. No answer to this letter had been received.
In the absence of any further word from Grant, the fate of the
Army hung on its ability to cut its way through the Federals, who
were across the road to Lynchburg. That, in turn, depended on
how strong the Federals were and whether they were cavalry or
infantry. A light force of cavalry could be swept aside, but if a
heavy force of infantry was encountered, then nothing remained
for Lee to do except . . . to surrender.

Plans were made for Gordon's infantry and Fitz Lee's cavalry
to attack in front the next morning. Behind these troops, the rest
of the Army was to proceed with few wagons and guns so that
the column, if it got away, could move fast. All this was arranged
by General Lee, who then lay down for a few hours of rest.

About 3 o'clock Lee arose, dressed himself in his best uniform,
tied his officer's red sash around his waist, and put on his finest
sword. When asked later in the morning why he did this, he said
simply: "I have probably to be General Grant's prisoner and
thought I must make my best appearance." Astride Traveller, he
rode to the front and soon heard the guns of Gordon's attack. The
fire swelled and dwindled and rose again and then continued un-
evenly. From the sound Lee could not tell whether Gordon was
gaining or losing ground. Consequently an officer was sent forward to get a report. It was 8 o'clock when the officer came back
with this message from Gordon: "Tell General Lee I have fought
my Corps to a frazzle, and I fear I can do nothing unless I am
heavily supported by Longstreet's Corps." Gordon had met both
infantry and cavalry in large numbers. These Federals had beaten
off his attack and now were trying to get between him and the
other Confederate troops. Longstreet could not help. His small
force was facing a great mass of Unionists who were closing from
the rear.

To the report of this situation, Lee listened in silence. A moment later he said in anguish of spirit: "Then there is nothing left for me to do but go and see General Grant, and I would rather die a thousand deaths."

His words were heard by numbers of his officers. For a minute or two they were overwhelmed with grief. "Oh, General," one of them broke out, "what will history say of the surrender of the Army in the field?"

"Yes," Lee replied, "I know they will say hard things of us." He went on: "They will not understand how we were overwhelmed by numbers. But that is not the question, Colonel: The question is, Is it right to surrender this Army? If it is right, then I will take all the responsibility."

Consciousness of this duty strengthened him for a short while, but soon he looked across the field toward the Federal position and said, as if to himself, "How easily I could be rid of this, and be at rest! I have only to ride along the line and it will be all over!" He paused and took a grip on his emotions: "But it is our duty to live. What will become of the women and children of the South if we are not here to protect them?"

He talked next with Longstreet and Mahone and found that they believed he should surrender, but one of the younger Generals, Porter Alexander, said he thought the Army should scatter and take to the woods and reassemble later. Two-thirds of the men, Alexander argued, could get away.

Lee answered that the number was too small to accomplish anything. After explaining that, Lee continued: "Then, General, you and I as Christian men have no right to consider only how this would affect us. We must consider the effect on the country as a whole. Already it is demoralized by the four years of war. If I took your advice, then men would be without rations and under no control of officers. They would become mere bands of marauders, and the enemy's cavalry would pursue them and overrun many sections they may never have occasion to visit. We would bring on a state of affairs it would take the country years to recover from. And, as for myself, you young fellows might go to bushwhacking, but the only dignified course for me would be to go to

General Grant and surrender myself and take the consequences of my acts."

In that spirit Lee rode to the rear, where he hoped Grant would meet him for the conference he had suggested the previous day. Instead, Grant sent word that he could not consider a general peace. Lee learned, also, that the powerful Union troops in rear of Longstreet had orders to advance and did not think they could wait for a further message to be sent General Grant. After several exchanges, the Northern officers agreed to a brief truce in order to permit Lee to dispatch a letter to the Federal commander. As Grant was believed to be on a road south of the Confederates, Lee was told that he might save time by having the paper carried to the front. Lee accordingly wrote a brief note in which he asked an interview.

While this message was being forwarded to Grant, there was a long, long wait under a tree in a small apple orchard by the side of the Lynchburg road. Lee had little to say. His companions did not attempt to talk to him because they understood how he was suffering. About 12:15, he saw a Federal officer coming down the road from the direction of Appomattox. With him was a Confederate. Everyone made the same guess: The man in blue brought a letter from Grant.

"General," said Longstreet, "unless he offers us honorable terms, come back and let us fight it out."

Lee made no answer, but Longstreet thought his chief looked firmer because of the advice. Quickly Lee read the letter from his opponent. It was an offer to meet Lee at any place the Confederate leader named. The preliminaries were ended; the time had come for the final act. It could be nothing less than the surrender of that gallant Army of devoted men. The thought was agonizing; the very word "surrender" was one that burnt any Southern lips that uttered it; but it had to be spoken.

With the Federal officer, a member of his own staff and a courier, Lee rode down to the little stream, where Traveller stopped for a long drink, and then up the slight grade and into the village. Another wait there was while Lee's staff officer, Col. Charles Marshall, searched for a house in which to hold the meeting with

Grant. The final choice was the two-story frame dwelling of Maj. Wilmer McLean who, by the strangest of chances, had moved from Manassas after the battle of July 21, 1861, and had come to Appomattox to escape all contact with war.

Lee rode into the yard of the McLean house, dismounted, climbed the steps, went into the parlor and took a seat near a table in the front, farther corner of the room. There he remained for half-an-hour, a terrible half hour of silence that must have seemed as long as a lifetime of misery. Then, from the road, came the clatter of horses' hoofs and the sound of many boots on the steps. Soon a thin, slightly stooped and bearded man of middle height walked into the room. It was Grant. He shook hands quietly. Then he sat down at a table in the middle of the room and spoke briefly to the staff officer who had accompanied him. The officer stepped out and came back in a moment with a dozen or more bluecoated Generals and Colonels, who silently lined the wall. These were Grant's lieutenants. He wanted them to be present at the death of the Army they had helped to kill.

There was a brief reference by the two leaders to the fact that they had been in Mexico at the same time. After a tense pause, Lee began: "I suppose, General Grant, that the object of our meeting is fully understood. I asked to see you to ascertain upon what terms you would receive the surrender of my Army." This was said with perfect courage and with flawless self-command, though everyone knew that Lee would have given his life to be spared the necessity of uttering those few words.

Grant was as courteous and considerate as a man could be. Not one note of exultation was in his answer; not one glance did he turn to the other officers, whose hearts were beating high. The Federal commander said simply that he would accept the surrender of the Army, would leave the officers their swords, and would let the men go to their homes. All arms, animals, and equipment must be given up.

When these generous terms were written out, Lee explained that in the Confederate Army the cavalrymen and some of the artillerists owned their horses. Would these men be permitted to take their animals? Grant reflected. He did not know, he said, that any of Lee's troops owned their horses, but he supposed most of the soldiers were small farmers who might not be able to raise a crop to carry them through the next winter unless they had their horses. "I will arrange it this way: I will not change the terms as now written, but I will instruct the officers I shall appoint to receive the paroles to let all the men who claim to own a horse or mule take the animals home with them to work their little farms."

Lee's face showed his relief: "This," he said, "will have the very best possible effect upon the men; it will be very gratifying and will do much toward conciliating our people."

One other painful explanation Lee was compelled to make: He had Federal prisoners he could not feed; in fact, he had no provisions for his own men, and he hoped Grant would permit the use of rations ordered from Lynchburg. Lee was ignorant of it, but these trains containing the food already had been captured. Grant did not humiliate Lee by announcing it. He merely said he would send rations to Lee's men but unfortunately had no forage for the horses.

In a few minutes, the terms of surrender were copied. Lee's acceptance was written by Colonel Marshall and was signed by the General. After a few more words, Lee rose, shook hands with Grant, bowed to the other officers and left the room. While waiting for his horse, he stood on the porch and, when he put on his gauntlets, he abstractedly smote his hands together as he looked across the fields to the hill where the remnant of his Army waited. Soon the horse was ready. Lee mounted. On the porch Grant and the other Federals took off their hats. Lee raised his without a word and rode slowly off.

The early halt in the fighting that day and the passage of the flags of truce had led some of the soldiers to suspect that a surrender was being arranged. Most of the higher officers knew this was true. Thousands of other Confederates had never admitted even to themselves the possibility of such a thing. Now, as they saw Lee coming up the road, they went to meet him. Anxious, doubtful, curious or confident, they crowded around the General, who steeled himself for the ordeal. The men started to cheer him, and then, when they saw in his face the agony of his spirit, they sensed the reason for it and choked their cheer. "General," some of them asked, "are we surrendered?" Others in startled voices repeated the inquiry. As they spoke, they closed around him in the road and took off their caps. He removed his hat and bowed, but he could make no answer. Still the question, "General, General, are we surrendered?" Painfully, Lee pulled in his horse and stopped in the midst of the throng. In shaken tones, struggling with his emotions, he said slowly: "Men, we have fought the war together, and I have done the best I could for you. You will all be paroled and go to your homes until exchanged." He tried to say more but all he could force from his trembling lips was a half-inaudible "Good-bye."

His misery made the soldiers forget theirs. They crowded even closer around him again as he started onward. Some stretched out trembling hands to him; some touched his arm, his uniform, his boots, his horse, and they gave him such comfort as they could. "General, we'll fight yet; General, say the word and we'll go in and fight 'em yet." When he reached the apple orchard, they came as close as the guards would permit and, later, when he rode back to his tent in the woods they followed him there, with blessings, with tears, with pledges and with appeals that he lead them once more against the enemy.

Rations came to some of the Confederate camps that night, and to others the next day. Rolls were made of the soldiers who remained to the last. Paroles were printed. All the details were arranged in exact accord with the terms Lee and Grant had signed. By Lee's direction an address was prepared and was read to all his troops. In this famous "General Order No. 9" or "last order," Lee told the men that he had not surrendered them because he doubted their willingness to fight but because "valor and devotion could accomplish nothing that could compensate for the loss that must have attended the continuance of the contest." Terms of surrender were explained again. The concluding words were these: "You will take with you the satisfaction that proceeds from the consciousness of duty faithfully performed; and I earnestly pray that a merciful God will extend to you His blessing and protection. With an unceasing admiration of your constancy and devotion to

your country, and a grateful remembrance of your kind and generous consideration for myself, I bid you all an affectionate farewell."

To this tribute, the Federals added that of their considerate
silence. They were as splendid as brave men could be in sparing
the feelings of a defeated adversary; but their commander insisted
that formal surrender be made. The Northern people must have
evidence that the most dreaded "rebel" Army had laid down its
arms and its flags in front of a Federal line. On the 11th, the artil-
lerymen yielded up their guns. The next morning, the Confederate
infantry came down the hill, crossed the little river and marched
between the open ranks of Union troops who chivalrously saluted
them. So few were the survivors that their battleflags were
crowded together until the heads of all the men appeared to be
under the red halo of their banners.

SUGGESTIONS FOR STUDY

1. You may have heard the expression: war brings out the beast
in man. What evidence is there in this selection that proves that
even in war human beings can be humane and honorable?

2. Contrast the techniques of warfare in 1865 with those of present
times. How does an understanding of these differences illuminate the
events of each time?

3. What easy-way-out came to Lee? How did Lee answer his own
question?

4. What were the terms of the surrender?

5. How does this selection dramatize the idea that from defeat
can come success?

6. Look up the word *magnanimous.* How does this word apply to
both Lee and Grant?

7. Describe the countryside around Appomattox. What atmosphere
prevailed there as Lee approached the site? In what respect was this
a suitable setting for the historical event which was to take place
there? What was ironical about the fact that the surrender arrangements were made in Major Wilmer McLean's home?

8. Find scenes that demonstrate that silence can speak louder than
words. What was your reaction to these scenes?

9. Write a paragraph based on this selection in which you show
what you think Robert E. Lee was like.

Mother to a King

JAMES POPE-HENNESSEY

The history books tell us that in December, 1936, King Edward VIII of England, forced to choose between love and his throne, chose love. But to understand this abdication as a crisis in the lives of real, living human beings, the British royal family, we must turn to biography.

Queen Mary; 1867–1953 is an entertaining and perceptive portrait of King Edward's mother, who led a very eventful life. As the charming Princess May of Teck she became engaged to the Prince of Wales; and after his death she married the new heir apparent to the throne, the brother of the dead prince. As wife of King George V, she was Queen of England for over twenty-five years, and later lived to see two sons and a granddaughter become ruling monarchs of her country. Through a long life which included two world wars, this wonderful woman "endeared herself to her own nation and to the world."

The following selection tells how this great queen, who was dedicated to duty and who all her life put her country before everything else, reacted to the shock of her son's abdication.

THAT SUMMER [1936], breaking with his father's tradition of spending August on the grouse moors, King Edward VIII had chartered a yacht, the *Nahlin,* in which, escorted by two destroyers, he proposed to cruise with a small staff and a few of his personal friends off the Adriatic coast. The King had at first hoped to board the yacht at Venice, but, in view of the anti-British feeling then current in Italy over the imposition of sanctions, the Foreign Office did not deem this wise. The King and his guests therefore joined the *Nahlin* at Sibenic, a small port on the Dalmatian coast. "I am glad you have chartered a yacht," wrote Queen Mary from Sandringham, "& I hope you will find sunshine & good weather abroad & be able to get out to Venice or wherever you

Reprinted from QUEEN MARY by James Pope-Hennessy, by permission of Alfred A. Knopf, Inc. Copyright 1959 by James Pope-Hennessy.

join the yacht in comfort, I hope too that this autumn may be free
from complications of which we have had more than our share for
years. It was a nice day today & less cold & no rain for a wonder."
In Queen Mary's usage, "complications" was a capacious word;
like the adjectives "tiresome" and "worrying," it could be made to
cover any number of awkward or critical situations, from an international crisis like that caused by the Italian attack on Abyssinia
to a matter of the most private family or domestic concern.

To the world at large, and most specifically to the public of the
United States of America, the short cruise of the *Nahlin* was the
subject of violent curiosity and loud conjecture, for it was known
that amongst the guests aboard the yacht was a married lady from
Baltimore, Mrs. Wallis Warfield Simpson; and to everyone but
the readers of the discreet and loyal British press it was equally
known that the bachelor King Edward VIII and Mrs. Simpson
were in love. Dogged by reporters, photographers, and tourists
wherever they landed, the party found their only true privacy on
board the yacht.

On 14 September King Edward got back to London. He went
that same night to dine with his mother at Buckingham Palace,
where Queen Mary was for the moment occupying the late King's
rooms. "Greeting her," he writes, "I wondered how much she knew
about the stories appearing in the American press. But her conversation told me nothing." . . .

The Coronation, in Westminster Abbey, of King Edward VIII
had been fixed for the 12th of May 1937. Preparations for this ceremony were already well advanced in the autumn of 1936. It was a
quarter of a century since there had been any Coronation in the
Abbey, and there had been none in living memory of a British
Monarch without a Consort. . . . Thus, to the generation which
had grown up during the First World War, and even to a good
many of their parents, the prospect of the crowning of the bachelor
King Edward seemed less that of the performance of an imme-
morial rite than the expectation of an interesting novelty. . . .

All this time Queen Mary was steadily and actively pursuing
her own plans for moving from Buckingham Palace to Marlborough House. "Things are getting on very slowly," she complained

to her Diary after one of her daily visits of inspection at Marlborough House in early September. She now hoped to achieve the final move in the last fourteen days of that month, while the King was entertaining at Balmoral. "The news that I intended to spend the last two weeks of September at Balmoral pleased her," writes the Duke of Windsor of his mother at that time. "To my mother the habits and customs of the family meant almost as much as the official obligations devolving upon us: she hoped now that I had become the head of the family that I would return more to the ways of my father." For Queen Mary this particular hope proved a forlorn one, since the King's September house-party at Balmoral seemed inspired more by the carefree spirit of the *Nahlin* cruise than by any conscious imitation of the staid, traditional hospitality which King George V and Queen Mary had dispensed year after year to certain chosen statesmen, to the Archbishop of Canterbury, and to King George's old friends. Upon the courtiers of the last reign, the very names officially announced in the newspapers as those of some of King Edward VIII's guests at Balmoral Castle that September of 1936 had a rather jarring effect. . . . The names of individuals, as history has repeatedly shown us, can suddenly and without warning assume an importance unexplained by any theory of semantics. For some time past the plain and unpretentious surname Simpson had taken on for Queen Mary and for her family an ominous ring.

Up at Balmoral some of the King's brothers began to feel that they no longer enjoyed the King's confidence. In especial, the heir-presumptive to the throne, the Duke of York, found himself, in his official biographer's words, "shut off from his brother, neglected, ignored, unwanted. . . . He felt that he had lost a friend and was rapidly losing a brother"; for King Edward VIII's emotions, strong and exclusive, were characteristically concentrated upon the person whom he loved. In the United States of America and in continental Europe the newspapers were now frankly predicting that when Mrs. Simpson, who had applied for a divorce that summer, should have become free, she would marry the King and mount the British throne as Queen Consort and Empress of India. In this country the London and provincial press still maintained, although with increasing difficulty, its voluntary silence on the subject, but the number of letters of shock and protest from British residents abroad which now poured into Buckingham Palace and 10 Downing Street, Lambeth Palace and *The Times* office in Printing House Square, grew daily in volume. Many such letters were addressed to Queen Mary at Marlborough House, urging her to act before it was too late. The letter-writers did not, however, indicate what action Queen Mary could take over a situation which was ambiguous and which, since it concerned her King, she would not discuss or acknowledge. Queen Mary read the letters, put them by, and tried to seek distraction from her agony of doubt in superintending the placing of furniture, of pictures, and of *objets d'art* in her new home, Marlborough House. . . .

Queen Mary had hardly been established at Marlborough House a fortnight when it became known that Mrs. Simpson's petition for divorce from her second husband would be heard towards the end of the month in the county court of Ipswich, in Suffolk. Like the three mallet-blows which precede the raising of the curtain in a French theatre, this brief announcement of the date for hearing the divorce petition—Tuesday, 27 October—declenched a drama which galvanized the literate world, and simultaneously revealed the elasticity and the inborn strength of the Constitution of the British Empire and of the British Monarchy.

The crisis of the autumn and winter of 1936 was, in fact, a triumphant proof that the life-work of King George the Fifth and of Queen Mary had not been in vain: "in any other country," Queen Mary wrote when all was over, "there would have been riots, thank God people did not lose their heads."

Much has been written about the abdication of King Edward VIII from the Imperial throne in December 1936; more will no doubt be written in the future. The Duke and the Duchess of Windsor have each of them published their narratives of the events which led up to the crisis. They have explained their motives and have indicated the emotional climate in which their parts in this drama were enacted. The chronology and the interplay of character in this startling episode in English history are, therefore, well established and, indeed, the documentation now available to students may be thought to be reasonably complete. In this chapter we are solely concerned with one aspect of the abdication of 1936: its effect upon the mother of two King-Emperors, Queen Mary.

It can be simply stated that Queen Mary greeted her son's decision to give up the throne with consternation, with anger, and with pain. To other members of the family she declared both at that time and subsequently that no single event in the whole of her life—which, we may recall, had not been an invariably happy one—had caused her so much real distress or left her with so deep a feeling of "humiliation." Even the pride she felt in watching the development as King and Queen of her second son and his wife failed to obliterate for her the memory of the shock which King Edward VIII's abdication had caused.

We have seen that although for many, many months Queen Mary had been subterraneously aware of King Edward VIII's love for Mrs. Simpson, she had never discussed the matter with him, hoping that with time the strength of the emotion might evaporate. She had, however, consulted one or two extraneous persons in her anxiety, and she had even urged the Cabinet to take some sort of "action" before Mrs. Simpson's divorce case came up for hearing. Queen Mary's anxiety arose, as is well known, from the fact that Mrs. Simpson, who was born of a good family in Maryland, had already divorced one husband and was on the verge of divorcing the second: Mrs. Simpson had, in fact, in Queen Mary's own phrase, "two husbands living," and she had, in Queen Mary's opinion, captivated the King. Queen Mary's views on divorce were clear and strict: one divorce could seldom or never be justified, and to divorce twice, on any grounds whatever, was to her unthinkable. As for the possibility of a lady "with two husbands living" marrying her eldest son and becoming Queen Consort, this was out of all question.

The sequence of events of the winter of 1936 showed that Queen Mary's standpoint was one that was shared by the British Cabinet and by the administrations of the Dominions, as well as by large sections of British and Imperial public opinion. The British public were prepared to accept innovations in kingship from King Edward VIII; they were not prepared for, nor did they want, a total break with the traditions of the past or the paradox evidently offered by the prospect of their King, who was at the same time Defender of the Faith, married to what was at that epoch called "a divorcee." Moreover, our political relations with the United States of America during the post-war years had been notably inharmonious, and the majority of the King's subjects did not relish the idea of a transatlantic successor to Queen Mary on the throne.

The daily developments of those weeks during which Mrs. Simpson's divorce suit was pending at Ipswich do not concern us here; we may, briefly, recall that the Prime Minister, Mr. Stanley Baldwin, first discussed the matter with King Edward VIII at Fort Belvedere on 20 October, that a week later the King saw Mr. Mackenzie King of Canada on the same subject, and that on 13 November the King's Private Secretary, Major Alexander Hardinge, wrote the King a letter apprising him that the British press was about to break the long silence it had hitherto preserved about himself and Mrs. Simpson, whose decree *nisi* had been granted to her on 27 October. On 16 November King Edward VIII again saw Mr. Baldwin, declaring that he intended to marry Mrs. Simpson and, to do so, would, if necessary, abdicate the throne. It was on the evening of this day that the King dined with his mother at Marlborough House. The King's sister, the Princess Royal, was also present at this meeting and, like Queen Mary, listened carefully to what the King had to say.

When, sitting in Queen Mary's boudoir after dinner, the King broached the subject of his feeling for Mrs. Simpson, he found his mother and his sister sympathetic; but when they learned that he was prepared to give up the throne in order to marry her, they were astounded and shocked. "To my Mother," writes the Duke of Windsor, "the Monarchy was something sacred and the Sovereign a personage apart. The word 'duty' fell between us. But there could be no question of my shirking my duty." The longer they talked, the more apparent became the divergence of their views. To Queen Mary her son had two alternatives, two choices which he could make: to give up marrying Mrs. Simpson or to give up the throne. To the King these choices did not seem to exist: he was convinced that he could not endure his present life unless he were married to Mrs. Simpson, that he could no longer carry on as King without her "help and support," and that therefore, in the last resort, he must go. In this sense it seemed to the King that his duty was to leave the throne, while to Queen Mary it seemed equally plain that it was his duty to stay upon it. This was, in essence, a conflict of realities. Not surprisingly, the discussion resulted in a deadlock, since neither party to it could give way. Queen Mary's arguments, which are of historical interest and which have not hitherto been published, were enumerated by her very clearly in a letter which she wrote to the Duke of Windsor eighteen months subsequently—that is to say, in July 1938:

> You ask me in your letter of the 23rd of June to write to you frankly about my true feelings with regard to you and the present position and this I will do now. You will remember how miserable I was when you informed me of your intended marriage and abdication and how I implored you not to do so for our sake and for the sake of the country. You did not seem able to take in any point of view but your own. . . . I do not think you have ever realised the shock, which the attitude you took up caused your family and the whole Nation. It seemed inconceivable to those who had made such sacrifices during the war that you, as their King, refused a lesser sacrifice. . . . My feelings for you as your Mother remain the same, and our being parted and the cause of it, grieve me beyond words. After all, all my life I have put my Country before everything else, and I simply cannot change now.

In his own book the Duke of Windsor has explained that in his final and irrevocable decision to abdicate he also was inspired by a purely patriotic motive—the wish to avoid splitting the country on the issue of his marriage, and thus endangering the Empire and the throne.

On the morning after this harrowing talk at Marlborough House —which had ended with Queen Mary's refusal of her son's suggestion that she should herself see Mrs. Simpson—Queen Mary sent the King a sorrowful, maternal little note. "As your mother," she wrote, "I must send you a line of true sympathy in the difficult position in which you are placed—I have been thinking of you all day, hoping you are making a wise decision for your future—I fear your visit to Wales will be trying in more ways than one, with this momentous action hanging over your head."

That same day Queen Mary received the Prime Minister, Mr. Stanley Baldwin. During the night the Queen's bewilderment and shock had crystallized into a positive exasperation. To give vent to her feelings she reverted, suddenly and unexpectedly, to a Cockney slang expression of her youth, picked up from her brothers in the distant, gay, Victorian days of life at White Lodge. "Well, Mr. Baldwin!" Queen Mary exclaimed, stepping briskly into the room, her hands held out before her in a gesture of despair, "*this* is a pretty kettle of fish!"

For Queen Mary these anxious winter days of 1936 were terrible and bleak. In common with a great many other people in positions of responsibility, the Queen had very natural fears of what damaging effect an abdication might have upon the position of the Monarchy and its influence throughout the British Empire. All that she valued and admired in life seemed threatened, all that for which she and King George V had patiently and steadfastly worked. With that overriding passion for the British throne which had illuminated her whole life since her girlhood, the idea that one Monarch should step down from his high position and another take his place appalled Queen Mary, for in her mind the very concept of "abdication" implied ceasing to do your duty.

All through these days Queen Mary did her utmost to help her two elder sons—the actual King, Edward VIII, and the King of the future, who was still the Duke of York. King Edward came to tea at Marlborough House on 24 November; after this further talk, which, like the first one, made no headway, Queen Mary did not see the King for another ten days, since, anxious to avoid public demonstrations, he withdrew quietly to Fort Belvedere. Queen Mary did, however, have news of the King from the Duke of York, whom she was seeing regularly and who, like the Duchess of York, was dreading his possible accession to the throne. Determined to maintain at least an outward appearance of calm, Queen Mary spent the last week of November in doing Christmas shopping, visiting exhibitions, and going to look at the London Museum. On

Monday, 30 November, the Crystal Palace on Sydenham Hill was burned down. "After dinner," Queen Mary noted, "Mary and I were horrified to hear the Crystal Palace was on fire with no hope of saving it. We saw the smoke from my window—What a pity, a great landmark gone."

It was on 3 December that the news of the constitutional crisis over the King's wish to marry Mrs. Simpson appeared in all the London papers. The Duke of York, who had been to Edinburgh for two days to be installed as Grand Master Mason of Scotland, has recorded the shock he experienced on reaching Euston Station that morning. "At Euston," he wrote, "I was both surprised & horrified to see that the posters of the Daily Press had the following as their headlines in block letters 'The King's Marriage.' Down at Fort Belvedere, where Mrs. Simpson, with her aunt Mrs. Merriman as chaperone, had taken refuge from a curious public, King Edward and his future bride were, as they have told us in their memoirs, equally astounded that morning by the tone of the press. At Marlborough House Queen Mary likewise was aghast; it was the first time that national newspapers had openly criticized or attacked a British Monarch since the jubilant obituary notices of George the Fourth in 1832 and the outcry raised in 1864 against Queen Victoria's seclusion in her widowhood. "Darling David," Queen Mary wrote at 2.30 p.m. to King Edward, "This news in the papers is very upsetting, especially as I have not seen you for 10 days—I would much like to see you, won't you look in some time today? I shall only be out from 3 to 5—Ever yr loving Mama, Mary."

Queen Mary was out that afternoon because she wished to see the smoking ruins of the Crystal Palace. She was accompanied by her brother, Lord Athlone, and her sister-in-law, Princess Alice (who were staying with the Queen to give her support in this crisis), as well as by the Princess Royal: "went to see what was left of the poor Crystal Palace—a very sad sight," she recorded. This deliberate visit to the burned-out shell on Sydenham Hill had, as Queen Mary intended it to have, a very salutary effect upon public morale and was an altogether typical gesture. "Since the crisis Queen Mary has paid two visits south of the river," recorded, for example, *The Yorkshire Post* on 8 December. "On Thursday she motored to Sydenham, to view the ruins of the Crystal Palace; and this excursion, so peculiarly irrelevant in the circumstances, was widely appreciated for its sedative effect upon an excited country. Today Her Majesty has been occupied in a fashion even more placid. She has been to Dulwich Park where she spent some time watching the birds in the aviary." But behind this façade of dignity and valour Queen Mary was waiting with frayed nerves and a ghastly apprehension for the decision of her eldest son.

On receiving Queen Mary's note that afternoon of 3 December, King Edward, exhausted as he was, drove late at night to Marlborough House, where he found the Duke and Duchess of York, who had been dining there. The King explained to his mother that he had refrained from seeing her during the preceding days because he had been anxious to avoid giving her pain. "As simply as I could," he writes, "I explained the reasons for my apparent aloofness. 'I have no desire to bring you and the family into all this. This is something I must handle alone.' If she had hoped to learn from me that I had changed my mind, she gave no sign. I left Marlborough House sorry to disappoint her." "David said to Queen Mary," the Duke of York recorded, "that he could not live alone as King & must marry Mrs.—. When David left after making this dreadful announcement to his mother he told me to come & see him at the Fort next morning."

The King did not in fact receive the Duke of York until three days later, the 7th of December. On the morning of the 8th the Duke called at Marlborough House, and on the following day, Wednesday, 9 December, the Queen drove down with her daughter to the Royal Lodge at Windsor, the home of the Duke and Duchess of York. "I met my brother at Royal Lodge & he & his mother were together some time," the Duke of York noted in his Memorandum. There, in the drawing-room of Royal Lodge, as the winter afternoon shortened to twilight and the fog closed in over the garden beyond the window-panes, Queen Mary heard of her eldest son's irrevocable decision to leave the throne.

She was already waiting in the drawing-room when I arrived [writes the Duke of Windsor]. I gave her a full account of all that had passed between Mr. Baldwin and myself during the six days since our last meeting on the Thursday before. She still disapproved of and was bewildered by my action, but now that it was all over her heart went out to her hard-pressed son, prompting her to say with tenderness: "And to me, the worst thing is that you won't be able to see her for so long."

Queen Mary's own Diary account of this momentous interview is laconic. "Rather foggy day," she wrote. "At 1.30 with Mary to meet David (on business) at the Royal Lodge—Back before 5— Georgie & Marina dined." After dinner the Duke of York arrived at Marlborough House and with Queen Mary looked over the draft Instrument of Abdication, a document which he himself re- garded with revulsion and his mother read with incredulity. "I went to see Queen Mary," the Duke recorded, "& when I told her what had happened I broke down & sobbed like a child." Unlike her mother, the Duchess of Teck, and unlike her mother-in-law, Queen Alexandra, Queen Mary had never been given to an exces- sive use of exclamation marks. Seldom does this useful form of punctuation interrupt or emphasize passages in the calm narrative of her Diary. In her account of the Duke of York's visit that night the Queen did, however, have recourse to the exclamation mark:

Bertie arrived very late from Fort Belvedere and Mr. W. Mockton brought him & me the paper drawn up for David's abdication of the Throne of this Empire because he wishes to marry Mrs. Simpson!!!!! The whole affair has lasted since Nov. 16th and has been very painful— It is a terrible blow to us all & particularly to poor Bertie [the Duke of York, afterward George VI].

On the following day, 10 December 1936, King Edward VIII signed the Instrument of Abdication in the presence of his broth- ers. King George VI succeeded to the throne. "Dark gloomy day," Queen Mary recorded. "I saw Ld Salisbury & the P M—At 3 to Piccadilly to see Elizabeth [the Duchess of York] who was in bed with a cold, too unlucky. The P M made his announcement in the house about David's final decision—which was received in silence & with real regret—The more one thinks of this affair the more regrettable it becomes."

SUGGESTIONS FOR STUDY

1. What do you find to admire in the way Queen Mary handled her son during this crisis? What do you find to criticize adversely?

2. What were the objections to Mrs. Simpson's becoming Queen of England? To what extent do you consider these objections justified?

3. What were the two different ideas of "duty" held by King Edward and his mother?

4. Why was the Duke of York distressed by his brother's abdication? From your history teacher, learn what sort of king he became.

5. What does Queen Mary's trip to the ruins of the Crystal Palace tell you of her character? What does her comment that "in any other country there would have been riots" tell you about British character?

6. Find out what you can of the lives of the Duke and Duchess of Windsor (Edward VIII and Wallis Simpson). Do you think that all their lives they were glad they acted as they did back in 1936? Why, or why not?

7. In recent years Princess Margaret (Elizabeth II's sister) decided not to marry a divorced man, with whom she was in love. How might the marriage of her uncle, Edward VIII, have been influential in this decision?

8. How is the word *abdication* used today besides in its formal meaning of giving up a throne?

9. Review the three "special contributions" of biography to history mentioned on page 40, and give an example of each from your reading of this section of *Portraits in Words*.

Selections from the Diary of Samuel Pepys

SAMUEL PEPYS

Among the so-called "primary sources" from which historians and biographers get their factual material, none is more prized by them than a good diary. Like an autobiography, a diary is written by the one person who knows the truth about such things as emotions, motives, and private actions; and because most diaries are not written to be published, they are generally more honest and more frank than most autobiographies.

Samuel Pepys, an able English government official, kept a diary from 1660 to 1669. Published in 1825, it quickly took undisputed first place among the world's great diaries. It reveals its author as a fascinating and genial personality, but, more importantly, it gives a vivid picture of seventeenth century events, large and little. As only a diary can, it applies a strong magnifying glass to the fabric from which history is made.

Pepys began the writing of his diary on a good date for beginning something important: Sunday, January 1st, 1660. The first entry that you will read in the following selection, January 16, 1660, was made on a Monday, a fact which may help to explain why Pepys' wife and maid were working so desperately to get the washing done before going to bed.

January 16th 1660   In the morning I went up to Mr. Crew's, and at his bedside he did talk to me concerning things of state. I went from thence, and in my way went into an alehouse and drank my morning draft with Matthew Andrews and two or three more of his friends, coachmen. From thence to my office, where nothing to do. At noon, Harry Ethall came to me and we had a very good dinner, and after dinner we went to the Green Dragon, on Lambeth Hill, and there we sang of all sorts of things, and I ventured with good success upon things at first sight; and after that I played on my flageolet, and staid there till nine o'clock, very merry and drawn on with one song after another till it came to be so late. So parted, and thence home, where I found my wife and maid a-washing. I staid up till the bell-man came by with his bell just under my window as I was writing of this very line, and cried, "Past one of the clock, and a cold, frosty, windy morning." I then went to bed, and left my wife and the maid a-washing still.

March 25th (Lady Day) 1661   This morning came workmen to begin the making of me a new pair of stairs up out of my parlor, which, with other work that I have to do, I doubt will keep me this two months and so long I shall be all in dirt; but the work do please me very well. After dinner I to Mrs. Turner, and there staid talking late. The. Turner being in a great chafe about being disappointed of a room to stand in at the Coronation. Then to my father's. So homewards and took up a boy that had a lanthorn, that was picking up of rags, and got him to light me home, and had great discourse with him, how he could get sometimes three or four bushels of rags in a day, and got three pence a bushel for them, and many other discourses, what and how many ways there are for poor children to get their livings honestly. So home and I to bed at 12 o'clock at night.

April 11th 1662   Up early to my lute and a song, then about six o'clock with Sir W. Penn by water to Deptford. So to Greenwich; and had a fine pleasant walk to Woolwich, having in our company Captn. Minnes. Among other things he tells me that Negroes drowned look white and lose their blackness, which I never heard before.

January 21st 1664   Up, and after sending my wife to my aunt Wight's to get a place to see Turner hanged, I to the office, where we sat all the morning. And at noon going to the 'Change, and seeing people flock in the city, I enquired and found that Turner was not yet hanged. And so I went among them to Leadenhall Street, and to St. Mary Axe, where he lived, and there I got for a shilling to stand upon the wheel of a cart, in great pain, above an hour before the execution was done, he delaying the time by long discourses and prayers one after another, in hopes of a reprieve; but none came, and at last was flung off the ladder in his cloak. A comely-looked man he was, and kept his countenance to the end:

I was sorry to see him. It was believed there were at least 12 or 14,000 people in the street. So I home all in a sweat, and dined by myself.

March 18th 1664   Up betimes, and walked to my brother's, where a great while putting things in order against anon; then to Madam Turner's and eat a breakfast there, and so to Wotton, my shoemaker, and there got a pair of shoes blacked on the soles against anon for me. So to church, and with the grave-maker chose a place for my brother to lie in, just under my mother's pew. But to see how a man's bones are at the mercy of such a fellow, that for sixpence he would, (as his own words were), "I will justle them together but I will make room for him," speaking of the fulness of the middle aisle, where he was to lie; and that he would, for my father's sake, do my brother that is dead all the civility he can. At noon home, where I dressed myself, and so did Besse; and so to my brother's again, whither, though invited, as the custom is, at one or two o'clock, they came not till four or five. But at last one after another they come, many more than I bid, and my reckoning that I bid was one hundred and twenty; but I believe there was nearer one hundred and fifty. Their service was six biscuits a-piece, and what they pleased of burnt claret. My cousin Joyce Norton kept the wine and cakes above, and did give out to them that served, who had white gloves given them. The men sat by themselves in some rooms, and women by themselves in others, very close, but yet room enough. Anon to church, walking out into the street to the Conduit and so across the street, and had a very good company along with the corpse. And being come to the grave as above, Dr. Pierson, the minister of the parish, did read the service for burial, and so I saw my poor brother laid into the grave; and so all broke up, and I and my wife and Madam Turner and her family to my brother's, and by and by fell to a barrel of oysters, cake, and cheese, being too merry for so late a sad work. But, Lord! to see how the world makes nothing of the memory of a man an hour after he is dead! And, indeed, I must blame myself; for though at the sight of him dead and dying, I had real grief for a while, while he was in my sight, yet presently after, and ever since, I have had very little grief indeed for him. By and by I took my wife and

Besse (who hath done me very good service in cleaning and getting ready every thing and serving the wine and things to-day, and
is indeed a most excellent good-natured and faithful wench, and I
love her mightily), by coach home, and so after being at the office
to set down the day's work home to supper and to bed.

May 5th 1665   To Woolwich and back to Blackewall, and
after dinner to Mr. Evelyn's. He being abroad we walked in his
garden, and a lovely noble ground he hath indeed. And among
other rarities a hive of bees, so as being hived in glass you may see
the bees making their honey and combs mighty pleasantly. This
day, after I had suffered my owne hair to grow long in order to
wear it, I find the convenience of periwiggs is so great that I have
cut off all short again, and will keep to periwiggs.

September 3rd (Lord's Day.)   1665   Up; and put on my col-
oured silk suit very fine, and my new periwigg, bought a good
while since but durst not wear because the plague was in Westminster when I bought it; and it is a wonder what will be the
fashion after the plague is done as to periwiggs, for nobody will
dare to buy any hair for fear of the infection, that it had been cut
off of the heads of people dead of the plague. To church, where a
sorry dull parson. I up to the Vestry at the desire of the Justices of
the Peace, in order to the doing something for the keeping of the
plague from growing; but Lord! to consider the madness of the
people of the town, who will (because they are forbid) come in
crowds along with the dead corpse to see them buried; but we
agreed on some orders for the prevention thereof. Among other
stories one was very passionate, methought, of a complaint brought
against a man in the town for taking a child from London from an
infected house. Alderman Hooker told us it was the child of a
very able citizen in Gracious Street, a saddler, who had buried all
the rest of his children of the plague, and himself and wife now
being shut up and in despair of escaping, did desire only to save
the life of this little child; and so prevailed to have it received
stark-naked into the arms of a friend, who brought it (having put
it into new fresh clothes) to Greenwich; where upon hearing the
story, we did agree it should be permitted to be received and kept
in the town.

August 14th (*Thanksgiving day.*[1]) *1666*   After dinner with
my wife and Mercer to the Bear-garden, where I have not been,
I think, of many years, and saw some good sport of the bull's
tossing of the dogs, one into the very boxes. But it is a very rude
and nasty pleasure. We had a great many hectors in the same box
with us (and one went into the pit and played his dog for a wager,
which was a strange sport for a gentleman), where they drank
wine, and drank Mercer's health first, which I pledged with my
hat off; and who should be in the house but Mr. Pierce the surgeon, who saw us and spoke to us. Thence home, well enough
satisfied however with the variety of this afternoon's exercise; and
so I to my chamber, till in the evening our company come to supper. And so we supped, and very merry. And then about nine
o'clock to Mrs. Mercer's gate, where the fire and boys expected
us, and her son had provided abundance of serpents and rockets;
and there mighty merry till about twelve at night, flinging our
fireworks, and burning one another and the people over the way.
And at last our businesses being most spent, we into Mrs. Mercer's,
and there mighty merry, smutting one another with candle grease
and soot, till most of us were like devils. And that being done, then
we broke up, and to my house, and there I made them drink; and
upstairs we went, and then fell into dancing (W. Batelier dancing
well) and dressing, him and I and one Mr. Banister (who with
his wife come over also with us) like women; and Mercer put on
a suit of Tom's, like a boy, and mighty mirth we had, and Mercer
danced a jigg; and Nan Wright and my wife and Pegg Pen put on
perriwigs. Thus we spent till three or four in the morning, mighty
merry; and then parted, and to bed.

November 2nd   1667   Up, and to the office, where busy all the
morning; at noon home, and after dinner my wife and Willett and
I to the King's playhouse, and there saw "Henry the Fourth:" and
contrary to expectation, was pleased in nothing more than Cart-
wright's speaking of Falstaff's speech about "What is Honour?"
The house full of Parliament-men, it being holyday with them: and
it was observable how a gentleman of good habit, sitting just before us, eating of some fruit in the midst of the play, did drop

[1] For the late victory at sea over the Dutch.

Samuel Pepys 83

down as dead, being choked; but with much ado Orange Moll [2] did thrust her finger down his throat and brought him to life again. After the play we home, and I busy at the office late, and then home to supper and to bed.

SUGGESTIONS FOR STUDY

1. The bellman referred to in the first entry in this selection was quite modern in his function. How is this true?
2. Explain the special significance of the coronation in 1661.
3. Although humble and insignificant persons do not get much attention in the pages of a history book, Pepys' diary portrays them well. Give briefly one or two episodes from this selection that provide the reader with a close look into the day-to-day life of an ordinary person in the 1600's.
4. Find, and write down, little evidences which reveal the nature of the times with regard to the general state of learning.
5. Summarize the various means of recreation and entertainment available to the 17th century person in England, to the extent that they are revealed in this selection.
6. The Mr. Evelyn to whom Pepys refers was John Evelyn, also a diarist. Find in an encyclopedia some other important things about him and report on them to the class.
7. Why are diaries especially valuable source material to biographers and historians? To a historian, what is the difference between a *primary* and a *secondary* source?
8. Some published diaries which might interest you are: *Diary of George Templeton Strong, The Diary and Sundry Observations of Thomas Alva Edison, The Diary of Selma Lagerlöf, The Diaries of Lewis Carroll,* and Thomas Merton's *The Sign of Jonas. The Treasury of the World's Greatest Diaries,* edited by Mel Evans and Philip Dunaway, is a gold-mine for readers interested in diaries.

FOR FURTHER READING

More biographies to shed light on history: *The Sword and the Spirit: A Life of John Brown,* Delight Ansley; *Tom Paine, Freedom's Apostle,*

[2] Moll, the orange-seller at the King's playhouse, was a well-known character.

Leo Gurko; *The DeGaulle Nobody Knows,* Alden Hatch; *The Great Lucifer: a Portrait of Sir Walter Raleigh,* Margaret Irwin; *Andrew Jackson, Frontier Statesman,* Clara Ingram Judson; *Hannibal: One Man Against Rome,* Harold Lamb; *Sherman, Fighting Prophet,* Lloyd Lewis; *Thomas Jefferson,* Gene Lisitzky; *The Empress Josephine,* Marguerite Vance.

To Widen Our Sympathies

IT MAY BE that you can recall that as a child you were not permitted to play with the children whose language or color was different from your own. Perhaps dad did not approve of that "goofey scientist" or that "wild foreign piano player." Perhaps as a child you whispered about the bars on the upstairs windows of the green house on the corner and thoughtlessly teased crazy Willie, who lived there. Perhaps filled with fear you ran home to mother when the mysterious old lady with the big black bag approached. Most of us, as children, are caught up and trapped by our own small interests, inherited prejudices, and blind fears.

Even when we become adults we have to be on guard against these poisons in the bloodstream of human understanding. Reading biography can help us to "put away childish things." It can help us to see that an Indian or Chinese or Russian is a human being with a sense of human values, and that such matters are greater than nationality or race. It can show us that labor leaders, industrialists, mental defectives, eggheads may be "enemies" only because of our ignorance. Reading the life story of someone who is different from us can teach us why these differences exist, and how insignificant they often are.

By extending and expanding your understanding, biography can widen your sympathies and enable you to say with a famous American humorist, "I never knew a man I didn't like."

A New Friendship

CYNTHIA BOWLES

When Cynthia Bowles was fifteen years old, she lived for almost two years in New Delhi, where her father, Chester Bowles, was United States Ambassador to India. In this foreign land, among a new people, from ordinary activities like going to school, seeing movies, attending weddings, buying clothes, she gained an unusual understanding of a people about whom many of us know much too little.

The following selection is from *At Home in India,* which Cynthia compiled from letters, notes, and a diary that she wrote while living there.

SAM, SALLY [her younger brother and sister] and I each felt differently about Delhi Public School. But we agree now that the friendships that we made there were the happiest and most valuable part of our experience in the school.

Although she was unlike me in every way, I came to know and like the best a pretty, outgoing girl named Suman. I remember that the first day I went to school she was the most outspoken and curious of all my classmates.

Just as I had formed a stereotype of Indian girls before I came to India, she had apparently formed a stereotype of American girls, largely from the numerous Hollywood movies she had seen. Therefore, she was a little disappointed that I, the first American her age she had ever really known, didn't act, talk and look as she had expected American girls to. But she was anxious to be friends and often, in the first few weeks of school, went out of her way to do things with me.

About a month after I started school, Suman introduced me to

From AT HOME IN INDIA by Cynthia Bowles, © 1956 by Harcourt, Brace & World, Inc.

the movies in New Delhi. The Rivoli Theater is very near Connaught Circle, the wealthier class's main shopping center, and we went there from school on the school bus. The theater was already crowded mostly with what Suman identified for me as college students and young, yet to be employed, graduates. There were few girls and I felt conspicuous and self-conscious in my American clothes and wished that I were wearing Suman's loose-fitting salvar and cumeez.

The salvar is an ankle length pantaloon affair, with a draw string at the waist that gathers in the two yards of material. It is usually made of white cotton material although sometimes of the same material, color and print as the cumeez.

Cumeez means shirt in Hindustani. The cumeez is very much like a man's shirt in that it is loose-fitting around the waist, but it is designed more like a dress and is worn over the salvar. Like the American girl's dress, the length, color, material and style differ with each person.

Suman usually wore a bright-colored, big print cotton cumeez which reached to her knees. Long cumeez were the fashion at that time and most of the school and college girls wore them down to, or a little below, their knees.

In addition to the salvar and cumeez, the Delhi girl wears a kind of shawl, called a chunni or dapatta, of lightweight material, about six feet long and two feet wide, which drapes around her shoulders and down her back or over her head as she likes.

The salvar and cumeez is the dress typical of the Punjab, a province just north of Delhi. But recently it has been adopted by many girls throughout India to take the place, in sports or work, of the more cumbersome sari.

That day at the movies, Suman, who I think would look beautiful no matter what she wore, was looking particularly lovely in a light and dark green cotton print cumeez with white cotton salvar and chunni. She was wearing lipstick, which just a few, more westernized, older girls have begun to wear, and had braided her jet black hair into two long braids. She had several jingling glass bracelets on each wrist and I felt quite conspicuously inferior to her as we went into the theater and up to the ticket window.

The theater was much the same as any movie theater in America although, I must say, more plush than any I had seen near our home in Connecticut. There were three groups of seats, each having a different priced ticket. If you bought a cheap ticket for one rupee, four annas (about 25 cents), you would sit right in front of the screen. Even this cheapest ticket is out of the reach of most Indians. The most expensive ticket was 3/12 (about 75 cents), and the ticket which we and most people bought cost 2/8 (about 50 cents).

We bought some coke and potato chips and went into the theater to listen to the music, both Indian and popular American, and wait for the show to begin.

There were three short newsreels, one that centered on Indian news, one on world news, and another that featured news in the United States. Next there were various advertisements and a cartoon, and then Hollywood's *Francis Goes to the Races.*

Many Hollywood movies are shown in New Delhi and the other big Indian cities. I seldom went but when I did it was usually with Suman who, like many upper-income Indian girls, went almost weekly. At one time or another I saw *Come Back Little Sheba, Gaslight,* with Ingrid Bergman, *Scaramouche* and a Bob Hope picture.

It is primarily on films such as these that most Indian moviegoers base their ideas and opinions of America. I remember being horribly embarrassed by certain scenes in *Come Back Little Sheba,* in which a high school boy acted aggressively toward his girl friend and was not very firmly repulsed.

In America I would have enjoyed the movie. I would not have given any thought to those particular scenes. But sitting in the New Delhi theater, I realized that I, unlike the other movie-goers, understood the attitudes that it portrayed. Without this understanding the Indian movie-goer could only attribute to Americans a great lack of modesty and morality.

However, *Come Back Little Sheba* was by no means the worst of the films Hollywood regularly sends to Delhi and other Indian and Asian cities. For example, some of our westerns, which often show a rough and arrogant attitude toward American Indians, while bad enough in the United States, looked much worse in New Delhi. Not only do these films give Indians false ideas about what American life is like; many of them present a picture of wealth and luxury so far out of the average Indian movie-goer's experience that he concludes, as one of my pen-friends did, that America is a "paradise on earth." The Hollywood movie serves as a kind of escape from the less attractive realities of his own environment.

There is yet another and perhaps more constructive reaction that these movies produce. Indian teen-age and college-age boys and girls see American young people enjoying a close and natural companionship, going to school, church, parties and dances together. This causes them to think about and to become discontented with the restrictions which the caste system, the joint family and the general high moral standards of their society place upon them.

Italian movies too are popular in India, and just as misleading. Suman and I saw *Bitter Rice* and *Bicycle Thief*. In February of 1952 the International Film Festival was held in Delhi and we saw Japanese and Russian films.

The Indian movie industry itself is the largest in the world outside that of U.S.A. With Suman and other of my friends I saw quite a few Indian films. Most of these, in their length, and variety and number of calamities—birth, death, marriage, illness and accident following one upon another—resembled Hollywood's *Gone with the Wind*. Many were a rather unsuccessful combination of comedy and tragedy. They exaggerated Indian life just as the Hollywood pictures do the life of America, and often they dwelt at great length on India's proud past.

I had long hoped to see an Indian wedding, so I was happy when one day toward the end of January Suman asked me if I would like to go to a wedding of a friend of hers. The wedding was to be the following night and Suman told me that she would pick me up early in the evening.

I was ready at 5:00 when she drove up. Suman was wearing a sari and looked wonderfully grown-up. The sari was silk, light pink, and had hundreds of tiny silver sequins sewed to the end that fell from the shoulder. She wore large sparkling earrings and a lovely plain gold bracelet.

In America such elaborate jewelry would suggest great wealth. But Suman's family was not particularly wealthy. Jewelry, even gold and silver, is relatively inexpensive in Delhi and it is customary for girls, even of families of modest incomes, to own expensive-looking pieces.

We drove through the crowded Delhi streets, past the parks filled with families and groups of young students, taking their rest from work and study as they do throughout the world, and across the city to the bride's house. Since the house was deep in the heart of Old Delhi, on a dirty, very narrow, crowded street, I was surprised to find the home large and comfortable and the people inside it English-speaking. When we arrived the house was already crowded with friends and relatives of the bride. We were taken into a room where some of the women and girls were sitting and talking.

Among them was the bride-to-be, dressed in her beautiful red bridal sari and not yet acting shy. As soon as the groom and his friends arrived she would have to assume an expression of shyness and modesty. Her closest relatives sat near her, continually fussing over her, fixing her sari or the brilliant flowers in her hair.

I thought of the newly-wed bride I had seen at a wedding reception Suman and I had gone to just a few weeks before. She had acted very shy, keeping her head bowed and her eyes lowered. I later learned that this shyness may have been genuine. But genuine or not, it was what was expected of her. She was married and had just entered a new household. She could no longer act as a young girl but must act as a modest, dutiful young wife should.

Women guests had come up to her one at a time, with a small gift or a word of congratulation. She would raise her eyes and, smiling, greet the person and accept the good wishes. Then she lowered her eyes once more.

The bride-to-be on this particular evening would soon have to assume this shyness for we were warned of the coming of the bridegroom and his party—his friends and relatives (called the barat)—by a clatter and sound of music outside in the street. Suman and I ran up to the second floor to get a good look from the balcony.

It is the Hindu custom that the bridegroom walk, or preferably, ride a horse from his house to that of the bride on the eve of the wedding. But this more modern groom came in a bright yellow, flower-bedecked convertible. We could see it and the small barat procession as we looked down the street.

Leading the procession was the wedding band—two drummers and two flutists who were making a great deal of noise and only a little music but enjoying themselves immensely. Following them was the new convertible in which the groom and his closet relatives were riding. We could see that the groom was dressed in a western suit and a marvelous glittering headdress that covered all his face except his eyes and came down over his shoulders. Behind the car was a crowd of people, the groom's friends and relatives and many curious, fun-loving onlookers.

When he arrived at the door of the house the groom was greeted by some of the bride's relatives. Climbing from the car, he lifted the brightly decorated mask from his face and representatives of the two families exchanged rosewater as a symbol of good wishes. Meanwhile we and others on the balcony showered the group with flower petals.

The groom and his party then came inside to have dinner and wait for the marriage ceremony to begin. Unfortunately since it had not started by 10:30 Suman and I had to leave without seeing it. Later we found that it had not begun until midnight and had continued many hours into the night.

During my stay in India I attended several Indian weddings, Hindu and Sikh. All were rather long religious ceremonies held outdoors at the home of the bride. The couple were married after completing seven steps around a small wood fire, the ends of their clothing tied together.

One of my best friends was married in Delhi. In her bright red and gold bridal sari she looked lovely. She wore several gold bracelets and a gold chain that rested in the part of her hair. At the end of the chain was an ornament that hung down on her forehead. Her eyes had been accentuated by black marking, and tiny white dots were painted on her forehead in a simple design.

After the wedding ceremony, which took place in the early evening there was a wedding dinner at the bride's home.

Suman and I had many good times together. Yet at first she was merely someone who was nice to me, who provided me with good times when they were much needed, and who somewhat awed me by her boldness in what I had soon discovered to be a modest country. Within a couple of months she was more than that. She was a real friend and I could talk with her as I talked with my friends at home.

I remember one of January's typically beautiful days. The sky was a deep blue and the sun shone warm and bright, just warm enough so that it felt good when you put your back to it and cool enough so that you wanted to stay out of the shade unless you were wearing a heavy sweater. Suman and I and some other girls and boys had "stayed back"—stayed after school—to play hockey.

The game had finished and Suman and I were sitting in the sun resting when we saw a big dump truck go by on the road past the school. It was gaily decorated and had big posters on the sides. On each of the posters was a picture of a bullock and "Vote for Patel—Vote Congress" written in English, Hindi and Urdu. The truck was filled with people singing and shouting "Vote for Congress." Delhi State's first election was just a week away and the campaigns of each of the major Delhi parties—the Congress, Socialist, Jan Sangh and Communist—were in full swing.

I asked Suman what the bullock on the posters meant. She told me that the bullock was the symbol of the Congress party. Illiterate people could associate the symbol with the Congress party as they could associate the banyan tree with the Socialists, the diwa (oil light) with the Jan Sangh, and the wheat spike and sickle with the Communists. And they could choose the ballot box marked with the symbols of the party for which they wished to vote.

Suman asked me if we had symbols representing the political parties in America. I told her about our Republican elephant and

Democratic donkey and about our two-party system, about our
elections and our political campaigns. We agreed that as far as
campaigns and elections go the two countries differ little.

"But," Suman said, "India has nothing resembling your two-
party system." She explained that the Congress party is the main
party in India and there is no other party equal or even nearly
equal to it in strength. The Socialist and the Communist parties
have some strength, and the Jan Sangh a little.

The rather emotional supporters of this last party believe that
India should be a purely Hindu country and that the Moslems
should be forced to leave India and make their homes in Pakistan
or some other Moslem state. "Besides these four parties," Suman
explained, "there are other smaller ones and many independent
candidates."

Suman was learning politics as I had learned them in America.
In this, India's first national election, her father was an independent candidate for the Delhi State Assembly from the constituency
in which he lives. "His symbol," Suman said, "is a ladder and his
campaign slogan 'We want progress. Down with Congress!' " I
was somewhat surprised at the slogan and told Suman I had
thought that the Congress party was one of the most progressive
parties in India.

"After independence we all thought it would be," Suman said,
"and, indeed, it has done much for our country. But Congress has
acted too slowly." Later this criticism of the Congress party was
often repeated to me. Most of the people I talked to were impatient
for "progress." India is in a hurry.

It was late in the afternoon when we finished talking but I felt
that I knew and liked Suman much better. She was not simply the
movie-going, westernized teen-ager I had previously thought her
to be.

One day near the first of February, after I had been in India
about three months, the girls at school decided that it was time
for me to have some Indian clothes. In India clothes are made to
order by men tailors called darzis. Suman suggested we go down
to the cloth market and then to the shop of the darzi who usually
made her clothes and have him make me a salvar and cumeez.

I agreed. I had, for some time, wanted to have a salvar and cumeez of my own. I had felt rather conspicuous in my American clothes, and a dress was *not* the best thing for bicycle riding. Suman and I made plans to meet in front of her home at 4:00 that afternoon.

Suman's home on Babar Road is a smallish, one-storied stucco building and she was waiting in front of it when I arrived on my bike. As we were only a short way from the market we decided to walk to the store. We walked along Babar Road, on down wide, tree-lined Barakamba Road to Connaught Circle, and around the circle to Queensway, one of New Delhi's main streets. Among the several small shops along Queensway, set up by Hindu refugees from what is now West Pakistan, there are many cloth shops and we knew that we could find something we liked there.

Soon we had bought three yards of white cotton for a salvar, two and a half yards of blue printed cotton for a cumeez, and a yard and three quarters of a light blue net-like material for a chunni. The darzi's shop was on a nearby street. We walked there, gave the tailor the cloth and told him the style I wanted. He measured me and told me to come by a week later and the clothes would be ready for me. From then on I wore Indian clothes regularly.

From the darzi's shop Suman and I went to a small stall in a bazaar nearer Suman's house where delicious-looking and, we found, delicious-tasting food was sold. We bought some indescribable spicy things and some sweets and so started a habit of which we could never break ourselves. From then on, every time I went to Suman's house we went to the little shop and filled ourselves with those delicacies.

It was not until about the first of March that I had a chance to visit Suman's home and meet her family. When I entered the house that afternoon I felt for a minute as if I were back in our usually busy home in Essex. I could hear babies crying, children laughing, the talk of grownups and the patter of many small bare feet.

The family was celebrating a young cousin's birthday and the house was overflowing with grandparents, parents, aunts and uncles, shouting children and feeding babies. There was a wonderful confusion and everyone was enjoying it, laughing and talking and having great fun. Suman introduced me to her mother and to her aunts and I entered into the confusion and was made to feel welcome.

When I left that day Suman invited me to come the next day for lunch. I had had odds and ends of Indian food and had often helped Suman and my other classmates finish their lunches at school. But not yet had I really sat down to a complete Indian meal.

When I knocked on Suman's door the next day, her small brother met me and shouted for Suman who came running, all smiles and with a grand "hi-ya" which she had recently learned from an American movie. "Hi-ya," I responded, and we sat down to talk until lunch was ready.

I asked her what members of her family were living in the house and she explained to me about the joint family system. At the head of the joint family, and at the head of Suman's family, is the grandfather and grandmother. Living with them are all their sons, married and unmarried, their married sons' wives and children, and their unmarried daughters.

"Most families in India are like this," Suman told me. "But many of the educated young people, wishing to feel independent of their parents, are making homes of their own." Suman thought, however, that the children owe much to their parents and the least they can do is look after them in their old age and respect and obey them until they die.

In Suman's household there are her grandparents (her father's mother and father), her own mother and father, her married uncle (father's brother) and his wife and children, her unmarried uncle, her unmarried aunt (father's sister), and her own two brothers and sisters.

I met almost all of them when we sat around the big dining room table to eat lunch. They greeted me shyly in English, of which they all knew at least a little, and then continued conversation among themselves in Hindustani.

Although the members of Suman's family are Hindus, like a great many Hindus, they are not vegetarians. However, like almost all Hindus, they do exclude beef from their diet. The lunch was as good as I had expected it would be. There was a highly spiced lamb curry, a delicious curry of potatoes and peas, and dhal. Dhal is a kind of mush made out of dried lentils. It is a very cheap, high-protein food and is eaten at almost every meal by people in most parts of India.

Both rice and chappaties—a round, flat, unleavened wheat bread—were served with the curries and dhal. Chappaties are a staple in almost every North Indian family and later I learned how to make them. They consist simply of whole wheat flour and enough water to make a stiff dough. The dough is kneaded well and made into small balls which are rolled out and baked for just a minute on a special iron pan on top of the fire. Other forms of unleavened bread can be made by adding oil to the dough and frying instead of baking the small discs. Rice is not eaten as much as wheat in North India. Suman's family did not have it every day.

Snowy white curds and different kinds of chutney were served with the meal and for dessert there was fruit—bananas, apples and luscious mangoes.

Suman and I spent much of the afternoon talking and then went down to the bazaar to get some of the spicy food that was so popular with us and two big handfuls—two cents worth—of deliciously sweet and juicy sugar cane.

Often after that I went to Suman's house for lunch or dinner and in those "after dinner" conversations learned much about a wonderful girl and her beautiful country.

Suman was sensitive, extremely friendly, kind and eager to learn. She was attracted by America, attracted by the America she saw in the movies, the movie magazines, and the comic books. And she tried to be as much like the American girl she found stereotyped there as she could without being what would be considered in India, with its very high moral standards, as "indecent."

She wore lipstick and rouge and eyebrow pencil and occasionally fingernail polish and American jewelry. She preferred shoes with heels to the simple sandals which I and most other people wore. In the privacy of her home she wore dungarees (which I contributed) and chewed bubble gum. She knew the names of many, many American movie stars, danced the waltz, the fox trot and the rhumba, and said "hi-ya" and dozens of other American slang expressions.

Therefore, Suman was sometimes considered a bold, almost immodest, extravagant girl. Some even thought from what she did and wore that she cared more for America than for her own country.

But in conversations with her I learned that she was much more than that. The surface impression was not the real Suman. I came to know that Suman was as true an Indian as any of my other friends.

It was Suman who took me to the Indian wedding, who often invited me to her home to eat and take part in her family activities, in their festivals and celebrations.

It was Suman who took me to the crowded bazaars and small restaurants where I saw and was part of the teeming life of an Indian city. And it was Suman who took me to the Ram Lila where I saw India's famous epic, the *Ramayana,* being reenacted.

I can only hope that I helped Suman to see America as well as she helped me to understand and see her own country. I tried to tell her about the America I knew, about small town America. I described my town to her, and how the people lived and worked. I described the schools and the system of education and explained how our town and state governments are run. I told her that many girls do not wear fingernail polish and not all chew bubble gum and know the names and life histories of all the movie stars.

Still, when it came time for me to leave India, to all outward appearances Suman was more American than I, and I, who had adopted her Indian clothing, her language and many of her customs, seemed quite Indian. But down underneath, in our hearts and in our minds, Suman was an Indian and I an American.

Before I left India, Suman told me that she knew a boy whom she liked very much and hoped to marry some day. But love-marriages are uncommon in India and I guessed that Suman would never disobey her parents' request that her husband be of the same caste as she. Suman's friend was not. So I was not surprised when I received a letter from her a while ago saying that she had become engaged, at her family's request, to a fellow of her own caste. Suman was the best of my Delhi Public School friends, but there were others. These friendships have proved to me, as similar friendships have proved to others, that the East and West need not be strangers to each other.

•

SUGGESTIONS FOR STUDY

1. What is meant by referring to Suman as an "outgoing girl"?

2. In this selection, in what way is the Indian attitude toward love and marriage different from ours?

3. What adverse and what constructive criticism did the two girls make of movies?

4. Why did Cynthia decide to wear Indian clothes?

5. Find evidence that Suman was aware of the political situation in her country. How well would you have been able to explain our American political situation to her?

6. Explain what Cynthia meant when she wrote: "The surface impression was not the real Suman." (p. 97)

7. What impression or "portrait" of herself has the author created?

8. How would you welcome an Indian boy or girl into your school? Would you invite him to your home? Why, or why not?

9. What constituted an Indian meal? In your community what restaurants specialize in foreign dishes? Be experimental: obtain a copy of a book of Indian recipes and prepare some of the dishes.

10. Write a theme explaining to what extent this selection has changed ideas you had of India, and to what extent it has fortified such ideas. (What is meant by a "stereotype"?)

John L. Lewis Unionizes the Auto Workers

SAUL ALINSKY

In the autumn of 1936, the accumulated grievances of the General Motors auto workers "had fused into deadly hatred against the industry." Early in 1937 they expressed this hatred in a series of "sit-down" strikes, which were promptly declared illegal by the courts. For a month tension mounted as the Union and General Motors maneuvered for power. On February 2, an injunction was issued by a federal judge ordering the sit-down strikers out of the General Motors Detroit plant by 3 p.m. the following day. Frank Murphy, the newly inaugurated governor of Michigan, was forced to act. The sit-downers must now get out or be forced out.

All of this you could read in the newspapers of 1937. But to comprehend and appreciate the strengths and weaknesses of the persons involved, you must turn to biography. The most amazing figure in the battle was John L. Lewis, president of the CIO. In an "unauthorized biography," *John L. Lewis*, Saul Alinsky, an eminent criminologist and sociologist, gives us his version of the highly controversial way this labor leader defeated General Motors and brought the workers of the whole auto industry into his CIO.

Whether you are inclined to be violently for or against unions, the following selection will introduce you to some of the human beings in the unions' rise to power. It should also give you some idea of the complexity of labor-management problems, and convince you that there is something to be said on both sides of this great controversy.

WITH LEWIS now hanging onto the union's demands with bulldog tenacity and General Motors demanding the enforcement of the court order, Governor Murphy was at the end of the road. No one could have done more than he did to help the union. He had stood by now for almost a week turning his back while thousands of strikers defied the law. Now he must give the fatal order.

Around Flint that night of February 9, 1937, the National Guard sprang into action. All units were alerted. Preparations were made to seal off all highways, railroads, and every entrance into Flint so as to prevent CIO members and sympathizers from reinforcing the strikers. The civilian police were mobilized and used for the first time.

In Chevrolet No. 4 and the Fisher Body plants that night, the men were depressed and angry. Was this the end? They nervously clutched sections of door hinges, bars, cushions for shields, and anything else they could hold in their hands. Some wanted to fight to the death, some wanted to run, and all were scared. There was that tightness in the air and inside their chests; the feeling that men have just before they do battle.

In Detroit, that night, the General Motors chieftains were on edge. With nerves at the breaking point they waited for Murphy's order. Maybe they had erred in forcing the Governor's hand. What if there was a horrible massacre? What if their plants were destroyed in the reign of terror that seemed certain to erupt with the Governor's decision? How long would it take them to rebuild their plants and how much more of their shrinking market would their competition raid? General Motors' customers were buying Ford, Chrysler, Studebaker, and Nash products. Was it too late to retract and sign a contract? The nerves of General Motors were snapping. If Murphy now did not put through the order they would recognize the union and avoid the nightmare that now enveloped them.

In Detroit, that night, John L. Lewis went to bed.

In Detroit, that night, Governor Murphy, torn up inside, prepared the order that was to convert Flint into a battlefield and sound the death knell of the union.

In Detroit, later that night, Lewis told the writer, he was awakened by a knock on the door. He opened it to find Governor Murphy standing there tense and pale. The Governor entered and turned to Lewis. "Mr. Lewis, I have here in my hand an official order as governor of the State of Michigan, declaring a state of insurrection and ordering the National Guard to enforce the injunction of the court of the State of Michigan to evict the sit-down strikers from those plants of General Motors which they are occupying by illegal seizure." Lewis, equally pale, glowered silently at the Governor. Governor Murphy continued, "I want to give you an advance copy of this order so that we can avoid violence."

Lewis took the order and read it carefully. It was a brief announcement by Frank Murphy that as the governor of the state he was sworn to uphold the laws of the state; that an injunction of a court of the State of Michigan was now being flouted and that he was sworn to uphold the law and therefore compelled to enforce this injunction. It went on to order officially that on that morning the sit-down strikers were to be asked voluntarily to evacuate the plants. If they refused there would be no alternative except forcible ousting.

Lewis wheeled on the Governor, thundering, "Governor, do you know what this means?"

Murphy, shaken, replied, "Yes, I do, but there is nothing else I can do."

Lewis then turned his back on the Governor, walked across the room, and stared broodingly out of the window.

For some minutes the silence in the room alone was audible and then Murphy said, "Well, Mr. Lewis, what are you going to do about it?"

Lewis turned on Murphy. "I repeat, Governor Murphy, why are you doing this?"

Murphy's voice trembled. "You know why I'm doing it. As governor of the State of Michigan, I have no recourse. I'm doing it because I am sworn as governor of this state to uphold the laws of this state, and I have to uphold the law. Now do you understand?"

Lewis fixed a stony stare upon the Governor and then began in a very low voice, "Uphold the law? You are doing this to uphold the law? You, Frank Murphy, are ordering the National Guard to evict by point of bayonet or rifle bullet, the sit-down strikers? You, Frank Murphy, by doing this are giving complete victory to General Motors and defeating all of the hopes and dreams of these men. And you are doing all of this because you say, *'to uphold the law!'*" Lewis continued with his voice rising with each sentence. "Governor Murphy, when you gave ardent support to the Irish revolutionary movement against the British Empire you were not doing that because of your high regard for law and order. You did not say then *'uphold the law!'* When your father, Governor Murphy, was imprisoned by the British authorities for his activity as an Irish revolutionary, you did not sing forth with hosannas and say, 'The law cannot be wrong. The law must be supported. It is right and just that my father be put in prison! Praise be the law!' And when the British government took your grandfather as an Irish revolutionary and hanged him by the neck until dead, you did not get down on your knees and burst forth in praise for the sanctity and the glory and the purity of the law, the law that must be upheld at all costs!

"But here, Governor Murphy, you do. You want my answer, sir? I give it to you. Tomorrow morning, I shall personally enter General Motors plant Chevrolet No. 4. I shall order the men to disregard your order, to stand fast. I shall then walk up to the largest window in the plant, open it, divest myself of my outer raiment, remove my shirt, and bare my bosom. Then when you order your troops to fire, mine will be the first breast that those bullets will strike."

Then Lewis lowered his voice. "And as my body falls from that window to the ground, you listen to the voice of your grandfather as he whispers in your ear, 'Frank, are you sure you are doing the right thing?'"

Governor Murphy, white and shaking, seized the order from Lewis's hand and tore out of the room. The order was not issued, and the next day General Motors collapsed and capitulated at 2:45 A.M.

With the defeat of General Motors, the CIO turned the flank of American industry. Now the CIO began to roll up the line of industry, and the war turned into a rout. The giants of commerce were successively and speedily toppled. The roll call of the CIO conquests was the listing of the New York Stock Exchange. Some of these made a hopeless last-ditch fight while others capitulated.

The Chrysler Corporation made a last stand. The Chrysler strike was far different from the General Motors one. The bitter hatred of General Motors workers against the heads of their corporation was not felt by the Chrysler employees. Walter P. Chrysler was regarded with admiration and affection by his workers. Lewis told the writer, "Walter Chrysler was a just, decent man, and I always respected him."

Almost immediately after the victory over General Motors, the Chrysler Corporation was gripped by the sit-down strike. Even at the height of the conflict, the slogan on the signs carried by the strikers read, "Mr. Chrysler, we still think you're fair. Prove it!" or, "Will Chrysler lead again with human rights?"

Again Lewis rode into Detroit, and again Murphy left the Governor's Mansion in Lansing. This time, when they met, it was not with General Motors' Knudsen or Smith under the icy shadow of Sloan. This time, it was with the humane, warm-hearted Walter Chrysler and his hard-boiled, anti-union production boss, K. T. Keller. Where in the General Motors situation Knudsen as production chief was the warm, human person and Sloan hostile and unapproachable, the roles were reversed in the Chrysler setting.

Again, Governor Murphy wearily sat at the head of the table. On one side was Lewis flanked by Lee Pressman and UAW's organizer Richard T. Frankensteen; on the other side sat Walter Chrysler with his high command, K. T. Keller and Nicholas Kelley, general counsel. Chrysler appeared helpless against the threats of Keller and Kelley to resign along with other key officials if any concession was granted the CIO. It was also known that Keller and Kelley had the full support of the Chairman of the Chrysler Corporation's Finance Committee. Chrysler was reported to have been in misery as his hands were tied by these threats.

Throughout these negotiations Chrysler's Keller sat sneering across the table, disdainfully looking beyond Lewis and his cohorts with cold arrogance. His insulting stares infuriated the CIO leaders. Finally Lewis decided to break down Keller.

The meeting on the day following this decision began as its predecessors had with a lame, strained conversation between Governor Murphy, Pressman, Frankensteen, and Kelley. Occasionally

Walter Chrysler would join in with a friendly, humorous story. Everyone was acutely uncomfortable and conscious of the frozen aloofness of Keller. His grimaces were beginning to tell on the nerves of Pressman and Frankensteen as they kept stealing glances at their impassive chief. The hours went by, with Lewis sitting in complete silence. Across from him sat Keller with his manifest scorn becoming more obnoxious to the CIO spokesmen with each passing minute. To Lewis and his associates, Keller's face began to symbolize the attitudes and position of a giant corporation toward its employees.

The tension heightened, and suddenly Keller broke his silence. Turning to Lewis, with a sneer in his voice, he said, "Mr. Lewis, you haven't said a word about this situation. Do you happen to have any comment or contribution?"

Lewis very slowly rose to his feet and with a murderous stare at Keller softly replied, "Yes, Mr. Keller, yes, I have. I am ninety-nine per cent of a mind to come around this table right now and with one fell swoop wipe that damn sneer off your face!"

There was a dead silence in the room. Governor Murphy hastily cleared his throat and announced a brief recess. The Governor got up quietly, nervously looking at Lewis and Keller. Keller seemed to be in a state of shock. Suddenly he shook his head and came around the table toward Lewis. Lewis deliberately turned his back on him and began to walk over to the other side of the room. Keller followed him, then put his arm around Lewis's shoulder. Everyone heard Keller in a pleading voice say, "I'm really not as bad as you make me out to be, Mr. Lewis, really I'm not as bad as that. Believe me, I'm not as bad as that."

Lewis turned to Keller and still with complete dignity said, "Well, Mr. Keller, in the heat of controversy, one is bound to be indiscreet." Keller's resistance cracked after this episode.

Lee Pressman, when questioned by the writer about this incident, remarked, "It is impossible to put into words just what everyone felt at that moment. Lewis, the man, was not threatening Keller, the man. Lewis's voice in that moment was in every sense the voice of the millions of unorganized workers who were exploited by gigantic corporations. He was expressing at that instant their resentment, hostility, and their passionate desire to strike back. There just was no question that Lewis's threat was not against Mr. Keller as a person, but against the Chrysler Corporation and every other giant, soulless corporation in this country. It was a moment of real greatness, because Lewis transcended his own person and was speaking out the deep yearning of millions to force a great, sneering, arrogant corporation to bend its knee to organized labor. I cannot remember when I have been so moved in my life. I had never before experienced anything so completely devoid of individual personality, for those two voices of Lewis and Keller were really the spokesmen of two opposing fundamental forces."

The next day Lewis cleared the decks as he demolished Nicholas Kelley. Although not possessed of Keller's icy arrogance, Kelley had constantly insulted Pressman and Frankensteen and gone out of his way to bait and goad them. Suddenly Lewis turned on him and began a bitter excoriation. He reminded Kelley of the different position on social issues which his mother had represented as over against Kelley's anti-union stand.

Lewis went on and on and on developing his denunciation in low, cold, withering words. Lewis continued driving and driving into him until everyone thought that Kelley was about to have a fit of apoplexy.

Finally Kelley leaped to his feet and screamed, "STOP IT, STOP IT, MR. LEWIS!" After a good deal more in this vein he finally ended up by shouting, "*Mr. Lewis, I want you to know, Mr. Lewis, that I—I—I am not afraid of your eyebrows.*"

Lewis's laughter rolled Kelley out of the fight, and Chrysler gave up.

SUGGESTIONS FOR STUDY

1. What is meant by an "unauthorized biography"?
2. What are sit-down strikes? How did the auto workers justify them? Why are they illegal? Why did some persons think they were inspired by communists?

3. What is your opinion of John L. Lewis's argument to convince Governor Murphy that he should not uphold the law in this case? How does Murphy's reaction to that argument affect your opinion of him?

4. Using *John L. Lewis* or some encyclopedia or social history, some member of the class should report on the workers' grievances which led to the sit-down strikes. What improvements in the lives of workers have been made by the unions?

5. What are some of the excesses of unions which many deplore? (Read "A Warning to Labor and to Management," by Eric Johnson, in *The Challenge of Ideas* for material to answer this question.)

6. Why is it important that you postpone taking a positive stand on the rights and wrongs of the labor-management controversy? Do you think, in the final analysis, labor and management will prosper or suffer reverses *together*, or that the success of one must mean the destruction of the other? Defend your answer.

7. How can biography help you to understand this struggle in a way that history and sociology cannot?

Space Man

GEORGE A. WALTZ, JR.

In Chapter I of *What Makes a Scientist?* (the book from which this selection is taken) the author reports that "in a recent nation-wide poll of thousands of high school students more than half the teen-agers interviewed expressed the feeling that scientists are 'odd-balls,' 'squares,' 'eggheads,' and 'longhairs,' who 'don't think and act like ordinary people.'" Mr. Waltz also quotes some results from a study of student opinion made by the eminent sociologist, Margaret Mead. Typical of student responses she received were these: "He [the scientist] neglects his family. . . . He has no social life, no other intellectual interests, no hobbies or relaxations. . . . He is always running off to his laboratory. . . . A scientist should never marry. . . . No one wants to be such a scientist or to marry him."

The reading of biography will teach you that such opinions are false. You will find from reading this profile of Dr. Fred Whipple that it *is* possible to be a normal happy man and still be a great scientist. Even though you may not work in the scientific field, you still may encounter many scientists and technicians in your day-to-day work. Your discovery that scientists are human should help to make you more successful working with them.

WITH SPUTNIKS, rockets, and moon missiles streaking through outer space, Fred Lawrence Whipple has been a busy man. For one thing, it was Dr. Whipple who laid the initial groundwork for setting up the vast Minitrack and Moonwatch networks that now gather the valuable and voluminous information made available by the man-made satellites.

But then Fred Whipple always has been a busy man. He couldn't be happy if he wasn't. For more than thirty years he has been probing into the secrets of space and exploring the nature of the heavenly bodies. As early as 1946, he was championing a plan to get a satellite into orbit.

In 1959, besides being the director of the famed Smithsonian Institution Astrophysical Observatory in Cambridge, Massachusetts, he is serving on dozens of committees and commissions, including the Technical Panel of Rocketry, the U. S. Rocket and Satellite Research Panel, and the Scientific Advisory Board to the Air Force. He is also head of Harvard University's Department of Astronomy.

During World War II, Dr. Whipple, like so many scientists, shifted his interest to a field where his abilities could be used more directly in the war effort. He became a member of the staff of the Radio Research Laboratory that was an important part of Dr. Vannevar Bush's far-flung OSRD. While there, he headed up a group that developed "Window," an ingenious anti-detection system that made it possible for American and Allied combat planes to jam the German ground radar stations that were being used to aim and control the Nazi anti-aircraft batteries with deadly accuracy. Thanks to the use of "Window," the AAF and the RAF were able to continue and even step up their relentless round-the-clock bombing of German industrial centers without staggering losses of crews and planes.

The system consisted of dropping huge quantities of sliver-thin aluminum strips from high-flying bombers. As the metallic strips fluttered slowly to the earth, they acted like millions of tiny reflectors in the path of the searching radar beams, and the reflected signals cluttered the enemy's radar screens with blizzards of meaningless blips and streaks. This same system was later used to foil Japanese radar stations.

In spite of a work schedule that has never been light, dark-haired, bespectacled Fred Whipple has always found time for a rewarding personal life. His average day consists of bicycling the three miles from his home to his Cambridge office (weather permitting), a morning filled with observatory affairs, a lunch at a local cafeteria where the chances are good that he will order sausages and mashed potatoes if they are on the menu that day, and an afternoon of lecturing at Harvard and working on his many astronomical projects. When the day's chores are done, he pedals his way back to his home and to his wife, Babette, and his two young daughters, Lolly and Sandy. Cycling is just one of the many forms of outdoor exercise that Whipple enjoys, and his well-built frame is good testimony of the fact.

Saturdays and Sundays he tries to reserve exclusively for his family so he can ice skate with them in winter, swim with them in summer (Whipple is also quite a skin diver), garden and raise prize roses, enjoy hi-fi recordings, and go to local square dances, where more often than not he is the "caller." Most weekday nights he relaxes by reading science fiction—he buys just about every new one he can find in the bookstalls around Harvard Square.

He is also a collector of neckties—not just ordinary ties, but astronomical cravats whose bright and bold designs consist of flaming comets, showers of meteors, galaxies, rockets, spacemen, and planets. His collection numbers well over a hundred, and no collector of old jade or rare stamps could be prouder. Oddly enough, this hobby of collecting and sporting astronomical neckties is popular with a good many astronomers. At professional meetings they like to compete with each other in the matter of outer-space neckwear. To date, Fred Whipple seems to be the top tie man.

Dr. Whipple spent his pre-teen and teen years on a farm near Red Oak in southwestern Iowa. He was born there on November 5, 1906. In 1922 his family moved to Long Beach, California. There he attended Long Beach High School and Occidental College, got his bachelor's degree from the University of California in Los Angeles, and his Ph.D. at the age of twenty-five from the University of California at Berkeley. In 1932 he moved to the East to take on an instructorship at Harvard and has been in and around Cambridge ever since. He became the director of the Smithsonian Astrophysical Observatory in 1955.

As a young energetic boy, Fred Whipple loved to tinker and invent things. In school his favorite subjects were mathematics and physics. It wasn't until his sophomore year at UCLA that he became interested in the universe and the solar system. From that point on, however, astronomy became his main interest, but with mathematics playing an important part in his work. Where many astronomers are, for the most part, observers, working with powerful telescopes and astronomical photos to probe the heavens, Dr. Whipple develops his concepts and theories at his office desk with a pad, a pencil, a small electric calculator, and his keen mathematical mind.

Fred Whipple's pockets are always stuffed with odd scraps of paper and old envelopes scribbled with formulas and calculations. When he gets an idea, regardless of where he happens to be at the moment, he works it out in mathematical shorthand. If the rough answer looks promising, he then goes to work in earnest at his desk.

Currently Fred Whipple has two pet ideas. First, to get telescopic observatories—perhaps manned observatories—into orbit around the earth so, as he tells it, "we'll have eyes in outer space so we can see more." What he proposes is a telescope mounted on a space platform so observations could be made from a point well above the earth's obscuring atmosphere. Second, he would like to prove his theory that the moon is not covered with a thick layer of dust as many other astronomers contend. One of the best ways to find out, according to Whipple, is to make a landing on the moon and bring back a sample of the "cosmic green cheese."

Dr. Whipple also has some very definite ideas about the scientist's role, privileges, and responsibilities in the national community, and he preaches them whenever he gets a chance. Although a scientist himself who numbers among his friends a large number of fellow scientists, he feels that too many scientists spend too much time in the company of other scientists. They should get out more, according to Whipple, and rub elbows mentally as well as physically with the rest of the world. He also feels that there should be a much wider spreading of scientific knowledge to the public, written in simple everyday words, that the layman can understand, and not in the complicated jargon of scientific reports. He is a great believer in letting the taxpayer know exactly how the scientific dollars are being spent.

And Dr. Whipple does a deal more than just preach. He puts his ideas into practice by writing down-to-earth articles for the national magazines, including *The Saturday Evening Post,* and authoring books like his *Earth, Moon and Planets* for the general publishers. He has the knack of being able to explain astronomical facts and theories simply, crisply, and with imagination. As a result, since the coming of the Space Age, Fred Whipple has been a much-quoted man in newspapers and on television and radio.

At home his theories about spreading the scientific word have worked well. In spite of the fact that his daughters have received no special prodding from their father, they started to show a special interest in science at an early age.

Although things have been a little hectic since October 4, 1957, when the first Russian sputnik began its trips around the earth, Mrs. Whipple—she also is a "Dr." and a psychologist—has been able to be with her husband more by working at the observatory when extra help is needed.

Oddly enough, it was Mrs. Whipple who was the first to break the news of Sputnik I to her husband. Dr. Whipple had been in Washington, D.C., attending a meeting, and although he always carries a small transistor radio with him when he travels so he can listen to the news, he couldn't get it to perk during the plane ride back to Boston. When he landed, Mrs. Whipple told him the news, and together they rushed over to the observatory.

Speaking about science and scientists not long ago to a large gathering of the Harvard Dames, an organization of faculty wives, Mrs. Whipple urged the ladies to make every effort to create a general atmosphere that will foster intellectual achievement in this country. "Let's promote the 'eggheads,'" she said. "After all, we're married to them."

Dr. Fred Lawrence Whipple, as one of the breed of modern scientists, is a forceful argument for "pure research"—research for research's sake. His theory proposing that comets are made up almost entirely of ice is widely accepted. Yet while he was evolving it and proving it, he seldom looked at a comet through a telescope. He proved it mathematically, not by observation.

Dr. Fred Whipple sees great new knowledge coming from our future explorations of space with orbiting satellites. For one thing, man, through electronic and optical eyes in the sky, will be able

112   Dr. Fred Whipple

to view the universe from outside the earth's blurring and often distorting atmosphere. Until now we have had no real means of obtaining clear views of Mars, Venus, Saturn, and the other planets. And until now, Dr. Whipple feels, our theories regarding the lack of life on such planets as Mars and Venus have been based on incomplete data. An observatory in the sky may unravel many astronomical riddles and might even upset some "established" astronomical theories.

At the moment Dr. Whipple's plans for "eyes in the skies" may seem farfetched. "But," say his friends and associates, "don't underestimate Fred Whipple. When he sets his sights on a project, things invariably begin to happen."

SUGGESTIONS FOR STUDY

1. What are some of Dr. Whipple's hobbies? Why is being a caller at a square dance good relaxation for a scientist?

2. What was Dr. Whipple's contribution to the war effort during World War II?

3. In this selection what evidence is there to make you think that Mrs. Whipple is a real partner to her husband and has a place in his career, instead of being solely a housewife and mother of his children?

4. What was Dr. Whipple's criticism of many of his colleagues? In what way have some scientists themselves contributed to the formation of uncomplimentary notions about scientists?

5. While on the plane to Boston, Dr. Whipple did something which would not now be permitted. What was it? What is the reason for this rule?

6. Look up in an encyclopedia and report to the class the story of the discovery of the planet Pluto. In what way does the discovery of this planet illustrate the scientific method used by Dr. Whipple? What is meant by "pure research"?

7. In what way has this selection "widened your sympathy"? Also, what additional information did you learn about the vocation of a scientist?

Doctor and Nurses Against Insanity

PAUL DE KRUIF

Some doctors specialize in working with mental diseases, and our picture of the psychiatrist analyzing his reclining patient's fears and complexes is becoming increasingly familiar. One striking indication of the growing need for doctors who specialize in mental illness is the commonly repeated statistic that more than half of all the hospital beds in our land are occupied by mental patients.

Unfortunately, the mentally disturbed person is not always understood. Many persons consider him a disgrace to the family, even an object of ridicule. In reality he is just a person who needs professional treatment and understanding.

Dr. Jack Ferguson, in his work with the insane at Traverse City [Michigan] State Hospital, has explored new methods of dealing with such patients. Beyond the fact of his medical pioneering, Dr. Ferguson himself is interesting because of mental illness in his own background. Paul de Kruif, in his book *A Man Against Insanity*, writes with a fresh and interesting style of Dr. Ferguson's battles in the struggle against mental illness.

But the Dr. Fergusons and their staffs cannot do all the work. You also can help, perhaps not as a doctor or as a nurse but as an understanding and sympathetic human being.

JACK FERGUSON betrays a smoldering pride when he says of his patients: "We treat them and love them and know we are doing right." But what would his colleagues on the staff of the Traverse City hospital think of Jack's kind of tall talk? Overenthusiasm, according to one's lights, can also be called arrogance.

"You're treating them and loving them in your own special way on your service," I said, "but have you tried to get other members of the staff to confirm your work, independently, on their own services?"

From A MAN AGAINST INSANITY, © 1957 by Paul de Kruif. Reprinted by permission of Harcourt, Brace & World, Inc.

"No, I haven't."

"But aren't they curious, aren't they excited about the way you're sending chronic schizophrenics home?"

"They don't seem to be," said Jack, and he didn't seem to care, only giving me a look that said so what.

"Their only reaction, so far," said Jack, "is one of them writing to a big Detroit newspaper hinting at bad habits on my part and incompetence in running my service." Jack smiled.

"That member of the Michigan State Medical Society," said Jack, "the doctor who warned you I was a barbiturate addict—this doctor got that story from one of my colleagues."

What was most remarkable about Jack Ferguson, telling me this imperturbably, calmly, was his lack of what, three years before in his time of troubles, would be called paranoia. There was about him an utter absence of worry that anyone in the world was down on him, against him, or gunning for him.

"But isn't the growing number of empty beds on your service going to make the other services look bad?"

"Oh, they'll have to come round to looking at our stuff, finally," said Jack. His nonchalance was exasperating. "Ask Miss Orcutt whether she thinks we're doing the right thing," urged Jack, "just ask her."

Bertha E. Orcutt, R.N., is the director of nursing at Traverse City State Hospital and has been so for thirty years. She is outwardly severe and primly New Englandish and she does not smoke and liquor has not touched her lips and the sweetness of her smile is precious because it is so rare. She has seen treatments of the insane come and go, and this is recorded in her face, a dedicated one in its austerity and asceticism carved there by thirty years of disillusion. "In one year's time," says Miss Orcutt, "there has been an unbelievable change in the nursing of custodial patients on Dr. Ferguson's service."

What astounds Miss Orcutt—who does not astound easily—is to see something stranger than the effect of the new medicines on patients so long lost. It is the constantly renewed inspiration that has been given to her nurse attendants. "You just can't imagine what a thrill it is," says Miss Orcutt—who is not quick to be thrilled—"when hopelessly withdrawn patients suddenly say to their attendant nurse . . . 'What time is it?' . . . or, 'I would like a blue dress' . . . or, 'Please let me help in the kitchen.' "

For Miss Orcutt this means only the first glow of the sunrise of a new day following years of black night. She explains it is the nurse attendants—not Dr. Ferguson—who are the first to hear these faint whispers of a coming up out of a nightmare world of mental confusion.

"Those first timid words are like doors opening," says Bertha Orcutt, "doors opening to the mind through which an understanding nurse attendant may work to draw the patient out to reality."

It was Jack's flash of discovery to understand that he must give his 107 nurse attendants the duties, the dignity, and the responsibility of doctors. For here was Jack Ferguson's situation as a doctor and clinical investigator: one M.D. serving a thousand patients, disturbed or dim-witted, incontinent or mute, violent or in despair, or all of these put together. There exists no microscope, no graph, no chemical test to trace the ups and downs of these tragedies, of this grotesque army of the lost. There exists only the watching of their behavior.

Who was going to spy out all the subtle, incessant, shifting ups and downs of behavior, watch them all like a hawk, night and day? Only the nurse attendants. Jack showed his deepest insight in regarding himself as multiplied more than a hundredfold. From one doctor into 108 doctors. Into 108 pairs of eyes and ears and hands and into 108 brains, working as one.

It's characteristic of Jack that he thinks himself in no way above his 107 nurse attendants. He makes you feel that he's the dispensable one. "If it weren't for these ladies, my work with the new medicines would amount to exactly nil," says Jack.

"You understand," says Jack, "it would be a half-baked experiment to test the new drugs as many are now doing—I mean throwing the chemicals into half the patients and leaving the rest for controls. Controls are only real controls if the sickness of the treated and untreated is identical." Jack went on to din it into me

that the disease of every one of his 1,000 patients *is different.*
That's why you've got to watch every one of them, constantly,
closely. That's why he's had to regard his nurse attendants as
doctors, and trust them.

"It isn't the new medicines, alone," said Jack. "They aren't much.
They only start up a mental awakening. By themselves they can't
carry the patients along. The nurse attendants have got to pour in
the confidence—they've got to wipe out the fear."

"Fear of what?" I asked.

"Fear of entering into new situations. For years they've been
told and helped to get up, to go to the bathroom, to dress, and to
eat. It's a deep conditioning. They're scared when they have to
start to do the simplest of things on their own."

I saw that. The nurse attendants must unscare them. But then
Jack explained they had to do far more than that. Did I remember
Bertha Orcutt describing one patient who showed her awakening
by saying she wanted a blue dress? All right. She is given the blue
dress. Then she tears the new blue dress off herself. She tears it to
shreds. She begins to eat it. Then what does this poor lady fear?
A bawling out. A return to the closed ward. But what does her
nurse attendant do? She is kind to this wild woman. She explains
she isn't sinful, only sick—and gets her another blue dress.

That's the medicine against fear. That's tender loving care,
bringing back a security long forgotten. "The nurse attendants
treat all their patients as if they were their little sisters," said Jack
—no doubt unscientifically, no doubt sentimentally.

Jack explained that by so doing, the nurse attendants have noticed a flicker of a rebirth of clear thought in their patients. When,
under the power of the medicines, they awaken to a saner condition, they begin to confide in the nurse attendant. "Yes, you can
get me another blue dress, thank you." Or—"No, you'd better put
me back in the closed ward—I'm not ready."

Jack feels his nurse attendants have made a fundamental discovery: "The awakening patients know far more about their sickness than we do. Here's an example—

"A fine girl had become clear under the new medicines plus
tender loving care," said Jack. "Except she couldn't get rid of a

nasty habit of pushing needles into her legs and finally into her belly. The needles had to be removed by surgery. At last she quit it. She was transferred to an open ward. She was ready for parole—"

"Has she gone home?" I interrupted. Jack smiled. "Let me finish my story. She hasn't gone home, not yet. The other day she told her nurse attendant she was scared she was going to needle herself again. She felt it coming on. She asked please to be put back in the semiclosed ward."

Jack revealed a deep technique of discovery in the homespun language of the country doctor that he is. "It isn't the nurse attendants who first tell me a patient is getting better or not. It's the patients, who first tell the nurse attendants, who then bring it to me."

Is it so strange that Ferguson should trust the patients themselves? But then he knew what it was to be insane.

Jack's faith in his 107 ladies is carried to what some physicians may consider a shocking extreme. They write the behavior profiles at the start and at the end of the treatment of all patients; they keep daily records of the doses of the medicines and changes in such doses; but here is what's more unorthodox: when a nurse attendant sees a patient getting better, or slipping, she reports to her ward supervisor, who regulates the doses or stops the medicines on her own responsibility. Then she reports to Dr. Ferguson, afterward.

"What am I, compared to these nurse attendants?" asks Jack Ferguson. "I'm nothing. All I've done is give them the new medicines to give their patients. And then they give the patients the love without which the medicines would be nothing."

Jack's smile glows bright when he tells me of the rewards now coming to his 107 lady doctors. For years they had to do the most menial, revolting, unspeakable things for the outcast, utterly forlorn, too muddled and lost to say as much as thank you. Now their resurrected patients love them back. "I've been here seven years —this is the first time anybody has tried to help me," says a woman on her way up into the light out of years of black nightmare. Her nurse corrects her gently: "This is the first time you've been well enough to know we were trying to help you."

In Hall Eleven at the Traverse City State Hospital the patients are proud of their two beautiful parakeets. They've named them Fergy and Francie—Fergy after Jack Ferguson and Francie after their beloved supervisor, Mrs. Frances Bare. Two years ago there could have been no Fergy and Francie in Hall Eleven—mischievous patients would have freed them or given them to the cat or maybe even killed them. In Hall Eleven in those days more than half of the patients were in specialing rooms in seclusion. In those pre-Ferguson days, among several disturbed wards, Hall Eleven was *the* disturbed ward, a dreaded and a dreadful place inhabited by beings who were noisy and untidy and fierce and wild—creatures too hot for other wards in the hospital to handle.

Mrs. Frances Bare has been at the hospital for more than fourteen years and is now the supervisor of the nurse attendants on Hall Eleven and she knows its horror in the old days and its hope as it is now. She is a wisp of a gray-eyed, grave-faced, yet easily smiling, lady and you sense in her pure moxie—a fighting heart.

For ten years Frances Bare has battled against much hopeless insanity but especially with the demons in the head of a magnificent woman whom we shall call Dolores—truly a lady of sorrows. Dolores is a college graduate, with an advanced degree, and had held a position of high responsibility in a Midwestern institution; she cracked up completely ten years ago—so thoroughly that the psychiatric professors could have diagnosed her to be suffering from all the psychoses in their textbooks and would then have had to invent yet other Latinities to describe adequately her multiform insanity.

Dolores as an athlete could have been a circus aerialist. In Hall Eleven she pulled open the top section of every other window and naked except for a towel draped round her middle, she delighted in swinging, high up, from window to window like a monkey, to the dim-witted delight and awe of those patients fit to act as an audience. She was an electrician; with cleverly hidden tools, slyly, she kept removing the coverings from light switches—announcing the wiring had been done improperly. Dolores had definite ideas about the therapy given her. When they tried to calm her by electro-shock, she knocked the doctor down and smashed the E.S.T. machine to bits. She ripped the uniform off a nurse attendant and took her keys away but immediately presented them to another nurse with the remark that the first one didn't have brains enough to work with crazy people. Dolores had strong feelings about her rights of personal privacy, and when, in a search for a very valuable piece of jade she was thought to be concealing, a doctor and attendants attempted an intimate examination of her person, Dolores literally threw the doctor across the room one way and the attendants the other. She was the victor: the examination was never made. She refused female attire and, being a clever seamstress, stitched herself slacks and jackets out of discarded hospital blankets. She was the guardian of the lives of all on Hall Eleven; she insisted that the pipe room was a breeding place for alligators and took her stand before the door, blocking the way in. Dolores was lionhearted. When she saw male help coming to seclude her, Dolores bellowed: "Here comes Mrs. Pillars and her thugs from Chicago!" And as she charged into them there ensued a Donnybrook that was a sight to behold.

At last Dolores was transferred to the back halls as hopeless. Frances Bare stuck with her and soothed her and never scolded her and tried to explain away every mad delusion patiently, and defended her most deplorable didoes stoutly to annoyed patients and exasperated attendants. Frances was good at ducking sudden left hooks and right swings appearing out of nowhere from the powerful fists of the incorrigible Dolores.

Then at last came Jack Ferguson with Serpasil and Ritalin and his confident smile, but Dolores would have no part of any medicine, so Frances Bare smuggled the chemicals—they are, providentially, tasteless—into every meal offered Dolores, and Frances saw to it they were all eaten. Soon Dolores was tranquil.

"It wasn't me at all, it was Mrs. Bare," said Jack. "She'd worked nine years, getting Dolores ready for the medicines to take action."

"Dr. Ferguson always talked with Dolores on his visits on Hall

Eleven," said Mrs. Bare. "It was something to see her now, not only calm but with her wonderful brain again thinking clearly."

To the astonishment of all the hospital at Dr. Ferguson's daring, Dolores was given grounds parole. She still had lingering ideas of remodeling the hospital and premises, and she stopped up the sewers and made a dam in the little river. But Dr. Ferguson would only smile and shake his finger and say: "Now—Dolores."

Now Dolores no longer had to be given her medicines concealed in her food, but took them as tablets, willingly. She discarded her make-it-yourself, fantastic raiment. And now she began to leave the hospital, on her own, three nights a week, to take care of her mother at home. She does all the shopping and banking for the family. Dolores, handsome and iron-gray-haired and with keen gray eyes, looks every inch the professional woman she was before her crack-up, ten years ago. "When you meet her downtown she looks like any other normal person," says Frances Bare.

Not long ago Dolores came to Jack's office. "Dr. Ferguson, I've gotten a job picking cherries. I got it on my own—will you give me permission for it?" asked Dolores, almost timidly.

"*Will* I give you permission!" said Jack.

"And she's just one of Frances Bare's patients," said Jack. "All from the bottom of the bottom of the barrel and getting jobs on their own.

"Frances Bare," mused Jack, "works exactly like the best kind of old family doctor. She gives her patients the medicines. She gives them PRN—*pro re nata*—as circumstances require."

Then vividly, if with dubious English usage, Jack Ferguson summed up what Frances means to him—"She's the eyes and ears and observations of my scientific papers that show how we're changing the habit patterns of the worst, so-called incurable insane."

On Jack Ferguson's service at Traverse City State Hospital before the new medicines, there were four locked wards for violently disturbed patients. There is only one disturbed ward now and that is Hall Eleven. There has to be one disturbed ward to receive the incorrigibles, the wild, the dangerous, the utterly derelict from other wards, from other state hospitals, problem cases from the Neuropsychiatric Institute at the University of Michigan and from the Hospital for the Criminal Insane at Ionia—homicidals who need what's called "maximum security."

"You say Hall Eleven doesn't look like the inside of a mental hospital?" asked Frances Bare. "You should have seen it the way it was two years ago—to really appreciate the way it is now."

In Hall Eleven there are pretty curtains and draperies now, and it is a rarity for a patient to try to tear them down. In Hall Eleven there is a record player and the patients dance—not wildly—to its music; there is a TV set with patients—not distractedly—looking and listening. There is a piano and there are patients who play it well to an appreciative audience. There are books, no longer to be thrown at other patients, but read. There are magazines and they are no longer used—mischievously—to stop up the plumbing.

"How can you keep it this way?" I asked Frances Bare. "You still get the toughest ones, the smashers, the wild ones—"

"Yes," said Frances, "but now we have the new medicines they don't stay that way very long."

Frances seems worried that, in my admiration for the nurse attendants, I'll forget Dr. Ferguson. At the end of a memo describing her work, Frances wrote:

"I would like to say that if all people that work with the mentally ill would have the same philosophy Dr. Ferguson has, namely—'But for the grace of God I might be in here myself without the keys'—they would be better able to help those so badly in need of help."

SUGGESTIONS FOR STUDY

1. What unusual responsibility did Dr. Ferguson give to his nurse attendants? What did their reaction reveal about human nature?

2. From the information you have been given about the staff and facilities at the Traverse City Hospital, what insight did you get about the work and responsibilities of a doctor?

3. What specific criticisms of Dr. Ferguson were made by others? To what extent do you think them justified?

4. Why did Dr. Ferguson not care whether his methods were followed by the other doctors at other hospitals?

5. How does your appreciation of Miss Orcutt's position and work contribute to your attitude toward the mentally ill?

6. What fear did Dr. Ferguson think is most prevalent in his patients? What was his solution?

7. From whom did the hospital get some of its most revealing information about each patient?

8. In what ways has reading and discussing this selection about Dr. Ferguson enlightened you or changed your attitude about the mentally ill? Recall Bob Hope's trip to a mental hospital. (p. 11) Why was Bob's visit so successful?

9. Assume that a member of your family or some friend has been released from a hospital that treats mental disorders. How can you help as an individual to make him, or her, feel at home?

10. Make a list of terms commonly applied in an uncomplimentary way to the insane. What is the effect of words of this kind upon the total situation of the mentally disturbed?

"The Day after Tomorrow I Must Die"

ICHIZO HAYASHI

Today Japan and America are friendly nations, but in World War II they were enemies; and even today it is hard for the Americans who fought in that war, and especially those Americans whose loved ones were killed by Japanese bullets, to understand that Japanese are human beings too.

Reading biographies of our "enemies" is one way to reduce and eventually eliminate the hatreds bred by wars. The selection you are about to read is a letter written by a kamikaze flyer to his mother just before he gave his life for Japan. You will find that he was a young man with problems, joys, sorrows, religious thoughts, strengths, weaknesses—just as were the Americans he was planning to kill.

Mother,

The time has come when I must give you sad news.

You love me more than I will ever be able to love you. What will you think of this letter? I am desperately sorry.

I have been really happy; perhaps I was too spoilt. But it is not my fault.

I am glad that I was selected as a pilot of a "specialized attack" group, but I can hardly restrain my tears when I think of you.

You did all you could to educate me, to help me to face the future. I am very sad that I must die without having given you anything in exchange—neither happiness nor serenity. I can hardly ask you to make the sacrifice of my life as well, nor to take pride in my death, however glorious it may be. It is better that I should not speak of all that to you.

I never dared to refuse the young girl you intended me to marry. I did not want to lose your affection, and I was so happy to receive your letters.

Reprinted from THE SUN GOES DOWN (KIKE WADATSUMI NO KOE) by permission of Orion Press, Tokyo, Japan.

123

I would have loved to see you once again. But the only place where I could have met you is Moji. For the day after tomorrow I must leave; the day after tomorrow I must die.

It is possible that I shall fly over Hakata. I will bid you farewell in silence from above the clouds. Mother, you used to dream of a splendid future for me, and I am going to disappoint you. I shall never forget your anxiety when I had to pass examinations. I joined this group in spite of your disapproval, but I can see now that I would have done better to follow your advice.

Try to comfort yourself by remembering that I am a very good pilot, and that it is very rare that a member of the air force with so few hours in the air to his credit is chosen for such a mission.

When I am dead, you will still have Makio. You preferred me because I was the elder, but believe me, Makio is worth far more than I. He is very good at looking after all the family interests. You will also have my sisters Chiyoko and Hiroko, and your grandchildren.

Cheer up. My soul will always be near you. Your joys will be mine, but if you are sad, I shall be sorrowful too.

Sometimes I feel tempted to come back to you, but that would be a cowardly action.

When I was baptized the priest said these words over me: "Renounce your own self." I can remember that very well. I will commit my soul to our Saviour before I die, pierced by American bullets. For everything is in God's hands. There is neither life nor death for those who live in God. Jesus Himself has said: "Thy will be done."

I read the Bible every day. Then I feel very close to you. When I crash to my death, I shall have the Bible and the Book of Psalms in my aircraft. I will also take along the mission badge which the director of the college gave me, and your medal.

Perhaps I did not take that marriage business as seriously as I should have done. I would not like to give the impression that I lacked respect for my betrothed and her family. Could you make her understand that it is better to make an end. I would really have liked to marry her: I would gladly have given you that happiness. I did not have time.

I ask only one thing of you: that you should forgive me. But I can go in peace, for I know that you always forgive me. Mother, how I admire you! You have always been so much braver than I. You are capable of forcing yourself to do painful things, and I find it impossible. Your only fault is that you spoilt me too much. But I myself wanted you to do so and I do not reproach you for that.

When I crash on to the enemy I will pray for you that all your prayers may be granted. I have asked Ueno to bring you this letter, but you must never show it to anybody. I am ashamed of it. I have the impression that it is not I whom death is waiting for. When I think that I shall never see you again, I am overcome with grief.

SUGGESTIONS FOR STUDY

1. What, as precisely as you can tell, was the action for which the writer was preparing?

2. What did you learn about the religious life of the Japanese?

3. What do you think the writer meant by saying, "I have the impression that it is not I whom death is waiting for"? Why can we never be absolutely sure what he meant?

4. What effect do you think this letter had upon the mother's emotions?

5. Do you feel more sympathy for the writer or for his mother? What in the letter made you feel the way you do? What statements were most surprising to you?

6. Among the many kinds of biographical material, letters are perhaps the most personal and revealing. In your library find a book of collected letters and read enough to convince yourself of the value of this type of literature. Perhaps you would enjoy one of the following:

Letters to His Son, Lord Chesterfield; *Letters to His Friends,* Cicero; *Letters of Emily Dickinson; Letters,* Ralph Waldo Emerson; *Letters of John Keats; Letters of Theodore Roosevelt; Letters,* Robert Louis Stevenson.

Collections: *Second Treasury of the World's Great Letters,* Wallace Brockway and Keith W. Bart; *Treasury of the World's Great Letters,* M. Lincoln Schuster, ed.; *Letters to Mother,* Charles Van Doren, ed.

FOR FURTHER READING

Other biographies that may widen your sympathies: *My Lord, What a Morning,* Marion Anderson; *My Several Worlds,* Pearl Buck; *It's Good to Be Alive,* Roy Campanella; *Our Son, Pablo,* Alvin Gordon; *George Washington Carver,* Rackham Holt; *Song of America,* George M. Mardikian; *Ben-Gurion,* Robert St. John; *Fifth Chinese Daughter,* Jade Snow Wong.

To Explore Vocations

ALMOST EVERY BIOGRAPHY discusses at some length the vocation of the person sitting for the biographical portrait. This information is of value for several reasons. It shows that interesting, and even exciting, persons may be found in every field of human endeavor. ("Rich man, poor man, beggarman, thief, doctor, lawyer, merchant, chief"—interesting personalities exist in every category.) Secondly, information about the history and the problems of various vocations can enable one better to understand and communicate with others. (For instance, would you be able to respond intelligently to a business man's casual reference to "Bernard Baruch's investment philosophy"? Yes, if you had read Baruch's *The Story of My Life*.)

Thirdly, the information on vocations in biographies can be of value to you by helping you choose a satisfactory lifework for yourself. Books giving statistics and other factual material about jobs of all sorts are probably available to you; but only by reading biographies can you become acquainted with the persons themselves who are engaged in these various vocations.

One way in which the reading of biography may guide you to the choice of a vocation is to acquaint you with new and helpful material about a career on which you have already set your heart. Such material may prove its value in a negative way: it may discourage you from giving further consideration to a vocation whose demands or difficulties you have not fully realized. To discover, for example, that the training of an F.B.I. agent is long, difficult, and expensive and that you are unwilling to pay its price will be helpful to you, if you have aspired to an F.B.I. career, but have not counted its cost. On the other hand, such material may have a positive value: knowledge of the rich rewards, both in money and in joy of service, of some vocation, may well strengthen your determination to pursue this career, whatever the cost in time, money, and effort.

A second way in which the reading of biography may guide you to a choice of vocation is to open your eyes to the rewards to be found in careers in fields to which you have previously not given serious consideration. The stage, the armed forces, politics, the church, business, union leadership, teaching, science,—the list is endless. Look them over before you settle for one.

A Cub Writer at Field's

EMILY KIMBROUGH

To prove herself competent and worthy of acceptance in the advertising bureau of a famous department store was Emily Kimbrough's vocational ambition. As you read this account of one of her first attempts to do advertising, test the appeal such work might have for you.

The Miss Gardner mentioned in the selection was the head of the advertising bureau, and was Miss Kimbrough's immediate boss. *Alice in Wonderland* is, of course, the famous tale by Lewis Carroll.

AT THE END OF A WEEK in the store I had gathered material for the page, "Little Things Noticed on a Walk. . . ." I had skirted round the Buyers as much as possible, but I had at arm's length got their sanction of the merchandise I wanted to use. Miss Gardner went over with me my notes on all the items I had selected, and then sent me on my rounds once more to check again a guarantee that this merchandise would be taken off sale and held back until the magazine came out, and assurance of a sufficient supply to take care of orders from the magazine readers.

This took nearly two weeks and almost countless trips, because of the difficulty of meeting with a Buyer, physically and temperamentally. Miss Gardner assured me I must not look on this as the standard of procedure for newspaper advertising—that had to be done on the double, from collecting merchandise to the finished proof. But *Fashions of the Hour* was special, and since it came out only six times a year, we could allow ourselves a longer period of preparation; though she warned that at the end, when we were ready to go to press, we would be involved in as big a rush as the newspaper people went through daily.

"The Buyers," she explained, "hate to hold back merchandise because a quick turnover is a mark of successful buying. But on the other hand they love to be represented in *Fashions of the Hour* because it means prestige and a wider range of customers than the daily in-the-store shoppers."

She suggested I go first to see the Personal Shopping Service in action, in order to learn at first hand something of how the store tried to satisfy a customer and what it took to provide that satisfaction. I went by way of Mr. Exley to ask how this service had started.

He could tell me, he said happily, as indeed I knew he could. It had begun when a derby-hatted bewhiskered LaSalle Street broker driving in his carriage to work had stopped at Field's on an errand for his wife. He'd found the store not yet opened and so had scrawled on the back of his calling card, "Baby needs new shoes, size two. And the Madame wants spool of thread to match attached sample." His coachman had pinned the card and attached sample to Charley's Door. Charley had filled the order himself that day, handing the package to the coachman when the carriage drew up as the store was closing.

The next day Charley had found three notes on the door from friends of the broker, the following day, eight. And after that the Personal Shopping Service was begun.

I found it to be a large room filled, except for communicating aisles, with rows of girls seated at telephone switchboards and facing two large screens suspended from the ceiling against a wall. The head of the Service told me every operator received daily a mimeographed sheet of the day's advertised items. On these sheets the items were described more fully than in the newspaper advertisement, because customers could think of many more things to ask than there was space for in the advertising copy. Reports on the changing supply of these items were flashed almost constantly on the screen; such as, "Size 10 out in all colors—Size 12 out in yellow."

The girls answered a phone call by saying, "May I help you?" One of the two or three supervisors to whom I talked said the girls formerly had answered calls with "Personal Shopping Service." It had been changed because many times a customer wanted to complain and thought she'd got the wrong desk. "That," the inspector looked a little frightened at such a prospect, "sometimes annoyed the customer." Therefore the girls expressed only a desire to help, and took complaints, passing them on to the proper adjustment bureaus or giving out information they were sure of. Stumped by requests for such things as timetable information on trains to California, and rates for shipping a dog to Hawaii, a girl would reroute those queries to the Travel Bureau on the third floor, and return to taking an order for anything from one spool of thread to be sent to Lake Forest, Special Delivery, because the customer wanted to finish a dress to wear for dinner that night, to a Chinese manservant to be interviewed, and if, in Field's estimation, found satisfactory, put on a train, destination a New York customer. Sables, I was told, and the most expensive jewelry had been ordered by telephone, as well as a five-cent Valentine to be selected "for my mother."

Following the dictum of Mr. Marshall Field, the slogan of the Personal Shopping Service was, a supervisor explained proudly, "We'll deliver a needle and we'll pick it up." She boasted further that it took a good deal to surprise this Service, but admitted the department had been a little dazed only the week before my visit when a customer had telephoned from a railroad station in Kansas City. The customer was somewhat agitated but had turned to Field's for help. She was on her way East from the Coast, she had explained somewhat breathlessly, had changed trains at Kansas City and learned there that all the baby's equipment, including a nursery icebox with bottles of the baby's formula, had been put on a wrong train and one that had already left Kansas City by the time she had discovered the error. Would the Shopping Service please buy other equipment, and she outlined the items needed, make up the stipulated number of bottles, and she dictated the formula, put them in a nursery icebox packed in ice, and deliver the whole to her when she got in to the Dearborn Street Station? The Shopping Service had filled the order.

Another supervisor, overhearing this recital, modified the record of the department a little by admitting to some mistakes. One customer ordering a vase had got a bag of marbles. Another requesting a color chart for paint had received a black corset. And only that morning a desperate plea had come from a customer who, having ordered a fruitcake from the tearoom bakery department, had not received it, but on reordering had, up to the time of her morning telephone call, received eight fruitcakes.

I was in something of a daze when I left the Personal Shopping Service, but I rallied sufficiently to recheck throughout the store the stock of every piece of merchandise destined for my *Fashions of the Hour* page.

Satisfied with this, Miss Gardner's comment was, "All right. Now write it."

And I was face to face with my typewriter and my first writing assignment, not counting—and I chose not to count it—my story that had been whittled to a single-line caption. I wanted to continue indefinitely selecting merchandise, to return fifty times for rechecking, to go on errands for all the people in the Bureau, even to meet Buyers I hadn't heretofore encountered and see again those I had. Anything, rather than write. There was, I knew dismally as I stared at the typewriter, no possibility of my keeping a job along those lines.

No one was happy about my career as it came off the machine. An enveloping ignorance of the way advertising should be written, and perhaps a persistent memory in the back of my mind of the Stationery Buyer and his gold watch, brought out of me a page done in the manner of *Alice in Wonderland*.

Miss Gardner was the first to express doubt about it. She was the first person who saw it. "We've never had advertising done in a humorous vein," she said.

"I don't think it's very humorous," I assured her mournfully.

"Perhaps not," was her answer, spoken kindly, "but I'm sure you meant it to be." She read it a second time while I sat beside her, sweating. I could think of nothing in all my life—and I tried to, as I sat there—not even Bryn Mawr College entrance examinations, that had exercised on me the fine torture provided by sitting and watching someone read words I had written. After what seemed like the time it takes one to drown, Miss Gardner looked up from the page and across at me. "I'm going to follow the Field policy," she said, "and take it. Everybody who gets a job here in the store is allowed to hang himself, and the management backs him all the way, while he's either achieving or avoiding that end. We've never run this kind of copy before, but I know I can get Mr. Schaeffer to go along with me on it, only you'll have to sell it to the merchandise people."

A kinder verdict would have been to turn down the piece, but that was not Miss Gardner's way. She accepted it and only sent Daniel Kimbrough right back again into the lions' den.

Mr. Tracy did not take it kindly that in return for a bottle of Blue Rose I should hand him an exposition of the fragrance entitled, "Take Care of the Scents and the Sounds Will Take Care of Themselves." He was not so angry as he was incredulous and grieved. He asked me to come back of the section to his desk. I think he felt a need to sit down and at a place of authority. There he took paper and pencil and worked laboriously and silently for perhaps ten minutes while I stood facing him. At the end of that time he turned the paper round, pushed it toward me and said, "This is more what I had in mind. I think you'll find it will catch the eye and make a snappy ad."

I read, "Blue Rose is the perfume choice of those who love fine things."

I assured him this was a catchy caption, but better perhaps for a newspaper than for the magazine. In my experience, I said, I had learned—but I did not tell him I had learned this only the preceding day and that my total experience was contained in the piece he was reading—"I have learned," I repeated emphatically, "that the principle in newspaper advertising must be that 'he who runs may read.'" But a magazine was a bit of reading that stayed on the living-room table and was gone over at leisure, perhaps reread several times; therefore you wanted something provocative in the caption that would lead on into the body of the piece, rather than tell the whole story at first glance.

Mr. Tracy shook his head but conceded mournfully that he would read on into the piece. The first line under the caption was, "Said the Duchess." That stopped him. It was not difficult to determine just where Mr. Tracy was in his reading because he formed with his lips each word as he came to it. He looked up, his eyes brightened, a happy smile spread over his face. "Well," he said, "that's not such a bad little ad after all."

There were eight paragraphs to my story—perfumes that month had been given the center spread with a cut. Mr. Tracy didn't read any of the paragraphs. He only ran his pencil down the page, stopping at each mention of a specific brand and price, nodding, "That's right, that's right." Reaching the bottom of the page and the end of the piece, he wrote a large OK and his signature under it. He handed it back to me across the desk and stood up. As I passed him on my way to the door he gave my shoulder a friendly little tap. "Bringing in our Carriage Trade like that," he said, "right at the top of your story. That's a good seller."

Until I took the copy for his OK, I had never met Mr. Harris of the second floor. He had been abroad on a buying trip when I'd gathered the merchandise and I had worked with his assistant, Jean Schureman. It was his opinion, Mr. Harris stated vehemently, that the assistant and I between us had betrayed him personally and done Marshall Field & Company no good. In the first place he had items that moved much faster than sundials, birdbaths, silk-covered celluloid desk sets and baskets for sugar bowl and cream pitcher. He didn't want to take up space advertising such items. "If," he added bitterly, "you can call advertising a thing that begins:

" 'Two days wrong. I told you butter wouldn't suit the works,' said the Mad Hatter gloomily." A sundial is the only safeguard against such mechanical difficulties . . . etcetera.

He looked up at this point, raised his eyebrows, shrugged his shoulders, resumed reading, and at the end of the passage observed bitingly, "I'm surprised you bothered to put in the prices." He handed back to me the sheet on which this was written and read again the second item:

"The bath was quite crowded. There was a duck, a dodo, a lory, and an eaglet." You might make just such an interesting, though different, collection with a birdbath . . . etcetera.

He wore the expression of one who has had put under his nose a particularly unpleasant odor. "You know what that will bring, don't you? Complaints from customers that our birdbaths haven't got dodos, lories and eaglets to go with them." He returned that page to me, holding it gingerly as if it were the source of the unpleasant odor.

The next one began:

" 'I shall sit here on and off for days,' said the Frog Footman." And so will everyone who plants a garden. A kneeling pad of oilcloth . . . etcetera.

His comment as he handed that one back to me was, "Our customers are certainly going to like being compared to frogs."

When he had finished reading:

" 'Why in a basket?' 'Why not?' said the Dormouse." And so the cream pitcher and sugar bowl are transported from tea wagon to tea guest in a basket especially designed for them . . . etcetera.

"Why don't you write advertising for the Zoo?" was Mr. Harris's comment as he returned the page.

And for:

"Why is a raven like a writing desk?" No answer—but as to why a desk set for your guest room—you'll know that when you see those of silk covered with celluloid . . . etcetera.

"Now," he said, "we're doing children's riddles. They might like that on the fourth floor. Miss Kimbrough, it seems to me you don't know just where you belong."

I felt he had a point there, but I didn't acknowledge it.

He took the pages back from me and riffled through them. "Did Miss Gardner see these?" he asked.

"Yes," I said eagerly, "and liked them." I knew this was pushing her comment but I was being pushed too.

Mr. Harris skimmed over the pages again. "Well," he said finally, "I don't know what on earth she's thinking of. But I have respect for Miss Gardner's judgment. She's a lady."

It had not before occurred to me that the two were synonymous, but I concurred enthusiastically.

"And," Mr. Harris continued, while I held my breath, "since I wasn't here in the beginning to set you straight about the merchandise, I guess I'll just have to OK these." He wrote the OK and his signature on each page.

On my way out of the section I ran into Mr. Schureman. He was waiting for me behind a display table that concealed us from Mr. Harris. "Did you get by?" he asked.

I showed him proudly the OK. Mr. Schureman told me I was lucky.

"I believe you," I assured him.

He invited me to come down to the section again. There were a lot of good stories there, he said, adding that he'd gathered from our conversations while we were collecting merchandise I was fascinated by what went on in the store.

He'd guessed exactly right, I told him, and I'd come down any chance I got.

I went off gaily, Mr. Schureman had been easy to talk to and pleasant to work with.

A few minutes later I was glad I had had the Schureman interlude. A Buyer on the first floor was standing in front of me, rattling my entire sheaf of papers in one hand and thumping them with the other. He had taken them all from me after reading those I'd handed him that pertained to his department. He wanted to see, he had said, if it was possible I had written about other departments as I had about his. Discovering I had, he announced vociferously his inability to convey to me what I was doing to Marshall Field & Company, and certainly to him. As if I had never seen any of them before, he read aloud in a trembling voice:

" 'Adventures first, explanations take such a dreadful time,' said the Gryphon." They need not if the passport is always ready in a leather case . . . etcetera.

At the end of the reading he opened and closed his mouth a few times, struggling, I was uncomfortably sure, to express his comment. He went on to the next paper, throwing the first to the floor.

"You couldn't deny, even if you tried with both hands"—that a keycase of soft leather with gold mountings . . . etcetera.

This page followed the first to the floor. His next selection was

" 'Must a name mean something?' Alice asked." Well petit point . . . has come to mean the newest thing in its combination with leather . . . etcetera.

As that page drifted to the floor he observed, and his voice sounded as if he were strangling, "Those beautiful cigarette and glove boxes I had made especially in Italy. All anyone needed to say was, 'Beautiful petit point and tooled leather boxes—first floor, Wabash Avenue,' and you would have had all Chicago, at least all of Chicago that matters, *flocking* in to my department. But instead they hire up there in the Advertising Bureau someone who deliberately makes fun of my merchandise."

I tried to protest this but he drowned me out with the vehemence of his next reading selection:

" 'They lived in an academy.' 'What did they live on?' asked Alice, always interested in questions of eating and drinking.

'They lived on the crops,' answered the Dormouse.

'It was a riding academy.' "

A slender crop of black leather . . . etcetera.

By the end of this reading the Buyer had recovered from his strangling attack. His voice instead took on the tone of a train-announcer. "Marshall Field & Company," he declaimed, "always stands for the finest quality in merchandise and dignity in presenting it. I should like to inquire, young lady, just who you think you are that you can flout, yes flout, such traditions. Can you answer me?"

I tried but I was unnerved. My voice came out like the squeak of a French locomotive. I said that Field's, I thought, had also stood for what was new and different. I hadn't meant to make fun of any of the merchandise. I was only trying to give its presentation a slightly different style.

The Buyer interrupted with a loud noise, expressing dissatisfaction with this explanation.

Miss Bredin came into my view down the aisle. She was almost on the run. Catching my eye, she lifted her arm and waved encouragingly to me. Someone, I realized, must have got word to her what was going on. She was to my fond eye the Northwest Mounties, the messenger galloping into the prison courtyard with a reprieve from the governor, and, when she spoke, St. Cecelia. "I hear," were the words she said, "Miss Kimbrough's done a little stunt for the magazine that's going to tickle our Carriage Trade."

Had Miss Bredin's announcement been that Mr. Simpson, the President of Marshall Field's, was scheduled that morning to do a fandango under the Tiffany dome, my opponent would have received the news with scarcely greater righteous horror. His jaw dropped, his eyes bulged slightly. "Since when," he inquired and his voice cracked on the query, "has Marshall Field & Company wished to tickle its customers?"

"It's a new style," Miss Bredin assured him soothingly, "one of our girls got it from a friend in Perfumes. Tracy over there says one of his finest customers let herself be quoted in the ad, a *Duchess*."
I silently but fervently promised Mr. Tracy I would, provided I wasn't fired in the meantime, write him an ad one day on Blue Rose perfume that would bring tears of happiness to his eyes.

Miss Bredin's boss pulled his watch from his pocket, looked at it, and gave a start. "Good gracious," he said, "they'll have my whole French shipment unpacked without my seeing it. I should be up in the stockroom this minute. You've wasted a good deal of my time, young lady," he added severely, "give me those pages."

Until this command I hadn't dared acknowledge the existence of the pages on the floor. I squatted down, scooped them together in my hands and handed them to him. I watched, scarcely daring to breathe, his signature over an OK go on every one of them. When he had written his signature on the last one, he gave the sheaf back to me, pulled his watch out again, clucked his tongue in annoyance at what he read, and scurried off without another word.

As I turned to go I said to Miss Bredin, "I'll never be able to thank you enough for what you did today."

"That's all right," she answered and her voice was brisk, "if Marshall Field's hadn't given young people a chance to hang themselves, the store wouldn't be where it is today. Anyway, I told the truth. They tell me Tracy's crowing like a rooster over his ad. Got anything for me?"

I pulled out a sheet from the pile and handed it to her over my shoulder. She read it aloud:

" 'If I am not the same, who in the world am I?' " For just such problems of identity, there is fashionable stationery with monogram to the left, address to the right . . . etcetera.

There was a pause. "Holy cat," she said finally, "if I'd known it was anything like this—why, our customers will think we're advertising stationery for lunatics, who don't know who they are."

I turned round from the counter to face her. "Miss Bredin," I said desperately, "that's a quotation from *Alice in Wonderland*. I did the whole page that way. They're all quotations. I've been fighting for them all over the store. But if you think it's terrible, standing up for me the way you did, I'll change the whole thing."

She suddenly put her hand out and squeezed my shoulder hard. "You probably wouldn't know in twenty-five years," she said, "what I know about engraving. Why should I think I know about advertising? If the ninth floor says it's all right, that's good enough for me. Now you go along, and don't pay attention to what *any-body* on the floor says."

I left the section on as close to a run as Marshall Field & Company rules would permit.

The remaining OK's were as easy to get as if the Buyers had really liked what they were signing. They didn't, but the sight of the signatures, "Tracy," "Harris," et al, brought them into line with only a mumbling of protest.

I walked into Miss Gardner's office, giddy with success, and without even asking in advance if I might see her. I spread the pages on the desk in front of her, and it was a gratifying sight to watch her eyes widen as she checked the OK's.

"I don't know how you ever got them," she said finally, and added, "I think that's something I'd better never know. You must have been either dishonest or immoral. Just don't tell me."

The OK'd pieces were put in a special file after I had made a copy for the printer, the Art Department, and one for myself. It was important, Miss Gardner explained, to keep the OK's separate, so they could not possibly be mislaid. Because not infrequently a Buyer going through the magazine at its publication would assert he had come upon merchandise from his section he had never authorized and had certainly not seen before what was written about it. At such moments, an OK'd copy was invaluable.

SUGGESTIONS FOR STUDY

1. Who or what are each of the following: Mr. Exley, the Slogan of the Personal Shopping Service, Mr. Harris, the Northwest Mounties?
2. What was the policy of the store toward new help? How would such a policy benefit the store? Other businesses? How would you, as an employee, react to such a policy?
3. What did Mr. Harris mean when he said of Miss Gardner, "She's a lady"?
4. How would you characterize the buyer who was Miss Bredin's boss?
5. What was the procedure that Miss Kimbrough had to follow to prepare each publication? How did she secure her O.K.'s?
6. Miss Kimbrough may seem to be too cocky and self-assured.

To what extent do you think the young worker should assume such
an air?

7. Of the people with whom Miss Kimbrough had to deal, which
ones had a sense of humor? Which ones lacked it? Do you think a
sense of humor is an asset, or a liability, in a business career?

8. Explain Miss Bredin's comment that the *Alice in Wonderland*
"stunt" would "tickle the carriage trade." Name some other books
which you think a merchant could refer to in his advertising and could
assume that the "carriage trade" would be familiar with. Look through
some magazines and see if you can find examples to bring to class.

9. Why did you find Miss Kimbrough interesting (or uninteresting)?
Why do you think her job would be a good one (or a poor one) for you?
Write a theme taking one side of one of these questions and giving
the reasons for your position.

FOR FURTHER READING

More biographical writings by Emily Kimbrough: *And a Right Good
Crew; Forty Plus and Fancy Free; How Dear to My Heart; It Gives
Me Great Pleasure; The Innocents from Indiana; Our Hearts Were
Young and Gay,* with Cornelia Otis Skinner.

Poor Little Rich Kid

JAMES MAC GREGOR BURNS

If democracy is to succeed (and it is challenged today as never before), more and more able men and women must make politics their life-work. But how does one get started on a political career? How did the mayor of your city get started? Your governor? Your congressman? Your senator? How did Franklin Roosevelt get started? Harry Truman? Dwight Eisenhower? The answers are found in the biographies of these successful politicians.

Read this chapter from *John Kennedy: A Political Profile* and discover how President Kennedy got started. Try to put yourself in his place and decide whether or not you would enjoy a similar experience. If so, you might well consider a career in politics.

The "Ambassador" (to England) whom you will find mentioned is President Kennedy's father, and "old Fitzgerald" is the President's maternal grandfather, one-time mayor of Boston, familiarly known as "Honey Fitz." Choate is the Episcopal preparatory school which Mr. Kennedy attended before going to Harvard.

ACCORDING TO A BOSTON LEGEND, Kennedy's decision to enter politics took place on a particular evening a few weeks after Joe, Jr.'s death. Jack, still recovering from his Navy injury, was summoned to his father's presence. In a dramatic scene, the Ambassador was supposed to have said that with Joe gone Jack must now carry on the family tradition of public service. He must be the champion of the Kennedy clan in politics. The whole family would unite to help him. And Kennedy, then and there, answered the family call.

Unhappily, things are always tidier and more dramatic in legend than in fact. To be sure, the Ambassador wanted his son to enter political life and made his views known on many occasions. But Jack was undecided. He still toyed with the notion of making

From JOHN KENNEDY: *A Political Profile*, © 1959, 1960, by James MacGregor Burns. Reprinted by permission of Harcourt, Brace & World, Inc.

a career of journalism; and he was attracted also to academic life and intellectual pursuits. On the other hand, newspaper work was an undependable trade for a beginner, and he had no graduate degree for teaching. Business lured him not at all.

He had mixed feelings about a political career. He liked the idea of being part of the top circles of government—making decisions, working on legislation, handling the affairs of state. But he was not at all sure that he would like politics at the level where he would have to start. He was still shy with people outside his social circle, a bit withdrawn and unassertive. He disliked the blarney, the exuberant backslapping and handshaking, the exaggerated claims and denunciations that went with politics, especially Boston politics. Nor was he convinced of his own talents as a speaker, or as a "mixer."

The issue was decided by, of all people, Jim Curley. In recent years the "Purple Shamrock" had been down on his luck. Vigorous young men had beaten him for the United States Senate, for governor, and even for mayor of Boston. Old and broke, under court orders to pay back to the city $42,000 as a result of a judgment of fraud, Curley had partly recouped his political fortunes in 1942 by winning a seat in Congress. But Washington was not his political forte. He hungered for one more crack at being mayor of Boston, one more chance to pay off political friends, to pay back political foes, and to refurbish the fading Curley legend. In the spring of 1945, he announced his candidacy for mayor in the fall election. If he won—and his chances looked good—the Eleventh Massachusetts Congressional District would be open. Kennedy eyed it with interest.

The Eleventh District was not an attractive one to a genteel political fledgling. Sprawling across East Boston, the North End and West End, and then over the Charles River into Charlestown, Cambridge, and part of Somerville, it enclosed a patchwork of some of the ugliest blighted areas in America. Irish, Italians, and a score of other immigrant groups were packed into grimy redbrick tenements sandwiched between smoking factories, oil tanks, elevated railways, dumps, and freight yards. In these tenements lived the thousands of longshoremen, teamsters, warehousemen, crane operators, and others who worked in or out of the docks and grain elevators of Boston Harbor that bounded the district on the east. Landmarks in the district were Bunker Hill monument and the grisly old State Prison. Boston's cesspool, some called the worst part of the area. The crime rate in sections of the district was among the highest in the country.

Tacked together by gerrymanders, the Eleventh had no resemblance to the "compact and contiguous" districts that the law enjoins. Quite the contrary, it fell into several distinct parts. East Boston—Pat Kennedy's old bailiwick—was now mainly Italian and dominated by street-corner politicians who promised to deliver their blocks for a consideration. Charlestown was peopled by varied groups, but all Catholic, who fought among themselves but united against outsiders, including those from across the Charles River. Cambridge and Somerville were more pleasant, lower-middle-class areas; the highest aspiration of many in East Boston or the North End was to move out of their slums into one of the huge frame "three-deckers" in these parts of the district.

Tucked into a corner of this district was a very different area—Harvard University and nearby precincts peopled by academics, old Yankee families, and executives commuting to the city.

Surely this was not a very inviting constituency for young Kennedy. But what else could he do? Some of his friends, knowing that he was looking around, urged him to run for statewide office—lieutenant governor, for example. Kennedy was cool to the idea. A host of politicians had their eye on the statehouse, men who had built up what Kennedy so painfully lacked—a political base of operations. Moreover, he far preferred office in Washington to Boston. So when Curley won the mayoralty early in November 1945, Kennedy decided to make the run for the Democratic nomination for Congress. In this district the Democratic nomination was equivalent to election.

Boston thought it had seen everything in politics, but here was something new. Kennedy was only twenty-eight years old. Still yellow from the Atabrine he had taken to fight malaria, reserved, gaunt, almost emaciated-looking, he was a polar opposite to the familiar image of the derby-hatted, loud-talking, paunchy Boston politician. Many of the latter did not take the young candidate very seriously. He would get a bad case of burned fingers, they told one another; Boston politics was for big boys. Wait till the pros got into the race. But he had the Kennedy name, money, and a determination to make good that became almost fanatical as the months passed.

Knowing he had to establish his claim to office in his own right, Kennedy got into the race early. In 1946, the Massachusetts primary elections took place in June. Kennedy campaigned for several months before the other candidates jumped off from the starting line. And in the process he began to build a big personal organization. It was this group that was most responsible for Kennedy's victory.

Its nucleus was a number of old friends from Choate, Harvard, and the Navy. Republicans or Democrats, liberals or conservatives, they converged on Bowdoin Street to "help out Jack." One Navy friend flew in all the way from San Francisco. Brother Bob, just out of the Navy, came in to take over some wards in East Cambridge. Les Billings, in from Pennsylvania, plunged into the campaign and even surprised himself with his zeal—a Republican working for a Democrat, an Episcopalian working in a Catholic district, a Pittsburgh native working in Boston, he later noted wryly.

Kennedy was shrewd enough, however, to know that he could not win with a bunch of non-Bostonians. It was bad enough that he himself was an outsider. Early in the operation, he began to hunt out people who had grown up in the different parts of his district. The men he found were much like himself—young, vigorous, politically inexperienced, not active in party politics, vaguely Democratic but uncommitted ideologically. His "junior brain trust," Kennedy called them.

At times they looked at their own candidate a bit anxiously. Could this slight, reserved, charming young man fight a Boston primary battle? One day Frank Morrissey found out. He drove Kennedy to Maverick Square, a gathering place for swarthy Sicilians, who stood about, coat collars turned up, hands in their pockets, broad-brimmed hats pushed low over their eyes, staring

coldly at the throng. Morrissey watched while Kennedy went up
to each of these characters, stuck out his hand, extracted a hand-
shake, and soon had them talking and even smiling. Kennedy,
Morrissey decided, would make out fine.

Primary elections are rather special affairs. Almost anyone who
has a mind to can run for the party nomination, which means that
a dozen or more politicians may join the race. Some jump in planning to be bought off to get out. Since all the contestants belong
to the same party, the battle is one of personalities and name-
calling rather than issues and program. Confused and bored, most
of the voters do not show up at the polls on primary day. All this
is doubly true of Boston primaries. In this most political of cities,
primaries are a hurly-burly of neighborhood vendettas, ethnic-
group rivalries, and obscure clashes of street-corner politicians,
occasionally enlivened by stunts and mudslinging.

Kennedy's primary was no exception. To make things worse,
the decision to hold primary election day in June meant that the
nomination of candidates came five months before Election Day
in November and hence at a time when the voters were even more
apathetic than usual. It was also apparent by early 1946, as candidate after candidate filed for the Democratic nomination for
Congress in the Eleventh District, that this race would be a typically wide-open affair.

Kennedy's rivals were a rather mixed lot. Best known was Mike
Neville, of Cambridge, an old-timer who had climbed the political
ladder to state legislator and mayor. Another favorite was John
F. Cotter, of Charlestown, who, as secretary to former Congressman Jim Curley, had built close contacts in the district. Of wholly
different cast was Joseph Lee, of Boston, a patrician Yankee who
valiantly ran for office year after year in this Catholic area and
occasionally won. Catherine Falvey, of Somerville, who had served
as a WAC major, lent color to the contest, for she liked to show
up at rallies in her gleaming white dress uniform. Also in the race
were a Somerville schoolteacher—an idealist who wanted to show
that he could campaign without accepting contributions—and four
Bostonians of Italian origin, *two* of whom were named Joseph
Russo.

At first the rest of the candidates laughed Kennedy off—at least tactically. "The poor little rich kid," Catherine Falvey dubbed him. Mike Neville offered him a job as a secretary if Kennedy would drop out. It became increasingly evident that Kennedy was working hard and running strong, and the taunts changed to indignation. Who was this kid who had invaded the Eleventh District? Nothing but an outsider trying to slide in on the Kennedy name and money. Kennedy's father, it was charged, was buying the election; according to one story, the old man claimed that with the money he was spending he could elect his chauffeur to Congress. And if the boy was a carpetbagger, he came by it naturally, for hadn't old Fitzgerald run for office while he was living in Concord?

Actually, the "kid" was taking no chances on the power of his name and money; he was relying on sheer hard work. Day after day, he made whirlwind tours of his district's endless sidewalks, darting into barbershops, saloons, grocery stores, factories, wharves, fire stations for quick handshakes. He turned more hollow-eyed and anemic-looking than ever, his war injury bothered him, and sometimes his harried workers wondered if he could get through the day. But he always did—though living on nervous energy.

Kennedy learned campaigning as he campaigned. At first his speaking was nervous and hesitant; he showed little poise and certainly no magnetism. But he slowly developed a style of direct, informal, simple speaking, without high-blown rhetoric or bombastic exaggeration, that to some of his listeners was in happy contrast to the oratory of the old-fashioned politicians. Kennedy's way of speaking was appropriate for what he talked about. Shunning personal attacks, ignoring his opponents altogether except toward the end, he talked factually about problems closest to the needs of the Eleventh District—jobs, housing, low rents and prices, medical care, veterans' benefits, social security, and other bread-and-butter matters. While on all these issues he took a New Deal–Fair Deal [1] position, he spoke not in generalities but in terms of concrete help that he could supply from Washington.

[1] *New Deal–Fair Deal:* Roosevelt-Truman.

The only foreign-policy issue of importance in the campaign was the British loan, which Kennedy supported and several other candidates opposed.

The young candidate learned, too, the power of suggestion and the quirks of voters. At one rally he was speaking vehemently for veterans' housing when an old character named Jackie Toomey suddenly stood up in the front row.

"What about the *non*-veteran?" Toomey hollered.

"Yes, sir, the *non*-veteran too," Kennedy shot back, and Toomey was seen going around to his pals afterward with the happy report, "You see—he's for the non-veteran, too."

With that cold realism that has marked his whole career, however, Kennedy saw early that orthodox campaigning was not good enough. People who turned out for rallies had already made up their minds. Sidewalk handshaking helped, but most voters quickly forgot his name, or at least what he was running for— hardly surprising, since there were nine other candidates in his own race, and several score other contestants for a dozen other state and local nominations. Radio time and newspaper advertising were useful, but much of this was wasted because these media covered all of Greater Boston.

How could he reach the thousands of apathetic voters who looked on politics as an odious business monopolized by crooks and windbags? If they would not come to him, he would go to them in their homes. So Kennedy, through his hundred or more volunteers, arranged for house parties in every corner of his district. There was nothing new in this—house parties were an old campaign technique—but what was different was the sheer number of parties, the care with which they were planned, and the scheduling that enabled Kennedy to cover at least half a dozen in one evening. In poorer neighborhoods, Kennedy workers supplied coffee and cookies, cups and saucers, silver and flowers. Names were carefully noted and added to mailing lists. Kennedy was at his best at these affairs—coming in a bit timidly but with his flashing, picture-magazine smile, charming the mothers and titillating their daughters, answering questions with a leg draped over an arm of his chair, wandering into the kitchen for a word with proud grandparents about news from the "old country," a final round of handshaking before leaving for the next affair. This social type of politicking was climaxed by a huge affair at a Cambridge hotel that featured, not the candidate, but his mother and sisters.

Kennedy reached the voters wherever he could—even on their way to and from work. It was said that his streetcar and subway advertising beat anything ever seen before in a congressional fight in Massachusetts. A single streetcar would have as many as four Kennedy placards, on which four different people—for example, a housewife, a dockworker, an executive, and a veteran—would explain "why I am for Jack Kennedy." A condensation of the *New Yorker* account of the PT-boat episode was widely distributed.

By now the slush and ice had long since gone from Boston's streets, spring was turning to summer, and the long campaign was nearing the end. The lesser candidates knew they were licked; one of them—the idealistic Somerville schoolteacher—obligingly played the piano to hold the crowd when Kennedy was late. But the tempers of the front runners grew short. When Miss Falvey, after peppering Kennedy with accusations at an outdoor rally, then whispered in his ear, "Don't pay any attention—it's just politics," Kennedy was not to be disarmed. He got up and delivered a biting counterattack on the lady. When one of Lee's supporters wrote humorous vitriolic pieces for an East Boston newspaper playing up the "rich kid" theme and, far worse, charging (falsely) that Kennedy's sister had married a descendant of Oliver Cromwell, despised by all good Irishmen, Kennedy begged Lee to have his friend lay off, and Lee reluctantly complied. By primary day, the race was rapidly developing into one of those zany, bellicose, and feverish battles so well described by Edwin O'Connor in *The Last Hurrah.*

On primary election day Kennedy went to the polls with Grandmother and Grandfather Fitzgerald, and squeezed in a movie— "*A Night in Casablanca*"—before the returns came in. The results showed how well Kennedy had done his work. By amassing a total of 22,183 votes, he almost doubled the vote of Neville, who came in second, and beat Cotter by better than three to one. Major

Falvey came in fifth. Kennedy ran ahead of all his opponents in Boston and Charlestown, and was beaten only by Neville in Cambridge. His share of the vote—about 42 per cent—was impressive for a ten-man race.

Jack took his victory with his usual self-possession. But Grandpa Fitz danced an Irish jig on a table and sang "Sweet Adeline."

SUGGESTIONS FOR STUDY

1. Explain the sentence: "Tacked together by gerrymanders, the Eleventh had no resemblance to the 'compact and contiguous' districts that the law enjoins."
2. What is a primary election?
3. Why was Mr. Kennedy "cool to the idea" of running for a state office? What is your opinion of his reasons?
4. Why did the other candidates not take Mr. Kennedy's campaign seriously at first? What changed their attitude?
5. Make a list of the things responsible for Mr. Kennedy's victory. How decisive was the fact that he was rich?
6. What were Mr. Kennedy's liabilities? How did he overcome them? (What is a carpetbagger?)
7. To what extent did this selection interest you in politics as a career for yourself?

A Clown's Debut

BUTCH REYNOLDS

You may have aspired to become a policeman, a baseball hero, a jet pilot, or even President of the United States, but I venture the guess that you have never dreamed of yourself as a circus clown. The lure of the circus has lessened in our age of radio and television, but still, all over the world, circuses offer the old-time jobs: roustabouts, animal trainers, acrobats—and clowns.

The following selection from Butch Reynolds' autobiography, *Broken-Hearted Clown,* tells how a famous English clown got his start in this profession.

IT WAS in the main street of a small Surrey town that a miracle happened to a boy of six. I had been shopping with my father, rather bored by the usual routine of chatting with men at counters and holding the bag open while my father put in one parcel after another. I was standing on the pavement, wishing he would hurry up and that the string of a parcel I was carrying did not cut my hand so much, when it happened. . . .

The humdrum world about me with its dull, basket-laden, Saturday morning shoppers, was filled with color and music, peopled with Red Indians in feathers, negroes, princesses, elephants, Arabs, Cossacks, snow-white horses with nodding plumes, grotesque clowns and gallant cowboys, and there, in the center of them all, was Britannia, glittering with gold as though on the back of a new penny, with a real, live lion on a golden chain sitting at her feet. She passed, and still they came, the fairy-tale people and animals in seemingly endless procession. To the little boy it was as though all the characters from the Arabian Nights, Just-So Stories, Chums and Hans Anderson had stepped into the High Street—actually Lord George Sanger's was passing by.

Present-day children count their blessings in television, cinema and radio, but here is a glory they have been denied—when the elephants are led from station to tober.[1] The banning of circus parades has meant that a little more of the color and gusto of living has been excluded from a world in which increasing control and mechanization have put a high rarity value on just those qualities.

Of course, I went to the show that afternoon—there would have been no holding me back, and my father, a writer of boys' books, knew his public too well to attempt such a thing. Seated near the sawdust ring, a little dazed with wonder, I confirmed that the morning's miracle was real. Here they were again, the colored people of the parade, and they were all supermen to me: the clowns were outrageously funny, the lady riders in pink spangled tights, royal princesses, the trapeze artistes, animal tamers and cowboys brave as lions, the jugglers, wizards of the rank of Merlin whose magic, for all I knew, was also responsible for the fact that, in this brave, new world, elephants played cricket and football and monkeys ate and drank from plates and cups like human beings.

I opened my eyes wide in horror when an elephant picked up one of the clowns and whacked him hard on the floor, split my sides with laughing the moment I realized that he was a dummy, and felt a delightful cold shiver run down my spine as the tiger sprang at his negro trainer, hitting the side of the cage with a hair-raising crash just as the trainer shut the door on the other side. I was much impressed, too, by the cohorts of Red Indians in full war paint who hopped round the ring first on one foot and then on the other, shaking their tomahawks menacingly at the audience and shouted their full-throated battle cry: "Ho, ho, ho!" All my ideas of Indians at that time came from Henty and Hiawatha, and these braves fitted the picture perfectly; later acquaintance with the Indians of Canada and the States leads me to suppose that they were tentmen dressed up for the purpose, very well achieved, of thrilling small boys.

Perhaps the germ of the circus really got into my blood on that day, and certainly from that time to this I have never missed a

[1] *tober:* circus ground.

chance to see the greatest show on earth; but I had a long way to
go before I found myself in the producing part of the ring.

"Tinker, tailor, soldier, sailor. . . ." We children used to count
our plum stones to see what life would offer us in the way of a
career. I didn't know at that time that I was going to take most of
the scheduled jobs in my stride, with a good many more thrown
in. . . . "Richman, poorman, beggarman, thief." I should certainly
have to cross "richman" and "thief" out of the list, but in their place
I could add ranch hand, painter, lumberjack, author, farm-man,
engineer, and a dozen or more minor occupations thrown in, before I finally became a circus clown. In fact you would need an
awful lot of plum stones to cover my checkered career. In an age
of increasing specialization, I dabbled with gusto here and there
and enjoyed it all immensely. In fact, I would recommend any
young fellow thinking about a career not only to "have a go" but
to have a lot of goes and enjoy them.

Leaving my little private school in Surrey at just under fourteen,
I took the humble, office beginnings of four careers in my stride,
and, with 11 pounds gleaned from the four ventures, shipped to
Western Canada, where much of the prairie was still open range.
Herding cattle in that lonely country I learned a lot about the ways
of animals, wild and domestic, my sole companions for weeks on
end, and this has helped me to understand all the various circus
creatures, horses, lions, bears, elephants, alligators, snakes, dogs,
etc., who were later to be my colleagues in the ring.

Ranching, farming, well-digging, logging, dredging, boring for
oil, hauling freight; life was strenuous, often hard, but never dull.
Sometimes I was dead broke, and my first impression of a lumberjack's life was one of good, abundant, beautiful, hot food, after a
spell of stark hunger. My twenty-first birthday saw me stranded
and penniless in a blizzard on the sort of night in which no human
being could stay out of doors and live. I kept going, with my side-
kick, Jack, by sleeping in a livery stable and helping with the
horses all day for twenty-five cents, in those days the price of a
meal. After that the logging camp, at sixty below zero and plenty
of it, with its abundant food and the satisfying rhythm of hard

work, very sound sleep and the peace of mind that goes with them, seemed pretty good to me.

In those Canadian days I never missed a chance to see a circus, including that of the famous Ringling Brothers. But still my vocation evaded me, and, with most of my young contemporaries, I got into a bigger show in 1914. With the Canadian forces I spent over nine hundred days in the firing line, and, as a signaller, had some good laughs and some sticky patches at Vimy Ridge, Passchaendale, Ypres, and the Somme. With peace I went back to Canada and the States, where an attack of after-the-war nerve trouble left me wondering who I was.

Recovering, I found that I could draw and paint, and plunged happily into art, balancing the budget meanwhile by making toys and games. Painting led me to a studio in Chelsea, England, and eventually back to my first love, the circus, taking in a few odd experiences (like a ten-thousand mile trip through the United States with a tent, a picture in the Academy, a journey to Finland on one of the last of the big sailing ships, building and decorating a Chelsea Club and working the South Coast with an old tug boat) on the way.

It was while I was walking through Kent, sketching, that I caught up with my circus career. I was up early before the bloom had been brushed off the summer day, sitting on the grass at the edge of a village green. As I sniffed the morning smells of woodsmoke and bacon, and listened to the clank of a pail, the sound of sticks being chopped, crockery put out and slow, country voices, as the cottage people got themselves into circulation, my ears picked out the pleasing and now rare sound of hooves. It was the sort of morning when you would expect something new and exciting to happen—the birds had been declaring for hours that life was a glorious adventure—but I was unprepared for the pantomime-pretty picture which my destiny presented as it came round the corner.

The little wagon was drawn by a pair of spotted ponies and a few more were hitched on behind; its gay colors were enhanced to enamel-like brilliance by the peculiar, transparent clarity of early morning sunlight. On the box sat a short stocky man with a large moustache pointed at either end. There is a feeling of fellowship between those who are up early on a fine morning, and, when he saw me, he stopped, unhooked his ponies to graze on the young grass of the green, and sauntered over to sit down beside me. That was how I met Fred (later known as Count) Rosaire of Rosaire's Circus. He and his wife, Florence (The Countess), had four boys and four girls, all outstanding performers, so that this family could put on a first-class show, including the band and the build-up, entirely by themselves. They must have a good claim to be the most versatile and self-contained circus family this country has ever seen.

Like most old-time circus homies,[2] Fred Rosaire was a very early riser and liked to take his horses on ahead of the motor transport. We sat and talked while he watched the road for the rest of his show, their next tober being nearby. When he found that I knew a bit about horses and was a good hand with a paint brush he invited me to travel with the show, and, attracted by the color and freedom of the life, I accepted with enthusiasm. That was the beginning of a career which has taken me from Land's End to John o' Groats and back again, with Tom Arnold's, Harringay, Prince Cox, Waverley Market, Skegness Winter Garden, Chipperfield-Sandow, Burns Supreme, Royal George and many other circuses, from the biggest residential shows, to the small, family tenting circus travelling the country fairgrounds.

The circus has a lot to offer to a painter; all through the tenting season it moves from tober to tober, its gaudy wagons crossing the colored counties. Setting out with the birds and blossom of Easter and pulling in through the burnished beeches and bracken of the fall, a painter with the summer circus has no shortage of subjects. There are plenty of odd jobs for him, too, putting the color into showfronts, wagons and signs, besides lending a hand with the thousand and one "backring" chores. These I found, like so many of the manual jobs carelessly classified as "unskilled" by white-collared statisticians who have never done them, required much real craftsmanship. I had to learn them the hard way and at first,

[2] *homies:* men.

being a very green "Josser," I did not know one tent pole from another, nearly jabbed the precious canvas with the spikes and missed a hole in lacing up so that the whole thing had to be done again and I was able to add a few circus man's additions to the wide vocabulary I had acquired in Canada and on the Western Front.

During the summer I got my circus name of "Butch" from a blue, striped apron, bought at a local shop when I was painting a side show. Someone called out: "What yer, butcher," and the shortened version stuck. Next year saw me with another show, as a cross between lorry-driver and nursemaid to a lot of horses, and from here I was "promoted" to a little of the front end of the business, putting strips of lightly colored cloth on the five shilling seats and taking the tickets at the door. It was while this show was touring Scotland that an accident led to my first, and very shaky, debut in the ring as a circus clown.

"Get into these, cul,³ somebody's got to come into the ring to-night." I looked from my colleague, a clown whose performance I had often admired from my seat among the flatties,⁴ to the armful of comedy clothes he had thrown on to the little bed in my wagon. "All right," I said, and then immediately wished I hadn't. It was half an hour before the night performance, and one of the clowns taking part in the "Honey Bee" entree had been packed off to the hospital. The Honey Bee was this homie's pet number, and he was not going to have it cut out of the program if he could help it; he knew I must have seen it often enough to know the patter and so I was to be the victim, I who had never been in the ring in my lifetime.

He was wise enough to go before I could retract, and, experimentally, I climbed into the clothes and looked in the mirror, feeling that I should probably make a perfect fool of myself, quite a different thing to being a perfect clown. I knew, too, that Scottish audiences, who cheer a good number well, have none of the Southerner's modesty about letting a duff ⁵ performer know their views

---

³ *cul:* friend; mate.
⁴ *flatties:* members of the audience.
⁵ *duff:* poor; bad.

of his act. I had no idea how to make up, but my colleague's wife, a woman born in the circus, did it for me so well that my morale was much boosted by the realization that I looked like a real clown at all events, and that my own brother would certainly not know me.

Feeling rather like a man who sits among the shiny periodicals waiting for a door to open and a white-coated dentist to say: "Next, please," I waited my turn. It was like Ferdinand the Bull, with eyes shut tight, that I finally charged into the ring, for the opening of the Honey Bee, and of my career as a clown. Too petrified to look at the flatties, who seemed to be crowded horribly close to the ring, I kept my eyes on my fellow clowns who helped me to make a start, covering up my hesitations with an easy run of patter. Gradually the mist cleared and the thing began to flow, the familiar words fell into place and the right kind of actions came with them. Half expecting boos, if not missiles, I heard a shout or two of the hearty laughter which is music to the ears of any clown. This was a favorite clown entree in which a lot of water gets squirted about, and I was the chief recipient. The volume of laughter grew and, greatly encouraged, I made my final exit with a feeling almost of elation. At least it was over, and I hadn't dried up—the thing most dreaded by any public performer. I was surprised, though, when the boss came up to me and said: "You are in the right place, you stay there"—and I have.

By now I was feeling like someone who has won a little in his first attempt at a football pool, and I was keen to have another go and venture a bit further. Next day I went into the Joey Pony act, and the day after, with greater daring, took a turn on the trampoline, that spring-bed affair which throws the performers up into the air and all over the place. It is made of a stretched canvas strung to an iron pipe frame with elastic cord, and a skilled artist can do neat backs and forwards and fall about at will. Some performers do a straight trampoline act, but mostly it is comedy. I was comedy all right. Not knowing the first thing about the art, I was thrown all over the place, on to the frame and off it, and though the trampoline looks soft and well sprung, it hurts quite a lot when you come down the wrong way, to say nothing of the times when you fail to hit the thing at all.

The flatties thought my antics were all part of the game and laughed well; in fact I got my biggest laugh when, jumping on the box to get on the trampoline, I missed my footing and disappeared underneath the contraption with the box on top of me. This was such a big success, especially with the chavies,[6] that I decided to keep that bit in for the future, only studying how to make it a bit easier on the shins.

My bit of success had a few unfortunate repercussions. The clown who had gone to the hospital for observation gave two free passes to the nurses and was furious when they came back with the report that the Honey Bee had gone on without him and had been a big success. Now no circus artist likes anyone else to take his place in an act; he prefers to feel unique and indispensable, and my colleague came out of hospital in double quick time, and was heard to mutter things about people like me dying in their sleep or getting hit over the head with a sledge hammer. However, so strange and unpredictable is human nature, that when I set myself and my wagon on fire with a primus stove, it was this clown who "put me out," and remained to drink all the whisky that had been brought to get me over the shock! This so changed his attitude towards me that we have been friends ever since and have often worked together in the ring.

My ambition thoroughly roused by this time, I began to think up an entree of my own, and, remembering something that had made me laugh at a polite garden party, I contrived a kind of deck chair that took a bit of opening and setting up and more than a bit of sitting in. After a few very private rehearsals I showed it to the boss who gave a little corner of the program to "Butch Reynolds and his Comedy Chair." My first appearance in the ring alone was a bit too hurried to be really effective, and the damned chair, which I had thought absolutely "fool proof," behaved too well. However the boss kept the number in, and I worked hard at worsening the chair and improving myself. Perhaps because it was

[6] *chavies:* children.

my first solo effort, this has always been my favorite number, and Butch and his chair have raised a laugh or two in most parts of the country from Earl's Court to Little Puddleton.

A favorite question of flatties is: "How do you get around to being a clown?" and this is generally followed by a rather regretful: "I suppose you have to be born to it." Well, a lot of good clowns are born in circus wagons, but there is always room for new blood. I think the recipe is to be either very short and fat or very tall and thin, to have, as a gift from the gods, that flair known among circus men as "ring sense" and to enjoy a good laugh yourself. I don't know where the popular legend about that brokenhearted clown arose, but I do know that real laughter is more infectious than the common cold, and can make a good act even when all the orthodox gags have somehow got out of hand.

This became mercifully clear to me during an encounter with a "hair-growing machine" while I was working with Parkins International in Jersey. Edgar Franks was carrying this wonderful contraption into the ring when he collided with young Percival (then with the High School Rider, Count de la Cour). Edgar did not realize that one of the three legs had been knocked off in the collision, and he kept trying to stand the machine up this way and that until finally the whole thing tipped over and shot all its telltale wigs into the ring. I and the other clowns were quite unable to go on with the show; we just sat in the sawdust and roared with helpless laughter—and so did the flatties! They were not too sure what it was all about but they "caught" our fit of laughing to such an extent that the act that went wrong was a big success.

The good clown's love of his craft sometimes leads to his practising it unofficially on his colleagues in the ring: When I was working with Henry (Koko) Pinder, Harry Pinder, Charlie Bale, Phil Williams, and Ray Higginson at Waverley Market, we all enjoyed doing a bit of this private clowning among ourselves at the same time as working our more orthodox gags for the benefit of the audience. For instance, I had a score of this kind to settle with Ray Higginson and was all set to squirt him with a good deal more water than the act demanded, but the others had "fixed" me in advance. As I walked away from the famous hair-growing machine, wearing an outsize in wigs, it suddenly flew off, in full view of the delighted flatties. It had been fastened (by Koko and Charlie Bale I suspect, though I never got to the bottom of the matter) to the machine by a thread. Again it was our private laughter that raised the biggest public laugh.

Clowns somehow have a knack of getting into accidentally funny situations in their private lives, perhaps just because no one is ever prepared to take them seriously: Most sensible tentmen fight shy of the job of wielding the sledge hammer (an unpopular tool for a hot summer build-up); only a couple of clowns would fight for the privilege of using the thing—and so it happened. I was touring the Lake District with Sandow's Circus, and we were late with the build-up on a tober near Kendal. Another clown, Mickey Cavanagh, had just one last stake to drive in; I had just to give a finishing tap to the stake holding up the damask curtain; we both reached the sledge hammer at the same moment. We were both hot, tired, about "through" with that job, and longing for a cup of tea. Our sense of humor was at very low ebb, and a tussle for possession soon developed into a rather bumble-fisted sort of a scrap. We clinched and staggered and ended by both falling through the seats with our heads down and our feet sticking up in the air, from which undignified position the boss rescued us. He then arbitrated in the best United Nations manner, letting me have my tap and then handing the sledge over to Mickey for his, after which we looked at each other and all burst out laughing. "Do that in the ring," the boss said, "and you'll bring the house down."

Once a clown, always a clown; clowning gets into your looks, your blood, and all your ways. I have found that out. Gone are my chances of being mayor of Chelsea, member of parliament or of the viewing committee at the Royal Academy. Betty Kayes, daughter of that old circus man, Buff Bill, said to me recently: "You are never so funny as when you are serious," and another friend remarked: "When you swear like that you are terribly funny." I had a flat tire and someone who had borrowed my pump had gone on ahead, taking it with him. Laugh, clown, laugh! I might as well. No one will ever take me seriously again.

SUGGESTIONS FOR STUDY

1. What do you think of Mr. Reynolds' advice "to have a lot of 'goes' and enjoy them"?

2. How did Butch Reynolds' various "goes" fit him for his career as a circus clown?

3. What so-called "unskilled" jobs can you name which really require much real craftsmanship?

4. Discuss with your father or some other relative or friend how he got his start in his career. Was it by accident, or by careful planning? Which do you think is the more usual?

5. Relate the example given of "professional jealousy." How was it overcome? How can a successful person prevent his colleagues from becoming jealous of him?

6. What do you think are the qualities that make a good circus clown? Which ones must be born in you? Which ones can be acquired? Do you think you would make a good clown? Why, or why not?

7. Name some other vocations which you have become interested in through the reading of biography.

8. If this selection interested you, read *Broken-Hearted Clown* and report to the class the significance of the title.

My Investment Philosophy

BERNARD BARUCH

In a free enterprise system such as ours, thrift and saving and investment are the life-blood of prosperity and of a high standard of living. Among the successful financiers who have made fortunes by "playing the stock market" none is more famous or respected than Bernard Baruch.

In his autobiography, *Baruch: My Own Story*, Mr. Baruch tells his investment philosophy. Whether you are interested in a career in finance, or just interested in the wise investment of your own savings, you will find his advice worth serious consideration.

IN RELATING MY FAILURES, I have hoped that others might profit from my errors. But I must confess that I am somewhat dubious how effective any advice I may give will prove.

Other people's mistakes, I have noticed, often make us only more eager to try to do the same thing. Perhaps it is because in the breast of every man there burns not only that divine spark of discontent but the urge to "beat the game" and show himself smarter than the other fellow. In any case, only after we have repeated these errors for ourselves does their instructive effect sink home.

Being so skeptical about the usefulness of advice, I have been reluctant to lay down any "rules" or guidelines on how to invest or speculate wisely. Still, there are a number of things I have learned from my own experience which might be worth listing for those who are able to muster the necessary self-discipline:

1. Don't speculate unless you can make it a full-time job.
2. Beware of barbers, beauticians, waiters—of anyone—bringing gifts of "inside" information or "tips."
3. Before you buy a security, find out everything you can

about the company, its management and competitors, its earnings and possibilities for growth.

4. Don't try to buy at the bottom and sell at the top. This can't be done—except by liars.

5. Learn how to take your losses quickly and cleanly. Don't expect to be right all the time. If you have made a mistake, cut your losses as quickly as possible.

6. Don't buy too many different securities. Better have only a few investments which can be watched.

7. Make a periodic reappraisal of all your investments to see whether changing developments have altered their prospects.

8. Study your tax position to know when you can sell to greatest advantage.

9. Always keep a good part of your capital in a cash reserve. Never invest all your funds.

10. Don't try to be a jack of all investments. Stick to the field you know best.

These "rules" mainly reflect two lessons that experience has taught me—that getting the facts of a situation before acting is of crucial importance, and that getting these facts is a continuous job which requires eternal vigilance.

I have heard, for example, that one of the Rothschilds, who certainly were among the wisest financiers of their day, set out to make secure the fortune of a loved one. He decided to invest this fortune in Austrian and German government bonds, English consols above par, and French rentes above par. When the story was told me many years later, this estate had shrunk to only a fifth of its original worth. The Austrian and German securities were completely valueless, of course, while the others had depreciated considerably.

One cannot, in other words, make an investment and take for granted that its worth will remain unchanged. New sources of supply coming from hitherto untapped areas of the world may transform the competitive position of a company, as will changes in people's habits or technological innovations. Often something will shrink in value because of one discovery, as coal did in relation to oil and electricity, only to be given new economic life by another development such as the new chemical uses being made of coal.

Actually one can point to only a few things whose value has resisted the change of time down through the centuries—and even then not without fluctuations. Among these I would list some minerals like gold, silver, and copper; precious stones; works of art; and crop-bearing lands.

Even with these things one must add the qualification "at least so far." The development of cultured pearls, for example, has nearly destroyed the old value of pearls. As for gold, some governments, including our own, have passed laws making its possession illegal.

This fact, that the value of an investment can never be counted upon as absolute and unchanging, is one reason why I urge everyone to make a periodic reappraisal of his or her investment position. It also explains why it is unwise to spread one's funds over too many different securities. Time and energy are required to come to a sound judgment of an investment and to keep abreast of the forces that may change the value of a security. While one can know all there is to know about a few issues, one cannot possibly know all one needs to know about a great many issues.

In no field is the old maxim more valid—that a little knowledge is a dangerous thing—than in investing.

In evaluating individual companies three main factors should be examined.

First, there are the real assets of a company, the cash it has on hand over its indebtedness and what its physical properties are worth.

Second, there is the franchise to do business that a company holds, which is another way of saying whether or not it makes something or performs a service that people want or must have.

I have often thought that perhaps the strongest force that starts an economy upward after it has hit bottom is the simple fact that all of us must somehow find a way to live. Even when we are sunk in the blackest despair, we have to work and eat and clothe ourselves; and this activity starts the economic wheels turning anew.

It is not too difficult to determine the things people must have if they are to continue to live. Such fields usually open up investments which are likely to hold their value over the long run.

Third, and most important, is the character and brains of management. I'd rather have good management and less money than poor managers with a lot of money. Poor managers can ruin even a good proposition. The quality of the management is particularly important in appraising the prospects of future growth. Is the management inventive and resourceful, imbued with a determination to keep itself young in a business way? Or does it have a sit-and-die attitude? I have learned to give less weight to big financial names at the head of a company than to the quality of its engineering staff.

These basic economic facts about various enterprises, to repeat, must be checked and rechecked constantly. Sometimes I have made mistakes and yet, by abandoning my position in time, still was able to emerge with a net profit.

Early in 1904, for example, I heard that the Soo line was planning to increase its wheat traffic by building a branch line from Thief River Falls in Minnesota to Kenmare, North Dakota, about three hundred miles westward. I asked Henry C. Davis to go West and explore the Soo's possibilities. On his return we shut ourselves up with a map. From the information Davis brought I concluded that enough wheat would come over the new rails to increase the Soo Line earnings greatly.

The Soo stock was selling at 60 or 65 and paying $4 a share, which was over 6 per cent on the investment. I began to buy the stock. Work on the Soo extension got started but soon the gossip spread through Wall Street that financial returns were a long way off and rather doubtful. I had learned that gossip of this sort often is put out to frighten people away from a good thing. And so I bought more Soo stock.

Along came a bumper wheat crop, which increased the Soo Line's revenues some 50 per cent. This jumped Soo stock to 110, nearly two thirds higher than it had been when I began to buy. All this was before the Thief River extension was even open.

Meanwhile, I had taken additional precautions to recheck my

facts on the prospects for the Soo extension. I had sent another man through the Northwest and adjacent parts of Canada to plot grain movements under a variety of actual and hypothetical conditions. He came back with pages of figures which I studied long and deeply.

My conclusion was that the Thief River extension would prove a disappointment since most of the wheat would move to the head of the Lakes and then east by water. Since this was contrary to the judgment on which I had started my operation, I began to sell, mostly to Soo insiders.

By discovering my error in time, I managed to retreat from the field of battle with a handsome profit before the stock broke. This feat, may I stress, was accomplished by superior research rather than the legerdemain so often attributed to speculators. . . .

In speculation, our emotions are constantly setting traps for our reasoning powers. It is far more difficult, for example, to know when to sell a stock than when to buy. Men find it equally hard to take either a profit or a loss. If a stock has gone up, a man wants to hold on to it in anticipation of a further rise. If a stock has gone down, he tends to hold on to it until an upward turn comes along so he will at least be even.

The sensible course is to sell while the stock still is rising or, if you have made a mistake, to admit it immediately and take your loss.

Some people, after selling, bedevil themselves with thoughts of "if only I had done this." To do this is both silly and demoralizing. No speculator can be right all the time. In fact, if a speculator is correct half of the time he is hitting a good average. Even being right three or four times out of ten should yield a person a fortune if he has the sense to cut his losses quickly on the ventures where he has been wrong.

In my younger days I heard someone, I forget who, remark, "Sell to the sleeping point." That is a gem of wisdom of the purest ray serene. When we are worried it is because our subconscious mind is trying to telegraph us some message of warning. The wisest course is to sell to the point where one stops worrying.

I have found it wise, in fact, to periodically turn into cash most of my holdings and virtually retire from the market. No general keeps his troops fighting all the time; nor does he go into battle without some part of his forces held back in reserve. After my first youthful reverses were behind me, I tried never to go into any speculation over my depth—beyond my financial capacity to pay for any error of judgment. By maintaining a large cash reserve, I have also been in a position to take advantage of unforeseen opportunities as they developed.

Another common illusion some people have is that they can do anything—buy and sell stocks, dabble in real estate, run a business, engage in politics—all at once. My own experience is that few men can do more than one thing at a time—and do it well. A skilled operator in any field acquires an almost instinctive "feel" which enables him to sense many things even without being able to explain them. In a few instances, as in coffee, where I went into speculations where I lacked this "feel," I have not done too well.

Success in speculation requires as much specialized knowledge as success in law or medicine or any other profession. It never would occur to anyone to open a department store in competition with Macy's or Gimbels or to make motor cars against Ford and General Motors without prior training or preparation. Yet the same man will cheerfully toss his savings into a market dominated by men who are as expert in their line as Macy's and the auto makers are in theirs.

What of the man or woman with modest savings who is simply looking for a fair return on his or her savings and who cannot give full time to a study of investments? My advice to such persons is to seek out some trusted investment counselor. The emergence of this new profession of disinterested and careful investment analysts, who have no allegiance or alliances and whose only job is to judge a security on its merits, is one of the more constructive and healthy developments of the last half century.

SUGGESTIONS FOR STUDY

1. Explain the difference between a gambler, a speculator, and an investor.
2. Why was Mr. Baruch reluctant to lay down any "rules" for investment? To what extent do you agree with him on the usefulness of advice?
3. Open your book to the ten "rules" which Mr. Baruch lists, and give his arguments for each.
4. What are the two lessons from experience which Mr. Baruch says his "rules" reflect?
5. Add to the examples in the book others which illustrate change of value in commodities. What are the "new chemical uses being made of coal"?
6. Name the three main factors by which Mr. Baruch evaluated individual companies.
7. Why is it difficult to sell stock when one should do so?
8. What is Mr. Baruch's advice to the man or woman of modest savings looking for a reasonable return on his money?
9. Why, or why not, do you think Mr. Baruch would be an interesting person to know?
10. To what extent has this selection changed your attitude toward financiers?
11. Why, or why not, do you think you would enjoy a career as a financier?

FOR FURTHER READING

Some biographies that tell about vocations: *Adventures of a Biographer,* Catherine Drinker Bowen; *A Goodly Fellowship,* Mary Ellen Chase; *And Promenade Home,* Agnes De Mille; *Leonard Bernstein,* David Ewen; *The Stars at Noon,* Jacqueline Cochran; *A Long Way from Missouri,* Mary Margaret McBride; *I Wanted to Write,* Kenneth Roberts; *The Singing Family of the Cumberlands,* Jean Ritchie; *My Adventures as an Illustrator,* Norman Rockwell; *The Years Were Good,* Louis B. Seltzer.

To Find the Good Life

IN YOUR SEARCH for the "good life"—the fine and complete life—you can look to the reading of biography for some of your surest guidance. Lives that have faced disasters, overcome difficulties, and strived toward high goals can give direction to your own mind and spirit. Many adults realize that the reading of one certain life-story gave them the mental equipment to make important judgments, or instilled in them the moral strength to perform right actions.

To live happily in our difficult and changing world is not an easy thing to do. The future looms ominously, both for nations and individuals. But out of the past, thanks to biography, you may find the compass and the chart that you will need to achieve the good life under any conditions:

> Lives of great men all remind us
> We can make our lives sublime,
> And, departing, leave behind us
> Footprints on the sands of time.

Two Boys on a Mountain

WILLIAM O. DOUGLAS

Mountain climbing has always mystified the non-mountain-climber. Why engage in this exhausting enterprise? Why deliberately put yourself into a dangerous position? Is that moment when you stand on the summit worth all the effort? People who are fond of this sport will tell you that it is an exciting and inspiring thing to do—that the challenge, the danger, the exhilaration of final victory come to symbolize for them the very pattern of a heroic life.

William O. Douglas, now an Associate Justice of the United States Supreme Court, grew up in the state of Washington, where he learned to love the outdoor life and became especially fond of mountain climbing.

Of Men and Mountains is his own recounting of the many adventures he had in this, his favorite sport. He tells in Chapter 22 how he and his close friend, Douglas Corpron, had many narrow escapes climbing Kloochman Rock. But more than this, they both derived inspirational meanings from their experiences. This climb meant a great deal to William Douglas at the time. But to understand his more mature appreciation of it, you will want to read carefully his account of Kloochman revisited in the second section of this selection.

KLOOCHMAN ROCK stands on the southern side of the Tieton Basin in the Cascades. It is an oval-shaped lava rock, running lengthwise northwest by southeast, a half-mile or more. It rises 2000 feet above the basin. The first third of its elevation is gained through gentle slopes of pine and fir. Next are a few hundred yards of tumbled rock. Then there is the cliff rising to the sky, 1200 feet or more—straight as the Washington Monument and over twice as high.

It was in 1913 when Doug was 19 and I was not quite 15 that the

"Kloochman" from OF MEN AND MOUNTAINS by William O. Douglas. Copyright 1950 by William O. Douglas. Reprinted by permission of Harper & Brothers.

two of us made this climb of Kloochman. Walter Kohagen, Doug, and I were camped in the Tieton Basin at a soda spring. The basin was then in large part a vast rich bottomland. We were traveling light, one blanket each. The night, I recall, was so bitter cold that we took turns refueling the campfire so that we could keep our backs warm enough to sleep. We rose at the first show of dawn, and cooked frying-pan bread and trout for breakfast. We had not planned to climb Kloochman, but somehow the challenge came to us as the sun touched her crest.

After breakfast we started circling the rock. There are fairly easy routes up Kloochman, but we shunned them. When we came to the southeast face (the one that never has been conquered, I believe) we chose it. Walter decided not to make the climb, but to wait at the base of the cliff for Doug and me. The July day was warm and cloudless. Doug led. The beginning was easy. For 100 feet or so we found ledges six to twelve inches wide we could follow to the left or right. Some ledges ran up the rock ten feet or more at a gentle grade. Others were merely steps to another ledge higher up. Thus by hugging the wall we could either ease ourselves upward or hoist ourselves from one ledge to another.

When we were about 100 feet up the wall, the ledges became narrower and footwork more precarious. Doug suggested we take off our shoes. This we did, tying them behind us on our belts. In stocking feet we wormed up the wall, clinging like flies to the dark rock. The pace was slow. We gingerly tested each toehold and fingerhold for loose rock before putting our weight on it. At times we had to inch along sidewise, our stomachs pressed tightly against the rock, in order to gain a point where we could reach the ledge above us. If we got on a ledge that turned out to be a cul-de-sac, the much more dangerous task of going down the rock wall would confront us. Hence we picked our route with care and weighed the advantages of several choices which frequently were given us. At times we could not climb easily from one ledge to another. The one above might be a foot or so high. Then we would have to reach it with one knee, slowly bring the other knee up, and then, delicately balancing on both knees on the upper ledge, come slowly to our feet by pressing close to the wall and getting such purchase with our fingers as the lava rock permitted.

In that tortuous way we made perhaps 600 feet in two hours. It was late forenoon when we stopped to appraise our situation. We were in serious trouble. We had reached the feared cul-de-sac. The two- or three-inch ledge on which we stood ended. There seemed none above us within Doug's reach. I was longer-legged than Doug; so perhaps I could have reached some ledge with my fingers if I were ahead. But it was impossible to change positions on the wall. Doug was ahead and there he must stay. The problem was to find a way to get him up.

Feeling along the wall, Doug discovered a tiny groove into which he could press the tips of the fingers of his left hand. It might help him maintain balance as his weight began to shift from the lower ledge to the upper one. But there was within reach not even a lip of rock for his right hand. Just out of reach, however, was a substantial crevice, one that would hold several men. How could Doug reach it? I could not boost him, for my own balance was insecure. Clearly, Doug would have to jump to reach it—and he would have but one jump. Since he was standing on a ledge only a few inches wide, he could not expect to jump for his hand-hold, miss it, and land safely. A slip meant he would go hurtling down some 600 feet onto the rocks. After much discussion and indecision, Doug decided to take the chance and go up.

He asked me to do him a favor: If he failed and fell, I might still make it, since I was longer-legged; would I give certain messages to his family in that event? I nodded.

"Then listen carefully. Try to remember my exact words," he told me. "Tell Mother that I love her dearly. Tell her I think she is the most wonderful person in the world. Tell her not to worry—that I did not suffer, that God willed it so. Tell Sister that I have been a mean little devil but I had no malice toward her. Tell her I love her too—that some day I wanted to marry a girl as wholesome and cheery and good as she.

"Tell Dad I was brave and died unafraid. Tell him about our climb in full detail. Tell Dad I have always been very proud of him, that some day I had planned to be a doctor too. Tell him I lived a clean life, that I never did anything to make him ashamed. . . . Tell Mother, Sister, and Dad I prayed for them."

Every word burned into me. My heart was sick, my lips quiv-

ered. I pressed my face against the rock so Doug could not see. I
wept.

All was silent. A pebble fell from the ledge on which I squeezed.
I counted seconds before it hit 600 feet below with a faint, faraway
tinkling sound. Would Doug drop through the same space? Would
I follow? When you fall 600 feet do you die before you hit the
bottom? Closing my eyes, I asked God to help Doug up the wall.

In a second Doug said in a cheery voice, "Well, here goes."

A false bravado took hold of us. I said he could do it. He said
he would. He wiped first one hand then the other on his trousers.
He placed both palms against the wall, bent his knees slowly,
paused a split second, and jumped straight up. It was not much of
a jump—only six inches or so. But that jump by one pressed against
a cliff 600 feet in the air had daredevil proportions. I held my
breath; my heart pounded. The suspense was over.

Doug made the jump, and in a second was hanging by two
hands from a strong, wide ledge. There was no toehold; he would
have to hoist himself by his arms alone. He did just that. His body
went slowly up as if pulled by some unseen winch. Soon he had
the weight of his body above the ledge and was resting on the
palms of his hands. He then put his left knee on the ledge, rolled
over on his side, and chuckled as he said, "Nothing to it."

A greater disappointment followed. Doug's exploration of the
ledge showed he was in a final cul-de-sac. There was no way up.
There was not even a higher ledge he could reach by jumping. We
were now faced with the nightmare of going down the sheer rock
wall. We could not go down frontwards because the ledges were
too narrow and the wall too steep. We needed our toes, not our
heels, on the rock; and we needed to have our stomachs pressed
tightly against it. Then we could perhaps feel our way. But as
every rock expert knows, descent of a cliff without ropes is often
much more difficult than ascent.

That difficulty was impressed on us by the first move. Doug had
to leave the ledge he had reached by jumping. He dared not slide
blindly to the skimpy ledge edge he had just left. I must help
him. I must move up the wall and stand closer to him. Though I
could not possibly hold his weight, I must exert sufficient pressure

to slow up his descent and to direct his toe onto the narrow ledge from which he had just jumped.

I was hanging to the rock like a fly, twelve feet or more to Doug's left. I inched my way toward him, first dropping to a lower ledge and then climbing to a higher one, using such toeholds as the rock afforded and edging my way crabwise.

When I reached him I said, "Now I'll help."

Doug lowered himself and hung by his fingers full length. His feet were about six inches above the ledge from which he had jumped. He was now my responsibility. If he dropped without aid or direction he was gone. He could not catch and hold to the scanty ledge. I had little space for maneuvering. The surface on which I stood was not more than three inches wide. My left hand fortunately found an overhead crevice that gave a solid anchor in case my feet slipped.

I placed my right hand in the small of Doug's back and pressed upward with all my might. "Now you can come," I said.

He let go gently, and the full weight of his body came against my arm. My arm trembled under the tension. My left hand hung onto the crack in the rock like a grappling hook. My stomach pressed against the wall as if to find mucilage in its pores. My toes dug in as I threw in every ounce of strength.

Down Doug came—a full inch. I couldn't help glancing down and seeing the rocks 600 feet below.

Down Doug moved another inch, then a third. My left hand seemed paralyzed. The muscles of my toes were aching. My right arm shook. I could not hold much longer.

Down came Doug a fourth inch. I thought he was headed for destruction. His feet would miss the only toehold within reach. I could not possibly hold him. He would plunge to his death because my arm was not strong enough to hold him. The messages he had given me for his family raced through my mind. And I saw myself, sick and ashamed, standing before them, testifying to my own inadequacy, repeating his last words.

"Steady, Doug. The ledge is a foot to your right." He pawed the wall with the toes of his foot, searching.

"I can't find it. Don't let go."

The crisis was on us. Even if I had been safely anchored, my cramped position would have kept me from helping him much more. I felt helpless. In a few seconds I would reach the physical breaking point and Doug would go hurtling off the cliff. I did not see how I could keep him from slipping and yet maintain my own balance.

I will never know how I did it. But I tapped some reserve and directed his right foot onto the ledge from which he had earlier jumped. I did it by standing for a moment on my left foot alone and then using my right leg as a rod to guide his right foot to the ledge his swinging feet had missed.

His toes grabbed the ledge as if they were the talons of a bird. My right leg swung back to my perch.

"Are you OK?" I asked.

"Yes," said Doug. "Good work."

My right arm fell from him, numb and useless. I shook from exhaustion and for the first time noticed that my face was wet with perspiration. We stood against the rock in silence for several minutes, relaxing and regaining our composure.

Doug said: "Let's throw our shoes down. It will be easier going." So we untied them from our belts and dropped them to Walter Kohagen, who was waiting at the rock field below us.

Our descent was painfully slow but uneventful. We went down backwards, weaving a strange pattern across the face of the cliff as we moved from one side to the other. It was perhaps midafternoon when we reached the bottom, retrieved our shoes, and started around the other side of the rock. We left the southeast wall unconquered.

But, being young, we were determined to climb the rock. So once more we started to circle. When we came to the northwest wall, we selected it as our route.

Here, too, is a cliff rising 1000 feet like some unfinished pyramid. But close examination shows numerous toe- and fingerholds that make the start at least fairly easy. So we set out with our shoes on.

Again it was fairly easy going for a hundred feet or so, when Doug, who was ahead, came to a ledge to which he could not step. On later climbs we would send the longer-legged chap ahead.

And on other occasions Doug himself has used a rope to traverse this spot. But this day success of the climb depended at this point on Doug's short legs alone. The ledge to which he must move was up to his hips. There were few fingerholds overhead, and none firm enough to carry his whole weight. Only a few tiny cracks were within reach to serve as purchase for him. But Doug would not give up.

He hitched up his trousers, and grasped a tiny groove of rock with the tips of the fingers of his left hand, pressing his right hand flat against the smooth rock wall as if it had magical sticking power. Slowly he lifted his left knee until it was slightly over the ledge above him. To do so he had to stand tiptoe on his right foot. Pulling with his left hand, he brought his right knee up. Doug was now on both knees on the upper ledge. If he could find good purchase overhead for his hands, he was safe. His hands explored the wall above him. He moved them slowly over most of it without finding a hold. Then he reached straight above his head and cried out, "This is our lucky day."

He had found strong rough edges of rock, and on this quickly pulled himself up. His hands were on a ledge a foot wide. He lay down on it on his stomach and grasped my outstretched hand. The pull of his strong arm against the drop of 100 feet or more was as comforting an experience as any I can recall. In a jiffy I was at his side. We pounded each other on the shoulders and laughed.

My own serious trouble was yet to come. For a while Doug and I were separated. I worked laterally along a ledge to the south, found easier going, and in a short time was 200 feet or more up the rock wall. I was above Doug, 25 feet or so, and 50 feet to his right. We had been extremely careful to test each toe- and fingerhold before putting our trust in it. Kloochman is full of treacherous rock. We often discovered thin ledges that crumbled under pressure and showered handfuls of rock and dust down below. Perhaps I was careless; but whatever the cause, the thin ledge on which I was standing gave way.

As I felt it slip, I grabbed for a hold above me. The crevasse I seized was solid. But there I was, hanging by my hands 200 feet in the air, my feet pawing the rock. To make matters worse, my camera had swung between me and the cliff when I slipped. It was a crude and clumsy instrument, a box type that I carried on a leather strap across my shoulders. Its hulk was actually pushing me from the cliff. I twisted in an endeavor to get rid of it, but it was firmly lodged between me and the wall.

I yelled to Doug for help. He at once started edging toward me. It seemed hours, though it was probably not over a few minutes. He shouted, "Hang on, I'll be there."

Hang on I did. My fingers ached beyond description. They were frozen to the rock. My exertion in pawing with my feet had added to the fatigue. The ache of my fingers extended to my wrists and then along my arms. I stopped thrashing around and hung like a sack, motionless. Every second seemed a minute, every minute an hour. I did not see how I could possibly hold.

I would slip, I thought, slip to sure death. I could not look down because of my position. But in my mind's eye I saw in sharp outline the jagged rocks that seemed to pull me toward them. The camera kept pushing my fingers from the ledge. I felt them move. They began to give way before the pull of a force too great for flesh to resist.

Fright grew in me. The idea of hanging helpless 200 feet above the abyss brought panic. I cried out to Doug but the words caught in my dry throat. I was like one in a nightmare who struggles to shout—who is then seized with a fear that promises to destroy him.

Then there flashed through my mind a family scene. Mother was sitting in the living room talking to me, telling me what a wonderful man Father was. She told me of his last illness and his death. She told me of his departure from Cleveland, Washington, to Portland, Oregon, for what proved to be a fatal operation. His last words to her were: "If I die it will be glory. If I live, it will be grace."

The panic passed. The memory of those words restored reason. Glory to die? I could not understand why it would be glory to die. It would be glory to live. But as Father said, it might take grace to live, grace from One more powerful than either Doug or I.

And so again that day I prayed. I asked God to save my life, to save me from destruction on this rock wall. I asked God to make my fingers strong, to give me strength to hang on. I asked God to give me courage, to make me unafraid. I asked God to give me guts, to give me power to do the impossible.

My fingers were as numb as flesh that is full of novocain. They seemed detached from me, as if they belonged to someone else. My wrists, my shoulders, cried out for respite from the pain. It would be such welcome relief if they could be released from the weight that was on them.

Hang on? You can't hang on. You are a weakling. The weaklings die in the woods.

Weakling? I'll show you. How long must I hang on? All day? OK, all day then. I'll hang on, I'll hang on. O God, dear God, help me hang on!

I felt someone pushing my left foot upwards. It was Doug. As if through a dream his voice was saying, "Your feet are 18 inches below your toehold." Doug found those toeholds for my feet.

I felt my shoes resting in solid cracks. I pulled myself up and leaned on my elbows on the ledge to which my hands had been glued. I flexed my fingers and bent my wrists to bring life back.

Doug came up abreast of me and said, "We're even Stephen now."

"Even Stephen?"

"Today each of us has saved the other's life."

It was shortly above the point where Doug saved my life that we discovered a classic path up Kloochman. It is a three-sided chimney chute, a few feet wide, that leads almost to the top. There are several such chutes on Kloochman. In later years Cragg Gilbert and Louis Ulrich went up Devil's Chimney on the northeast face in a seven-hour nerve-wracking climb with ropes. Clarence Truitt and many others have gone up the chimney chute that Doug and I discovered. Then as now this chute was filled with loose rock that had to be cleared away. To negotiate the chute we took off our shoes and tied them to our belts. We climbed the chute in stocking feet, pressing our hands and feet against the opposing walls as we kept our backs to the abyss below us. This day we went up the chute with ease, stopping every eight feet or so to measure our progress.

The sun was setting when we reached the top. We were gay and buoyant. We talked about the glories of the scene in front of us. We bragged a bit about our skill in rock work—how we must be part mountain goat to have reached the top. We shouted and hallooed to the empty meadows far below us.

On Kloochman Rock that July afternoon both Doug and I valued life more because death had passed so close. It was wonderful to be alive, breathing, using our muscles, shouting, seeing.

We stayed briefly at the top. We went down as we came up, in stocking feet. We raced against darkness, propelled by the thought of spending the night on Kloochman's treacherous wall.

I climbed Kloochman again in 1948. This time my steps were more cautious and measured than they had been in 1913. There was less dash, less abandon in this adult ascent. I took my ease, feeling my way with care. But the memories of the earlier trip were still fresh in my mind as if it had happened only the previous week instead of thirty-five years ago.

As I climbed, I realized how conservative man became in his physical endeavors as he passed his thirties. I was not thinking of wind or stamina, for mine were both good. I was thinking of the subtle forces that control the reflexes. It struck home why only young men make good fighter pilots—how it is that age fast takes the daredevil out of man. There was a thrill in this adult climb, but the reckless, carefree attitude of the earlier day had gone.

Yet I relived the experience of 1913. Places, as well as smells and shapes and sounds, can be symbols of fear and terror. He who, after long years of absence, revisits a place associated with sadness or guilt or suffering is likely to relive for a moment the sensations he experienced there. The forces at work are subtle; and unless he is aware of their influences, he may be painfully disturbed or upset. Unless he recognizes the part these imponderables play in human emotions, he may indeed be seized with a new discomfiture greater than the one that seized him earlier at the selfsame place.

The day I climbed Kloochman as a man, all the sensations of the earlier trip returned to me. There was the trembling excitement of the start. Doug's messages to his family raced once more through my mind, as if he had just uttered them. I saw Doug make his jump up the side of the cliff while he was 600 feet in the air. I saw him hanging on the ledge, doomed to die. I felt the weight of his body against my arm. I felt myself slipping slowly from the rock to destruction. It seemed once more that demons were pulling at my feet with a power too great for flesh and blood to resist. Once again little vestiges of the old fear passed through me.

Those, however, were fleeting sensations. When I came to the top a sense of calm came over me, a deep peace, the feeling a man has when he is with the woman he loves. And with the calm came pride.

Kloochman was in my very heart. Here we had accomplished the impossible. We had survived terrible ordeals on her sheer walls. We had faced death down; and because of our encounter with it, we had come to value life the more. On these dark walls in 1913 I had first communed with God. Here I had felt the presence of a Mighty Force, infinitely beyond man. Here I had known the strength of unseen hands helping me along ledges.

I wondered if Kloochman had been a testing ground for other lads. I wondered if others had met on her walls the challenge of life and death. I knew now what a boy could not know, that fear of death was the compound of all other fears. I knew that long years ago I had begun to shed on Kloochman's walls the great, overpowering fear.

Kloochman became that day a symbol of adversity and challenge—of the forces that have drawn from man his greatest spiritual and physical achievements.

When man knows how to live dangerously, he is not afraid to die. When he is not afraid to die, he is, strangely, free to live. When he is free to live, he can become bold, courageous, reliant. There are many ways to learn how to live dangerously. Men of the plains have had the experience in the trackless blizzards that sweep in from the north. Those who go out in boats from Gloucester have known it in another form. The mountains that traverse this country offer still a different way, and one that for many is the most exciting of all. The mountains can be reached in all seasons. They offer a fighting challenge to heart, soul, and mind, both in summer and winter. If throughout time the youth of the nation accept the challenge the mountains offer, they will help keep alive in our people the spirit of adventure. That spirit is a measure of the vitality of both nations and men. A people who climb the ridges and sleep under the stars in high mountain meadows, who enter the forest and scale the peaks, who explore glaciers and walk ridges buried deep in snow—these people will give their country some of the indomitable spirit of the mountains.

SUGGESTIONS FOR STUDY

1. How does the author say that the challenge to climb Klooch-man Rock came to him and his friend? Does their response to that challenge seem to you rash, or noble? Does their second attempt at the mountain seem foolhardy?

2. What made Doug's six-inch leap so dangerous? In the message Doug gave to Bill to be delivered in the event of death, what areas of life did he touch upon? In what way can this statement of Doug's be related to the chapter headings of *Portraits in Words?*

3. Read aloud the two excellent descriptive parts of the selection in which Douglas tells of near falls from the cliff. (pp. 171–4 and p. 175) What physical sensations do you experience vicariously as you read of these narrow escapes?

4. How do the young Douglas' inner thoughts—as the author retells them here—reveal his character?

5. What did the boys do when they reached the top of the mountain? What do you think you would do upon reaching the top of a fairly high mountain?

6. William Douglas says, ". . . both Doug and I valued life more because death had passed so close." What deeper lessons did Douglas get from the consideration of death 35 years later? To what extent do you share his ideas on the subject?

7. You may have heard the statement made that when a person is in imminent danger of death, his whole life flashes before his eyes. What flashed before William O. Douglas' eyes before Doug came to his rescue?

8. How does the author defend daredeviltry?

9. William Douglas calls Kloochman Rock a "symbol of adversity and challenge." In your opinion, what challenges might these boys have met later in life which could be directly related to their experience on Kloochman Rock? What in your life up to now has been both tough and challenging?

10. Write a composition about an experience you or someone close to you had which made life seem more valuable.

Johnny Gunther Graduates

JOHN GUNTHER

Though we all hope to avoid misfortunes, nevertheless we must develop courage for the defeats and frustrations of life. Learning how others faced their troubles courageously can inspire us to prepare our own reservoir of fortitude against ill fortune.

Death Be Not Proud is in the form of a memoir written by Johnny Gunther's father to commemorate his 17-year-old son's valiant struggle with death. Chapter Five of that memoir, most of which is presented here, opens toward the end of Johnny's 14-month fight to live. By that time both he and his parents knew—without speaking of it, however —that he could not expect to recover. Reading of Johnny Gunther's courage as he faced death from a brain tumor, you can develop your own spiritual resources.

SMOOTHLY, steadily, ominously, the next two weeks slipped by. The bulge disappeared entirely for an interval and was replaced by what we had prayed for for a year, a concavity. Johnny was worried, though. The bandage was too big for him to feel through. He said to a visitor, "I wonder if the bump is still there. I'm not convinced." Also he began to inquire with great earnestness why a plate had not been inserted, which must have meant that, finally, he had given up hope that the bone would grow back of itself. He said indignantly to one friend, "If only they'd put in a plate, one of the new types of plate made of tantalum, at least I'd be able to swim and sail."

Frances [Johnny's mother], who was holding up wonderfully under a strain that had become unendurable, went off to Florida for a brief rest, and, with my sister standing by, I got away later for a week in Virginia. There came one violent hour in the solarium before I left. Johnny was passionate and stormy. He exploded,

"I'm always in a haze! I was in a haze up in school last year! The tumor must have been starting then, only nobody knew it! People kidded me about it, and it was very disagreeable. I talked it over with Steve [one of his classmates] but came to no conclusion. I'm sensitive about being kidded. I didn't like it, and I don't like it now! It wasn't my fault that I was in such a haze!" . . .

But there were lighter moments. One nurse said, "I'll be just like your mother to you." He answered, "Okay, provided you don't go too far." . . .

"Did you sleep well?" the nurse asked one morning.

"Like an octopus."

This is, I believe, the last letter he ever wrote. He had pleaded with his mother to get away for her brief holiday, and while she was in Florida he telephoned her a couple of times and then wrote this:

DEAR MOTHER,

Today is the last day at this—hospital! Thanks for your letters, and be sure to remember the words of wisdom which I tried to impart to you a few minutes before your departure. I feel fine but seem to be struck with a most monstrous attack of lazyness. What a job it is for my poor nurse to get me up in the morning! I've gotten into an awful habit of drinking coffee in the morning, and find it necessary to keep me awake—at least enough so I don't fall asleep and drown in the bathtub!

It made me happy to hear that you will be returning soon. In a week or so I will go back to Deerfield to take the exams, and to say hello and goodbye!

O! How wonderful food is again! Bacon and eggs! salt! steaks! How I eat! mushrooms! last night I played poker with some fellow patients! —great fun! I've almost finished the English anthology which we were reading

lots of love and kisses

JOHNNY

He was cleared to go home on May 15, only two weeks after the operation. So for the last time Johnny checked out of Neurological. He ended the experience with a wry wisecrack. We marched out and I said the hospital knew us so well by this time that they sent the bill by mail. Johnny jibed: "You mean by parcel post." . . .

He remained pretty well, but now it became increasingly difficult for him to fix his belt or shoelaces. He was too proud to admit this, and Marie, our admirable housekeeper, helped him to put on his shoes one morning. Johnny said, "I'm only giving way to your maternal instinct." Carl, our old elevator man, wept once when he saw how warped his face was and how difficult it was for him to walk. Johnny said to him coolly, "I haven't had any chance to exercise, and so my foot is tired."

Marie told me of another colloquy. A schoolmate whom he had not seen for years called up.

JOHNNY: "I should warn you that my head is bandaged because I have a brain tumor."

BOY: "I've never known anybody with a brain tumor."

JOHNNY: "You know me."

BOY: "What's it like?"

JOHNNY: "I've been lucky. I have no pain, and there has been no impairment of my faculties."

The boy came over that afternoon, and Johnny cleaned him up in a game of chess.

The effort to pretend that the tumor was nothing cost him dearly; the price of his invincible fight was great fatigue. It took a miserable lot out of him to pretend to ignore what he must have now known to be the truth, that he wasn't getting any better. The faraway look was in his eyes more often now. But it was impossible for us not to support his optimism, because any discouragement would have been a crushing blow. All he had now was his will to live. We had to keep that up at any cost. The cord of life was wearing very thin, and if we took away hope, it would be bound to snap.

After a struggle one morning he gave up trying to tie his tie, and things would drop out of his left hand more frequently. "My left hand is a mess." The hand cupped sharply and he looked frightened. "The nerves are crazy in this left hand. I can't get it open."

He always loved to joke with me about my size. I said one day that I was tired enough to stay asleep until I starved to death. Reply: "That would take quite some time, Father." I had a massage and reported that I had lost some weight. Comment: "How much did the masseur lose?"

He read the papers carefully and with Frances listened to every important broadcast. He said, "The reason why the Republicans don't offend and oppose those Southern Democrats is because they may need their help some day." Some friends talked once about the great vitality of the United States. He asked, "But may not vitality end in smugness? Isn't it possible, too, that vitality could express itself in reaction, in the wrong direction?" He turned to me. "In Volume Two, hit them hard, Father!" I can tell you all right whom he meant by "them"—anybody cheap, anybody shoddy or vulgar, anybody selfish and corrupt, anybody on-the-make or feathering his nest in the name of false principle.

He dropped a pill.

"Is it still all right?" I asked stupidly enough, reaching for it.

"It will be if you pick it up off the floor."

On Sunday mornings Frances read to him from the Hebrew Bible, the Christian Gospels, the Hindu scriptures, Confucius, and other eastern sages. One of the last things he read was the Psalms. I read to him, too, though not so much. One of the books he was going through for English was a poetry anthology; he would look bored or turn away whenever we chanced on a poem about Death.

One day came an unbearably moving moment when he announced, as if casually, that perhaps he was having the bump for *us!*

The phone rang on May 25 and Mr. Boyden's cheerful, assured voice came through. "I've gone through Johnny's papers and examinations," he said. "You know he did extra work in his freshman year and has some surplus credits. He has caught up to his class in everything except one examination, and we are going to give him a diploma. This isn't a favor. It is Johnny's right. Come up next week, and he will graduate with his class."

Johnny yawned and tried to look casual, and we all burst into tears.

We drove to Deerfield on May 27, and Johnny graduated on June 4, though he had not been to school for fourteen months. The days passed in a proud procession, and I think probably it was the happiest week of his life.

It seemed chilly when we started, and Johnny, as always extracting compensation out of any ill fortune, said, "Well, at least we don't have a heat wave." We passed through Hartford and he asked, "Were you here when you did your research?—I wouldn't dream of asking how long you stayed, probably half an hour." I was full of nerves as we got near Deerfield with its stiff old houses and great fanlike elms, and impatiently I asked him if I had overshot the side road and did he recognize any landmarks. He replied gently, "You know I don't see well out of my left eye."

Then without the slightest self-consciousness he took his place in his class. He sat between old friends in the dining hall (the instructors had warned them) and Frances whispered that they should inconspicuously cut his meat if necessary. The boys stared at him for a second as if he were a ghost—of course his hair had not grown back fully after the last operation and he wore a white turban—and then accepted his appearance without question.

Every evening after dinner an informal ceremony takes place at Deerfield which is one of the distinguishing marks of this magnificent school; each boy from Freshman to Senior meets with Mr. Boyden, and the roll of the entire school is called. The boys are heaped together on the floor. Usually there is a casualty or two—some youngsters hurt in a football game—for whom there are big leather chairs. Johnny eased himself into one of these, and his name was called in the roll exactly as if he had never been absent for a moment. Then he limped slowly and proudly to the Senior Dorm where he would have been living this past year, and looked at what should have been his room with a piercing yearning. Boys were moving back and forth in the orderly bustle that precedes commencement. Johnny had the attitude of one who is both a participant in and a spectator of a great event. Mr. Boyden crept up to us and asked if we were sure he would not get too tired. Then he joined calmly in a bull session.

It was decided that he should sleep in the infirmary—a building he knew only too exasperatingly well. The next morning we came to pick him up at what we thought was a reasonable hour. But he had left the building before eight, alone, and was at that moment taking the final exam in chemistry! He passed it B Minus—though he had never taken a regular chemistry course in his life.

Later that day I bumped into him accidentally on the bright sunlit grass as he dragged himself from behind a hedge in shadow. His left shoulder sagged; his arm hung almost useless; his mouth was twisted with effort; the left side of his lip sank down; his eyes were filmy; he was happy. "Oh, pardon me, sir," Johnny said. He had not recognized me, and thought that I was some master he did not know.

Everybody tried hard to keep him from being too active. But he said, "Walking around this way helps the wound heal." Frances told him to sit around in the sun—how they both loved the sun!—and get brown and he answered, "All you are interested in, Mother, is my color!" When he had trouble with knife and fork one evening, he told her in exquisite parody of what she often said, "Be patient. Believe in calmness and Nirvana." It was a lovely day the next day and Johnny spent an hour learning some calculus from a fellow student. He worked out the equations on the bottom of a paper plate during a picnic lunch in the soft grass. Frances remonstrated that he might be getting tired. He replied briefly, "There's no future to just sitting."

The day before graduation was strenuous, with a lunch for the parents at noon and then a baseball game which Johnny watched with serious interest for about four innings. The dress-up banquet that night, to celebrate among other things Mr. Boyden's forty-fifth year as headmaster, lasted three hours; Johnny did not miss a minute of it. He tramped across the lawn afterward, with his classmate Henry Eisner holding his hand, for the off-the-record talk Mr. Boyden gives each graduating class. Then the class, standing under the trees in a night grown chilly, serenaded the Boydens on the front porch. Johnny, on the outskirts of the massed pack of boys, looked suddenly exhausted, and I slipped away from the adults to join him inconspicuously, standing just behind him. He did not mind, though as a rule he loathed having us anywhere near him at school. I was afraid he might fall. Then I heard his light, silvery tenor chime in with the other voices. The song floated

across the lawn and echoed back. We hiked to the infirmary and
Johnny ran into a classmate who had won an award. "Congratula-
tions!" he snapped briskly.

The next morning the boys assembled early for the quarter-mile
walk to the white-frame Deerfield church, arranging themselves
four abreast in order of their height. I did not think Johnny could
manage such a march. He shook us off and disappeared. The procedure is that the boys, reaching the church, line up behind the
pews, and then walk one by one down the center aisle, as each
name is called. Mr. Flynt, the president of the board of trustees,
then shakes hands with each boy, giving him his diploma in the
left hand. We explained that Johnny might not be able to grasp
the smooth roll of diploma with his left fingers, and asked Mr.
Flynt to try to slip it into the right hand instead. The boys began
to march in slowly, and though Johnny should have been conspicuous with his white bandage, we did not see him and I was in an
agony fearing that he had fallen out. Mr. Boyden, sweeping the
assembly with his all-embracing sharp affectionate glance, caught
Frances's eye and nodded to her reassuringly. One by one the
names were called out, and each boy dissociated himself from the
solid group and marched forward alone. The call was alphabetical,
and by the time the G's were reached we were limp with suspense,
since we did not know for sure that Johnny had even got into the
church. As each boy passed down the aisle, there was applause,
perfunctory for some, pronounced for others. Gaines, Gillespie,
Goodwin, Griffin, Gunther. Slowly, very slowly, Johnny stepped
out of the mass of his fellows and trod by us, carefully keeping
in the exact center of the long aisle, looking neither to the left nor
the right, but straight ahead, fixedly, with the white bandage flashing in the light through the high windows, his chin up, carefully,
not faltering, steady, but slowly, so very slowly. The applause
began and then rose and the applause became a storm, as every
single person in that old church became whipped up, tight and
tense, to see if he would make it. The applause became a thunder,
it rose and soared and banged, when Johnny finally reached the
pulpit. Mr. Flynt carefully tried to put the diploma in his right
hand, as planned. Firmly Johnny took it from right hand to left,

as was proper, and while the whole audience rocked now with release from tension, and was still wildly, thunderously applauding, he passed around to the side and, not seeing us, reached his place among his friends.

That evening we talked of Harvard. Some of the boys were getting their admission notices, and Johnny, now that he had actually been graduated, wondered when his would come. He was impatient. He had a great sense of the passage of time.

Everything that Johnny suffered was in a sense repaid by the few heroic moments of that walk down the center aisle of that church. This was his triumph and indomitable summation. Nobody who saw it will ever forget it, or be able to forget the sublime strength of will and character it took.

SUGGESTIONS FOR STUDY

1. Find evidence that Johnny at least suspected that his struggle was a losing one. What surer evidence do you find that his parents and others knew that it was?

2. What do you find remarkable about Johnny's attitude, considering that the incidents which you have been reading about occurred just 30 to 40 days before his death?

3. In what ways, other than not discussing the subject, might this same problem be faced? Which way would you prefer?

4. What is the implication of "Johnny yawned and tried to look casual, and we all burst into tears"? (p. 184)

5. The death of the fine, intelligent son in the Gunther family was a bitter experience. What gain or benefit to the world do you find from the fact that John Gunther, Sr., wrote this memoir? What benefit personally to you? Write out your answer to this last question.

6. Johnny's father is an eminent American writer and political analyst. What famous books has he written?

7. Just one year before his death Johnny wrote an "Unbeliever's Prayer" *:

* "Unbeliever's Prayer" by John Gunther, Jr. from DEATH BE NOT PROUD by John Gunther. Copyright 1949 by John Gunther. Reprinted by permission of Harper & Brothers.

Almighty God
forgive me for my agnosticism;
For I shall try to keep it gentle, not cynical,
nor a bad influence.

And O!
if Thou art truly in the heavens,
accept my gratitude
for all Thy gifts
and I shall try
to fight the good fight. Amen.

What is the difference between an atheist and an agnostic? Do you
believe Johnny could have written this prayer if he had been a real
agnostic?

Robert A. Taft

JOHN F. KENNEDY

When President Kennedy was serving as the Junior Senator from Massachusetts, he used a period when he was hospitalized to write *Profiles in Courage*. This book relates a series of incidents in each of which some man took a bold stand for principle in the face of danger to his person or his career.

The chapter on Senator Robert A. Taft of Ohio records how "Mr. Republican" (or "Mr. Integrity," as Mr. Kennedy prefers to name him) called down upon himself the wrath of a nation by daring to criticize the execution of the Nazi war criminals. Taft felt that the offenses of these men occurred at such a time and under such conditions that to bring the offenders to trial and pronounce sentence upon them was not in keeping with the principles set forth in the United States Constitution. Risking his own political future, he made "a bold plea for justice in a time of intolerance and hostility." Such courage in an age of expediency is unusual and impressive.

This selection is a "profile" rather than a complete "portrait"; but it is an inspiring picture of a man of principle, who believed in the "liberty of the individual to think his own thoughts." In his own life, Robert A. Taft thought for himself and stood by his conclusions, regardless of consequences.

THE LATE SENATOR ROBERT A. TAFT of Ohio was never President of the United States. Therein lies his personal tragedy. And therein lies his national greatness.

For the Presidency was a goal that Bob Taft pursued throughout his career in the Senate, an ambition that this son of a former President always dreamed of realizing. As the leading exponent of the Republican philosophy for more than a decade, "Mr. Republican" was bitterly disappointed by his failure on three different occasions even to receive the nomination.

But Robert A. Taft was also a man who stuck fast to the basic principles in which he believed—and when those fundamental principles were at issue, not even the lure of the White House, or the possibilities of injuring his candidacy, could deter him from speaking out. He was an able politician, but on more than one occasion he chose to speak out in defense of a position no politician with like ambitions would have endorsed. He was, moreover, a brilliant political analyst, who knew that during his lifetime the number of American voters who agreed with the fundamental tenets of his political philosophy was destined to be a permanent minority, and that only by flattering new blocs of support—while carefully refraining from alienating any group which contained potential Taft voters—could he ever hope to attain his goal. Yet he frequently flung to the winds the very restraints his own analysis advised, refusing to bow to any group, refusing to keep silent on any issue.

It is not that Bob Taft's career in the Senate was a constant battle between popularity and principle as was John Quincy Adams'. His principles usually led him to conclusions which a substantial percentage of his constituents and political associates were willing to support. Although on occasions his political conduct reflected his political ambitions, popularity was not his guide on most fundamental matters. The Taft-Hartley Labor Management Relatons Act could not have gained him many votes in industrialized Ohio, for those who endorsed its curbs on union activity were already Taft supporters; but it brought furious anti-Taft reprisals during the 1950 Senate campaign by the unions in Ohio, and it nourished the belief that Taft could not win a Presidential contest, a belief which affected his chances for the nomination in 1952. Simultaneously, however, he was antagonizing the friends of Taft-Hartley, and endangering his own leadership in the Republican party, by his support of education, housing, health and other welfare measures.

Those who were shocked at these apparent departures from his traditional position did not comprehend that Taft's conservatism contained a strong strain of pragmatism, which caused him to support intensive Federal activity in those areas that he believed not adequately served by the private enterprise system. Taft did not believe that this was inconsistent with the conservative doctrine; conservatism in his opinion was not irresponsibility. Thus he gave new dimensions to the conservative philosophy: he stuck to that faith when it reached its lowest depth of prestige and power and led it back to the level of responsibility and respectability. He was an unusual leader, for he lacked the fine arts of oratory and phrasemaking, he lacked blind devotion to the party line (unless he dictated it), and he lacked the politician's natural instinct to avoid controversial positions and issues.

But he was more than a political leader, more than "Mr. Republican." He was also a Taft—and thus "Mr. Integrity." The Senator's grandfather, Alphonso Taft, had moved West to practice law in 1830, writing his father that "The notorious selfishness and dishonesty of the great mass of men you find in New York is to my mind a serious obstacle to settling there." And the Senator's father was William Howard Taft, who knew well the meaning of political courage and political abuse.

So Bob Taft, as his biographer has described it, was "born to integrity." He was known in the Senate as a man who never broke an agreement, who never compromised his deeply felt Republican principles, who never practiced political deception. His bitter political enemy, Harry Truman, would say when the Senator died: "He and I did not agree on public policy, but he knew where I stood and I knew where he stood. We need intellectually honest men like Senator Taft." Examples of his candor are endless and startling. The Ohioan once told a group in the heart of Republican farm territory that farm prices were too high; and he told still another farm group that "he was tired of seeing all these people riding in Cadillacs." His support of an extensive Federal housing program caused a colleague to remark: "I hear the Socialists have gotten to Bob Taft." He informed an important political associate who cherished a commendatory message signed by Taft that his assistant "sent those things out by the dozen" without the Senator even seeing, much less signing them. And a colleague recalls that he did not reject the ideas of his friends by gentle indirection, but by coldly and unhesitatingly terming them "nonsense." "He had," as William S. White has written, "a luminous candor of purpose that was extraordinarily refreshing in a chamber not altogether devoted to candor."

It would be a mistake, however, to conclude from this that Senator Taft was cold and abrupt in his personal relationships. I recall, from my own very brief service with him in the Senate and on the Senate Labor Committee in the last months of his life, my strong impression of a surprising and unusual personal charm, and a disarming simplicity of manner. It was these qualities, combined with an unflinching courage which he exhibited throughout his entire life and most especially in his last days, that bound his adherents to him with unbreakable ties.

Perhaps we are as yet too close in time to the controversial elements in the career of Senator Taft to be able to measure his life with historical perspective. A man who can inspire intensely bitter enemies as well as intensely devoted followers is best judged after many years pass, enough years to permit the sediment of political and legislative battles to settle, so that we can assess our times more clearly.

But sufficient time has passed since 1946 to enable something of a detached view of Senator Taft's act of courage in that year. . . . As a piece of sheer candor in a period when candor was out of favor, as a bold plea for justice in a time of intolerance and hostility, it is worth remembering here.

In October of 1946, Senator Robert A. Taft of Ohio was the chief spokesman for the Republicans in Washington, the champion of his party in the national political arena and the likely Republican nominee for the Presidency in 1948. It was a time when even a Senator with such an established reputation for speaking his mind would have guarded his tongue, and particularly a Senator with so much at stake as Bob Taft. The party which had been his whole life, the Republicans of the Congress for whom he spoke, now once again were nearing the brink of success in the fall elections. Capturing for his party control of both Houses of Congress would enhance Bob Taft's prestige, reinforce his right to the Republican Presidential nomination and pave the way for his triumphant return to the White House from which his father had been somewhat ungloriously ousted in 1912. Or so it seemed to most political observers at the time, who assumed the Republican leader would say nothing to upset the applecart. With Congress out of session, with the tide running strongly against the incumbent Democrats, there appeared to be no necessity for the Senator to make more than the usual campaign utterances on the usual issues.

But Senator Taft was disturbed—and when he was disturbed it was his habit to speak out. He was disturbed by the War Crimes Trials of Axis leaders, then concluding in Germany and about to commence in Japan. The Nuremberg Trials, in which eleven notorious Nazis had been found guilty under an impressively documented indictment for "waging an aggressive war," had been popular throughout the world and particularly in the United States. Equally popular was the sentence already announced by the high tribunal: death.

But what kind of trial was this? "No matter how many books are written or briefs filed," Supreme Court Justice William O. Douglas has recently written, "no matter how finely the lawyers analyzed it, the crime for which the Nazis were tried had never been formalized as a crime with the definiteness required by our legal standards, nor outlawed with a death penalty by the international community. By our standards that crime arose under an *ex post facto* law.[1] Goering *et al.*[2] deserved severe punishment. But their guilt did not justify us in substituting power for principle."

These conclusions are shared, I believe, by a substantial number of American citizens today. And they were shared, at least privately, by a goodly number in 1946. But no politician of consequence would speak out—certainly not after the verdict had already been announced and preparations for the executions were already under way—none, that is, but Senator Taft.

The Constitution of the United States was the gospel which guided the policy decisions of the Senator from Ohio. It was his source, his weapon, and his salvation. And when the Constitution commanded no "*ex post facto* laws," Bob Taft accepted this pre-

[1] See Suggestions for Study, Number 7.
[2] *et al.: et alii:* and others (Latin).

cept as permanently wise and universally applicable. The Constitution was not a collection of loosely given political promises subject to broad interpretation. It was not a list of pleasing platitudes to be set lightly aside when expediency required it. It was the foundation of the American system of law and justice and he was repelled by the picture of his country discarding those Constitutional precepts in order to punish a vanquished enemy.

Still, why should he say anything? The Nuremberg Trials were at no time before the Congress for consideration. They were not in any sense an issue in the campaign. There was no Republican or Democratic position on a matter enthusiastically applauded by the entire nation. And no speech by any United States Senator, however powerful, could prevent the death sentence from being carried out. To speak out unnecessarily would be politically costly and clearly futile.

But Bob Taft spoke out.

On October 6, 1946, Senator Taft appeared before a conference on our Anglo-American heritage, sponsored by Kenyon College in Ohio. The war crimes trial was not an issue upon which conference speakers were expected to comment. But titling his address "Equal Justice Under Law" Taft cast aside his general reluctance to embark upon startlingly novel and dramatic approaches. "The trial of the vanquished by the victors," he told an attentive if somewhat astonished audience, "cannot be impartial no matter how it is hedged about with the forms of justice."

I question whether the hanging of those who, however despicable, were the leaders of the German people, will ever discourage the making of aggressive war, for no one makes aggressive war unless he expects to win. About this whole judgment there is the spirit of vengeance, and vengeance is seldom justice. The hanging of the eleven men convicted will be a blot on the American record which we shall long regret.

In these trials we have accepted the Russian idea of the purpose of trials—government policy and not justice—with little relation to Anglo-Saxon heritage. By clothing policy in the forms of legal procedure, we may discredit the whole idea of justice in Europe for years to come. In the last analysis, even at the end of a frightful war, we should view the future with more hope if even our enemies believed that we had treated them justly in our English-speaking concept of law, in the provision of relief and in the final disposal of territory.

In ten days the Nazi leaders were to be hanged. But Bob Taft, speaking in cold, clipped matter-of-fact tones, deplored that sentence, and suggested that involuntary exile—similar to that imposed upon Napoleon—might be wiser. But even more deplorable, he said, were the trials themselves, which "violate the fundamental principle of American law that a man cannot be tried under an *ex post facto* statute." Nuremberg, the Ohio Senator insisted, was a blot on American Constitutional history, and a serious departure from our Anglo-Saxon heritage of fair and equal treatment, a heritage which had rightly made this country respected throughout the world. "We can't even teach our own people the sound principles of liberty and justice," he concluded. "We cannot teach them government in Germany by suppressing liberty and justice. As I see it, the English-speaking peoples have one great responsibility. That is to restore to the minds of men a devotion to equal justice under law."

The speech exploded in the midst of a heated election campaign; and throughout the nation Republican candidates scurried for shelter while Democrats seized the opportunity to advance. Many, many people were outraged at Taft's remarks. Those who had fought, or whose men had fought and possibly died, to beat back the German aggressors were contemptuous of these fine phrases by a politician who had never seen battle. Those whose kinsmen or former countrymen had been among the Jews, Poles, Czechs and other nationality groups terrorized by Hitler and his cohorts were shocked. The memories of the gas chambers at Buchenwald and other Nazi concentration camps, the stories of hideous atrocities which had been refreshed with new illustrations at Nuremberg, and the anguish and suffering which each new military casualty list had brought to thousands of American homes—these were among the immeasurable influences which caused many to react with pain and indignation when a United States Senator deplored the trials and sentences of these merely "despicable" men.

In New York, the most important state in any Presidential race, and a state where politics were particularly sensitive to the views of various nationality and minority groups, Democrats were joyous and Republicans angry and gloomy. The 1944 Republican Presidential nominee, and Taft's bitter rival for party control and the 1948 nomination, New York's Governor Thomas E. Dewey, declared that the verdicts were justified; and in a statement in which the New York Republican nominee for the Senate, Irving Ives, joined, he stated: "The defendants at Nuremberg had a fair and extensive trial. *No one* can have any sympathy for these Nazi leaders who brought such agony upon the world." The Democratic State Campaign Manager in New York challenged Taft

to come into this state and repeat his plea for the lives of the Nazi war criminals. . . .

The Democratic Party has a perfect right to ask if the public wants the type of national administration, or state administration, favored by Senator Taft, who indicated he wants the lives of the convicted Nazis spared and who may very well be preparing the way for a Republican propaganda campaign to commute the death sentences of the Nazi murderers.

New York Republican Congressional candidate Jacob K. Javits sent a telegram to Taft calling his statement "a disservice to all we fought for and to the cause of future peace." The Democratic nominee for United States Senator in New York expressed his deep shock at the Taft statement and his certainty it would be repudiated by "right-thinking and fair-minded Americans." And the Democratic nominee for Governor told his audiences that if Senator Taft had ever seen the victims of Nazi concentration camps, he never would have been able to make such a statement.

Even in the nation's Capital, where Taft was greatly admired and his blunt candor was more or less expected, the reaction was no different. G.O.P. leaders generally declined official comment, but privately expressed their fears over the consequences for their Congressional candidates. At a press conference, the Chairman of the Republican Congressional Campaign Committee refused to comment on the subject, stating that he had "his own ideas" on the Nuremberg trials but did not "wish to enter into a controversy with Senator Taft."

The Democrats, however, were jubilant—although concealing their glee behind a façade of shocked indignation. At his weekly press conference, President Truman smilingly suggested he would be glad to let Senator Taft and Governor Dewey fight the matter out. Democratic Majority Leader in the Senate (and later Vice President) Alben Barkley of Kentucky told a campaign audience that Taft "never experienced a crescendo of heart about the soup kitchens of 1932, but his heart bled anguishedly for the criminals at Nuremberg." Typical of Democratic reaction was the statement of Senator Scott Lucas of Illinois, who called Taft's speech "a classical example of his muddled and confused thinking" and predicted it would "boomerang on his aspirations for the Presidential nomination of 1948."

11,000,000 fighting veterans of World War II will answer Mr. Taft. . . . I doubt that the Republican National Chairman will permit the Senator to make any more speeches now that Taft has called the trials a blot on the American record. . . . Neither the American people nor history will agree. . . . Senator Taft, whether he believed it or not, was defending these culprits who were responsible for the murder of ten million people.

Even in Taft's home bailiwick of Ohio, where his strict constitutionalism had won him immense popularity, the Senator's speech brought anger, confusion, and political reverberations. The Republican Senatorial candidate, former Governor John Bricker, was not only a close ally of Taft but had been the Vice Presidential nominee in 1944 as running mate to Governor Dewey. His Democratic opponent, incumbent Senator James Huffman, challenged Bricker to stand with either Taft or Dewey, declaring:

A country that has suffered the scourge of modern war, lost more than 300,000 of its finest men, and spent $300,000,000,000 of its resources because of the acts of these convicted gangsters can never feel that the sentences meted out have been too severe. . . . This is not the time to weaken in the punishment of international crimes. Such criticism, even if justified, should have been offered when the international tribunals were being set up.

The Toledo *Blade* told its readers that "on this issue, as on so many others, Senator Taft shows that he has a wonderful mind which knows practically everything and understands practically nothing. . . ."

The Cleveland *Plain Dealer* editorialized that Taft "may be technically correct," but turning "loose on the world the worst gang of cutthroats in all history . . . would have failed to give the world that great principle which humanity needs so desperately to have established: the principle that planning and waging aggressive war is definitely a crime against humanity."

Senator Taft was disheartened by the voracity of his critics— and extremely uncomfortable when one of the acquitted Nazi leaders, Franz Von Papen, told interviewers upon his release from prison that he agreed with Taft's speech. A spokesman for Taft issued only one terse statement: "He has stated his feelings on the matter and feels that if others want to criticize him, let them go ahead." But the Ohio Senator could not understand why even his old supporter, newspaper columnist David Lawrence, called his position nothing more than a "technical quibble." And he must have been particularly distressed when respected Constitutional authorities such as the President of the American Bar Association, the Chairman of its Executive Committee, and other leading members of the legal profession all deplored his statement and defended the trials as being in accordance with international law.

For Robert Taft had spoken, not in "defense of the Nazi murderers" (as a labor leader charged), not in defense of isolationism (as most observers assumed), but in defense of what he regarded to be the traditional American concepts of law and justice. As the apostle of strict constitutionalism, as the chief defense attorney for the conservative way of life and government, Robert Alphonso Taft was undeterred by the possibilities of injury to his party's precarious position or his own Presidential prospects. To him, justice was at stake, and all other concerns were trivial. "It illustrates at once," a columnist observed at that time, "the extreme stubbornness, integrity, and political strongheadedness of Senator Taft."

The fact that thousands disagree with him, and that it is politically embarrassing to other Republicans, probably did not bother Taft at all. He has for years been accustomed to making up his mind, regardless of whether it hurts him or anyone else. Taft surely must have known that his remarks would be twisted and misconstrued and that his timing would raise the devil in the current campaign. But it is characteristic of him that he went ahead anyway.

The storm raised by his speech eventually died down. It did not, after all the uproar, appear to affect the Republican sweep in 1946, nor was it—at least openly—an issue in Taft's drive for the Presidential nomination in 1948. The Nazi leaders were hanged, and Taft and the country went on to other matters. But we are not concerned today with the question of whether Taft was right or wrong in his condemnation of the Nuremberg trials. What is noteworthy is the illustration furnished by this speech of Taft's unhesitating courage in standing against the flow of public opinion for a cause he believed to be right. His action was characteristic of the man who was labeled a reactionary, who was proud to be a conservative and who authored these lasting definitions of liberalism and liberty:

Liberalism implies particularly freedom of thought, freedom from orthodox dogma, the right of others to think differently from one's self. It implies a free mind, open to new ideas and willing to give attentive consideration. . . .

When I say liberty, I mean liberty of the individual to think his own thoughts and live his own life as he desires to think and live.

This was the creed by which Senator Taft lived, and he sought in his own fashion and in his own way to provide an atmosphere in America in which others could do likewise.

SUGGESTIONS FOR STUDY

1. Name some ways in which Taft stuck to principle in spite of political consequences. In which of these do you agree with him in principle?

2. A good, though incomplete, definition of an *ex post facto* law was written by Supreme Court Justice Samuel Chase: "A law that makes an act which was done before the passing of the law and which was innocent when done, criminal, and punishes such action." State exactly why the law under which the Nazi leaders were convicted and executed was an *ex post facto* law. Would you have opposed these convictions and executions for this reason? Why or why not?

3. State some of the criticisms of Taft's position. Which ones of these criticisms do you think were not justified? Why?

4. What was the difference between the reaction of the Republicans and that of the Democrats? Give the reason for this difference. To what extent do you think either group was sincere? Try to think of some statement made recently by a candidate for office which was later used insincerely for political advantage by his opponents.

5. Henry Clay said, "I would rather be right than President." Why would this quotation serve as a good title for a biography of Robert A. Taft?

6. Name some statements which men of principle have made or might make today and which would create an uproar equal to that which Taft caused.

7. What persons in public life today do you think might be called "Mr. Integrity"?

8. What would have been Taft's opinion of persons who today advocate suspension of the Bill of Rights in order to combat communism more successfully? What is your opinion?

9. If you were following a political career, and confronted a situation like the one Senator Taft faced, would you do as he did, or would you keep silent for the sake of getting elected to an office? What is the meaning of expediency? Give reasons for your stand on this question. What does your choice reveal about your own personality?

The Pursuit of Moral Perfection

BENJAMIN FRANKLIN

Through his long active life Benjamin Franklin maintained an active interest in moral principles. To him the good life has its roots in morality, a term which he analyzed into thirteen virtues, stressing both man's duty to society and improvement of the individual. Franklin believed that, in spite of human weaknesses, we should set up goals and try to achieve them. Turn off the television, radio, and record player; listen to and think with this Solid American Citizen as he speaks from the pages of his classic *Autobiography*.

IT WAS ABOUT THIS TIME I conceived the bold and arduous project of arriving at moral perfection. I wished to live without committing any fault at any time; I would conquer all that either natural inclination, custom, or company might lead me into. As I knew, or thought I knew, what was right and wrong, I did not see why I might not always do the one and avoid the other. But I soon found I had undertaken a task of more difficulty than I had imagined. While my care was employed in guarding against one fault, I was often surprised by another; habit took the advantage of inattention; inclination was sometimes too strong for reason. I concluded, at length, that the mere speculative conviction that it was our interest to be completely virtuous, was not sufficient to prevent our slipping; and that the contrary habits must be broken, and good ones acquired and established, before we can have any dependence on a steady, uniform rectitude of conduct. For this purpose I therefore contrived the following method.

In the various enumerations of the moral virtues I had met with in my reading, I found the catalogue more or less numerous, as different writers included more or fewer ideas under the same name. Temperance, for example, was by some confined to eating and drinking, while by others it was extended to mean the moderating of every other pleasure, appetite, inclination, or passion, bodily or mental, even to our avarice and ambition. I proposed to myself, for the sake of clearness, to use rather more names, with fewer ideas annexed to each, than a few names with more ideas; and I included under thirteen names of virtues all that at that time occurred to me as necessary or desirable, and annexed to each a short precept, which fully expressed the extent I gave to its meaning.

These names of virtues, with their precepts, were:

1. TEMPERANCE.—Eat not to dullness; drink not to elevation.
2. SILENCE.—Speak not but what may benefit others or yourself; avoid trifling conversation.
3. ORDER.—Let all your things have their places; let each part of your business have its time.
4. RESOLUTION.—Resolve to perform what you ought; perform without fail what you resolve.
5. FRUGALITY.—Make no expense but to do good to others or yourself; *i.e.*, waste nothing.
6. INDUSTRY.—Lose no time; be always employed in something useful; cut off all unnecessary actions.
7. SINCERITY.—Use no hurtful deceit; think innocently and justly, and, if you speak, speak accordingly.
8. JUSTICE.—Wrong none by doing injuries, or omitting the benefits that are your duty.
9. MODERATION.—Avoid extremes; forbear resenting injuries so much as you think they deserve.
10. CLEANLINESS.—Tolerate no uncleanliness in body, clothes, or habitation.
11. TRANQUILLITY.—Be not disturbed at trifles, or at accidents common or unavoidable.
12. CHASTITY.
13. HUMILITY.—Imitate Jesus and Socrates.

My intention being to acquire the *habitude* of all these virtues, I judged it would be well not to distract my attention by attempting the whole at once, but to fix it on one of them at a time; and, when I should be master of that, then to proceed to another, and so on, till I should have gone through the thirteen; and, as the previous acquisition of some might facilitate the acquisition of certain others, I arranged them with that view, as they stand above. *Temperance* first, as it tends to procure that coolness and clearness of head, which is so necessary where constant vigilance was to be kept up, and guard maintained against the unremitting attraction of ancient habits, and the force of perpetual temptations. This being acquired and established, *Silence* would be more easy; and my desire being to gain knowledge at the same time that I improved in virtue, and considering that in conversation it was obtained rather by the use of the ears than of the tongue, and therefore wishing to break a habit I was getting into of prattling, punning, and joking, which only made me acceptable to trifling company, I gave *Silence* the second place. This and the next, *Order,* I expected would allow me more time for attending to my project and my studies. *Resolution,* once become habitual, would keep me firm in my endeavors to obtain all the subsequent virtues; *Frugality* and *Industry* freeing me from my remaining debt, and producing affluence and independence, would make more easy the practice of *Sincerity* and *Justice,* etc., etc. Conceiving then, that daily examination would be necessary, I contrived the following method for conducting that examination.

I made a little book, in which I allotted a page for each of the virtues. I ruled each page with red ink, so as to have seven columns, one for each day of the week, marking each column with a letter for the day. I crossed these columns with thirteen red lines, marking the beginning of each line with the first letter of one of the virtues, on which line, and in its proper column, I might mark, by a little black spot, every fault I found upon examination to have been committed respecting that virtue upon that day.

FORM OF THE PAGES

TEMPERANCE

Eat not to dullness; drink not to elevation

	Sun.	M.	T.	W.	Th.	F.	S.
Tem.							
Sil.	*	*		*		*	
Ord.	*	*			*	*	*
Res.		*				*	
Fru.		*				*	
Ind.			*				
Sinc.							
Jus.							
Mod.							
Clea.							
Tran.							
Chas.							
Hum.							

I determined to give a week's strict attention to each of the virtues successively. Thus, in the first week, my great guard was to avoid every least offence against *Temperance,* leaving the other virtues to their ordinary chance, only marking every evening the faults of the day. Thus, if in the first week I could keep my first line, marked T, clear of spots, I supposed the habit of that virtue so much strengthened, and its opposite weakened, that I might venture extending my attention to include the next, and for the following week keep both lines clear of spots. Proceeding thus to the last, I could go through a course complete in thirteen weeks, and four courses in a year. And like him who, having a garden to weed, does not attempt to eradicate all the bad herbs at once, which would exceed his reach and his strength, but works on one

of the beds at a time, and, having accomplished the first, proceeds
to a second, so I should have, I hoped, the encouraging pleasure
of seeing on my pages the progress I made in virtue, by clearing
successively my lines of their spots, till in the end, by a number
of courses, I should be happy in viewing a clean book, after a
thirteen weeks' daily examination.

The precept of *Order* requiring that *every part of my business
should have its allotted time,* one page in my little book contained
the following scheme of employment for the twenty-four hours of
a natural day.

THE MORNING. *Question.* What good shall I do this day?	5 6 7	Rise, wash and address *Powerful Goodness!* Contrive day's business, and take the resolution of the day; prosecute the present study, and breakfast.
	8 9 10 11	Work.
NOON.	12 1	Read, or overlook my accounts, and dine.
	2 3 4 5	Work.
EVENING. *Question.* What good have I done to-day?	6 7 8 9	Put things in their places. Supper. Music or diversion, or conversation. Examination of the day.
NIGHT.	10 11 12 1 2 3 4	Sleep.

I entered upon the execution of this plan for self-examination, and continued it with occasional intermissions for some time. I was surprised to find myself so much fuller of faults than I had imagined; but I had the satisfaction of seeing them diminish. To avoid the trouble of renewing now and then my little book, which, by scraping out the marks on the paper of old faults to make room for new ones in a new course, became full of holes, I transferred my tables and precepts to the ivory leaves of a memorandum book, on which the lines were drawn with red ink, that made a durable stain, and on those lines I marked my faults with a black-lead pencil, which marks I could easily wipe out with a wet sponge. After a while I went through one course only in a year, and afterward only one in several years, till at length I omitted them entirely, being employed in voyages and business abroad, with a multiplicity of affairs that interfered; but I always carried my little book with me.

My scheme of *Order* gave me the most trouble; and I found that, though it might be practicable where a man's business was such as to leave him the disposition of his time, that of a journeyman printer, for instance, it was not possible to be exactly observed by a master, who must mix with the world, and often receive people of business at their own hours. *Order*, too, with regard to places for things, papers, etc., I found extremely difficult to acquire. I had not been early accustomed to it, and, having an exceeding good memory, I was not so sensible of the inconvenience attending want of method. This article, therefore, cost me so much painful attention, and my faults in it vexed me so much, and I made so little progress in amendment, and had such frequent relapses, that I was almost ready to give up the attempt, and content myself with a faulty character in that respect, like the man who, in buying an ax of a smith, my neighbor, desired to have the whole of its surface as bright as the edge. The smith consented to grind it bright for him if he would turn the wheel; he turned, while the smith pressed the broad face of the ax hard and heavily on the stone, which made the turning of it very fatiguing. The man came every now and then from the wheel to see how the work went on, and at length would take his ax as it was, without further grinding. "No," said the smith, "turn on, turn on; we shall have it bright by-and-by; as yet, it is only speckled." "Yes," says the man, *"but I think I like a speckled ax best."* And I believe this may have been the case with many, who, having, for want of some such means as I employed, found the difficulty of obtaining good and breaking bad habits in other points of vice and virtue, have given up the struggle, and concluded that *"a speckled ax was best";* for something, that pretended to be reason, was every now and then suggesting to me that such extreme nicety as I exacted of myself might be a kind of foppery in morals, which, if it were known, would make me ridiculous; that a perfect character might be attended with the inconvenience of being envied and hated; and that a benevolent man should allow a few faults in himself, to keep his friends in countenance.

In truth, I found myself incorrigible with respect to *Order;* and now I am grown old, and my memory bad, I feel very sensibly the want of it. But, on the whole, though I never arrived at the perfection I had been so ambitious of obtaining, but fell far short of it, yet I was, by the endeavor, a better and a happier man than I otherwise should have been if I had not attempted it; as those who aim at perfect writing by imitating the engraved copies, though they never reach the wished-for excellence of those copies, their hand is mended by the endeavor, and is tolerable while it continues fair and legible. . . .

My list of virtues contained at first but twelve; but a Quaker friend having kindly informed me that I was generally thought proud; that my pride showed itself frequently in conversation; that I was not content with being in the right when discussing any point, but was overbearing, and rather insolent, of which he convinced me by mentioning several instances; I determined endeavoring to cure myself, if I could, of this vice or folly among the rest, and I added *Humility* to my list, giving an extensive meaning to the word.

I cannot boast of much success in acquiring the *reality* of this virtue, but I had a good deal with regard to the *appearance* of it. I made it a rule to forbear all direct contradiction to the sentiments of others, and all positive assertion of my own. I even forbid my-

self, agreeably to the old laws of our Junto, the use of every word
or expression in the language that imported a fixed opinion, such
as *certainly, undoubtedly,* etc., and I adopted, instead of them,
I conceive, I apprehend, or I imagine a thing to be so or so; or it
so appears to me at present. When another asserted something
that I thought an error, I denied myself the pleasure of contradict-
ing him abruptly, and of showing immediately some absurdity in
his proposition; and in answering I began by observing that in
certain cases or circumstances his opinion would be right, but in
the present case there *appeared* or *seemed* to me some difference,
etc. I soon found the advantage of this change in my manner; the
conversations I engaged in went on more pleasantly. The modest
way in which I proposed my opinions procured them a readier
reception and less contradiction; I had less mortification when I
was found to be in the wrong, and I more easily prevailed with
others to give up their mistakes and join with me when I happened
to be in the right.

And this mode, which I at first put on with some violence to
natural inclination, became at length so easy, and so habitual to
me, that perhaps for these fifty years past no one has ever heard
a dogmatical expression escape me. And to this habit (after my
character of integrity) I think it principally owing that I had early
so much weight with my fellow-citizens when I proposed new
institutions, or alterations in the old, and so much influence in
public councils when I became a member; for I was but a bad
speaker, never eloquent, subject to much hesitation in my choice
of words, hardly correct in language, and yet I generally carried
my points.

In reality, there is, perhaps, no one of our natural passions so
hard to subdue as *pride.* Disguise it, struggle with it, beat it down,
stifle it, mortify it as much as one pleases, it is still alive, and will
every now and then peep out and show itself; you will see it, perhaps, often in this history; for, even if I could conceive that I had
completely overcome it, I should probably be proud of my humility.

SUGGESTIONS FOR STUDY

1. Which ones of Franklin's 13 virtues would you omit from your own list? Which ones would you add? What would your complete list be?
2. Find evidence in this selection for each of the following traits of Franklin: his sharp wit, his candor, his wisdom, his understanding, his humility.
3. What virtues caused Franklin great trouble? Why?
4. On page 208, the long sentence that begins, "And I believe this may have been the case. . . ." is worth rereading. Tell in your own words what it means.
5. What distinction does Franklin make between the *reality* and the *appearance* of acquiring a virtue?
6. Why did Franklin list temperance first? (What is the difference between *temperance* and *abstinence?*)
7. Find indications that Franklin had a genuine awareness of his own limitations. To what extent can this awareness be helpful to the individual? Detrimental?
8. How much or how little do you find yourself inclined to admire and imitate Franklin's project? What aspects of it most catch your imagination?
9. What value is there in setting up a project for arriving at moral perfection, when perfection is unattainable?
10. Review the five "values" to be obtained from reading biography which are listed in Part One of this book. Write a theme giving specific examples of how you personally have profited from your study of this book so far.

FOR FURTHER READING

More biographies to guide you to a better life: *Twenty Years at Hull House*, Jane Addams; *Cyclone in Calico*, Nina Brown Baker; *Small Woman*, Alan Burgess; *Dr. Schweitzer of Lambaréné*, Norman Cousins; *The Story of My Boyhood and Youth*, John Muir; *Junipero Serra*, Agnes Repplier; *The Thread That Runs So True*, Jesse Stuart; *Valiant Companions: Helen Keller and Anne Sullivan*, Helen Waite.

PART TWO

The "Seven Ages" of Man

The "Seven Ages" of Man

IN THIS SECOND PART of our book, you will find an approach to biography entirely different from the one used in Part One. The material has been arranged in the pattern found in full-length biographies. You will first read selections telling about the family background and the early home life of the persons written about. The next section of Part Two shows the importance of schooldays and education. The third major area in life, and one that you yourselves are swiftly nearing, is the time for love and marriage. You will next read biographical excerpts selected for the information they can give you concerning the subjects' adult life. Death makes the logical concluding section of Part Two; and here you will see how the closing pages of biography often take a look in perspective at the way a life may have intensified and matured in values, like the slow mellowing of wine with aging. In your own life these five periods, extending from the cradle to the grave, can be a thrilling sequence; and in Part Two you should increase your understanding of what it means to have a full, rich, abundant, complete life. I hope you will be convinced that you must not settle for less!

In Part Two you will find material similar to that used in Part One. That is, there will be selections from full-length biographies and from other writings that are biographical in nature. And you will have opportunities to practice skills that you learned in Part One and also to get a wider sampling of existing biographies. In addition, you will, I hope, better understand what a full life consists of. You will begin to sense the sweep of life, from the beginning to the end, as Shakespeare did when he wrote his famous lines on man's "seven ages":

213

All the world's a stage,
And all the men and women merely players;
They have their exits and their entrances;
And one man in his time plays many parts,
His acts being seven ages. At first the infant,
Mewling and puking in the nurse's arms,
Then the whining school-boy, with his satchel
And shining morning face, creeping like snail
Unwillingly to school. And then the lover,
Sighing like furnace, with a woeful ballad
Made to his mistress' eyebrow. Then a soldier,
Full of strange oaths, and bearded like the pard,
Jealous in honour, sudden and quick in quarrel,
Seeking the bubble reputation
Even in the cannon's mouth. And then the justice,
In fair round belly with good capon lin'd,
With eyes severe and beard of formal cut,
Full of wise saws and modern instances;
And so he plays his part. The sixth age shifts
Into the lean and slipper'd pantaloon,
With spectacles on nose and pouch on side,
His youthful hose, well sav'd, a world too wide
For his shrunk shank; and his big manly voice
Turning again toward childish treble, pipes
And whistles in his sound. Last scene of all,
That ends this strange eventful history,
Is second childishness and mere oblivion;
Sans teeth, sans eyes, sans taste, sans everything.

As You Like It: Act II, Scene 7

Heredity, Home, and Family

BY THIS TIME in your life most likely you have been asked to write an autobiography. In such an account you have mentioned some things about your father and mother, your home, and your family, including pets and reunions and favorite cousins. You may or may not now treasure these sentiments and young memories of your childhood. But the fact remains that, whether these recollections are joyous or sad, they persist in the memory as you grow up. (Remember grandmother's repeated narrations —sometimes enthralling, sometimes boring—of her childhood?) Childhood is life's home plate. True, some persons, for various reasons, may want to escape their memories of childhood; but many, many persons fondly look back upon their entrances into life with warmth and gratitude and kindly humor.

The next three selections show you how each of three very different persons with varying backgrounds plays his part in Act One of man's seven ages.

Memories of My Childhood

ELEANOR ROOSEVELT

Although Eleanor Roosevelt has been a wife, a mother, a former First Lady of the United States, she is perhaps best known as a great woman. But the great woman of today was once a little girl—a fact easy to forget.

In this excerpt from *This Is My Story,* Mrs. Roosevelt sets down with charming candor those facts, impressions, and little incidents which she remembers about her childhood in a family of wealth, position, and culture.

MY MOTHER was one of the most beautiful women I have ever seen. The Halls were noted for their beauty and charm in the days when New York City was small enough to have a society spelled with a capital S! She had been largely brought up by her father, who died when she was seventeen. It must have been a curious household, for my Grandfather Hall never engaged in business. He lived on what his father and mother gave him. . . .

My Grandfather Hall's great interest was in the study of theology, and in his library were immense books dealing with religion. Most of them were of little interest to me as a child, but the Bible illustrated by Doré occupied many hours—and I think, probably gave me many nightmares!

A clergyman, Mr. C. P. Rhodes, lived with my grandfather in order that he might have some one with whom to talk on equal terms! My Grandmother Hall, a beauty and a belle, was treated like a cherished but somewhat spoiled child. She was expected to bring children into the world and seven children were born, but she was not expected to bring them up. My grandfather bought her clothes and adornments of every kind, but he told her nothing about business, never even taught her to draw a check, and died without a will, leaving her with six children under seventeen years of age, a responsibility for which she was totally unprepared.

The two eldest children, my mother and Tissie—whose real name was Elizabeth—bore the marks of their upbringing by their father. They were deeply religious; they had been taught to use their minds in the ways that my grandfather thought suitable for girls. He disciplined them well. For instance, in the country they walked from the house to the main road with a stick across their backs in the crook of their elbows, to improve their carriage—and that was done not only once, but several times a day! He was a severe judge of what they read and wrote and how they expressed themselves, and held them to the highest standards of conduct. The result, as far as my mother was concerned—and I think the same holds good of Tissie—was strength of character, with very definite ideas of right and wrong, and a certain rigidity in conforming to a conventional pattern which had been put before them as the only proper existence for a lady.

Suddenly the strong hand was removed, and the two boys and two younger girls knew no discipline, for how could a woman who had never been treated as anything but a grown-up child suddenly assume the burden of training a family?

I have been told that my mother, for the first year or so after my grandfather died, was the guiding spirit of the household, but girls were married young in those days, and at nineteen she was married to my father.

My mother belonged to that New York City Society which thought itself all-important. Old Mr. Peter Marié, who gave choice parties and whose approval stamped young girls and young matrons a success, called my mother a queen, and bowed before her charm and beauty, and to her this was important.

In that Society you were kind to the poor, you did not neglect your philanthropic duties in whatever community you lived, you assisted the hospitals and did something for the needy. You accepted invitations to dine and to dance with the right people only, you lived where you would be in their midst. You thought seriously about your children's education, you read the books that everybody read, you were familiar with good literature. In short, you conformed to the conventional pattern.

My father, Elliott Roosevelt, charming, good-looking, loved by all who came in contact with him, high or low, had a background and upbringing which were a bit alien to her pattern. He had a physical weakness which he himself probably never quite understood. As a boy of about fifteen he left St. Paul's School after one year because of illness, and went out with Dr. Metcalf, a friend of the family, to what was then the "wild and woolly west" of Texas. He made friends with the officers of Fort McKavit, a frontier fort, and stayed with them, hunting wild turkeys and game of every sort, and scouting in search of hostile Indians. He loved the life and was a natural sportsman, a good shot and a good rider. I think the life left an indelible impression on him. The illness left its mark on him, too, on those inner reserves of strength which we all have to call on at times in our lives. He returned to his family in New York apparently well and strong.

My Grandfather Roosevelt died before my father was twenty-one and while my father's older brother, Theodore—later to be President of the United States—fought his way to health from an asthmatic childhood, and went to Harvard College. Elliott, with the consent of an indulgent mother and two adoring sisters, took part of his inheritance and went around the world. He hunted in India when few people from this country had done anything of the kind. In his letters, which I collected and published a few years ago (*Hunting Big Game in the '80's*), the story of these early years, both in the West and in India, is told.

My father returned from his trip around the world to be at the wedding of his little sister, Corinne, to his friend, Douglas Robinson. Then he married Anna Hall, and, as is so often the case in life, tragedy and happiness came walking on each other's heels.

He adored my mother and she was devoted to him, but always in a more reserved and less spontaneous way. I doubt that the background of their respective family lives could have been more different. His family was not so much concerned with Society (spelled with a big S) as with people, and these people included the newsboys from the streets of New York and the cripples whom Dr. Schafer, one of the most noted early orthopedic surgeons, was trying to cure.

My father's mother, whom he adored, and his brother Theodore's young wife, Alice Lee, died within a few days of each other. The latter left only a little Alice to console the sorrowing young father and the other members of the family. My father felt these losses deeply, not only for himself but for those whom he loved. Very soon, however, in October, 1884, I came into the world, and from all accounts I must have been a more wrinkled and less attractive baby than the average—but to him I was a miracle from Heaven.

I was a shy, solemn child even at the age of two, and I am sure that even when I danced, which I did frequently, I never smiled.

My earliest recollections are of being dressed up and allowed to come down into what must have been a dining room and dance for a group of gentlemen who applauded and laughed as I pirouetted before them. Finally, my father would pick me up and hold me high in the air. All this is rather vague to me, but my father was never vague. He dominated my life as long as he lived, and was the love of my life for many years after he died.

With my father I was perfectly happy. He would take me into his dressing room in the mornings, or when he was dressing for dinner, and let me watch each thing he did. There is still a woodeny painting of a child with a straight bang across her forehead, very solemn, with an uplifted finger and an admonishing attitude, which he always enjoyed and referred to as "Little Nell scolding Elliott."

We had a country house at Hempstead, Long Island, so that he could hunt and play polo. He loved horses and dogs, and we always had both. During this time he was in business, and with this, added to the work and the sports, the gay and popular young couple lived a busy, social life. Some of the older members of my father's family have told me since that they thought the strain on his health was very great, but my mother and he himself probably never realized this. I knew only that he was the center of my world, and that all around him loved him.

One other thing I remember of this early period. We were on a steamer, and a collision occurred when we were one day out. The story has been told me many times, but I remember only that there was wild confusion. My father stood in a boat below me, and I was dangling over the side to be dropped into his arms. I was terrified and shrieking, and clung to those who were to drop me. Finally, I was safely in the little boat, and we transferred to the boat which had run us down in the fog, and were taken back to New York.

My father and mother and Tissie started out again for Europe a few days later, but a terrified and determined little girl refused to go near a boat again, so I was left for the summer with my father's aunt, Mrs. James King Gracie, my Grandmother Roosevelt's sister. That summer I remember: the pretty house and grounds at Oyster Bay, the bantam chickens which were called mine, and the eggs I brought in for breakfast. Occasional "Br'er Rabbit" stories, told me by sweet and gentle Auntie Gracie, visits to Auntie Bye, my father's older sister, who, it seems to me, had a cottage in the woods near by.

When the European trip was over, I returned to my family, and one little brother must have been born about that time, Elliott Roosevelt, Junior, but of his arrival I have no recollection whatsoever.

A short time after must have come a serious accident. My father was riding in a society circus. His leg was broken, and later it had to be rebroken and reset. I remember the day well, for we were alone in his room when he told me about it. Little as I was, I sensed that this was a terrible ordeal, and when he went hobbling out on crutches to the waiting doctors, I was dissolved in tears and sobbed my heart out for hours. From this illness my father never quite recovered.

Whether it was some weakness from his early years which the strain of the life he was living accentuated, whether it was the pain he endured, I do not know, for of course at that time I had no realization that anything was wrong—he began, however, to drink, and for my mother and his brother Theodore and his sisters began the period of harrowing anxiety which was to last until his death in 1894.

My father and mother, my little brother and I went to Italy for the winter of 1890 as the first step in the fight for his health and the power of self-control. Of this trip I have only vague pictures in my mind. I remember my father acting as gondolier, taking me out on the Venice canals, singing with the other boatmen, to my intense joy. I think there never was a child who was less able to carry a tune and had less gift for music than I. I loved his voice, however, and, above all, I loved the way he treated me. He called me "Little Nell," after the Little Nell in Dickens' *Old Curiosity Shop.* Later he made me read the book, but at that time I only knew it was a term of affection, and I never doubted that I stood first in his heart.

He could, however, be annoyed with me, particularly when I disappointed him in such things as physical courage—and this, unfortunately, I did quite often. We went to Sorrento and I was given a donkey and a donkey boy so I could ride over the beautiful roads. One day the others overtook me and offered to let me go with them, but at the first steep descent which they slid down I turned pale, and preferred to stay on the high road. I can remember still the tone of disapproval in his voice, though his words of reproof have long since faded away.

I was about five and a half and very sensitive to physical suffering, and quite overcome by the fact that my little donkey boy's feet were always cut and bleeding. On one occasion we returned with the boy on the donkey and I was running along beside him, my explanation being that his feet bled too much!

I remember my trip to Vesuvius with my father and one other person, and the throwing of pennies which were returned to us encased in lava, and then an endless trip down. I suppose there was some block in the traffic, but I can only remember my utter weariness and my effort to bear it without tears so that my father would not be displeased.

Two other experiences stand out in my mind. One was in Germany, where my father went to a sanitarium. Perhaps it illustrates how one's childhood marks one's future life!

We often went to the cafés, and the older people drank steins of beer with the delicious looking foam on top. I saw little German children drinking it, too. I begged my father to let me have one of the small mugs, as the other children. He refused for a while and then said; "Very well, but remember, if you have it, you have to drink the whole glass." I promised without a suspicion of the horror before me. When I took my first taste, instead of something sweet and delicious, I found I had something very bitter which I could hardly swallow. I was a disillusioned and disappointed child, but I had to finish the glass! Never since then have I cared for beer.

I remember, too, that we children were left to travel into Paris following the older members of the family. My father's man and our nurse looked after us. The nurse and I got out at one of the stations and managed to be left behind! Such excitement on the part of the nurse, for, of course, she had neither money nor tickets! Such terror for me and exasperation on the part of the station master! Finally, after much telegraphing, we were put on a train and met later that night by a worried but distinctly annoyed father and mother in Paris.

My mother took a house in Neuilly, outside of Paris, and settled down for several months, as another baby was expected the end of June. My father entered a sanitarium while his older sister, Anna, our Auntie Bye, came to stay with my mother.

The house was small, so it was decided to put me in a convent to learn French, and to have me out of the way when the baby arrived. In those days children were expected to believe that babies dropped from Heaven, or were brought in the doctor's satchel.

The convent experience was a very unhappy one. Of course, I was not yet six years old, and I must have been very sensitive, with an inordinate desire for affection and praise—perhaps brought on by the fact that I was fully conscious of my plain looks and lack of manners. My mother was always a little troubled by my lack of beauty, and I knew it as a child senses those things. She tried very hard to bring me up well so my manners would in some way compensate for my looks, but her efforts only made me more keenly conscious of my shortcomings.

The little girls of my age in the convent could hardly be expected to take much interest in a child who did not speak their language and did not belong to their religion. They had a little shrine of their own and often worked hard for hours beautifying it. I longed to be allowed to join them, but was always kept on the outside and wandered by myself in the walled-in garden.

Finally, I fell prey to temptation. One of the girls swallowed a penny. The excitement was great, every attention was given her, she was the center of everybody's interest. I longed to be in her place. One day I went to one of the sisters and told her that I had swallowed a penny. I think it must have been evident that my story was not true, but I could not be shaken, so they sent for my mother and told her that they did not believe me. She took me away in disgrace. Understanding as I do now my mother's character, I realize how terrible it must have seemed to her to have a child who would lie!

I finally confessed to my mother, but never could explain my motives. I suppose I did not really understand them then, and certainly my mother did not understand them.

I remember the drive home as one of utter misery, for I could bear swift punishment of any kind far better than long scoldings. I could cheerfully lie any time to escape a scolding, whereas if I had known that I would simply be put to bed or be spanked I probably would have told the truth.

My father had come home for the baby's arrival, and I am sorry to say he was causing my mother and his sister a great deal of anxiety—but he was the only person who did not treat me as a criminal!

The baby, my brother Hall, was several weeks old when I finally left the convent, and soon we sailed for home, leaving my father in a sanitarium in France where his brother, Theodore, had to go and get him later on.

SUGGESTIONS FOR STUDY

1. What time span in the life of Eleanor Roosevelt is covered in this selection?

2. Contrast the attitude toward life's values held by the family of Anna Hall with those respected by the family of Elliott Roosevelt. What do you feel these different backgrounds contributed to the early life of Eleanor Roosevelt? How has your own background varied from hers? Why, or why not, would you have been happy growing up under such a background as hers?

3. Explain how Elliott Roosevelt dominated his daughter's life. How did this domination affect Eleanor? In what way is Eleanor critical of her mother?

4. What does Eleanor's frankness about her father's weakness add to this selection?

5. What self-portrait of the child emerges from this word-picture?

6. Why as a child did Eleanor lie? Recall similar instances from your own experience. How do you defend yourself? Write a composition concerned with the problem of lying.

7. For the ambitious student: Read more about the life of Eleanor Roosevelt. Then explain to what extent this brief selection supports the poet Wordsworth's line "The child is father of the man."

8. For the ambitious student: Read Dickens' novel *The Old Curiosity Shop.* What do you suppose Mrs. Roosevelt's reaction to the book might have been?

FOR FURTHER READING

Autobiographical writings by Eleanor Roosevelt: *This Is My Story; This I Remember; On My Own; Autobiography of Eleanor Roosevelt* (selections from her three previous books with recent additions).

Dublin Quays

ROBERT BRISCOE

Robert Briscoe, an orthodox Jew, attained international fame by being elected Mayor of Dublin, the capital of Roman Catholic Ireland.

In Chapter II of his interesting autobiography, *For the Life of Me,* he tells of his Jewish and Irish heritages, both of which had great influence upon his thinking and upon his activities.

MY FATHER, Abraham William Briscoe, was born in the village of Zagar, province of Kovno, in Lithuania. In a way he was fortunately placed for a subject of the Czar, because Zagar was too small to have a ghetto. Besides, Jews were generally better off in Lithuania than in most other parts of Russia. There were never any pogroms [1] there, and living by the Baltic Sea, they traveled a good deal in the course of business to Russian ports and even to other countries. They were considered the intellectuals of Russian Jewry.

But make no mistake about it, a Russian Jew was always a second- or third-class citizen. There were many professions which he was forbidden to follow. He could not own land, but must rent it at exorbitant prices from the great landlords; and he was not allowed to live in either Moscow or St. Petersburg. . . .

Of course our people were subject to conscription like all Russians, and in the army they were liable to all sorts of indignities. They were given the dirtiest jobs; and never could they hope to become regular officers. In short, there was no freedom and no future for a Russian Jew.

When Father was about fourteen years old, my grandfather, who had a small mill in Zagar, scraped up enough money to send

[1] *pogroms:* organized massacres of helpless people.

him to Dublin, where some relatives already held a beachhead, so to speak. This made him that rare bird, an immigrant *to* Ireland, whose best young people are always leaving her. To Father the soft green hills of Dublin Harbour were the sheltering arms of justice, and Ireland seemed the very land of liberty—though he soon learned to think differently.

Nevertheless, compared to Lithuania, it was indeed a land of freedom, where a man could worship and work and rise unfettered by the stigma of race; where a Jew could freely associate with his fellow citizens; which was, I think, the freedom Father valued most of all. He took the country as his own and never once looked back. At least, from my earliest memory he thought of himself as an Irishman.

When he landed in Dublin he had only a few shillings in the pocket of his only decent suit—of course his cousins gave him shelter. He had no knowledge of English at all. In this connection, people wonder how we came to have such an English-sounding name as Briscoe. I have wondered myself; but I never thought to ask Pappa. I know he did not change his name, but I think it may have been spelled differently in Lithuania. Since at this time Father could only write Yiddish and Russian, which use quite different alphabets from ours, the immigration officer most likely asked his name and spelled it phonetically, Briscoe. In any event it is a good name.

The first thing my father had to do was to learn the language as quickly as possible. With the last of his money, or more likely some he borrowed, he engaged, of all things, a Protestant minister to tutor him. This amiable gentleman also taught him to play the violin. All his life my father loved to play that instrument. But he was very shy about it. Nobody, not even my mother, ever *saw* him play. He would lock himself in his room and through the door would come the faint strains of his fiddle.

As soon as he could speak English at all, Father got a job as a traveler in brushes—a sort of Irish Fuller Brush man. He was a very hard worker and had an engaging personality. Medium tall he was, with sandy hair, a big straight nose and bright blue eyes. To this was soon added a neatly trimmed beard. Charm and hard work must have sold a lot of brushes, for by the time he was twenty-one he was able to start a little brush factory of his own. Each year after that he traveled to the great fair at Leipzig in Germany to buy bristles for his brushes. On the way he fell into the habit of staying in Frankfurt with a Jewish family named Yoedicke, who became my grandparents. The Yoedickes had emigrated from Russia for a very different reason than my father.

My grandmother's family, the Klonskis, were great swells in Russian Jewry. Some of them were doctors in the Russian Navy with the status of officers, an almost unheard of thing; and they were allowed to live in St. Petersburg. When their daughter married my grandfather, it was a terrible misalliance, and the young couple left the country to avoid embarrassing the stylish Klonskis.

There were five Yoedicke daughters. Father fell in love with Ida, the third. His once-a-year courtship prospered despite a noticeable lack of enthusiasm on the part of Grandfather Yoedicke. But in accordance with our custom Father first had to help the old man get the two older daughters married off before he could claim his bride.

Having served, not as long as Isaac, but long enough, the time finally came. Stylishly clothed in a Prince Albert coat and a shining new topper, Father was married to Ida Yoedicke. They went straight back to Ireland, and when the Irish mail boat left them on Kingstown pier, my father was obliged to confess to his bride that his business had gone bad. In addition to his wedding garments he had exactly one shilling.

Self-confidence is an ineradicable attribute of the Briscoes. However his bride may have felt, Pappa was not at all worried. He went back to traveling again; but he kept his eyes and ears open for opportunity's knock. It came in the shape of a cargo of tea, which had been damaged by a fire at sea, and was advertised to be sold at auction "as was." Pappa examined the tea in Becker's warehouse and found many of the chests to be in good condition. At the auction he was the highest bidder, and the cargo was knocked down to him.

The following day he went to the Royal Insurance Company, which had sold the tea, and told them he had no money to pay for it. The officials raised a tremendous row, to which he meekly listened. When their anger had cooled a little, he said, "Gentlemen, all this excitement is unnecessary; I have a plan, and you don't have to trust me at all. Put all the tea in a warehouse, and I will take delivery, either chest by chest, or lorry by lorry. I will pay cash for each delivery as I take it. In this way you will get the highest bid for your tea and still be protected."

Abraham Briscoe was indeed a salesman, for he persuaded the indignant insurance men to accept his proposition. He then rented a small shop near Terenure Bridge, and installed his bride behind the counter to sell tea, measuring it out into pound and half-pound packets. Meanwhile he took to the road to sell it wholesale.

That deal was the foundation of his little fortune. He cleared enough profit to buy an interest in the Lawlor furniture business. The firm became Lawlor Briscoe. When Mr. Lawlor died, Pappa bought his share and became sole owner of the greatly expanded business. If you walk on Lower Ormond Quay today, you will still see the sign of Lawlor Briscoe, though we no longer have an interest in the firm.

My mother was a great help to her young husband. She was a beautiful and charming lady who wrote poetry and taught in the Jewish Hebrew school, and was an even better salesman than he. She knew quality when she saw it, in furniture, rugs, and pictures. In Lawlor Briscoe, as in the little shop by the bridge, she often sold behind the counter. Many of our customers refused to be served by anyone else. She was a shrewd judge of people's reactions. One thing she told me was, "If a customer praises something he is sure not to buy it; but if he runs it down, he is really interested."

The one treasure that my father brought to Ireland and kept inviolate was his religion. He was an Orthodox Jew who implicitly followed the Law as given to our people by their great prophets and the priests of our church. The dietary rules, so complicated and difficult to follow in a non-Hebraic country, were the absolute rule of our house. You may realize how strictly they were observed when I tell you that such great orthodox rabbis as Doctor Isaac Herzog who is now Chief Rabbi in Israel, his father who was

Chief Rabbi of Paris, and his father-in-law Rabbi Hillman who succeeded Herzog senior in Paris, often sat down to eat at my father's table.

To us of the younger generation, who tended to become impatient with such minutiae as special dishes for Passover, the ritual of purification and the ordinance against using dairy products and meat at the same meal, Pappa said, "Our Jewish laws and customs have been preserved by our ancestors for two thousand years or more, at the cost of great hardship, suffering and extreme peril. They are a precious heritage. Are we in our comparative comfort and ease lightly to abandon these things they strove so hard to hand down to us merely because they are inconvenient?"

And again he said, "We are the people chosen by God to suffer and strive and serve him; let us do so thankfully."

Of course Pappa taught us Hebrew so that we could read our prayers and study the Torah, which is the Old Testament. We learned many of the Psalms by heart. The poetry of David, which is so beautiful even in the King James translation, is even lovelier in the liquid syllables of its original tongue. We also learned many of the solemn, resonant verses of the different rituals, which we offer in the temple on our holy days.

When I was in America in 1923, on the eve of the anniversary of Pappa's death, I went to a synagogue and asked the beadle [2] if I might come the next day to say the memorial prayers. He assented, and then asked, "Where are you from?"

I answered, "I am an Irishman."

"Then I will keep close to you," he said, "so that I can prompt you."

When the time came I put on the praying shawl and intoned the full service of morning prayer. In the evening, I again was able to complete the prayers without once faltering.

After the service the beadle came smiling to me. "You said you came from Ireland," he remarked, "but I've never known a man from that country with such a knowledge of Hebrew and so great a capacity for prayer. I think you're phony!"

[2] *beadle:* a minor synagogue official.

Indeed, Pappa loved all great literature in any language. He read and reread the plays of Shakespeare and these he taught us, as well as many of the other English classics.

However, this gives too solemn a picture of him, for he had an irrepressible sense of fun. He liked to have people around him. After service on the Sabbath he stayed home all day, and people kept dropping in. The house would be full of laughter. Often in the evening his great friend Joseph Isaacs would come by, and the two of them would sit talking and drinking far more than Mother thought was good for them. It must be admitted that Pappa was very fond of drink, though he never let it interfere with business. Often people tried to get him tipsy to soften up his judgment. On these occasions Pappa used to sit with an umbrella over his arm taking glass for glass. But when they were not looking he poured the drinks into his slightly open umbrella.

Nor was our religion always as somber as you might think. I remember several occasions when Pappa's sense of humor considerably irritated his co-religionists. One was at our festival celebrating the saving of the Jews by Esther. It is always a gay, even raucous ceremony. When the name of our oppressor, Haman, who was something of an early Hitler, is mentioned, we express our opinion of him with very rude noises. It is a time when you can have a bit of fun in church.

Pappa particularly disliked one rather pompous member of our synagogue, and on this Queen Esther festival he incited us boys and our cousins to come with our pockets full of chestnuts. We sat at some distance from him. At the right moment he gave us the signal. We all stood up and began throwing chestnuts at the pompous gentleman's high silk hat. Pappa rose in a righteous indignation and called upon the beadle to throw those rowdy boys out. As he finished, he gave us the high sign again, and another cascade of chestnuts rattled off that silken topper.

Just as he did not leave his love of practical jokes outside the synagogue, he did not leave his morals in church. His integrity in his business was absolute; his word was, in truth, his bond. Shady practices filled him with rage.

It may seem odd to those whose ideas of the business methods of our race are formed by the unfortunate Merchant of Venice; but the people my father abhorred most of all were unscrupulous moneylenders. The first time I came back from America, cutting a rather dashing figure in my New York clothes, I began going out with a certain very beautiful Jewish girl. When my father learned of it he called me to his room, and said, "I hear you are keeping company with Esther. You know her father is a money lender, and I am sure you know how much I love you. Now I solemnly tell you this, rather than see you married to a moneylender's daughter, I would prefer to see your right arm cut off at the shoulder."

Mother shared this feeling of his. One time a moneylender died who had never paid his subscription to the Jewish cemetery of which Pappa was a trustee. His relatives, who were forced to pay a large capital sum to get him buried there, came to Pappa to complain. Mother hearing the argument, said to them, "Those good Jews who lie in the cemetery will rise when the Messiah comes. But your uncle will be there forever. He's getting a bargain."

I was so impressed by Pappa's abhorrence of moneylenders that when I first went into the Dail,[3] I joined with Patrick J. Little to introduce a bill which would put an end to their worst abuses. They often juggled loans so that they received as much as a thousand per cent interest, and once in their clutches a man had as little chance of escaping as a rabbit in a boa constrictor's jaws. My bill regulated the interest that could be charged, and also made it illegal for a married woman to borrow money without the knowledge and consent of her husband, for these foolish ones are always the easiest prey of the moneylenders. The act was passed and is today the law of Ireland.

As my father got better off, he played a leading part in the community. He was instrumental in raising funds to build the synagogue in Adelaide Road, where we still worship. Before that we went to an old ramshackle converted dwelling on a narrow slit of a street, oddly known as Mary's Abbey. You could say that

[3] *Dail:* short for *Dail Eireann,* lower house of Parliament in Irish Free State.

the new synagogue was the beginning of the modern history of Dublin Jewry.

Father also helped to get the land for our cemetery, and established the Board of Shechita, the controlling body of Kosher butchering, so that our people could live according to the dietary laws.

But all these things that he did for the community were simply expressions of his religious faith, not his race. His nationality was Irish, and all the time I was growing up I was also learning from my father—I was being steeped in—the dark, storm-wracked, light-shot history of my country—of Eire. I learned about the mysterious druids, and the prehistoric Firbolgs, and of the great days of the Irish kings, though I confess there was also terrible fighting among them and seldom peace for long; of Saint Patrick, and the time that followed when Ireland was the only center of learning and culture in these northern lands and the spear point of the Christian faith.

It is remarkable to think what she has survived since then until now. I learned how one marauding race after another crossed the narrow northern seas to plunder and tyrannize, until at last came the English, who were the worst of all. The reason I say that is because, of them all, only England made a systematic effort to destroy the Irish people or assimilate them into the Anglo-Saxon race.

At first they were content only to rule and exploit us. But when they found us stubbornly resisting, they passed the Penal Laws—that was after the Battle of the Boyne in 1690, when King William's Orangemen beat Prince Charles Stuart. These laws were aimed at the very souls of the Irish. Any kind of teaching, whether religious or secular was denied to all who would not forswear the Catholic Church. We survived even that; for the children gathered to be taught behind the tall hedges or in the hay barns in what were called the hedge schools, in which the great scholars taught, unpaid and hunted.

Finally came the effort to destroy the Irish language, and that came near to succeeding. It was forbidden to write it. Shopkeepers who put up their signs in it were prosecuted and imprisoned, and children were beaten in the schools for speaking it.

On top of that there was the great potato famine of 1847, in

which nearly a million Irish died of starvation, and more millions
emigrated, so the population fell from eight million to four, while
the British landlords, who held all the best land, shipped boatloads
of wheat and cattle out of the country and began driving the people out of their miserable, thatched-roof, single-room cottages,
because they wanted to enclose their lands, and turn them from
tillage to grazing cattle, which was more profitable.

My father told me tales of the great Irish leaders who had resisted these things; of Wolfe Tone leading his scythe-swinging
peasants in 1798, and poetic Robert Emmet, dangling from the
gibbet at Dublin Castle. He spoke of the moral force of Daniel
O'Connell, a member of the British Parliament, who secured the
repeal of the penal laws and Catholic Emancipation Act in 1832;
and of the leaders of the Young Ireland movement of 1841, from
whom the Irish learned to hope again. He ardently supported the
new Gaelic League, founded the year before I was born, which
provided centers where those who loved the best things of the old
days could gather and spread Irish ideals; and relearn our lovely
language that was being lost. Our native tongue became, and still
is, the symbol of Irish freedom.

Most of all, I learned about the great patriot, Charles Stewart
Parnell, who had been untimely dead only a little while when I
was born.

My father was foremost a man of peace, who loved deeply. He
loved his wife and his children; and I believe he truly loved humanity. And he hated the killing of men. So Parnell was his chosen
leader; because he did not preach revolution and war against England; but the achievement of freedom for Ireland by constitutional means. He asked only dominion status like Canada; and he
nearly succeeded in getting it. I think that if England had granted
it then, we would have been her faithful ally in the great wars.
But by the time she was willing to give it, the toll of spilt blood
was too great, the tide of bitterness too high for us to accept less
than complete freedom.

When I said Parnell nearly won dominion status, I mean that
Britain's great Prime Minister, William Gladstone, twice staked
his government on Home Rule. Once the House of Lords beat
him. The second time it was the scandal of Parnell and Kitty

O'Shea, whose husband sued the Irish statesman for adultery.

Father always thought, as many Irish did, that the O'Shea scandal was a Tory British plot. And when Parnell died by his own hand, or so they said, Father would not think that he was dead; but implicitly believed the legend that the body of a black man had been buried in Parnell's coffin, and that the great Irish leader had been spirited away to Australia; from whence he would some day return to lead the Irish people peacefully to freedom.

Peacefully is the key word here; for after Parnell there was no man who had a chance to set us free without war, and, as I said, my father was a man of peace. In his last days this caused a breach between us; for by then I knew that only by bloodshed could the Irish break loose from British domination. I was already enlisted in the fight.

This, I think, was the one big thing in which I went against his wishes. In most of the things which I have done in my lifetime, the major decisions I have made, I have acted as I believed he would have done, and decided in the way he would have wished.

SUGGESTIONS FOR STUDY

1. What is meant by "having served, not so long as Isaac"? Look up the story of "the saving of the Jews by Esther" in the Book of Esther in the Bible.

2. Give the details of Briscoe's Jewish heritage. Of his Irish heritage.

3. What do you think about the ethics of the elder Briscoe when he bid on a shipload of tea without having money to pay for it?

4. What truth is there in Ida Briscoe's statement about customers' interest in buying?

5. Let various members of the class report on the lives of the Irish patriots mentioned: Wolfe Tone, Robert Emmet, Daniel O'Connell, Charles Stewart Parnell.

6. Read again the last sentence of the selection. To what extent can you say this of yourself?

7. Write a theme answering one of these questions: What customs or characteristics have you (and America) inherited from the nationality of your ancestors? In what way has your life been influenced by the family situation into which you were born?

Boy Life on the Prairie

HAMLIN GARLAND

In the early chapters of *A Son of the Middle Border*, Hamlin
Garland gives a full account of his boyhood. He tells about his ancestors (particularly the McClintocks, his mother's people), his schooling, his recreation, and many of the other activities related to his life
on the farm in Iowa in the year 1872.

Bear in mind that you are reading what a mature, successful author
is recalling about his own boyhood. The language is that of a person
who is very skilled in the use of words (a skill which he developed
over his entire life), while the things he is talking about are those
which are of interest to young boys and girls.

If you have ever lived on a farm, or visited one, you still will not
be acquainted with the kind of life Hamlin Garland lived, because
modern farm life is quite different from what it was a century ago.
In those days people endured many hardships, but they also found
time for exciting and satisfying enjoyment.

THE SNOWS FELL deep in February and when at last
the warm March winds began to blow, lakes developed with magical swiftness in the fields, and streams filled every swale, trans-
forming the landscape into something unexpected and enchanting.
At night these waters froze, bringing fields of ice almost to our
door. We forgot all our other interests in the joy of the games
which we played thereon at every respite from school, or from the
wood-pile, for splitting fire-wood was our first spring task.

From time to time as the weather permitted, father had been
cutting and hauling maple and hickory logs from the forests of
the Cedar River, and these logs must now be made into stove-
wood and piled for summer use. Even before the school term

ended we began to take a hand at this work, after four o'clock and on Saturdays. While the hired man and father ran the cross-cut saw, whose pleasant song had much of the seed-time suggestion which vibrated in the *caw-caw* of the hens as they burrowed in the dust of the chip-yard, I split the easy blocks and my brother helped to pile the finished product.

The place where the wood-pile lay was slightly higher than the barnyard and was the first dry ground to appear in the almost universal slush and mud. Delightful memories are associated with this sunny spot and with a pond which appeared as if by some conjury, on the very field where I had husked the down-row so painfully in November. From the wood-pile I was often permitted to go skating and Burton was my constant companion in these excursions. However, my joy in his companionship was not unmixed with bitterness, for I deeply envied him the skates which he wore. They were trimmed with brass and their runners came up over his toes in beautiful curves and ended in brass acorns which transfigured their wearer. To own a pair of such skates seemed to me the summit of all earthly glory.

My own wooden "contraptions" went on with straps and I could not make the runners stay in the middle of my soles where they belonged, hence my ankles not only tipped in awkwardly but the stiff outer edges of my boot counters dug holes in my skin so that my outing was a kind of torture after all. Nevertheless, I persisted and, while Burton circled and swooped like a hawk, I sprawled with flapping arms in a mist of ignoble rage. That I learned to skate fairly well even under these disadvantages argues a high degree of enthusiasm.

Father was always willing to release us from labor at times when the ice was fine, and at night we were free to explore the whole country round about, finding new places for our games. Sometimes the girls joined us, and we built fires on the edges of the swales and played "gool" and a kind of "shinny" till hunger drove us home.

We held to this sport to the last—till the ice with prodigious booming and cracking fell away in the swales and broke through the icy drifts (which lay like dams along the fences) and vanished, leaving the corn-rows littered with huge blocks of ice. Often we came in from the pond, wet to the middle, our boots completely soaked with water. They often grew hard as iron during the night, and we experienced the greatest trouble in getting them on again. Greasing them with hot tallow was a regular morning job.

Then came the fanning mill. The seed grain had to be fanned up, and that was a dark and dusty "trick" which we did not like anything near as well as we did skating or even piling wood. The hired man turned the mill, I dipped the wheat into the hopper, Franklin held sacks and father scooped the grain in. I don't suppose we gave up many hours to this work, but it seems to me that we spent weeks at it. Probably we took spells at the mill in the midst of the work on the chip pile.

Meanwhile, above our heads the wild ducks again pursued their northward flight, and the far honking of the geese fell to our ears from the solemn deeps of the windless night. On the first dry warm ridges the prairie cocks began to boom, and then at last came the day when father's imperious voice rang high in familiar command. "Out with the drags, boys! We start seeding tomorrow."

Again we went forth on the land, this time to wrestle with the tough, unrotted sod of the new breaking, while all around us the larks and plover called and the gray badgers stared with disapproving bitterness from their ravaged hills.

Maledictions on that tough northwest forty! How many times I harrowed and cross-harrowed it I cannot say, but I well remember the maddening persistency with which the masses of hazel roots clogged the teeth of the drag, making it necessary for me to raise the corner of it—a million times a day! This had to be done while the team was in motion, and you can see I did not lack for exercise. It was necessary also to "laphalf" and this requirement made careful driving needful, for father could not be fooled. He saw every "balk."

As the ground dried off the dust arose from under the teeth of the harrow and flew so thickly that my face was not only coated with it but tears of rebellious rage stained my cheeks with comic lines. At such times it seemed unprofitable to be the twelve-year-old son of a western farmer.

One day, just as the early sown wheat was beginning to throw a tinge of green over the brown earth, a tremendous wind arose from the southwest and blew with such devastating fury that the soil, caught up from the field, formed a cloud, hundreds of feet high, a cloud which darkened the sky, turning noon into dusk and sending us all to shelter. All the forenoon this blizzard of loam raged, filling the house with dust, almost smothering the cattle in the stable. Work was impossible, even for men. The growing grain, its roots exposed to the air, withered and died. Many of the smaller plants were carried bodily away.

As the day wore on father fell into dumb, despairing rage. His rigid face and smoldering eyes, his grim lips, terrified us all. It seemed to him (as to us), that the entire farm was about to take flight and the bitterest part of the tragic circumstance lay in the reflection that our loss (which was much greater than any of our neighbors) was due to the extra care with which we had pulverized the ground.

"If only I hadn't gone over it that last time," I heard him groan in reference to the "smooch" with which I had crushed all the lumps making every acre friable as a garden. "Look at Woodring's!"

Sure enough. The cloud was thinner over on Woodring's side of the line fence. His rough clods were hardly touched. My father's bitter revolt, his impotent fury appalled me, for it seemed to me (as to him), that nature was, at the moment, an enemy. More than seventy acres of this land had to be resown.

Most authors in writing of "the merry merry farmer" leave out experiences like this—they omit the mud and the dust and the grime, they forget the army worm, the flies, the heat, as well as the smells and drudgery of the barns. Milking the cows is spoken of in the traditional fashion as a lovely pastoral recreation, when as a matter of fact it is a tedious job. We all hated it. We saw no poetry in it. We hated it in summer when the mosquitoes bit and the cows slashed us with their tails, and we hated it still more in the winter time when they stood in crowded malodorous stalls.

In summer when the flies were particularly savage we had a way of jamming our heads into the cows' flanks to prevent them from kicking into the pail, and sometimes we tied their tails to their legs so that they could not lash our ears. Humboldt Bunn tied a heifer's tail to his boot straps once—and regretted it almost instantly. No, No, it won't do to talk to me of "the sweet breath of kine." I know them too well—and calves are not "the lovely, fawn-like creatures" they are supposed to be. To the boy who is teaching them to drink out of a pail they are nasty brutes—quite unlike fawns. They have a way of filling their nostrils with milk and blowing it all over their nurse. They are greedy, noisy, ill-smelling, and stupid. They look good when running with their mothers in the pasture, but as soon as they are weaned they lose all their charm—for me.

Attendance on swine was less humiliating for the reason that we could keep them at arm's length, but we didn't enjoy that. We liked teaming and pitching hay and harvesting and making fence, and we did not greatly resent plowing or husking corn but we did hate the smell, the filth of the cowyard. Even hostling had its "outs," especially in spring when the horses were shedding their hair. I never fully enjoyed the taste of equine dandruff, and the eternal smell of manure irked me, especially at the table.

Clearing out from behind the animals was one of our never ending jobs, and hauling the compost out on the fields was one of the tasks which, as my father grimly said, "We always put off till it rains so hard we can't work out doors." This was no joke to us, for not only did we work out doors, we worked while standing ankle deep in the slime of the yard, getting full benefit of the drizzle. Our new land did not need the fertilizer, but we were forced to haul it away or move the barn. Some folks moved the barn. But then my father was an idealist.

Life was not all currying or muck-raking for Burt or for me. Herding the cows came in to relieve the monotony of farm-work. Wide tracts of unbroken sod still lay open to the north and west, and these were the common grazing grounds for the community. Every farmer kept from twenty-five to a hundred head of cattle and half as many colts, and no sooner did the green begin to show on the fire-blackened sod in April than the winter-worn beasts left the straw-piles under whose lee they had fed during the cold months, and crawled out to nip the first tender spears of grass in the sheltered swales. They were still "free commoners" in the eyes of the law.

The colts were a fuzzy, ungraceful lot at this season. Even the best of them had big bellies and carried dirty and tangled manes, but as the grazing improved, as the warmth and plenty of May filled their veins with new blood, they sloughed off their mangy coats and lifted their wide-blown nostrils to the western wind in exultant return to freedom. Many of them had never felt the weight of a man's hand, and even those that had wintered in and around the barn-yard soon lost all trace of domesticity. It was not unusual to find that the wildest and wariest of all the leaders bore a collar mark or some other ineffaceable badge of previous servitude.

They were for the most part Morgan grades or "Canuck," with a strain of broncho to give them fire. It was curious, it was glorious to see how deeply-buried instincts broke out in these halterless herds. In a few days, after many trials of speed and power the bands of all the region united into one drove, and a leader, the swiftest and most tireless of them all, appeared from the ranks and led them at will.

Often without apparent cause, merely for the joy of it, they left their feeding grounds to wheel and charge and race for hours over the swells, across the creeks and through the hazel thickets. Sometimes their movements arose from the stinging of gadflies, sometimes from a battle between two jealous leaders, sometimes from the passing of a wolf—often from no cause at all other than that of abounding vitality.

In much the same fashion, but less rapidly, the cattle went forth upon the plain and as each herd not only contained the growing steers, but the family cows, it became the duty of one boy from each farm to mount a horse at five o'clock every afternoon and "hunt the cattle," a task seldom shirked. My brother and I took turn and turn about at this delightful task, and soon learned to ride like Comanches. In fact we lived in the saddle, when freed from duty in the field. Burton often met us on the feeding grounds, and at such times the prairie seemed an excellent place for boys.

As we galloped along together it was easy to imagine ourselves Wild Bill and Buckskin Joe in pursuit of Indians or buffalo.

We became, by force of unconscious observation, deeply learned in the language and the psychology of kine as well as colts. We watched the big bull-necked stags as they challenged one another, pawing the dust or kneeling to tear the sod with their horns. We possessed perfect understanding of their battle signs. Their boastful, defiant cries were as intelligible to us as those of men. Every note, every motion had a perfectly definite meaning. The foolish, inquisitive young heifers, the staid self-absorbed dowagers wearing their bells with dignity, the frisky two-year-olds and the lithe-bodied wide-horned truculent three-year-olds all came in for interpretation.

Sometimes a lone steer ranging the sod came suddenly upon a trace of blood. Like a hound he paused, snuffling the earth. Then with wide mouth and outthrust, curling tongue, uttered voice. Wild as the tiger's food-sick cry, his warning roar burst forth, ending in a strange, upward explosive whine. Instantly every head in the herd was lifted, even the old cows heavy with milk stood as if suddenly renewing their youth, alert and watchful.

Again it came, that prehistoric bawling cry, and with one mind the herd began to center, rushing with menacing swiftness, like warriors answering their chieftain's call for aid. With awkward lope or jolting trot, snorting with fury they hastened to the rescue, only to meet in blind bewildered mass, swirling to and fro in search of an imaginary cause of some ancestral danger.

At such moments we were glad of our swift ponies. From our saddles we could study these outbreaks of atavistic rage with serene enjoyment.

In herding the cattle we came to know all the open country round about and found it very beautiful. On the uplands a short, light-green, hair-like grass grew, intermixed with various resinous weeds, while in the lowland feeding grounds, luxuriant patches of blue-joint, wild oats, and other tall forage plants waved in the wind. Along the streams and in the "sloos" cat-tails and tiger-lilies nodded above thick mats of wide-bladed marsh grass. Almost without realizing it, I came to know the character of every weed, every flower, every living thing big enough to be seen from the back of a horse.

Nothing could be more generous, more joyous, than these natural meadows in summer. The flash and ripple and glimmer of the tall sunflowers, the myriad voices of gleeful bobolinks, the chirp and gurgle of red-winged blackbirds swaying on the willows, the meadow-larks piping from grassy bogs, the peep of the prairie chick and the wailing call of plover on the flowery green slopes of the uplands made it all an ecstatic world to me. It was a wide world with a big, big sky which gave alluring hint of the still more glorious unknown wilderness beyond.

Sometimes of a Sunday afternoon, Harriet and I wandered away to the meadows along Dry Run, gathering bouquets of pinks, sweet-williams, tiger-lilies, and lady-slippers, thus attaining a vague perception of another and sweeter side of life. The sun flamed across the splendid serial waves of the grasses and the perfumes of a hundred spicy plants rose in the shimmering midday air. At such times the mere joy of living filled our young hearts with wordless satisfaction.

Nor were the upland ridges less interesting, for huge antlers lying bleached and bare in countless numbers on the slopes told of the herds of elk and bison that had once fed in these splendid savannahs, living and dying in the days when the tall Sioux were the only hunters.

The gray hermit, the badger, still clung to his deep den on the rocky unplowed ridges, and on sunny April days the mother fox lay out with her young, on southward-sloping swells. Often we met the prairie wolf or startled him from his sleep in hazel copse, finding in him the spirit of the wilderness. To us it seemed that just over the next long swell toward the sunset the shaggy brown bulls still fed in myriads, and in our hearts was a longing to ride away into the "sunset regions" of our song.

All the boys I knew talked of Colorado, never of New England. We dreamed of the plains, of the Black Hills, discussing cattle raising and mining and hunting. "We'll have our rifles ready, boys, ha, ha, ha-ha!" was still our favorite chorus, "Newbrasky" and Wyoming our far-off wonderlands, Buffalo Bill our hero.

David, my hunter uncle who lived near us, still retained his long old-fashioned, muzzle-loading rifle, and one day offered it to me, but as I could not hold it at arm's length, I sorrowfully returned it. We owned a shotgun, however, and this I used with all the confidence of a man. I was able to kill a few ducks with it and I also hunted gophers during May when the sprouting corn was in most danger. Later I became quite expert in catching chickens on the wing.

On a long ridge to the north and west, the soil, too wet and cold to cultivate easily, remained unplowed for several years and scattered over these clay lands stood small groves of popple trees which we called "tow-heads." They were usually only two or three hundred feet in diameter, but they stood out like islands in the waving seas of grasses. Against these dark-green masses, breakers of blue-joint radiantly rolled. To the east some four miles ran the Little Cedar River, and plum trees and crabapples and haws bloomed along its banks. In June immense crops of strawberries offered from many meadows. Their delicious odor rose to us as we rode our way, tempting us to dismount and gather and eat.

Over these uplands, through these thickets of hazel brush, and around these coverts of popple, Burton and I careered, hunting the cows, chasing rabbits, killing rattlesnakes, watching the battles of bulls, racing the half-wild colts and pursuing the prowling wolves. It was an alluring life, and Harriet, who rode with us occasionally, seemed to enjoy it quite as much as any boy. She could ride almost as well as Burton, and we were all expert horse-tamers.

We all rode like cavalrymen—that is to say, while holding the reins in our left hands we guided our horses by the pressure of the strap across the neck, rather than by pulling at the bit. Our ponies were never allowed to trot. We taught them a peculiar gait which we called "the lope," which was an easy canter in front and a trot behind (a very good gait for long distances), and we drilled them to keep this pace steadily and to fall at command into a swift walk without any jolting intervening trot. We learned to ride like circus performers standing on our saddles, and practised other of the tricks we had seen, and through it all my mother remained unalarmed. To her a boy on a horse was as natural as a babe in the cradle. The chances we took of getting killed were so numerous that she could not afford to worry.

Burton continued to be my almost inseparable companion at school and whenever we could get together, and while to others he seemed only a shy, dull boy, to me he was something more. His strength and skill were remarkable and his self-command amazing. Although a lad of instant, white-hot, dangerous temper, he suddenly, at fifteen years of age, took himself in hand in a fashion miraculous to me. He decided (I never knew just why or how) that he would never again use an obscene or profane word. He kept his vow. I knew him for over thirty years and I never heard him raise his voice in anger or utter a word a woman would have shrunk from—and yet he became one of the most fearless and indomitable mountaineers I ever knew.

This change in him profoundly influenced me and though I said nothing about it, I resolved to do as well. I never quite succeeded, although I discouraged as well as I could the stories which some of the men and boys were so fond of telling, but alas! when the old cow kicked over my pail of milk, I fell from grace and told her just what I thought of her in phrases that Burton would have repressed. Still, I manfully tried to follow his good trail.

Cornplanting, which followed wheat-seeding, was done by hand, for a year or two, and this was a joyous task. We "changed works" with neighbor Button, and in return Cyrus and Eva came to help up. Harriet and Eva and I worked side by side, "dropping" the corn, while Cyrus and the hired man followed with the hoes to cover it. Little Frank skittered about, planting with desultory action such pumpkin seeds as he did not eat. The presence of our young friends gave the job something of the nature of a party and we were sorry when it was over.

After the planting a fortnight of less strenuous labor came on, a period which had almost the character of a holiday. The wheat needed no cultivation and the corn was not high enough to plow. This was a time for building fence and fixing up things generally. This, too, was the season of the circus. Each year one came along from the east, trailing clouds of glorified dust and filling our minds with the color of romance.

From the time the "advance man" flung his highly colored posters over the fence till the coming of the glorious day we thought of little else. It was India and Arabia and the jungle to us. History and the magic and pomp of chivalry mingled in the parade of the morning, and the crowds, the clanging band, the haughty and alien beauty of the women, the gold embroidered housings, the stark majesty of the acrobats subdued us into silent worship.

I here pay tribute to the men who brought these marvels to my eyes. To rob me of my memories of the circus would leave me as poor as those to whom life was a drab and hopeless round of toil. It was our brief season of imaginative life. In one day—in a part of one day—we gained a thousand new conceptions of the world and of human nature. It was an embodiment of all that was skillful and beautiful in manly action. It was a compendium of biologic research but more important still, it brought to our ears the latest band pieces and taught us the most popular songs. It furnished us with jokes. It relieved our dullness. It gave us something to talk about.

We always went home wearied with excitement, and dusty and fretful—but content. We had seen it. We had grasped as much of it as anybody and could remember it as well as the best. Next day as we resumed work in the field the memory of its splendors went with us like a golden cloud.

Most of the duties of the farmer's life require the lapse of years to seem beautiful in my eyes, but haying was a season of well-defined charm. In Iowa, summer was at its most exuberant stage of vitality during the last days of June, and it was not strange that the faculties of even the toiling hay-maker, dulled and deadened with never ending drudgery, caught something of the superabundant glow and throb of nature's life.

As I write I am back in that marvellous time. The cornfield, dark-green and sweetly cool, is beginning to ripple in the wind with multitudinous stir of shining, swirling leaf. Waves of dusk and green and gold, circle across the ripening barley, and long leaves upthrust, at intervals, like spears. The trees are in heaviest foliage, insect life is at its height, and the shimmering air is filled with buzzing, dancing forms, and the clover is gay with the sheen of innumerable gauzy wings.

The west wind comes to me laden with ecstatic voices. The bobolinks sail and tinkle in the sensuous hush, now sinking, now rising, their exquisite notes filling the air as with the sound of fairy bells. The king-bird, alert, aggressive, cries out sharply as he launches from the top of a poplar tree upon some buzzing insect, and the plover makes the prairie sad with his wailing call. Vast purple-and-white clouds move like stately ships before the breeze, dark with rain, which they drop momentarily in trailing garments upon the earth, and so pass in majesty amidst a roll of thunder.

The grasshoppers move in clouds with snap and buzz, and out of the luxurious stagnant marshes comes the ever-thickening chorus of the toads, while above them the killdees and the snipe shuttle to and fro in sounding flight. The blackbirds on the cat-tails sway and swing, uttering through lifted throats their liquid gurgle, mad with delight of the sun and the season—and over all, and laving all, moves the slow wind, heavy with the breath of the far-off blooms of other lands, a wind which covers the sunset plain with a golden entrancing haze.

At such times it seemed to me that we had reached the "sunset region" of our song, and that we were indeed "lords of the soil."

SUGGESTIONS FOR STUDY

1. Hamlin Garland says that he pronounced *maledictions* on the tough northwest forty acres. What tasks which you must perform do you find deserving of *maledictions?*

2. Which tasks did Hamlin Garland dislike the most? Which tasks did he most enjoy?

3. What were the reasons that the circus was important to the Garland children? Which of your pleasures, if any, do you think are dulled because they occur too frequently?

4. How successful was Hamlin Garland in following in the foot-

steps of his friend Burton—especially in the matter of reforming his language?

5. Why didn't Mrs. Garland worry about the boys' behavior and dangerous feats on horseback?

6. What features of these early days on the farm do you think were probably important in shaping the character of Hamlin Garland? What features of your own early life do you think have been important in the formation of your character?

7. What did Hamlin Garland find objectionable in the portrayal of farm life by most authors of his day? What method did he himself use to describe farm life? (See *Romance and Realism, An Introduction to the Study of the Novel,* for a complete explanation of these two approaches to any given subject.)

Schooldays and Education

SCHOOL LIFE, with its great variety of joys and sorrows, successes and failures, frustrations and fulfillments, is a part of everyone's life, and therefore a part of every complete biography. You have doubtless been told many times that schooldays ("Schooldays, schooldays, dear old golden rule days") are "the happiest days of your life," but experience with the problems of the teen-years may have convinced you that this statement is a bit of romantic nonsense. Shakespeare spoke of the second age of man somewhat less enthusiastically:

> Then the whining school-boy, with his satchel
> And shining morning face, creeping like snail
> Unwillingly to school.

The selections in this section give you some idea of the many ways in which the reading of biography can help you to understand the meaning and the importance of schooling and education —which are not necessarily the same thing—in the lives of all persons, including yourself.

Nixon's Years at School and College

WILLIAM COSTELLO

Richard M. Nixon, Vice-President of the United States from 1953 to 1961, was born at Yorba Linda, a settlement near Los Angeles, California, on January 9, 1913.

The Facts About Nixon, published in 1960, when Mr. Nixon was the Republican candidate for President, was frankly acknowledged as "unauthorized." Although to some Nixon supporters this "campaign biography" possessed an anti-Nixon bias, the chapter reprinted here was quite generally approved. This chapter relates the details of Nixon's school and college life. Among these you will probably find many similarities to your own experiences. At any rate, you will be interested in the sort of schooling and schoolday activities which prepared a young American for a spectacularly successful political career.

FRANK, Richard's father, after the failure of his lemon grove worked at carpentering and various other jobs. Richard was reared in the strict Quaker tradition, for Frank had adopted his wife's profession of faith. All attended church three times on Sunday and every Wednesday evening, and when Richard grew old enough, he played the organ at meeting house and taught Sunday school. Card-playing and dancing were forbidden. Richard was remembered as sober, serious, and disciplined, even as a child. He walked half a mile to school each day; before and after school he performed the normal chores of a farmer's son; he seldom played. He had a record of perfect attendance as a second-grader, skipped the third grade, and missed but a single day in the fourth grade.

Years later, when oil was discovered under his orchard, Frank Nixon was to learn that Yorba Linda could have made him a millionaire, but in 1922 he gave up trying to make a living from his lemon grove and sold out.

Back in Whittier, his old home-town, the rolling stone came to rest. Frank and Hannah Nixon bought a filling station, three miles outside town, one of the first gasoline pumps in the area, a stroke of enterprise that helped greatly to stabilize the family fortunes

"The house was a simple one," Nixon recalled many years later. But "in the living room was a mahogany upright piano that Mother insisted on having although I was the only one in the family who played it. Next door was the garage with connecting stairs that led to three bedrooms and a bath above the garage. The downstairs bedroom off the living room was where two of my brothers died."

Nixon spent a frugal, hard-working boyhood in Whittier, but it was by no means the poverty-stricken household that some have reported.

"My father was fairly successful," Nixon has said. "The filling station was going two or three years when the old Quaker church nearby was put up for sale. My Dad bought it, moved it close to our filling station, and made it into Nixon's Market, a country store. If it hadn't been for the expense of my brothers' sickness we would have been fairly well off.

"I remember that my Dad sold half of the acre on which our house was located in order to pay medical bills. My Dad was an individual—he'd go to his grave before he took government help. This attitude of his gave us pride. Maybe it was false pride, but we had it."

Richard was the second of five sons. A younger boy, Arthur, died of tubercular meningitis at seven when Richard was in his first year of high school. Soon after that the oldest brother, Harold, suffered a second attack of tuberculosis, which resulted in his death five years later. Those five years were a tragic time for the Nixons. Hannah first took her son to the mountains a hundred miles from Whittier and then, in a desperate effort to find a more beneficent climate, moved him to Prescott, Arizona. There, to help meet the added expense, she ran a nursing home for Harold and three other tubercular bed patients.

During the years of Mrs. Nixon's absence, father and sons sold groceries and gasoline and cared for themselves. Meals and house-keeping amenities were sketchy except on Sundays, when there was time for a roast. The store stayed open until nine or ten o'clock at night, and the boys were expected to carry their share of work. After hours, Richard would sit in the kitchen, beside the gas oven, studying until two or three in the morning.

After Whittier grammar school, Richard entered Fullerton High School, transferring to Whittier High for his last two years. In Richard's junior year, to give him the pocket money he needed and at the same time keep faith with the Quaker philosophy of individual self-sufficiency and personal dignity, his father gave him complete charge of the vegetable counter in the family store. Richard did the buying, driving to the Los Angeles public market before sunrise to bargain with the local produce growers and hurrying back to arrange his displays before leaving for school. All the profit he could make was his, and all he could save went into a college bank account, for he had already become interested in studying law.

Neighbors recall him during those years as a shy, serious boy who applied himself as avidly to his school books as he did to his household duties. The adjectives applied to him were always complimentary: determined, methodical, diligent, resourceful, conscientious; but no one ever called him a prodigy.

It was perhaps partly through the Nixon store that young Richard acquired his first interest in public affairs. His father (who died in 1956), was an extroverted personality who suffered from ulcers; a hard-driving, fiery-tempered man with outspoken views on political issues and a taste for vigorous argument. His store, an anachronistic hangover of the vanishing cracker-barrel era, became a neighborhood rendezvous; and although Richard and his brothers learned not to challenge their father in debate, they had the stimulus of the provocative environment he provided.

Richard's shyness in boyhood gave way to a new self-confidence when he acquired what was to be a lifelong interest in debating. From the first he was outstanding. As a Fullerton High sophomore he won the Constitutional Oratorical Contest, and the school yearbook in 1928 praised him as the sophomore representative of West Coast high schools in the National Oratorical Contest. At Whittier High he won the same contest in both his junior and senior years, and as a testimonial to his classroom efforts his diploma bore the gold seal awarded for scholarship by the California Interscholastic Federation.

His high-school debating coach, Mrs. Norman Vincent, remembers she used to feel "disturbed" at his superiority over his teammates. "He had this ability," she said, "to kind of slide round an argument instead of meeting it head on, and he could take any side of a debate."

In his final year at high school Nixon also ran for and won his first political office—general manager of student-body affairs. One of his biographers refers to him even then as a "controversial" member of the student body, one who had definite opinions and expressed them. His Whittier high-school principal, O. C. Albertson, recalls, "Dick was a marked man when he transferred to us. He was a leader in scholastic and student activities—a self-starter —very popular. I think of Dick as a 'fighting Quaker.'" . . .

The years 1930–1934 saw Nixon as an undergraduate at Whittier College, a local Quaker institution, majoring in history, covering himself with distinction as a debater, still helping to pay his way by running the fresh-vegetable counter at the family store.

The pattern of diligence, seriousness, and aggressive sociability that had been established in high school repeated itself. Nixon seldom went to parties; no one remembers his telling a joke or squandering time on frivolities. He had work and books to occupy him. But he understood his classmates and their drives and motivations perfectly.

During all four college years he went out doggedly for football and never made the team except as a freshman when only eleven men turned out. Besides lacking weight and speed, he had two left feet. Nevertheless, he refused to give up. He said later, "I got a good seat on the fifty-yard-line." His coach, Wallace Newman, recalling the weeks that would go by without Richard's ever playing a minute, said, however, "He was wonderful for morale, because he'd sit there and cheer the rest of the guys, and tell them how well they'd played. To sit on the bench for the better part of four seasons isn't easy. I always figure, especially in the case of Dick, who excelled in everything else, that kids like that have more guts than the first-string heroes."

His frustrated football ambition did, however, give birth to a legend that was to be applauded subsequently by his political enemies. Once in a long while Richard would be permitted to play in the last few minutes, and one of his classmates, who was a linesman, recalled later: "When Dick went in, I always got out the five-yard penalty marker. Dick was so eager I knew he'd be offside just about every play."

One of the fields in which Nixon excelled was campus politics. He started by being elected president of the freshman class, and by the time he was a senior he was president of the entire student body.

He had a talent for picking an issue. One such, in his senior year, was the student appeal for permission to hold school dances on the campus. The strict Quaker authorities had always forbidden dancing, "were horrified at the idea" of sanctioning such self-indulgence on school property. Personally Nixon had little interest. He himself had not learned to dance until he was a sophomore and then not well and never with pleasure. Many years later, when he represented the United States at the 1957 Ghana independence ceremonies, he carried his early Quaker aversion to the point of avoiding dancing with the Duchess of Kent at a state ball in Accra. But, at Whittier, as student president, he used all the arts of debate and argumentation to carry the day, and eventually won over the board of directors by pointing out that college dances were being held anyway "in Los Angeles dens of iniquity."

He was graduated second in Whittier College's class of 1934. Harvard might have been his goal—he had been eligible to apply for a Harvard scholarship four years earlier—but Duke University was starting its law school that year and to establish high academic standards it offered nineteen scholarships for its first class of thirty-six students. Nixon was awarded one of these—a two-hundred-dollar tuition grant; to keep it he had to maintain a B average.

He was a slim, boyish twenty-one, with dark, heavy eyebrows and sparkling eyes, innocent of eccentricities in manner or appearance, when he arrived at Durham, North Carolina, in September 1934. Those were the middle years of the Great Depression, and Nixon's allowance from his family was only thirty-five dollars a month. That income he supplemented, under a grant from the New Deal's National Youth Administration, by doing research in the law library, at thirty-five cents an hour.

"I couldn't afford the dormitory," Nixon recalled later, "so at first I stayed at a downtown boardinghouse with fourteen preachers. But I had to move because of the noise." . . .

Early in his first year Nixon with three other students rented a room in a white ramshackle farmhouse set in the tall pines a mile from the campus. The four shared two double beds in a big bare room without lights or water and with only an old pot-bellied sheet-iron stove for heat.

Their landlady was a Mrs. Henderson who lived with her small son in a separate part of the house. Nixon's roommates were William R. Perdue, who eventually became vice-president of the Ethyl Corporation, Fred S. Albrink, who rose to a Navy captaincy, and Lyman Brownfield, who settled down to a prosperous law practice in Columbus, Ohio.

The virtue of "Whippoorwill Manor," as they called their lodgings, was that the rent was nominal—Nixon's recollection later was that they paid $5.00 a month apiece, but Brownfield set the figure much lower at $50 a year, or $12.50 apiece. Yet for all its primitiveness the place had its own pastoral attractions. Its remoteness bespoke a sense of physical and psychological elbowroom. In spring and fall the weather was mild and the walk through the woods was lovely. On winter nights they stoked the stove with papers and fired it red hot to break the chill while they undressed.

Part of the time they took their meals at Mrs. Pierce's boardinghouse—25 cents for a meal of "strictly home style cooking, serving, and eating," with fifteen or more crowded cheerfully around the table, all dedicated to the boardinghouse reach. To save money, the four bought secondhand textbooks, sometimes cooperatively.

For lack of heat and lights at the rooming house, they did their studying at the law library and took their showers at the gym. For three years, Nixon used his trunk for a closet.

Now and then Nixon had a half-hour to listen to one of the campus bands or to play handball, now and then an afternoon to go to a football game, or even more rarely an evening and the price of a date with a girl. He wrote for the law review, and during the summer between his second and third years he stayed on at Duke to do research on a long article. The one luxury he allowed himself was politics; as a senior he ran for the presidency of the Duke Bar Association and won.

At their graduation in 1937, Perdue, Brownfield, and Nixon headed the class in that order and automatically won election to the Order of the Coif, the national honorary law fraternity. In his choice of a career Nixon had first turned hopefully toward New York; there during the 1936 Christmas holidays, with two classmates, he applied for admission to some of the biggest and best-known law firms in the country. When this feeler drew only one provisional reply, he turned a speculative eye on the FBI.

One of Richard's lasting friendships at Duke was with Dean Horack, who wrote in a letter of recommendation to J. Edgar Hoover of the FBI: "Mr. Richard Nixon is one of the finest young men . . . that I have ever had in my classes. He is a very superior student, alert, aggressive, a fine speaker and one who can do an exceptionally good piece of research when called on to do so."

Hoover in reply promised Nixon an interview and an examination and careful consideration for an appointment, but in a quick shift of plans Nixon decided against the FBI and chose instead to practice law in his home state. To qualify he took a summer cram course for the California bar examinations. He was one of the 46 per cent that passed, and on November 9, 1937, he was sworn in as a member of the bar at San Francisco. Immediately afterward he joined the law offices of Wingert and Bewley, at the Bank of America Building, in Whittier.

SUGGESTIONS FOR STUDY

1. What is meant by "an anachronistic hangover of the vanishing cracker-barrel era"?

2. What characteristics of Nixon as a schoolboy and college man do you admire? Would you have wanted him for a friend? Why, or why not?

3. What does Nixon's comment about his father's refusal to take government help tell you about Nixon?

4. How often have you studied till two or three in the morning on your homework? What is your opinion of a school in which assignments require so much time for home study?

5. What is the value of a money-making job to a high-school student? The disadvantage?

6. What is your opinion of the value of high-school debating? How can it be helpful in later life? How can it be harmful?

7. Do you agree or disagree with the football coach's admiration for the boys who "sit on the bench"? Why?

8. Find statements which, though presented with disarming objectivity, are, in your opinion, selected and stated in such a way as to give a bad impression of Mr. Nixon. What bearing do your findings have upon your evaluation of campaign biographies?

Anne Frank's Diary

ANNE FRANK

Normally we think of school days as a happy time: the pleasant association with friends, the joy of learning in the stimulating atmosphere of the classroom and the library, sports, and much time devoted to just plain fun. Think, however, of what it would have been like to live these ordinarily pleasant years, say from age thirteen to fifteen, during World War II. And imagine further what these adolescent years would have been like if you had lived in Germany or Holland and had been a Jew.

The diary of Anne Frank is the moving and dramatic record of a girl who found herself in this unfortunate situation. Her own and another Jewish family, in order to escape the Gestapo, were forced to hide for two years and one month in an attic in Amsterdam. During this time Anne kept a diary, each entry of which she addressed to her diary, which she called Kitty. Over the two-year period Anne had a great deal of time to think and to mature mentally. She committed many of her innermost thoughts to the diary. And because she fell deeply in love with Peter, who was imprisoned with her, she had an opportunity to mature emotionally as well.

The following is a selection of "letters" taken from her complete diary. Although the letters presented here are in chronological order, not every letter for the time covered in Anne's life is included. You will, therefore, want to note carefully the date of each letter to see if any time has elapsed.

Sunday, 14 June, 1942

On Friday, June 12th, I woke up at six o'clock and no wonder; it was my birthday. But of course I was not allowed to get up at that hour, so I had to control my curiosity until a quarter to seven. Then I could bear it no longer, and went to the dining room, where I received a warm welcome from Moortje (the cat).

Soon after seven I went to Mummy and Daddy and then to the sitting room to undo my presents. The first to greet me was *you*, possibly the nicest of all. Then on the table there were a bunch of roses, a plant, and some peonies, and more arrived during the day.

I got masses of things from Mummy and Daddy, and was thoroughly spoiled by various friends. Among other things I was given *Camera Obscura*, a party game, lots of sweets, chocolates, a puzzle, a brooch, *Tales and Legends of the Netherlands* by Joseph Cohen, *Daisy's Mountain Holiday* (a terrific book), and some money. Now I can buy *The Myths of Greece and Rome*—grand!

Then Lies called for me and we went to school. During recess I treated everyone to sweet biscuits, and then we had to go back to our lessons.

Now I must stop. Bye-bye, we're going to be great pals!

Saturday, 20 June, 1942

I haven't written for a few days, because I wanted first of all to think about my diary. It's an odd idea for someone like me to keep a diary; not only because I have never done so before, but because it seems to me that neither I—nor for that matter anyone else—will be interested in the unbosomings of a thirteen-year-old schoolgirl. Still, what does that matter? I want to write, but more than that, I want to bring out all kinds of things that lie buried deep in my heart.

There is a saying that "paper is more patient than man"; it came back to me on one of my slightly melancholy days, while I sat chin in hand, feeling too bored and limp even to make up my mind whether to go out or stay at home. Yes, there is no doubt that paper is patient and as I don't intend to show this cardboard-covered notebook, bearing the proud name of "diary," to anyone, unless I find a real friend, boy or girl, probably nobody cares. And now I come to the root of the matter, the reason for my starting a diary: it is that I have no such real friend.

Let me put it more clearly, since no one will believe that a girl of

thirteen feels herself quite alone in the world, nor is it so. I have
darling parents and a sister of sixteen. I know about thirty people
whom one might call friends—I have strings of boy friends, anxious to catch a glimpse of me and who, failing that, peep at me
through mirrors in class. I have relations, aunts and uncles, who
are darlings too, a good home; no—I don't seem to lack anything.
But it's the same with all my friends, just fun and joking, nothing
more. I can never bring myself to talk of anything outside the
common round. We don't seem to be able to get any closer, that
is the root of the trouble. Perhaps I lack confidence, but anyway,
there it is, a stubborn fact and I don't seem to be able to do anything about it.

Hence, this diary. In order to enhance in my mind's eye the picture of the friend for whom I have waited so long, I don't want to
set down a series of bald facts in a diary like most people do, but I
want this diary itself to be my friend, and I shall call my friend
Kitty. No one will grasp what I'm talking about if I begin my letters to Kitty just out of the blue, so albeit unwillingly, I will start
by sketching in brief the story of my life.

My father was thirty-six when he married my mother, who was
then twenty-five. My sister Margot was born in 1926 in Frankfort-
on-Main, I followed on June 12, 1929, and, as we are Jewish, we
emigrated to Holland in 1933, where my father was appointed
Managing Director of Travies N.V. This firm is in close relationship with the firm of Kolen & Co. in the same building, of which
my father is a partner.

The rest of our family, however, felt the full impact of Hitler's
anti-Jewish laws, so life was filled with anxiety. In 1938 after the
pogroms, my two uncles (my mother's brothers) escaped to the
U.S.A. My old grandmother came to us, she was then seventy-
three. After May 1940 good times rapidly fled: first the war, then
the capitulation, followed by the arrival of the Germans, which is
when the sufferings of us Jews really began. Anti-Jewish decrees
followed each other in quick succession. Jews must wear a yellow
star, Jews must hand in their bicycles, Jews are banned from trains
and are forbidden to drive. Jews are only allowed to do their shopping between three and five o'clock and then only in shops which

bear the placard "Jewish shop." Jews must be indoors by eight
o'clock and cannot even sit in their own yards after that hour.
Jews are forbidden to visit theaters, movies, and other places of
entertainment. Jews may not take part in public sports. Swimming
baths, tennis courts, hockey fields, and other sports grounds are
all prohibited to them. Jews may not visit Christians. Jews must
go to Jewish schools, and many more restrictions of a similar kind.
So we could not do this and were forbidden to do that. But life
went on in spite of it all. Jopie used to say to me, "You're scared
to do anything, because it may be forbidden." Our freedom was
strictly limited. Yet things were still bearable.

Granny died in January 1942; no one will ever know how much
she is present in my thoughts and how much I love her still.

In 1934 I went to school at the Montessori Kindergarten and
continued there. It was at the end of the school year, I was in form
6B, when I had to say good-by to Mrs. K. We both wept, it was
very sad. In 1941 I went, with my sister Margot, to the Jewish
Secondary School, she into the fourth form and I into the first.

So far everything is all right with the four of us and here I come
to the present day.

Sunday morning, 5 July, 1942

Dear Kitty,

Our examination results were announced in the Jewish Theater
last Friday. I couldn't have hoped for better. My report is not at
all bad, I had one *vix satis*,[1] a five for algebra, two sixes, and the
rest were all sevens or eights. They were certainly pleased at home,
although over the question of marks my parents are quite different
from most. They don't care a bit whether my reports are good or
bad as long as I'm well and happy, and not too cheeky: then the
rest will come by itself. I am just the opposite. I don't want to be a
bad pupil; I should really have stayed in the seventh form in the
Montessori School, but was accepted for the Jewish Secondary.

[1] *vix satis:* scarcely satisfactory; barely passing.

When all the Jewish children had to go to Jewish schools, the headmaster took Lies and me conditionally after a bit of persuasion. He relied on us to do our best and I don't want to let him down. My sister Margot has her report too, brilliant as usual. She would move up with *cum laude* if that existed at school, she is so brainy. Daddy has been at home a lot lately, as there is nothing for him to do at business; it must be rotten to feel so superfluous. Mr. Koophuis has taken over Travies and Mr. Kraler the firm Kolen & Co. When we walked across our little square together a few days ago, Daddy began to talk of us going into hiding. I asked him why on earth he was beginning to talk of that already. "Yes, Anne," he said, "you know that we have been taking food, clothes, furniture to other people for more than a year now. We don't want our belongings to be seized by the Germans, but we certainly don't want to fall into their clutches ourselves. So we shall disappear of our own accord and not wait until they come and fetch us."

"But, Daddy, when would it be?" He spoke so seriously that I grew very anxious.

"Don't you worry about it, we shall arrange everything. Make the most of your carefree young life while you can." That was all. Oh, may the fulfillment of these somber words remain far distant yet!

Yours, Anne

Wednesday, 8 July, 1942

Dear Kitty,

Years seem to have passed between Sunday and now. So much has happened, it is just as if the whole world had turned upside down. But I am still alive, Kitty, and that is the main thing, Daddy says.

Yes, I'm still alive, indeed, but don't ask where or how. You wouldn't understand a word, so I will begin by telling you what happened on Sunday afternoon.

At three o'clock (Harry had just gone, but was coming back later) someone rang the front doorbell. I was lying lazily reading a book on the veranda in the sunshine, so I didn't hear it. A bit later, Margot appeared at the kitchen door looking very excited. "The S.S. have sent a call-up notice for Daddy," she whispered. "Mummy has gone to see Mr. Van Daan already." (Van Daan is a friend who works with Daddy in the business.) It was a great shock to me, a call-up; every one knows what that means. I picture concentration camps and lonely cells—should we allow him to be doomed to this? "Of course he won't go," declared Margot, while we waited together. "Mummy has gone to the Van Daans to discuss whether we should move into our hiding place tomorrow. The Van Daans are going with us, so we shall be seven in all." Silence. We couldn't talk any more, thinking about Daddy, who, little knowing what was going on, was visiting some old people in the Joodse Invalide; waiting for Mummy, the heat and suspense, all made us very overawed and silent.

Suddenly the bell rang again. "That is Harry," I said. "Don't open the door." Margot held me back, but it was not necessary as we heard Mummy and Mr. Van Daan downstairs, talking to Harry, then they came in and closed the door behind them. Each time the bell went, Margot or I had to creep softly down to see if it was Daddy, not opening the door to anyone else.

Margot and I were sent out of the room. Van Daan wanted to talk to Mummy alone. When we were alone together in our bedroom Margot told me that the call-up was not for Daddy, but for her. I was more frightened than ever and began to cry. Margot is sixteen; would they really take girls of that age away alone? But thank goodness she won't go, Mummy said so herself; that must be what Daddy meant when he talked about us going into hiding.

Into hiding—where would we go, in a town or the country, in a house or a cottage, when, how, where . . .?

These were questions I was not allowed to ask, but I couldn't get them out of my mind. Margot and I began to pack some of our most vital belongings into a school satchel. The first thing I put in was this diary, then hair curlers, handkerchiefs, schoolbooks, a comb, old letters; I put in the craziest things with the idea that we were going into hiding. But I'm not sorry, memories mean more to me than dresses.

At five o'clock Daddy finally arrived, and we phoned Mr. Koophuis to ask if he could come around in the evening. Van Daan went and fetched Miep. Miep has been in the business with Daddy since 1933 and has become a close friend, likewise her brand-new husband, Henk. Miep came and took some shoes, dresses, coats, underwear, and stockings away in her bag, promising to return in the evening. Then silence fell on the house; not one of us felt like eating anything, it was still hot and everything was very strange. We let our large upstairs room to a certain Mr. Goudsmit, a divorced man in his thirties, who appeared to have nothing to do on this particular evening; we simply could not get rid of him without being rude; he hung about until ten o'clock. At eleven o'clock Miep and Henk Van Santen arrived. Once again, shoes, stockings, books, and underclothes disappeared into Miep's bag and Henk's deep pockets, and at eleven-thirty they too disappeared. I was dog-tired and although I knew that it would be my last night in my own bed, I fell asleep immediately and didn't wake up until Mummy called me at five-thirty the next morning. Luckily it was not so hot as Sunday; warm rain fell steadily all day. We put on heaps of clothes as if we were going to the North Pole, the sole reason being to take clothes with us. No Jew in our situation would have dreamed of going out with a suitcase full of clothing. I had on two vests, three pairs of pants, a dress, on top of that a skirt, jacket, summer coat, two pairs of stockings, lace-up shoes, woolly cap, scarf, and still more; I was nearly stifled before we started, but no one inquired about that.

Margot filled her satchel with schoolbooks, fetched her bicycle, and rode off behind Miep into the unknown, as far as I was concerned. You see I still didn't know where our secret hiding place was to be. At seven-thirty the door closed behind us. Moortje, my little cat, was the only creature to whom I said farewell. She would have a good home with the neighbors. This was all written in a letter addressed to Mr. Goudsmit.

There was one pound of meat in the kitchen for the cat, breakfast things lying on the table, stripped beds, all giving the impression that we had left helter-skelter. But we didn't care about impressions, we only wanted to get away, only escape and arrive safely, nothing else. Continued tomorrow.

Yours, Anne

Sunday, 13 December, 1942

Dear Kitty,

I'm sitting cozily in the main office, looking outside through a slit in the curtain. It is dusk but still just light enough to write to you.

It is a very queer sight, as I watch the people walking by; it looks just as if they are all in a terrible hurry and nearly trip over their own toes. With cyclists, now, one simply can't keep pace with their speed. I can't even see what sort of person is riding on the machine.

The people in this neighborhood don't look very attractive. The children especially are so dirty you wouldn't want to touch them with a barge pole. Real slum kids with running noses. I can hardly understand a word they say.

Yesterday afternoon Margot and I were having a bath here and I said, "Supposing we were to take the children who are walking past, one by one, hoist them up with a fishing rod, give them each a bath, wash and mend their clothes, and then let them go again, then . . ." Margot interrupted me, "By tomorrow they would look just as filthy and ragged as before."

But I'm just talking nonsense; besides, there are other things to see—cars, boats, and rain. I like particularly the screech of the trams as they go by.

There is no more variety in our thoughts than there is for ourselves. They go round and round like a roundabout—from Jews to food and from food to politics. By the way, talking of Jews, I saw two Jews through the curtain yesterday. I could hardly believe my eyes; it was a horrible feeling, just as if I'd betrayed them and was now watching them in their misery. There is a houseboat immediately opposite, where a bargeman lives with his family. He has a small yapping dog. We only know the little dog by his bark and his tail, which we can see when he runs round the deck. Ugh! Now it's started to rain and most of the people are hidden under umbrellas. I see nothing but raincoats and occasionally the back of someone's hat. Really I don't need to see more. I'm gradually getting to know all the women at a glance, blown out with potatoes, wearing a red or a green coat, trodden-down heels and with a bag under their arms. Their faces either look grim or kind— depending on their husbands' dispositions.

Yours, Anne

Wednesday, 13 January, 1943

Dear Kitty,
Everything has upset me again this morning, so I wasn't able to finish a single thing properly.

It is terrible outside. Day and night more of those poor miserable people are being dragged off, with nothing but a rucksack and a little money. On the way they are deprived even of these possessions. Families are torn apart, the men, women, and children all being separated. Children coming home from school find that their parents have disappeared. Women return from shopping to find their homes shut up and their families gone.

The Dutch people are anxious too, their sons are being sent to Germany. Everyone is afraid.

And every night hundreds of planes fly over Holland and go to German towns, where the earth is plowed up by their bombs, and every hour hundreds and thousands of people are killed in Russia and Africa. No one is able to keep out of it, the whole globe is waging war and although it is going better for the Allies, the end is not yet in sight.

And as for us, we are fortunate. Yes, we are luckier than millions of people. It is quiet and safe here, and we are, so to speak, living on capital. We are even so selfish as to talk about "after the war," brighten up at the thought of having new clothes and new shoes, whereas we really ought to save every penny, to help other people, and save what is left from the wreckage after the war.

The children here run about in just a thin blouse and clogs; no coat, no hat, no stockings, and no one helps them. Their tummies are empty, they chew an old carrot to stay the pangs, go from their cold homes out into the cold street and, when they get to school, find themselves in an even colder classroom. Yes, it has even got so bad in Holland that countless children stop the passers-by and beg for a piece of bread. I could go on for hours about all the suffering the war has brought, but then I would only make myself more dejected. There is nothing we can do but wait as calmly as we can till the misery comes to an end. Jews and Christians wait, the whole earth waits; and there are many who wait for death.

Yours, Anne

Friday, 24 December, 1943

Dear Kitty,

I have previously written about how much we are affected by atmospheres here, and I think that in my own case this trouble is getting much worse lately.

"*Himmelhoch jauchzend und zum Tode betrübt*" [2] certainly fits here. I am "*Himmelhoch jauchzend*" if I only think how lucky we are here compared with other Jewish children, and "*zum Tode betrübt*" comes over me when, as happened today, for example, Mrs. Koophuis comes and tells us about her daughter Corry's hockey club, canoe trips, theatrical performances, and friends. I don't think I'm jealous of Corry, but I couldn't help feeling a great longing to have lots of fun myself for once, and to laugh until my tummy ached. Especially at this time of the year with all the holidays for Christmas and the New Year, and we are stuck here like outcasts. Still, I really ought not to write this, because it seems ungrateful and I've certainly been exaggerating. But still, whatever

[2] A famous line from Goethe: "On top of the world, or in the depths of despair."

you think of me, I can't keep everything to myself, so I'll remind you of my opening words—"Paper is patient."

When someone comes in from outside, with the wind in their clothes and the cold on their faces, then I could bury my head in the blankets to stop myself thinking: "When will we be granted the privilege of smelling fresh air?" And because I must not bury my head in the blankets, but the reverse—I must keep my head high and be brave, the thoughts will come, not once, but oh, countless times. Believe me, if you have been shut up for a year and a half, it can get too much for you some days. In spite of all justice and thankfulness, you can't crush your feelings. Cycling, dancing, whistling, looking out into the world, feeling young, to know that I'm free—that's what I long for; still, I mustn't show it, because I sometimes think if all eight of us began to pity ourselves, or went about with discontented faces, where would it lead us? I sometimes ask myself, "Would anyone, either Jew or non-Jew, understand this about me, that I am simply a young girl badly in need of some rollicking fun?" I don't know, and I couldn't talk about it to anyone, because then I know I should cry. Crying can bring such relief. . . .

Yours, Anne

Wednesday, 23 February, 1944

Dear Kitty,

It's lovely weather outside and I've quite perked up since yesterday. Nearly every morning I go to the attic where Peter works, to blow the stuffy air out of my lungs. From my favorite spot on the floor I look up at the blue sky and the bare chestnut tree, on whose branches little raindrops shine, appearing like silver, and at the seagulls and the other birds as they glide on the wind.

He stood with his head against a thick beam, and I sat down. We breathed the fresh air, looked outside, and both felt that the spell should not be broken by words. We remained like this for a long time, and when he had to go up to the loft to chop wood, I knew that he was a nice fellow. He climbed the ladder, and I followed; then he chopped wood for about a quarter of an hour, during which time we still remained silent. I watched him from where I stood, he was obviously doing his best to show off his strength. But I looked out of the open window too, over a large area of Amsterdam, over all the roofs and on to the horizon, which was such a pale blue that it was hard to see the dividing line. "As long as this exists," I thought, "and I may live to see it, this sunshine, the cloudless skies, while this lasts, I cannot be unhappy."

The best remedy for those who are afraid, lonely, or unhappy is to go outside, somewhere where they can be quite alone with the heavens, nature, and God. Because only then does one feel that all is as it should be and that God wishes to see people happy, amidst the simple beauty of nature. As long as this exists, and it certainly always will, I know that then there will always be comfort for every sorrow, whatever the circumstances may be. And I firmly believe that nature brings solace in all troubles.

Oh, who knows, perhaps it won't be long before I can share this overwhelming feeling of bliss with someone who feels the way I do about it.

Yours, Anne

A thought:

We miss so much here, so very much and for so long now: I miss it too, just as you do. I'm not talking of outward things, for we are looked after in that way; no, I mean the inward things. Like you, I long for freedom and fresh air, but I believe now that we have ample compensation for our privations. I realized this quite suddenly when I sat in front of the window this morning. I mean inward compensation.

When I looked outside right into the depth of Nature and God, then I was happy, really happy. And Peter, so long as I have that happiness here, the joy in nature, health and a lot more besides, all the while one has that, one can always recapture happiness.

Riches can all be lost, but that happiness in your own heart can only be veiled, and it will still bring you happiness again, as long as you live. As long as you can look fearlessly up into the heavens,

as long as you know that you are pure within and that you will
still find happiness.

Thursday, 6 April, 1944

Dear Kitty,
You asked me what my hobbies and interests were, so I want
to reply. I warn you, however, that there are heaps of them, so
don't get a shock!
First of all: writing, but that hardly counts as a hobby.
Number two: family trees. I've been searching for family trees
of the French, German, Spanish, English, Austrian, Russian, Nor-
wegian, and Dutch royal families in all the newspapers, books,
and pamphlets I can find. I've made great progress with a lot of
them, as, for a long time already, I've been taking down notes from
all the biographies and history books that I read; I even copy out
many passages of history.
My third hobby then is history, on which Daddy has already
bought me a lot of books. I can hardly wait for the day that I shall
be able to comb through the books in a public library.
Number four is Greek and Roman mythology. I have various
books about this too.
Other hobbies are film stars and family photos. Mad on books
and reading. Have a great liking for history of art, poets and painters. I may go in for music later on. I have a great loathing for algebra, geometry, and figures.
I enjoy all the other school subjects, but history above all!
Yours, Anne

Saturday, 15 July, 1944

"For in its innermost depths youth is lonelier than old age." I
read this saying in some book and I've always remembered it, and
found it to be true. Is it true then that grownups have a more difficult time here than we do? No. I know it isn't. Older people have

formed their opinions about everything, and don't waver before they act. It's twice as hard for us young ones to hold our ground, and maintain our opinions, in a time when all ideals are being shattered and destroyed, when people are showing their worst side, and do not know whether to believe in truth and right and God.

Anyone who claims that the older ones have a more difficult time here certainly doesn't realize to what extent our problems weigh down on us, problems for which we are probably much too young, but which thrust themselves upon us continually, until, after a long time, we think we've found a solution, but the solution doesn't seem able to resist the facts which reduce it to nothing again. That's the difficulty in these times: ideals, dreams, and cherished hopes rise within us, only to meet the horrible truth and be shattered.

It's really a wonder that I haven't dropped all my ideals, because they seem so absurd and impossible to carry out. Yet I keep them, because in spite of everything I still believe that people are really good at heart. I simply can't build up my hopes on a foundation consisting of confusion, misery, and death. I see the world gradually being turned into a wilderness, I hear the ever approaching thunder, which will destroy us too, I can feel the sufferings of millions and yet, if I look up into the heavens, I think that it will all come right, that this cruelty too will end, and that peace and tranquillity will return again.

In the meantime, I must uphold my ideals, for perhaps the time will come when I shall be able to carry them out.

Yours, Anne

SUGGESTIONS FOR STUDY

1. What reasons does Anne give for wanting to keep a diary? (See p. 78 for a discussion of the diary as biographical material.)
2. What is the "stubborn fact" mentioned on page 259? In what way does Anne's recognition of this fact show maturity on her part?

3. What did Anne take with her into hiding? Under similar circumstances, what would you take?

4. What was Anne's favorite subject in school? What is there about her circumstances which enables you to understand why she would prefer this subject?

5. According to Anne, who have the more difficult time in life, adults or adolescents? Give reasons why you agree or disagree with her on this point.

6. What is the belief which keeps Anne hanging on to her ideals? In her opinion what causes young people to lose their ideals? List some ideals which you have now. What can you do to keep from losing them in later life?

7. When the Gestapo broke into the attic where the Franks were hiding, they did so with orders to destroy or confiscate every thing of importance. In what way did the secret police fail in their mission?

8. What advantages are there to keeping a personal diary? Why do most people insist that their diaries be secret documents?

9. Keep a diary for a week. Then write a composition relating your experience as a diarist and telling whether or not you'd wish others to see your diary, either now or later—and why!

Prince Akihito Visits an American School

ELIZABETH GRAY VINING

Less than one year after the end of World War II, an American woman, Mrs. Elizabeth Gray Vining, was offered a position as tutor for the 12-year-old Crown Prince of Japan. She accepted the post and spent four years, 1946 to 1950, at her duties. In making her decision Mrs. Vining based her action on the fact that, in her own words, "Here was an opportunity to uphold the hands of those who were willing to risk greatly for peace, and to bring before the Emperor's son in his formative years the ideals of liberty and justice and good will upon which peace must be based if it is to endure."

In the following selection from Mrs. Vining's *Windows for the Crown Prince*, the tutor takes her pupil to visit an American school, one that was built in Japan and was staffed to teach children of American families in that country. The account of that visit and its effect on Prince Akihito and his associates will give you a refreshing view of American education.

WASHINGTON HEIGHTS was a housing project for Occupationaires, a jerry-built [1] community erected in a few months upon the former Yoyogi Military Parade Ground. It looked like an American company town with rows of box-like stucco houses set at careful angles to insure play space and clothes-drying areas, and scrubby little transplanted trees and sparse bushes struggling for life. There was a commissary, a PX, a gas station, a movie house, a chapel center, a club, and a school, and the people who lived there need never know they were in Japan, except for the profusion of Japanese servants, who were Americanizing themselves as rapidly as possible.

The school was very bright and cheerful, well equipped and

From WINDOWS FOR THE CROWN PRINCE, by Elizabeth Gray Vining. Copyright 1952 by Elizabeth Gray Vining. Published by J. B. Lippincott Company.

[1] *jerry-built:* built cheaply and unsubstantially.

well run, and with its rows of orange school buses, which collected children from American houses all over Tokyo, it looked like any one of countless elementary schools in the United States. When I visited it I was impressed by the zest with which teachers and children worked together with no apparent discipline but self-discipline, yet without confusion or waste energy. In June I took the Crown Prince and five of his classmates to visit it.

Two boys went from each section, and except for the Crown Prince they were elected by the boys themselves. The teachers had asked me to appoint the five boys, as was customary in such cases, but I seized the opportunity to give them a little practice in democratic procedures.

I began by putting on the blackboard the words *representative, nominate, vote, elect, ballot,* and *teller,* which I told them to look up in their dictionaries. Then I told them what they were to elect and had them discuss desirable qualities in their representatives, which also I wrote upon the blackboard. The boys who were chosen must be able, they decided, to speak and understand English; they must be interested in the American school and able to show their interest; they must be polite, saving their comments in Japanese for a later time; and they must be able to observe carefully and to report to the class afterwards. Then we had nominations and took the vote. The boy the Crown Prince nominated was not elected. He was a good boy, but his English was really not at that time quite adequate. It interested me that the rest of his section did not feel that they must vote for the Prince's choice. In all three sections the boys elected were among those I should have considered myself, if I had done the appointing.

All six boys were excused from classes for the occasion, and we met at Harajuku Station a little after nine one sunny morning. Besides the six boys and Tane and myself, the party included Mr. Nomura, Mr. Sumikura, the bright-eyed Zen Buddhist chamberlain, Dr. Sato, the senior doctor, Mr. Kikuchi, and Viscount Mori, who was a friend of teachers in both schools and had been one link in the arrangements.

In three cars we proceeded through the monotonous streets of Washington Heights. Word of the imperial visitor had somehow got around among the Japanese servants, many of whom were out bowing. A few extra policemen were on duty, but the Americans appeared oblivious.

Bill Carty of the Paramount News just happened to come out of his house at the moment when the three cars passed. A very quick-witted young man, he took in the situation at a glance, and I have never seen anyone move faster. He jumped into his blue jeep, turned it around on two wheels, and whizzing past us was on the school steps in time to photograph our arrival.

Miss Marjorie Fox, the blond young acting principal, a very able and attractive girl, was at the door to meet us. She took us first to the teachers' room, where we all sat down and she explained to us very simply and slowly the history and organization of the school. The boys all listened intently and understood practically everything that was said, more, in fact, than the grownups did.

The school was accustomed to entertaining Japanese visitors, mostly teachers who came to see in practice some of the new methods which they had previously encountered only in theory, and the children went ahead with their work without paying any attention to them.

We visited a sixth grade studying South America, listened to a singing lesson in the library, where a group was learning a Japanese song, and passed on to the fourth grade, which was doing a unit on Japan under the imaginative leadership of Miss Fern White. Here we stayed for half an hour, and there was quite an interchange between the American children and the Japanese boys.

The American children were making reports on silkworm culture when we came in. After they had finished those, they showed us the costumes and properties of the play, *Momotaro*, which they had presented a few days before. *Momotaro* is one of the oldest of Japanese folk tales, and concerns a boy who was found as a baby bobbing down the river inside a peach and was brought up by the old man and old woman who found him and who finally, with the help of a dog, a monkey and a pheasant, rescued Japan from the inroads of a pack of devils from another island.

The next day, when the Crown Prince had his regular lesson

alone with me, I asked him what had interested him most at the American school. He answered promptly, "The classrooms." To my "Why?" he replied, "Because the children were so free." After a thoughtful pause, he asked, "Why are they so free?"

I struggled to find simple words. "Because they are going to be free when they grow up," I said, "and they must learn how to be free now. They must learn how to work together, and how to be free without disturbing or hurting other people. The time to learn that is when they are in school."

A little later he said, "Which is better, the American way or the Japanese way?"

I never liked to make a direct comparison, and I tried to side-step. "Which do you think?" I asked.

The Prince laughed, and countered quickly, "No, I asked you."

So I answered honestly, "There are many fine things about Japanese schools, but I think the American way is better. If people are going to be free when they grow up, they must learn how when they are young."

He nodded thoughtfully, then asked me about English and French schools. I told him that I had never visited English or French schools and had only read about them, but that I thought they studied more Latin, more mathematics, and so forth, but did not have so much practice in doing things as American schools did.

While the Crown Prince and I were having this conversation, Tane was talking it all over with Mr. Sumikura. He told her that the men who visited the school with the boys had been much impressed by the kindness and courtesy and friendliness which they had met there, both from teachers and pupils. I in my turn was impressed by the fact that it was the spirit of the school that had struck them so much more than the equipment. It would have been so easy and natural for them to say in effect, "Yes, of course you can have a good school when you have such superior equipment," but there was nothing of that kind.

At various times later we discussed the question of freedom and discipline. They could not understand why the informality and spontaneity in the classrooms did not deteriorate into disorder.

There was one aspect of the Japanese schools that never ceased to trouble me. In all the American schools that I had ever known, the students could be depended on, if a teacher was called from the room, to carry on quietly by themselves. If they did not work, they at least played without disturbing other people. In a Japanese school, on the contrary, if a teacher is called out, pandemonium promptly ensues, and neighboring classes can scarcely hear themselves think. As long as the teacher is present, however, rigid decorum prevails, and it is a rare student who speaks without being called upon or who asks a question or volunteers an opinion of his own.

Our visit to the American school was returned the following September, when six children and four teachers from both Washington Heights and the still larger development called Grant Heights came to Koganei. Dr. Yoshinari Abe, the white-haired, genial president of the Gakushuin, who had succeeded Mr. Yamanashi, came to Koganei to meet them. Two of the children were girls and four were boys.

They visited my English class first. I was teaching the Crown Prince's section at that time. I had divided the class into pairs, and each pair in turn delivered a conversation on the subject of the Olympic Games. I called on the Crown Prince and his partner while the visitors were in the room and they acquitted themselves well.

They went next to the calligraphy class, where the boys were practising difficult characters with brush and *sumi* (charcoal ink) while the teacher lectured on the order of the strokes and the meaning and philosophy of the character, and then to a geography class which was studying the Kanto region, in which Tokyo is situated. They visited also the Kokaden,[2] on the steps of which a drawing class was making sketches of the trees and the playground and the fence around the Crown Prince's house. The gate was opened for the visitors and they looked in. From there they went to a gym class in which the Crown Prince took part. But the high point of the day turned out to be the chestnut grove, where they

[2] *Kokaden:* "Palace of Glorious Light," a ceremonial building, now used for the Crown Prince's private lessons.

were turned loose and allowed to gather all the chestnuts that they wanted. The gardener had made some simple bamboo tongs with which to pick up the burrs, and one small boy climbed up into a tree to shake the boughs. They collected burrs to take back to school to show the others, and they stuffed their own pockets with nuts.

"Here," said one youngster, presenting his rear elevation to Tane, "you put 'em in. It's too tight for me." So she poked and pushed until she squeezed the fat brown nuts into two very small hip pockets. She told me about it later with amusement.

As time went on there were still other exchanges between the two schools, a baseball game at Grant Heights in which each team was composed of both Japanese and Americans, so that there should be no possibility of international rivalry, followed by a feast in the lunch-room. The Crown Prince did not attend this event, but Prince Masahito went to another one with a group from his class, and played in a lively game of dodgeball and afterwards conquered a nourishing sandwich of staggering proportions and a mug of hot chocolate.

Further pleasant relations developed when the mothers of the Japanese boys gave a party for the American mothers and this was returned. More than one young woman from Grant Heights spoke to me of her disappointment that she had so few opportunities to meet Japanese people and her pleasure in the occasional contacts that she had.

SUGGESTIONS FOR STUDY

1. How did Mrs. Vining use the trip to Washington Heights as a teaching device before the trip? After the trip? Which of the two lessons seemed to you to be more effective?

2. What features of the American school which Prince Akihito visited were typical of American education? What ones were not typical?

3. Why did the Japanese boys visiting the American school understand the principal's explanation better than their Japanese elders did?

4. By describing the reactions of at least two persons, show that people get different impressions during a visit such as the one made to Washington Heights. What impressed Mrs. Vining as she observed the others' reactions to the things they had seen?

5. Do you agree with the author in what she says about the dependability of American students in the absence of a teacher? Why, or why not?

6. How might you have answered if you had been asked by the Prince, "Which is better, the American way or the Japanese way?"

7. Write a letter to some imaginary foreigner who has written to you, "Tell me some interesting things about your school."

8. From the selections in this section of *Portraits in Words* what new have you learned about the importance of schooling and education in most lives? What have you learned which you can apply to your own education? Write out your answer to the last question.

Love and Marriage

SOMEONE HAS SAID that marriage is like a pair of scissors—so joined that they cannot be separated, often moving in opposite directions, yet punishing anyone who comes between them. Perhaps you have oftener heard married life compared to harmony in music. In whatever way people may choose to describe marriage, most of them agree that it has a central and important place on the stage of life. To read about it is, therefore, both satisfying and helpful.

Poets, playwrights, essayists, and story-tellers have written voluminously about love and marriage. From the true-confessions magazine on the newsstand to the realistic psychological study, such as Henry James's novel, *Washington Square*, love and marriage figure in all types of literature. Among these different types, the picture of matrimony which the biographer can give holds great interest and value for us.

Stop to consider: in no part of your life are you less likely to be guided by reason—or to be more in need of it—than when you are head over heels in love. The biographer can bring to your attention many aspects of this bewildering, though thrilling, experience in what he tells of how a person met, loved, wooed, and wed his life-partner. To what extent were love and intelligence balanced? How were conflicts over family approval met? Why did or did not the marriage succeed? In discovering the answers to these questions you will be adding much profit to the pleasure of reading good biography.

Father Gives In

IRVING STONE

More often than not the making of a marriage includes some unhappy hours. The separation of a person from one family in order to create another seems to require some tension, some strained emotion. In your reading of biography you would like the author to present these moments of friction honestly.

The American biographer, Irving Stone, has written interestingly of such matters in the popular biography, *Immortal Wife*. In this life story of Jessie Benton Fremont, a book which has become a favorite with teen-agers, you can read how the young Jessie Benton used courage and intelligence to defend the man she loved against the disapproval of her father. Her father was a famous 19th century statesman whose spirit and integrity have been celebrated in John F. Kennedy's *Profiles in Courage*. The famed explorer of the American West, John Fremont, was the man whom Jessie loved, whose future greatness she foresaw, and to whom she became a devoted, a helpful—an "immortal"—wife.

To tell the story of love and conflict among these three strong-willed and individualistic persons, the author has "reimagined" much of the dialogue. The style of writing he uses has been called "fictionalized" biography; that is, he creates details of action, conversation, and thought which give life to the basic, though rather bare, historical facts.

SHE WAS SITTING at her desk in the small, characterless bedroom allotted to her at Miss English's Academy when she heard a throaty voice singing a plodding spiritual; it was the song that announced the presence of the washerwoman below. All laundry was delivered up the side of the building by means of a rope and pulley attached to each of the window sills; Jessie never could figure why, except that it saved tracking through the schoolhouse. She left the desk, a fragile one designed to hold only light books and light thoughts, and walked to the open window where

From IMMORTAL WIFE, by Irving Stone. Copyright 1944 by Irving Stone. Reprinted by permission of Doubleday & Company, Inc.

she could watch the woman tie the rope through the cross-handles of the basket and slowly haul it up to the rhythm of her song.

Leaning over the sill to take in her own basket, she was surprised to see a piece of writing paper resting on top of the crisply ironed clothes. She read, "I couldn't seem to wait until next Sunday. Isn't there some place we can talk? J. C. F."

Once again she looked out the window. This time she saw John Fremont standing beside the mulberry tree.

"Hello," she said, "this is a surprise."

"Can you come down?"

"No, but you can come up."

"Up?"

He gazed in bewilderment.

"Yes, up the mulberry tree. I'll come out from here and meet you in the top branch. That is, if you're not afraid of ripping those lovely blue breeches."

His delighted laughter drifted up to her as she watched him catch a high branch and swing himself onto it. She gathered her skirts tightly about her and climbed over the window sill onto a crisscross of sturdy limbs which formed a platform beneath her. She had no sooner seated herself than John Fremont's head appeared through the green leaves; with quick, graceful movements he was seated beside her. He had left his hat on the ground, and his hair was tousled from pushing upward through the foliage. They overlooked the rolling lawns of the school and the dark green forests along the Potomac. Sitting in the tree swinging her legs through the branches, Jessie Benton would have had difficulty convincing anyone she was almost seventeen.

"Isn't this a mild case of mutiny, Lieutenant Fremont," she asked, her eyes sparkling, "interfering with the curriculum of a girls' school? And how does it happen that the Army lets you wander around loose of a Wednesday afternoon?"

He smiled broadly.

"Messieurs Nicollet and Hassler held a conference over me at lunch today and decided that I had an acute attack of spring fever. That was the only way they could figure why I should be drawing girls' faces on my maps, instead of mountains and rivers."

"But it seems perfectly normal for a young man to draw girls' faces," she answered. "Haven't you ever done that before?"

"Oh, yes, but not for a number of years. Not since I was suspended from Charleston College."

To herself she said, I'm not going to like this, but it will be better to hear it now than later. Aloud she asked, "Who was the girl, Lieutenant Fremont?"

His dark eyes became serious. "Cecilia. She was the oldest daughter of a Creole family that escaped to Charleston in the midst of the San Domingo massacres. I grew up with her brothers; when we were sixteen, Cecilia and I decided we were in love."

"And were you?" she interrupted.

He hesitated for a moment, then said softly, "It wouldn't be right to disavow Cecilia; yes, I loved her as a boy loves his first sweetheart. She was beautiful with flashing eyes and a magnificent smile."

Completely jealous, Jessie struggled with herself not to ask, Was she prettier than I? She said instead, "But why did being in love cause you to be suspended from school?"

"I'm an impetuous man, Miss Jessie—"

"—or you wouldn't be at the top of a mulberry tree at three o'clock—"

"—and I just couldn't stay in the classrooms when there were green hills covered with wild flowers, and a boat to take out into the harbor to fish and swim from in secluded lagoons. And that was why I was never graduated. You see, Miss Jessie, I'm not one to take love lightly. When I fall in love, I throw over everything for it."

"I think I approve of that, Lieutenant. I have never been in love, but I should feel much the same way about it." She hesitated, embarrassed, then deciding to brave it through, added quickly, "Speaking of love, I had the most exciting news this morning; my friend Harriet Williams is going to marry Count Bodisco, the Russian minister."

"Count Bodisco?" he asked, with a puzzled, almost pained expression. "Isn't he the pretentious one who drives to his Embassy every day in a snow-white barouche drawn by four black horses?"

"Yes, I suppose he is pretentious, but in a kindly sort of way that does no one any harm. He's just trying to maintain the dignity of the Russian aristocracy in what some of the other ambassadors call a mudhole capital."

"But," he exclaimed angrily, "he's an old man. He must be past sixty!"

"Just sixty. And Harriet is just sixteen. But he is so terribly kind, the Count Bodisco. He has been most generous to her parents, who are having a difficult time with their large family. The Count is going to educate the children and see that they have a brilliant future. Just think, Lieutenant, last week Harriet wasn't good enough to be the May queen at this school and in a couple of weeks she will be Countess Alexander de la Bodisco, cousin to the Czar, with a state wedding and President Harrison giving away the bride."

He did not reply. Not a muscle of his face twitched, but she felt a withdrawing, as though he were sorry he had come out to the school today, as though the spirit of the man had flown from the mulberry tree back to the workroom of the Hassler home. When he spoke his voice had a metallic edge.

"You seem to approve all this, Miss Jessie."

She put a finger lightly as a falling leaf on his sleeve. "I would not want it for myself, Lieutenant Fremont," she said quietly. "But do you think it fair of us to judge Harriet Williams? The Count is an entirely charming and cultivated man, one whom everyone respects. I know that Harriet likes him and is grateful to him. She's being generous, Lieutenant; don't you think that we might be equally generous to her?"

He picked up the finger resting on his sleeve and kissed it. "Forgive me, Miss Jessie; it was boorish of me, but I turned cold when I thought that you—might approve—that is you yourself—"

"No, Lieutenant, not I myself. I will marry a young man, one whom I can love with all my heart. A man at the very beginning of his career, who has an uphill fight to attain the ends he wants, and who will let our marriage be a partnership in the fullest sense of the term."

He did not answer, looking instead toward the west where the sun was setting behind an early spring heat haze to deep purple. Jessie's eyes followed his gaze; they sat quietly in their bower taking in the beauty of the spring sunset and the fragrance of the budding foliage about them. She was the first to speak.

"Lieutenant, would you come to Harriet's wedding? I am sure it will be very gay."

"But I don't know Count Bodisco—"

"I was in the middle of a letter to Harriet when your note came up in the basket. Won't you let me ask her to have the Count invite you? There will be a ball after the wedding supper. Do you like to dance, Lieutenant Fremont?"

[Lieutenant Fremont had been invited to dinner. The first warmth of impending summer was in the drawing room, a hint of the intense heat that soon would settle over Washington City. Jessie had put on a cool gown. After the demitasse she suggested to John that they go into the back garden for a breath of air. They walked along the hedge-lined path to the summerhouse. It was shaded by tall sycamores and much of it was covered by a deep green ivy. They sat side by side on the hard white bench, the air filled with the fragrance of honeysuckle, and chatted lightly about the people at the dinner table.]

They smiled, conscious of each other, of the sharp smell of the night earth, the scent of late spring. The words were all gone. They moved close. Their hands touched, her hair touched his lips as she leaned her head on his shoulder.

Suddenly she looked up to see her father and Nicollet standing on the path. Nicollet smiled, murmured something to Thomas Benton. Her father stiffened. There was a hostile pause, then he came to the door of the summerhouse and announced in a cold voice:

"Jessie, come into the house."

She rose and, with John Fremont at her side, trailed her father and Nicollet up the garden path. In the light of the foyer she saw that her father's face had frozen, that Nicollet was apologetic. Ignoring Lieutenant Fremont's presence, Tom Benton said, "Jessie, will you excuse yourself, please? It is growing late."

In the strained silence the unspoken words of these four leaped out to each other and clashed and were withdrawn. Lieutenant Fremont spoke out in a small voice. "I too must excuse myself. Thank you for your hospitality, Senator Benton, and for your excellent dinner."

He bowed formally, took his hat from a corner stand and left the house.

Tom Benton and his daughter stood gazing at each other. Nicollet murmured his adieus and left.

Jessie trailed her father up the stairs to the library, watching his broad, angry back. After he had slumped far down in his chair, his hand covering his face, she asked softly, "What have I done?"

He looked at her, his face seeming haggard and old.

"Jessie," he said, "I'm stunned."

"What is it that you feel so strongly about?" she queried.

"That is a silly and evasive question," he replied harshly. "You were so obvious that even Nicollet commented on it. I've been so absorbed in my work that I failed to notice,—"

Her voice too became firm. "I've done nothing but enjoy Lieutenant Fremont's company. You've done as much yourself. What is it you are accusing me of?"

"Of falling in love with him," he shot back.

There it is, she thought, out in the open at last. I have never let myself think it, and now Father has put it into words.

"You may be right," she answered quietly. "I had not let that word come into my consciousness. I knew that Lieutenant Fremont was the most delightful and sympathetic young man I had ever met. But you never approved of romantic novels, and there is very little in the literature of exploration to tell a young girl when she is in love. Now that you face me with it, I think I am in love with him."

With a tight voice Tom Benton pronounced, "Lieutenant Fremont will not come to this house any more; he will not be invited; and you will not see him again."

"But why are you punishing him?" she demanded.

"He has made you fall in love with him."

"Made me!" Her face was as taut and pale as his. "Have I no

mind of my own? Really, Father, that's unworthy of the years of training you have given me; you know that I am not a weak or silly child—"

"Nevertheless he is not coming here any more. You will not see him. It's far too advantageous a marriage to tempt the young lieutenant with."

"Lieutenant Fremont is no adventurer. He is one of the most talented and promising men in Washington. You said so yourself."

"Perhaps. But he is not so promising that he can't see the benefits of a marriage to Senator Benton's daughter."

Jessie's eyes flashed her indignation. She walked to the window, put aside the draperies and stared out over the dark green fields.

"So you think you have produced a daughter so unattractive and so unstimulating that the lieutenant could not fall in love with me for my own sake?"

Tom Benton said more quietly, "Forgive me, my dear, I did not mean to disparage your charms or your worth." But the coldness did not leave his voice. "Jessie, it is my job to protect you. You are too young to know—"

"Senator," she said deliberately, "that's the worst piece of sophistry you've ever been guilty of: Did you think I was too young at four to learn how to read, or too young at seven to go on hunting and camping trips with you, too young at eight to watch you from the Senate galleries, to read these heavy, serious books with you; too young at ten to begin writing down your speeches, too young at fourteen to become your adviser and confidante, to walk the streets of Washington at night while you were thrashing out your problems, using me as a sounding board? And now suddenly you thrust a calendar in my face, tell me that I am undeveloped, not quite seventeen, a child who doesn't know what she is doing."

She did not pause to give him an opportunity to answer, but pursued her advantage ruthlessly, even as Tom Benton did when his own desires were at stake.

"I've never questioned your judgment; when you praised me for some good work I had done, I worked ten times harder to earn more praise, until you said that you'd soon be going to school to me. And now, at the first turn of events that displeases you, you become heavy-handed, the outraged father laying down the law."

Tom eyed her calmly. "That was quite a speech, Jessie; perhaps you should be the senator from Missouri."

She walked quickly to her father's side, her manner conciliatory.

"I don't want to be the senator from Missouri; I want to be the daughter of the senator. You know how much I love you, Father; we have never had to talk about that. You've led me gently by the hand through all these happy years; you can't suddenly put a ring through my nose on the pretext that it's for my own good."

"What has Lieutenant Fremont said to you?"

"Nothing—not with his lips anyway. Perhaps I've been reading his mind, but that kind of evidence isn't admissible in a court of law, is it?"

"I am not amused."

"Lieutenant Fremont has been very circumspect," she continued. "You are forcing issues, Father, and it has never been your tactic to bludgeon your way through delicate situations."

"I've taught you too well," he moaned.

"Come now, Tom," she chided. "You gave me weapons with which to fight; did you think I was not going to use them whenever my happiness was threatened?"

"Your happiness! But this is fantastic, Jessie! It is the first time you have had a romantic attachment, and you talk to me about your happiness! Lieutenant Fremont simply will not be invited to this house any more."

They stood in silence staring at each other, two pairs of brooding eyes, as alike as a reflection in a gold-backed mirror. Their wills met too, their stubbornness. Then Jessie turned and went to her room.

If not for the presence of Grandmother McDowell, who had arrived for her annual spring visit with the Bentons, the following weeks would have been unendurable for Jessie. Both at school and at home she suffered the agonizing experience of having Lieutenant Fremont's face fade from her mind. The separation had been the more painful because there was no one in the Benton home with whom she could talk about John Fremont. That was why she had been happy to see Grandmother McDowell again.

Jessie had not needed to say more than a few sentences about Lieutenant Fremont before Grandmother McDowell had nodded her head and commented:

"So it has come to my Jessie at last. I was getting worried about you; by the time I was your age I already had a daughter."

The death of President William H. Harrison only one month after his inauguration furnished Jessie with her first opportunity to see John.

The morning of the funeral dawned cold and rainy. Though Grandmother McDowell wore a black silk dress with a wadded black cape, Jessie's mother permitted her to wear a dress and coat of dark green velvet. Tom Benton dropped his daughter and mother-in-law outside the Hassler house, then hurried on to the Senate for the official ceremonies. When the front door was opened by Lieutenant Fremont dressed in his full regimentals, Jessie exclaimed:

"Lieutenant, why aren't you with your regiment?"

"I developed a cold. The doctor at the armory did not consider it wise for me to march in this rain."

They stood smiling at each other, an eager smile. Then Jessie turned to her grandmother.

"This is the young lieutenant I have been telling you about."

"I'm glad to meet you, young man. I must confess I came more to see you than to get a better view of the funeral. At my age one is not overly partial to funerals."

"But Grandmother," Jessie exclaimed, "you couldn't have known that Lieutenant Fremont would be here. He was supposed to be marching with his regiment."

"Do tell!" murmured Grandmother McDowell.

John bent over to kiss the old woman's hand, then led them up to the second-floor workroom which had been cleared of its tables and working paraphernalia. He had placed potted azaleas on the window sills and there were many vases filled with geraniums and roses. A bright fire was burning in the fireplace, the cedar wood giving off a pungent fragrance. Before the fireplace a low table had been set for tea; comfortable chairs had been placed in front of the windows overlooking Pennsylvania Avenue. Jessie watched

John as he received two ladies who also had been invited to this vantage spot. She sat at the big windows with the other women listening to stories about William Henry Harrison, but John was standing behind her chair and her head was spinning; the feeling that ran between them was strong and certain.

In the distance could be heard faintly the dirge of the funeral march; in another moment six white horses could be seen pulling the plumed hearse which was carrying the body of President Harrison up the slope of Capitol Hill. As two more women were ushered into the room, Jessie quickly rose to offer her chair, and John led her to the fireplace. Here they sat opposite each other over the tea table gazing into the yellow-red flames. The women assembled at the windows had their eyes on the solemn scene below; Jessie could not have felt their privacy more complete had they been alone.

"I've been to the Senate twice while Senator Benton was speaking," he said. "I hoped I might catch a glimpse of you there."

"But I am still attending Miss English's Academy."

"I knew our separation was only temporary. I knew that nothing could keep us apart, not even—forgive me—Senator Benton."

Jessie did not speak; she could not have uttered a word if her life had been at stake. He took her hand between his.

"Miss Jessie, perhaps a funeral procession is not the best possible background to speak of love, but I am so full of the subject that I am afraid I would find any moment and any background a good one."

"Always the impetuous one," she murmured.

"You have a way of reading my eyes," he said. "I think you've read what I feel for you."

"No," she mocked gently, "when it comes to love, I'm illiterate. Or so Father thinks."

"Do you know the first thing I said to Mr. Nicollet when I returned from the musicale at Georgetown? I said, 'I have fallen in love at first sight.' When you stormed into the reception room, indignant because an injustice had been done to your friend, I knew at once that something important was happening to me; when you laughed and your laughter enveloped me with its warmth I knew that the rest of my life would be barren unless I could be with you always. My one thought was how and where I might meet Miss Jessie again. I love you," he said very quietly. "I loved you from that very first instant. I think you love me too."

Her eyes glowed.

"Surely you too believe that it's all part of a design, that if we searched the world, both of us, spent years looking for the one man or woman who would be our most perfect mate—"

"Yes, I believe that," she replied softly.

"Mr. Benton is telling the truth when he says I am a penniless lieutenant with only modest prospects—"

"Modest prospects! You have the most brilliant prospects of any young man in America; you will do great things—"

"We will do them together, Jessie."

She withdrew her hand from his, sat up stiffly in her chair, her slight body rigid.

"You are serious about that?" she demanded. "I must warn you, I can't live without work to do. I could not marry a man who would not let me work by his side as an equal and his partner. I am not a feminist, you will never hear me cry for equal rights for women. I believe that the greatest job a woman can do in the world is to be a good wife, but I believe that to be a good wife a woman must stand shoulder to shoulder and brain to brain alongside her husband." Her voice faltered. "I simply must have a man who will have faith in my judgment, who will make me his confidante, who will not try to exclude me because I am a woman, tell me to go out into society and amuse myself."

She relaxed in her chair, but her hazel eyes were still intense.

"I will never embarrass you, John Fremont; I want no credit or limelight or public acclaim; I will never stalk the street with a bundle of causes in my hand so that my friends will duck down side alleys when they see me coming. But I want to help you, I want to make my own small contribution to your work, I want to extend your reach by just a little bit, that little bit of which I am capable."

She cast down her eyes and sat laving her small hands as though in anguish.

"There, I've said it all. I hope it hasn't repulsed you, that you will not think it unwomanly of me."

She looked up at him. His eyes were closed, his twenty-eight-year-old face had lines in it, his forehead was furrowed.

"I hope I'm not being romantic about this," she said. "I know that from the viewpoint of the outside world it is an unwanted task. I know that most men prefer an amusing and charming wife who will bear their children and manage their houses and be there when they come home from a day's or a year's work. It is a full-time task to bear children and raise them and watch after the health of the family and keep the home beautiful and peaceful so that they can grow up to be fine human beings. It is enough for any one woman. But can you understand, Lieutenant, that it is not enough for me? I am my father's daughter; if I were a man I would be deep in a profession already. Since I am a woman I must work through my husband, and so I must find a husband who will let me achieve this ambition, who will allow me to become as indispensable in his work as in his life."

The slowly dying dirge of the funeral procession could be heard in the room; several of the women at the window were weeping quietly. Lieutenant Fremont had started to speak.

"I love you, Jessie," he was saying. "I would not want an Anne Royall, but your radiance and charm dissipate my fears. Jessie, I will always love you, of that you may be sure. I may make other mistakes, I may fail you in other things, I may never come up to your full expectations, but I will always love you."

A flicker of tender amusement came into her eyes, and she was glad to feel her spirit lighten; she did not want this sacred moment which she would never forget, no matter how old she grew, to be too deadly in earnest.

"Spoken as a true French poet, Monsieur Fremont," she said with a twinkle.

"I will confess I have been writing verse to you. Bad verse, Miss Jessie, astonishingly bad verse, considering how deep a love it sprang from."

"I am not marrying you as a poet, Lieutenant Fremont, and I will not hold your bad verses against you."

With one of those lightning changes to which she had not yet grown accustomed, his eyes clouded.

"You really ought not to accept me, you know," he said sternly. "I am suspect in this affair. You can see how it would be a marriage of convenience: being Senator Benton's son-in-law would be of tremendous help to me in my career; the senator would use his influence in the Congress and the War Department to get me promoted quickly, put in command of expeditions—"

Jessie answered with mock seriousness:

"Yes, of course, but then you realize, Lieutenant Fremont, that I am too young to know what I am doing."

"Quite! At sixteen you are an irresponsible child."

"—it will be several years yet before I will be old enough to make up my mind."

His dark mood had vanished.

"Since you are not marrying me as a poet," he asked eagerly, "when can I expect that you will marry me as a second lieutenant in the Topographical Corps?"

"That is the one answer I don't know. You must promise me to keep this secret until I can talk with Father."

"Will we have to wait long? You will forgive me if I appear impatient."

"We won't have to wait as long as he waited: Mother kept refusing him for six years. She said, 'I'll never marry a redhead, an army man, or a Democrat.' Father replied, 'I can't change the color of my hair and I can never be anything but a Democrat, but I will get out of the army: I only went into it to lick the British.' Let us allow circumstances to precipitate the right moment for telling him."

"I will keep our engagement a secret," he smiled; "what a beautiful word, engagement. My darling Jessie, now we are engaged to be married, and all our lives we will be engaged, engaged in valuable work, engaged in being happy and loving each other."

The funeral procession had passed out of view. Lieutenant Fremont threw another log on the fire, brought the chairs from the windows and made his guests comfortable. The air had grown warmer; the rain was beautiful as it slanted angularly over Pennsylvania Avenue. He disappeared for a moment, returning with a tray of ices, French *gateaux* [1] and a Russian samovar. He chatted happily as he poured the tea.

Heavens, thought Jessie, is my happiness that apparent too? If it is, our secret will be all over Washington within an hour.

"How was the funeral cortege?" she asked her grandmother.

"I would say that it served its purpose," Grandmother McDowell replied.

The next morning she awoke and burst into song, then realized that she might as well tell her father everything that had happened as go into his presence unable to contain her happiness. She put on a blue flannel robe, combed her hair, tied it on top of her head with a ribbon and went downstairs.

She had no sooner joined the family at the breakfast table than Josheem and Joshaam came in, each carrying two potted azalea plants. Tom Benton looked at the card which accompanied them, failing to note that it had been addressed to Mrs. Benton. He laid down his knife and fork, pushed aside the cutlet he had been vigorously dispatching and stared at his daughter.

"Was Lieutenant Fremont at home yesterday, by any chance?"

"Yes," admitted Jessie, "he was."

"Why wasn't he marching in the procession?"

"He had a cold."

"Did you know when you went to Hassler's that Lieutenant Fremont would be there?"

"No, Father, I don't enjoy second sight. But to be quite honest with you, I did hope—"

"I don't like this kind of deception, Jessie, even when it seems so innocent on the surface. I forbade you to see Lieutenant Fremont, and you have disregarded my wishes."

The rest of the family had silently finished breakfast and slipped out of the room. Jessie and her father were alone.

"Will you kindly tell me what took place at Hassler's yesterday? For it is apparent that something did take place."

---

[1] *gateaux:* cakes (French).

She was unwilling to tell a deliberate lie. Since she saw that she must expose her hand, she played it the bold way.

"I'll let you in on a secret, Father, if you promise not to tell anyone."

"A secret from whom?"

"From you, darling. I am engaged to Lieutenant John Charles Fremont!"

When Thomas Benton's anger was red hot he could get off the most profane diatribes to be heard in Washington; but when his anger was icy he held this emotion in leash and chose his words fastidiously.

"So you are engaged! Without my knowledge, without my consent, and against my express orders that you were not to see Lieutenant Fremont."

She could think of no reply, but only hung her head.

"Do you think your life is going to end that you must rush precipitately into clandestine arrangements? What has happened to your sense of perspective, Jessie?"

She realized with a shock that this was her first major difference with her father. She didn't like it, she didn't want to create a change in their relationship, but neither could she avoid this scene. Should her father gather that she was heavyhearted at quarreling with him, he would bludgeon her emotionally until she gave in. She had to keep the contest in the mood in which she could best and most effectively oppose him.

Pushing aside the plate before her, she stretched out her arms across the table.

"If I felt that my marriage to Lieutenant Fremont would separate me from you, Father, or in any way hurt you, I would do what you ask: I would give him up. I would give up whoever it might be, without your asking. But John Fremont is the fulfillment of your own ambitions. He will explore and conquer the wilderness. He will open the West, create the empire you have been tracing on maps and have had me tracing since I was five."

Joshaam padded in with a ham steak, grits baked in a casserole with orange honey, and a silver pitcher of chocolate. Jessie let him put the food down, then pushed her chair back from the table. Her young face was sober.

"Tom Benton, you should be the one pleading for this marriage, and I should be the one holding out: for I know what your dreams and plans will do to him. I know of the hardships and ever present dangers that will face him; I know of the long and bitter separations which your collaboration will bring about. It's a hard and painful future to think about, Father, but I rush out to meet it with open and loving arms."

"The first thing I know, you'll be telling me you are marrying him for my sake." After a pause, he cried, "Jessie, would you really set yourself up against my wishes? Would you oppose me in anything so critical?"

"If I let you deprive me of the most important thing in my life, Papa, my love for you might turn to hatred. I want you to protect and counsel me, but in the end it must be I and not you who determine my life. Surely you can see the justice of that?"

Thomas Benton alone had taught her to respect logic instead of people, to form her opinions on the basis of fact, and then stand by them through hell and high water. But Tom Benton shouted in his rage:

"And who is this sixteen-year-old that dares to defy her father?"

"A little girl who cries, 'Hurrah for Jackson!' " [2]

His anger was caught up, stopped short by the summoning of their past.

Jessie drew her chair to the table, helped herself to the breakfast. She spoke quietly.

"All I can say, Tom Benton, is that you underestimate yourself. If I am a misguided fool and romantic idiot at seventeen, then your efforts and work are wasted, and I shall still be a fool at twenty-seven or sixty-seven. Let us say instead that I matured early owing to the fact that my father was a maturing influence, owing to the fact that his intensive education had a sobering influence on me. Perhaps if during those years I had been thinking

[2] At three Jessie had won her father's smile when, after some childish mischief, she said these same words, playing on his strong political loyalties.

about nothing but pretty manners and conquering the hearts of
young men, instead of wildernesses, lost rivers, and hostile Indian
tribes, I would not have found it only natural to fall in love with
the one man who I think is going to do more to open that West
than anyone alive today."

Her voice carried a touch of bitterness. "Perhaps you should
have let me have a normal childhood of dolls and games and gig-
gling. Perhaps that would have been better for me."

Tom passed a heavy hand over his eyes.

"Jessie, my dear, have I really robbed you of your childhood?
Your mother—"

With a tinkling laugh she dropped her fork, ran around the
table and sat herself on her father's lap.

"For heaven's sake, Papa, don't let me take you in with my
ridiculous feminine logic. By this time tomorrow you would know
I had tricked you out of your opposition. You gave me the most
wonderful and exciting childhood any girl ever had. All I'm trying
to say is that I don't feel like a child, that you didn't leave much
for the finishing school to finish. That it is possible for some people to live more and learn more and enjoy and suffer more, within
the passage of time, than others."

"Yes, of course."

But when he looked up at her with hurt eyes, she realized that
he was not thinking along with her; that he was feeling the impending loss not only of his favorite daughter, but as he himself
often had told her, of his favorite human being. Intuitively she
understood by imagining what her world would be like with
Thomas Hart Benton gone out of it. She stroked his hot brow.

"You don't understand, child," he groaned; "a man needs time
to prepare in his mind for changes as important as this. In the back
of my head there was always the idea that when you fell in love
and wanted to marry, I would be ready for it. It wouldn't descend
upon me when I was unprepared."

"But, Father, we have no control over when we will meet the
person we love: it might be at fifteen or fifty—or never. Would it
be better to wait until I was eighteen or nineteen or twenty, when
your mind would be prepared, and marry someone with whom

you had little in common, than to marry a bit earlier than you had anticipated, and make a perfect marriage?"

She walked to the window and stood leaning against the sill, the sun warming her back.

"Whenever I have thought of marriage, it was to a man whose work I could be excited about. I have always believed that the woman who is excluded from a man's work has no contact with the best part of her husband's life. Where could I find anyone better suited to me than Lieutenant Fremont?"

Her father grunted, "Jessie, you have too many answers."

SUGGESTIONS FOR STUDY

1. What signs are there, early in the selection, that Jessie Benton loved John Fremont? That John loved Jessie?

2. What do Jessie and John reveal about their own ideas of marriage during their discussion of the approaching marriage of Jessie's friend Harriet to the Russian Count?

3. Follow the arguments between Senator Benton and his daughter over the latter's early interest in Lieutenant John Fremont. With whom do you agree and why?

4. In the first discussion that Jessie has with her father about Fremont, what facts do you learn about Jessie's earlier life?

5. Who comforted Jessie the most in her isolation from Fremont? What other signs of understanding did that person show?

6. During their meeting at the funeral, John told Jessie (p. 290), "surely you too believe that it's all part of a design, that if we searched the world, both of us, spent years looking for the one man or woman who would be our most perfect mate—." Jessie agrees with him. Do you agree or disagree with him? Why?

7. On the morning after the funeral Jessie and her father had a quarrel. State the arguments used on both sides and point out the merits of each.

8. What does this selection reveal of the history of our nation during the 1840's?

9. Read the section on Senator Thomas Hart Benton in *Profiles in Courage,* by John F. Kennedy. State ways in which the picture of him given there agrees or disagrees with the characterization made by Irving Stone.

10. What details of this selection are obviously fictionalized? Why do you like (or dislike) fictionalized biography?

FOR FURTHER READING

Adversary in the House; Clarence Darrow for the Defense; Jack London, Sailor on Horseback; Love Is Eternal; Lust for Life; Passionate Journey; President's Lady; The Agony and the Ecstasy, all by Irving Stone.

Scientists in Love

EVE CURIE

It is quite likely that you have heard of Marie and Pierre Curie, the discoverers of radium. And it is probable that you have read about them as scientists—but not as a young man and a young woman. This selection from *Madame Curie* (written by their younger daughter Eve) tells about the meeting of Pierre Curie, a promising young French scientist, and Marie Sklodovska, a brilliant young Polish girl, and the events which led to their marriage. Because of previous disappointments in young love, both had forsworn love and marriage. Moreover, in the way of their love there also stood their dedication to science and their sense of loyalty both to their native countries and to their families, in which prevailed a strong sense of comradeship. Read to discover how this gifted young couple overcame these obstacles and found happiness in marriage.

MARIE HAD RULED love and marriage out of her life's program.

There was nothing extremely original in that. The poor girl, disappointed and humilitated in the failure of her first idyll, swore to love no more; still more, the Slavic student exalted by intellectual ambitions easily decided to renounce the things that make the servitude, happiness, and unhappiness of other women, in order to follow her vocation. In all ages women who burn to become great painters or great musicians have disdained the norm, love and motherhood. Most often they are converted to family life when their dreams of glory come to nothing; or else, when they do make careers, it is in fact at the sacrifice of their sentimental life.

Marie had built for herself a secret universe of implacable rigor, dominated by the passion for science. Family affection and the attachment to an oppressed fatherland also had their place in it, but this was all. Nothing else counted, nothing else existed. Thus had she decreed, the beautiful creature of twenty-six who lived alone in Paris and met young men every day at the Sorbonne [1] and in the laboratory.

Marie was obsessed by her dreams, harassed by poverty, overdriven by intensive work. She did not know leisure and its dangers. Her pride and timidity protected her, as did her distrust: ever since the Z.'s had rejected her as a daughter-in-law she had had the vague conviction that poor girls found no devotion or tenderness among men. Stiffened by fine theories and bitter reflections, she clung fiercely to her independence.

No, it is not surprising that a Polish girl of genius, isolated by her arid existence, should have preserved herself for her work. But it is surprising, indeed wonderful, that a scientist of genius, a Frenchman, should have kept himself for that Polish girl, should have unconsciously waited for her. It is wonderful that at the time when Marie, still almost a child in the narrow apartment of Novolipki Street, dreamed of coming to study some day at the Sorbonne, Pierre Curie, returning home from that same Sorbonne, where he was already making important discoveries in physics, should have written down in his diary these melancholy lines:

. . . Woman loves life for the living of it far more than we do: women of genius are rare. Thus, when we, driven by some mystic love, wish to enter upon some anti-natural path, when we give all our thoughts to some work which estranges us from the humanity nearest us, we have to struggle against women. The mother wants the love of her child above all things, even if it should make an imbecile of him. The mistress also wishes to possess her lover, and would find it quite natural to sacrifice the rarest genius in the world for an hour of love. The struggle almost always is unequal, for women have the good side of it: it is in the name of life and nature that they try to bring us back. . . .

Years had passed. Pierre Curie, devoting body and soul to scientific research, had married none of the insignificant or nice little girls who had come his way. He was thirty-five years old. He loved nobody.

When he was idly running through his diary, abandoned long ago, and re-read the notes once made in ink that was already growing pale, a few words full of regret and dull nostalgia caught his attention: ". . . women of genius are rare. . . ."

When I came in, Pierre Curie was standing in the window recess near a door leading to the balcony. He seemed very young to me, although he was then aged thirty-five. I was struck by the expression of his clear gaze and by a slight appearance of carelessness in his lofty stature. His rather slow, reflective words, his simplicity, and his smile, at once grave and young, inspired confidence. A conversation began between us and became friendly; its object was some questions of science upon which I was happy to ask his opinion.

Such were the words Marie was to use to describe their first meeting, which took place at the beginning of 1894.

A Pole, M. Kovalski, professor of physics in the University of Fribourg, was visiting Paris with his young wife, whom Marie had met at Szczuki. It was their honeymoon, but a scientific expedition as well. M. Kovalski gave some lectures in Paris, and attended the sessions of the Physics Society. On his arrival he had inquired after Marie and had asked her how she was. Marie had confided in him her worries of the moment: the Society for the Encouragement of National Industry had ordered a study from her on the magnetic properties of various steels. She had begun the researches in Professor Lippmann's laboratory; but she had to analyze minerals and group samples of metal, which required a cumbersome equipment—too cumbersome for the already crowded laboratory. And Marie did not know what to do, where to conduct her experiments.

"I have an idea," Joseph Kovalski said to her after some moments of reflection. "I know a scientist of great merit who works in the School of Physics and Chemistry in the Rue Lhomond. Perhaps he might have a workroom available. In any case he could give you some advice. Come and have tea tomorrow evening, after dinner, with my wife and me. I will ask the young man to come. You probably know his name: it is Pierre Curie."

In the course of the calm evening passed in the young couple's room in a quiet boardinghouse, immediate sympathy brought the French physicist and the Polish student together.

Pierre Curie had a very individual charm made up of gravity and careless grace. He was tall. His clothes, cut on ample, old-fashioned lines, hung a bit loosely about his body, but they became him: he had much natural elegance. His hands were long and sensitive. His regular, almost motionless face, lengthened by a rough beard, was made beautiful by his peaceful eyes with their incomparable look, deep and serene, detached from all things.

Although this man maintained a constant reserve and never lifted his voice, it was impossible not to notice his expression of rare intelligence and distinction. In a civilization in which intellectual superiority is seldom allied to moral worth, Pierre Curie was an almost unique specimen of humanity: his mind was both powerful and noble.

The attraction he felt from the first moment for the foreign girl who spoke so little was doubled by intense curiosity. This Mlle. Sklodovska was truly a rather astonishing person. . . . She was Polish, come from Warsaw to study at the Sorbonne, had passed first in the physics examination last year, would pass her mathematics examination in a few months. . . . And if between her ashen-gray eyes a little preoccupied wrinkle appeared, was it not because she didn't know where to install her apparatus for the study of magnetism in steel?

The conversation, at first general, was soon reduced to a scientific dialogue between Pierre Curie and Marie Sklodovska. Marie, with a shade of timidity and deference, asked questions and listened to Pierre's suggestions. He in turn explained his plans, and described the phenomena of crystallography which fascinated him and upon which he was now engaged in research. How strange it was, the physicist thought, to talk to a woman of the work one loves, using technical terms, complicated formulæ, and to see that woman, charming and young, become animated, understand, even discuss certain details with an infallible clear-sightedness. . . . How sweet it was!

He looked at Marie's hair, at her high, curved forehead and her hands already stained by the acids of the laboratory and roughened by housework. He was disconcerted by her grace, which the absence of all coquetry made more surprising. He dug from his memory all that his host had told him about the girl when he had invited them together: she had worked for years before being able to take the train for Paris, she had no money, she lived alone in a garret. . . .

"Are you going to remain in France always?" he asked Mlle. Sklodovska, without knowing why.

A shadow passed over Marie's face, and she replied in her singing accent:

"Certainly not. This summer, if I succeed in my master's examination, I shall go back to Warsaw. I should like to come back here in the autumn, but I don't know whether I shall have the means to do so. Later on I shall be a teacher in Poland; I shall try to be useful. Poles have no right to abandon their country."

The conversation, in which the Kovalskis joined, turned toward the painful subject of Russian oppression. The three exiles evoked memories of their native land and exchanged news of their families and friends. Astonished, vaguely dissatisfied, Pierre Curie listened to Marie speak of her patriotic and social duties.

A physicist obsessed by physics, he could not imagine how this amazingly gifted girl could devote even one thought to anything outside of science, and that her plan for the future should be to use her strength in a struggle against Tsarism.

He wanted to see her again. . . .

The physicist had been immediately captivated by Marie Sklodovska and had understood what was unique in her. Pierre Curie, with gentle tenacity, endeavored to get on friendly terms with the girl. He saw her again two or three times at the sessions of the Physics Society, where she was listening to the reports of scientists on new research. He sent her, by way of compliment, a reprint of his latest publication, *On Symmetry in Physical Phenomena: Symmetry of an Electric Field and of a Magnetic Field;* and on the first page he wrote in his awkward hand, "To Mlle. Sklodovska, with the respect and friendship of the author, P. Curie." He had seen her in Lippmann's laboratory, in her big linen smock, bent silently over her apparatus.

And then he asked if he could visit her. Marie gave him her address, 11 Rue des Feuillantines. Friendly but reserved, she received him in her little room, and Pierre, his heart constricted by so much poverty, nevertheless appreciated, in the depths of his spirit, the subtle agreement between the character and the setting. In an almost empty attic, with her threadbare dress and her ardent, stubborn features, Marie had never seemed more beautiful to him. Her young face, thin and worn from the effort of an ascetic life, could not have found a more perfect frame than this denuded garret.

A few months passed. Their friendship strengthened, their intimacy increased, admiration and confidence grew greater. Pierre Curie was already the captive of the too-intelligent, too-lucid Polish girl. He obeyed her and followed her advice. He was soon urged and stimulated by her to shake off his indolence, write out his experiments on magnetism, and pass a brilliant thesis for the doctor's degree.

Marie still believed herself to be free. She did not seem disposed to listen to the final words which the scientist did not dare to pronounce.

This evening, for perhaps the tenth time, they were together in the room in the Rue des Feuillantines. It was warm: it was the end of an afternoon in June. On the table, near the mathematics books with the help of which Marie was preparing her approaching examination, there were some white daisies in a glass, brought back from an excursion Pierre and Marie had made together. The girl poured out tea, made on her faithful little alcohol lamp.

The physicist had just been speaking at length about a piece of work that preoccupied him. Then, without transition:

"I wish you would come to know my parents. I live with them, in a little house at Sceaux. They are charming."

He described his father for her: a tall, ungainly old man with lively blue eyes, very intelligent, hasty and impetuous, apt to boil over like a quick soup, but extremely kind—and his mother, weighed down by infirmities, but still an expert housekeeper, brave, gay, and courageous. He recalled his fantastic childhood, his interminable jaunts in the woods with his brother Jacques. . . .

Marie listened with surprise. What mysterious likenesses and coincidences! By changing a few details, transporting the little house at Sceaux to a street in Warsaw, you could turn the Curies into the Sklodovski family. Aside from religion—Dr. Curie, an anticlerical freethinker, had not had his children baptized—it was the same sort of circle, wise and honorable, with the same respect for culture, the same love of science, the same affectionate alliance between parents and children, the same passionate liking for nature. Smiling and more at her ease, Marie told the tale of her merry holidays in the Polish countryside—that countryside which she was going to see again in a few weeks.

"But you're coming back in October? Promise me that you will come back! If you stay in Poland you can't possibly continue your studies. You have no right to abandon science now. . . ."

These commonplace words of solicitude betrayed profound anxiety. And Marie felt that when Pierre said, "You have no right to abandon science," he meant, above all, "You have no right to abandon me."

They were silent for a time. Then Marie, lifting her ash-gray eyes to Pierre, answered gently, in a voice that still hesitated:

"I believe you are right. I should like to come back—very much."

Pierre spoke of the future several times again. He had asked Marie to be his wife; but the answer was not a happy one. To marry a Frenchman and leave her family forever, to renounce all political activity and abandon Poland, seemed to Mlle. Sklodovska like so many dreadful acts of betrayal. She could not and must not. She had passed her examination brilliantly; and now she must go back to Warsaw for the summer at least, perhaps forever. She offered the discouraged young scientist a friendship which was no longer enough for him, and took her train, having promised nothing.

He followed her in thought; he would have liked to join her in Switzerland, where she was passing a few weeks with her father who had come to meet her; or else in Poland—in that Poland of which he was jealous. But it could not be. . . .

So, from afar, he continued to urge his suit. Wherever Marie went, during the summer months, to Crettaz, Lemberg, Cracow or Warsaw, letters in uncertain and rather childish handwriting followed, on inexpensive paper headed by the name of the School of Physics, attempting to convince her and bring her back: to remind her that Pierre Curie was waiting for her.

October came. Pierre's heart swelled with happiness: Marie, according to her promise, had returned to Paris. She was to be seen again at the lectures in the Sorbonne and at Lippmann's laboratory. But this year—her last in France, as she believed—she no longer lived in the Latin Quarter. Bronya had given her a room adjoining the office she had opened for consultation at 37 Rue de Chateaudun. As the Dluskis still lived in La Villette and Bronya came to the Rue de Chateaudun only during the day, Marie could thus work in peace.

It was in this dark and rather dismal lodging that Pierre Curie resumed his tender entreaties. He bore within him the same faith as his future wife, a faith which was even more wholehearted, purer by its lack of alloy. For Pierre, science was the only aim. Thus his was a strange and almost incredible adventure, for it mixed the essential aspiration of his mind into the movement of his heart. He felt himself drawn toward Marie by an impulse of love and at the same time by the highest necessity.

He was even ready to sacrifice what people call happiness to another happiness known to him alone. He made Marie a proposal which at first seems fantastic, which might pass for a ruse or an approach, but which was characteristic of his nature. If Marie had no love for him, he asked, could she resolve upon a purely friendly arrangement at least, and work with him "in an apartment in the Rue Mouffetard, with windows giving on a garden, an apartment which could be divided into two independent parts?"

Or else (since necessity names its own price) if he, Pierre, went to Poland and obtained a position would she marry him? He could give French lessons; then, with whatever means at their disposal, he would engage in scientific research with her . . .

Before the former governess who had once been disdained by a Polish squireen [2] family, this man of genius became an humble supplicant.

Marie confided her perplexities and anxieties to Bronya, speaking of Pierre's offer to exile himself. She did not feel that she had the right to accept such sacrifice, but she was troubled and moved by the idea that Pierre loved her enough to have thought of it.

When he learned that the girl had spoken of him to the Dluskis, Pierre tried a new attack on that side. He went to see Bronya, whom he had already met several times; he won her over completely; he asked her to come with Marie to his parents' house at Sceaux. Dr. Curie's wife took Bronya aside and in a gentle, touching voice asked her to speak to her younger sister.

"There isn't a soul on earth to equal my Pierre," Mme. Curie insisted. "Don't let your sister hesitate. She will be happier with him than with anybody."

Ten more months had to pass before the obdurate Pole accepted the idea of marriage. Like a true Slavic "intellectual," Marie was encumbered with theories of life and duty. Some of her theories were generous and fine; others were only childish. Above all—and Pierre had understood this for a long time—it was not her theories that made Marie a superior being. The scientist made quick work of principles which Marie shared with several thousands of her cultivated compatriots. What held and fascinated him was her total devotion to work; it was her genius that he felt; it was also her courage and nobility. This graceful girl had the character and gifts of a great man.

Principles? He, too, had lived on principles for a long time, and life had undertaken to demonstrate their absurdity. He, too, had sworn never to get married. He had no Poland to defend, but he had always believed marriage to be incompatible with an existence devoted to science. The tragic end of an ardent youthful love had turned him in upon himself, and had kept him away from women. He no longer wanted to love: a salutary principle which had saved

[2] *squireen:* country gentleman.

him from commonplace marriage and made him wait for this meeting with an exceptional woman, a woman "made for him"— for Marie. And now he would not be stupid enough to let the chance of great happiness and a wonderful collaboration escape him for the sake of a "principle." He would win the girl, the Pole and the physicist, three persons who had become indispensable to him. . . .

Thus he gently reasoned with Mlle. Sklodovska. By such words and by others more tender, by the protection he offered her and by the deep, irresistible charm of his daily presence, Pierre Curie gradually made a human being out of the young hermit.

On July 14, 1895, Marie's brother Joseph sent her the affectionate absolution of the Sklodovski family:

. . . As you are now M. Curie's fiancée, I offer you first of all my sincerest good wishes, and may you find with him all the happiness and joy you deserve in my eyes and in the eyes of all who know your excellent heart and character.

. . . I think you are right to follow your heart, and no just person can reproach you for it. Knowing you, I am convinced that you will remain Polish with all your soul, and also that you will never cease to be part of our family in your heart. And we, too, will never cease to love you and to consider you ours.

I would infinitely rather see you in Paris, happy and contented, than back again in our country, broken by the sacrifice of a whole life and victim of a too-subtle conception of your duty. What we must do now is try to see each other as often as possible, in spite of everything.

A thousand kisses, dear Manya; and again let me wish you happiness, joy and success. Give my affectionate regards to your fiancé. Tell him that I welcome him as a future member of our family and that I offer him my friendship and sympathy without reserve. I hope that he will also give me his friendship and esteem.

A few days later Marie wrote to Kazia, her girlhood friend, and announced the decision she had taken:

When you receive this letter your Manya will have changed her name. I am about to marry the man I told you about last year in

Warsaw. It is a sorrow to me to have to stay forever in Paris, but what am I to do? Fate has made us deeply attached to each other and we cannot endure the idea of separating.

I haven't written, because all this was decided only a short time ago, quite suddenly. I hesitated for a whole year and could not resolve upon an answer. Finally I became reconciled to the idea of settling here. When you receive this letter, write to me: Madame Curie, School of Physics and Chemistry, 42 Rue Lhomond.

That is my name from now on. My husband is a teacher in that school. Next year I shall bring him to Poland so that he will know my country, and I shall not fail to introduce him to my dear little chosen sister, and I shall ask her to love him. . . .

On July 26, Marie awoke for the last time in her lodging in the Rue de Chateaudun. It was a marvelous day. The girl's face was beautiful. Something her student comrades had never seen was alight in her face: today Mlle. Sklodovska was to become Mme. Pierre Curie.

She dressed her lovely hair and put on her wedding dress, a present from Casimir Dluski's aged mother, who now lived in the Rue d'Allemagne. "I have no dress except the one I wear every day," Marie had said. "If you are going to be kind enough to give me one, please let it be practical and dark, so that I can put it on afterwards to go to the laboratory."

Guided by Bronya, Mme. Glet, a little dressmaker in the Rue Dancourt, had made the dress: a navy-blue woollen suit and a blue blouse with lighter blue stripes, in which Marie was pretty, fresh, and young.

Marie loved the idea of her wedding, which was to be, in every detail of the great day, different from all other weddings. There would be no white dress, no gold ring, no "wedding breakfast." There would be no religious ceremony: Pierre was a freethinker and Marie, for a long time past, had ceased the practices of religion. There were no lawyers necessary, as the married pair possessed nothing in the world—nothing but two glittering bicycles, bought the day before with money sent as a present from a cousin, with which they were going to roam the countryside in the coming summer.

It was to be a wonderful wedding indeed, for neither indifference nor curiosity nor envy were to be present. At the city hall in Sceaux and in the little garden at Pierre's parents' house in the Rue des Sablons there would be Bronya and Casimir, a few very close friends—university people—and Professor Sklodovski, who had come from Warsaw with Hela. . . . The professor made it a point of honor to talk to old Dr. Curie in the most correct and careful French; but first of all he would say, in his lowest tone, very moved, these words straight from his good heart: "You will have a daughter worthy of affection in Marie. Since she came into the world she has never caused me pain."

Pierre came to get Marie. They had to go to the Luxembourg station for the train to Sceaux, where their parents were waiting. They went up the Boulevard Saint-Michel on the top of an omnibus in the bright sun, and from the height of their triumphal chariot looked down on the passing of familiar places.

In front of the Sorbonne, at the entrance to the Faculty of Science, Marie squeezed her companion's arm a little and sought his glance, luminous and at peace.

SUGGESTIONS FOR STUDY

1. In what ways were Marie Sklodovska and Pierre Curie ordinary human beings? In what ways were they exceptional?
2. What element of chance brought these two together?
3. What things in Marie did Pierre admire? What things did she admire in him? Which of these admirable qualities become building blocks for a successful marriage?
4. Why did Marie hesitate for a whole year before finally accepting Pierre's proposal? Why had this delay not discouraged Pierre Curie?
5. Do you approve or disapprove of Marie's plans for her wedding day?
6. Marie Curie is the only person who has twice won the Nobel Prize. Read *Madame Curie* or some other biography of this remarkable woman. Prepare a good oral report about her contributions to science.

7. Compare and contrast the difficulties met by Pierre and Marie during their courtship with those met by John Fremont and Jessie Benton.

8. For the ambitious student: Their older daughter, Irene Joliot-Curie, also won the Nobel Prize. You might like to read about her life.

"Northfield!"

RICHARD STODDARD ALDRICH

To her millions of admirers, Gertrude Lawrence was one of the greatest actresses of all time. To her husband, Richard Aldrich, himself an important theatrical producer, she was "Adoringly, Mrs. A."

Mr. A's account of their life together, *Gertrude Lawrence as Mrs. A,* from which the following selection is taken, is an illuminating insight into the married life of two strong personalities. Besides the normal difficulties which beset most marriages, Mr. and Mrs. A added the special ones involved in the life of a theatrical star and in the tensions and separations caused by a terrible World War. But these two persons, deeply in love, were determined to make a success of their marriage, and they worked at the job. "Success in marriage is not something you can contract for in advance," says Mr. A, "a man needs to keep his marriage in repair."

This article is particularly impressive because it is a frank report of the battle of the sexes by the man involved, the husband himself.

WHEN GERTRUDE AND I were married, a good many people announced flatly—and gratuitously—that it would not last. Everything, they said, was against it: our backgrounds, our values—and above all, our temperaments. The optimists gave our marriage two years; the pessimists counted its chances for survival in months.

That it would last for life, and become more richly rewarding year by year, is something nobody—not even Gertrude and I— could have foretold; success in marriage is not something you can contract for in advance.

As time went by, the oracles reacted with increasing peevishness to our stubborn refusal to fulfill their gloomy prophecies. One gossip broadcaster publicly rebuked Gertrude for permitting a mere husband to keep her out of the spotlight of Cafe Society. The entire brood rejoiced, like vultures wheeling over dying prey, whenever reasons of career or wartime service forced Gertrude and me momentarily to go separate ways. Someday the columnists may learn the facts of life: two adults can enjoy an enduring love, even when they are not holding hands under the table at the Stork Club.

This is not to say that Gertrude and I never had our differences. In this account of our life together, I cannot pass them over. For they were a vital part of our relationship—tests that we had to meet together and for which we had to find our own solutions.

Some of our quarrels were heated, even violent. In the early years of our marriage Gertrude occasionally flew into a hysterical tantrum, at the height of which she might hurl at me whatever was nearest at hand. My own temper, though slower than hers, works up, like my father's, to fairly stormy proportions. And, like my father, I am apt to shout. . . . An additional irritant was the essentially different way in which we reacted to grievances. Gertrude got all the anger out of her system in one fine pyrotechnic outburst, after which she was all smiles and forgiveness. My tendency, by contrast, is to sulk and smolder at great length over something that irks me.

We were able to overcome these conflicts of personality, and the equally serious strains imposed by external circumstances, only because we were both fundamentally determined to make our marriage work. We realized that a successful union is an achievement accomplished not all at once, in a month, or a year; but little by little, day by day. It was Samuel Johnson, I believe, who said that "a man needs to keep his friendships in constant repair." The same might be said, with more telling truth, about a marriage. Gertrude and I were each prepared to give our relationship as much attention—if not more—than we gave to our individual careers.

The first major test of our resolution came in the summer of 1945, when we had an unexpected wartime reunion in Chicago. Paradoxically enough, whereas the deprivations of war had revealed to us our deep need of each other, our coming together again brought us to the verge of separation.

I cannot explain the tensions we both felt; though I suspect they will be familiar to any couple who were forced apart for long periods by the war. I only know that, deeply in love as I was with Gertrude, and as I believe she was with me when we said goodbye in London in the autumn of 1944, by the following July, when we came together in Chicago, our relationship was painfully askew.

We met in Chicago as a result of a wartime coincidence between unexpected naval orders issued to me, and Gertrude's return from Honolulu.

In the Navy everything moves at two speeds: either with exasperating slowness, or at a pace that doesn't allow you to catch your breath between the issuance of your orders and your arrival somewhere half the world away. I had had every expectation of being kept on in the ETO [1] for some time when, early in July, I was suddenly ordered to attend a naval conference then convening in Chicago. Before taking off from England there was no time or opportunity to get in touch with Gertrude, whom I supposed to be in Honolulu.

Not until I reached the United States and called David Holtzmann by telephone did I learn that Gertrude had arrived in San Francisco two days earlier. With that city playing host to the organizational meeting of the United Nations, Gertrude had found it impossible to get a hotel room. She had gone directly to Fanny Holtzmann, who was there as counsel to the Chinese delegation. Fanny gave her a bed in her suite at the Mark Hopkins and put her to work in place of an absent secretary. Gertrude enjoyed making herself useful to the diplomats and political advisors, among them Adlai Stevenson; she was working there when she received my wire asking her to join me in Chicago.

My message, as I later learned, caused a dramatic commotion. Until she ripped open the yellow envelope, Gertrude was under the impression that I was six thousand miles away.

The Overland Limited was due to leave from Oakland in exactly forty minutes. Gertrude made a mad dash across town and managed to get aboard the last of the Limited's five sections. She left her chances of getting a berth to luck.

[1] *ETO:* European Theater of Operations (World War II).

Brief but affectionate wires from Mrs. A announced the Limited's progress from stop to stop. Meanwhile Fanny had communicated with Gertrude's New York publishers, telling them that their author would be in Chicago on the day her book, *A Star Danced*, was to be released. The publishers, on their own, dispatched a publicity man to Chicago to promote book and author.

Thus, when I took time off from the naval conference to hurry down to the station to meet my wife, I walked into a huddle of newsmen, photographers, radio broadcasters, lights, microphones and several hundred gaping spectators. Our reunion promised to have about as much privacy as the proverbial goldfish in a bowl.

Irritation made me self-conscious, awkward, and brusque. More than three years of being in uniform, and being treated with the respect it commands, did not fit me to deal imperturbably with a swarm of reporters who buzzed around demanding what it felt like to be the husband of Gertrude Lawrence, what I thought of my wife's book, what she had said in it about me, and—were I to write a book—what I would tell the world about her.

I was having my first taste of being "Mr. Gertrude Lawrence," and not finding it very palatable.

I was there to meet Mrs. A, not the author of a potential bestseller. To have half a dozen cameramen snapping our first embrace, while shouting at us to "Hold It!", did not lessen my annoyance. I felt myself freeze up.

Gertrude looked at me wonderingly. And smiled at the cameras.

"But, Richard darling," she protested when I called over a cab and told the driver to take her to the Ambassador East, "aren't you coming, too?"

I explained that I had already been absent from my conference longer than I should have been.

"But you're meeting your wife."

I replied that the Navy was entirely uninterested in that. As far as it—the Navy—was concerned, I was in Chicago on duty. That came first. I would join her at the Ambassador as soon as I was free to do so.

"What will the press think if we separate at once, like this?" Gertrude demanded. "They'll hint all sorts of things. That you don't love me. That there is some other man, or other woman."

I said that for all of me, the press could think and say whatever it chose. I had not asked any of them to be there.

It was close to the dinner hour when the conference broke up and I was at liberty to rejoin Gertrude. Before I reached the door of our suite I heard her singing happily. Inside, I found her unpacking the clothes which her maid had sent on from New York; she was surrounded by flowers, with more being delivered as the news spread through Chicago of her arrival.

The phone rang repeatedly. Everyone, it seemed, was eager to welcome her, to fete her. I heard her promising to lunch with one caller; to meet another for cocktails. To dine at someone's house, "Not tomorrow night. We have an engagement. What about Thursday? Wonderful! My husband and I will be delighted. . . ."

"*Gertrude!*"

I found myself shouting at her. It seemed the only means of breaking through the glittering shell which enveloped her, to the reality of my Mrs. A.

"Don't make engagements for me," I roared. "I can't promise to go here, there, and everywhere."

"What do you mean—here, there, and everywhere?" she retorted. "I met the Hughston McBains on an Atlantic crossing. They want to meet my husband. Especially, considering all the nice things I've said to them about you."

Again I repeated what I had said at the station—that even in Chicago I was still in the Navy and subject to orders.

"But you and the captains and admirals can't be conferring all the time," Gertrude observed with clipped sarcasm. "They must let you have some time off. Suppose you devote a little of it to your wife—or are you too busy taking care of your friends in the Waves?"

"What do you mean, Waves?"

"Don't forget, darling," she replied with such cloying sweetness that I felt an impulse to slap her, "I've been around. I've seen a few Navy boys out in the Pacific."

I retorted that for my part I'd be glad of a chance to have a little time alone with my wife. If her friends and well-wishers and her publicity man would permit it. "After all," I pointed out, "this isn't the sort of thing I looked forward to when I asked you to meet me here."

"I know," she said, still with that annoying sweetness. "But, you must remember, all this is terribly good for my book."

I said I didn't care if it was. I wanted my wife. Not a successful author.

There were several copies of *A Star Danced* on the desk waiting for her to autograph. She took one, opened it, and showed me the dedication: *"For Richard."*

"This book is as much yours as it is mine," she said. "There's no need to be jealous."

"I'm not jealous," I snapped. My tone, I realized with some shame, was that of the Officer of the Day bawling out an incompetent yeoman. It did not salve my feelings to realize that Gertrude had put her finger unerringly on my weak spot. I *was* jealous.

The naval conference went on for several days, during which Gertrude kept the appointments her publishers made for her, and *A Star Danced* shot high among the best-sellers. I had applied for and was granted a one-month leave. As soon as the conference closed, Gertrude and I returned to New York, preparatory to going up to the Cape. I had every expectation that when my leave was up I would be sent out to the Pacific Theatre.

A month would have been little enough time for us, but, as I discovered as soon as we reached New York, we were not to have even that to ourselves in peace.

It was not only that the publishers were determined to make Gertrude's book sell more copies in New York than in Chicago, and showed an ingenuity in publicizing it that allowed us almost no privacy; but the publicity was producing an overwhelming amount of mail. Gertrude's fans demanded autographs, signed photographs, and personal mementos.

Although two secretaries were hastily installed to deal with the mail, Gertrude insisted on signing each letter herself.

The rattle of the secretaries' typewriters, the ringing of the telephone, and the appearance at all hours of interviewers, photographers, and persons soliciting Gertrude's endorsement of every sort of product drove me out of the apartment early in the morning, not to return until evening.

Meanwhile my few days of freedom were slipping by. I would have insisted on Gertrude's leaving all this and going with me up to the Cape but for the recollection of her remark to me in Chicago: "There's no need to be jealous." I felt unwilling to say anything that Gertrude might interpret as a return of the emotion which had possessed me there.

So we stayed on in New York.

If I had had an office of my own to go to and business of my own to engross me I might have been more philosophical about the delay. But this was 1945. During the four years I had been in the service a great many changes had taken place on Broadway, including the temporary dissolution of my own firm. The war had not only drawn hundreds of young actors into the services but had radically altered production conditions. I found myself in an alien land, without ties or prospects. I drifted aimlessly from the Players Club to the Harvard Club, to the Union Club.

As long as the Navy had use for me, I was able to tell myself that I was serving my country. What would happen when the war ended and I, along with millions more, was demobilized and had to start out looking for something to do? Frankly, I did not know.

I had pointed out to Gertrude before we married that play producing is a precarious livelihood. I had been out of production and consequently out of possible profits since December, 1941. I was now four years older, and enough wiser to realize that getting started again in the only business I knew was going to be the most difficult step of my career.

Meanwhile, I was the uniformed husband of the successful star and author, Gertrude Lawrence.

I did not like it.

However, for the present, there was nothing I could do about it. In desperation, and to take my mind off my own problems, of which I said nothing to Gertrude, I undertook to help plough through the mass of fan mail cluttering our apartment. It might help us get off to the Cape before my entire leave was up.

Gertrude welcomed my assistance. Going through her mail, I became aware of something which disturbed me.

Gertrude had been writing letters and sending packages—and unwittingly creating sentimental attachments—among English, Canadian, and American fighting men scattered all along the various fronts. Some she had met at the Stage Door Canteens, others in Normandy, in the camps in Britain, and in the South Pacific and in veterans' hospitals. When these lonely and home-sick men had started writing her, she had replied with character-istically generous warmth. In more than one instance this had been misinterpreted by her correspondent as a romantic interest in him.

True, the majority of letters from overseas (they came from colonels and corporals; Gertrude's notes and parcels were sent with proud disregard of rank) were simply genuine expressions of gratitude. A G.I. in Cairo thanked Gertrude for trying to place two songs he had written; another in the Marianas forwarded to her an invention which he wanted marketed (she promptly had it sent to a patent lawyer).

But there were more personal letters that bothered me; obvi-ously, the writers had no idea Gertrude was married. I showed one or two to Gertrude with the observation that she had gone beyond the bounds of common sense.

"But Richard!" she exclaimed. "I just sent those boys warm, friendly notes. You couldn't possibly take such letters seriously, could you?"

"I couldn't . . . but what about the boys? Do *they* realize that all those lavish 'darlings' in your letters mean nothing at all—that they are just part of the patter of the theatrical world?"

Gertrude appeared momentarily impressed. Then she said lightly, "Don't be so *glum* about it, darling—it's all past."

The whole thing would probably have ended there had it not been for the annoying insistence of one of her overseas admirers who suddenly turned up in New York. Answering the telephone one morning, I heard a high-pitched male voice with a distinct southern drawl ask for Miss Lawrence. The speaker identified himself as "an old friend—a close personal friend" of Gertrude's from overseas.

I explained that Miss Lawrence was not taking any calls, but that I would be glad to relay a message to her.

"Oh, she'll want to take this call, all right."

"I'm afraid that's not quite possible."

"Now, look here . . ." the voice paused impressively. "You just go on and tell her it's R— D— calling. She'll come quick enough," he added confidently.

I repeated with a slight edge of impatience that I could not disturb Gertrude; she was fulfilling a heavy schedule.

"You just don't understand." The tone became irritatingly patronizing. "Miss Lawrence is looking forward to my call. We have been corresponding back and forth for months."

"And *you* don't understand"—I realized I was raising my voice —"that Miss Lawrence has been corresponding with a number of young men in several Allied armies. I am sure it was all very pleasant at the time, and a help to morale, but now the war's almost over. Miss Lawrence has returned to her own life. I suggest that you do the same!" I slammed down the receiver and turned around to see Gertrude standing in the doorway. The look in her eyes left no doubt that she had heard my final remarks.

"So it's censorship now, is it?" she inquired acidly.

"Not censorship," I corrected her. "Just common sense. I am trying to protect you from possible embarrassment."

"How very, *very* chivalrous!" She glared. "Who was on the telephone—if I may pierce the veil of secrecy?"

"Oh, one of your pen pals. A rather . . ." I groped for a word that would annoy her—"dull-witted young man who said he was R— D—"

Gertrude bristled. "He's *not* dull-witted; he's very talented and intelligent."

She caught my skeptical glance. "He writes poetry," she added defiantly. "Free verse."

"Dedicated, no doubt," I said drily, "to that modern Helen of Troy, Miss Gertrude Lawrence."

Gertrude's head went up—a familiar storm warning. "It happens that some of them *were* dedicated to me—and it also happens that I would like to see R— again." She advanced a step toward the telephone. "He's in Army Public Relations. Their people can tell me where to reach him."

I grabbed her wrist. "You're not touching that phone!"

"How *dare* you stop me!"

Eyes blazing, she tried—unsuccessfully—to wrench herself away. For a few seconds we struggled, our fury rising. Then the doorbell started ringing insistently. The mood was broken.

I went to the door. It was one of the typists, apologetic for being a few minutes late. I left the apartment and went downtown.

I did not see Gertrude again until that evening, when I returned home. The apartment was filled with people—when they left, we had to hurry out to keep a dinner engagement. This was hardly the occasion for us to pursue our difference. But throughout the evening I could not forget the morning's unpleasantness; I felt that some decisive action had to be taken—at a time and place of my own choosing. Later, when I had a few moments to myself, I telephoned Fanny Holtzmann and asked her to let me have her apartment the following day.

"What for?"

I said I found it necessary to have a serious talk with Gertrude. Because it was a matter of importance, I preferred not to use our own apartment, where we might be overheard by secretaries or interrupted by visitors.

"Very well. My apartment is at your disposal from ten o'clock on; the housekeeper will let you in and disappear. You and Gee can then fight it out in peace and privacy."

Gertrude came along docilely enough, when I told her there was something I wanted to discuss in complete privacy. I am quite sure she had a very good idea what the subject would be.

Mrs. Jenkins, Fanny's motherly housekeeper, left us alone in the living room. Far off, I heard a door close.

"Well." Gertrude said rather too brightly.

"I want to talk to you about the man who phoned yesterday—among other things. Not that I think *he* himself is very important."

"If you're aware of that, why bring him up?"

"Because of what he represents."

Gertrude laughed. It was a brittle laugh, and it irritated me.

"Oh, Richard, don't tell me you're being jealous again!"

"No," I said grimly. "Not jealous. Disgusted."

"Disgusted?" Her quick reaction told me the shot had found its mark.

"Yes, disgusted. You're supposed to be a grown woman, a responsible adult. You've achieved great things in your profession. Yet at times you behave as if you had no respect for your position in the world—no respect for yourself—and no respect for your husband. In fact, you behave like a juvenile delinquent!"

She turned on me, white-faced, and stony-gray-eyed with anger.

"How *dare* you presume to speak to me like that, Richard Aldrich?" she demanded.

"Because I'm your husband," I shot back. "And don't forget it."

"What if you are—do you think that gives you the right to find fault with me? Criticize what I do? Scold me? Give me orders? I'm not one of your men, Commander Aldrich. How dare you presume to tell anyone that he shall not write to me, or call me up, or come to see me in my own home?"

"Your home is my home," I reminded her, "while you and I are married, and I want you to know it."

"And I want you to know," Gertrude flared back, "that, married or not, I'll see whom I like, and when I like. And where. I don't need anyone to manage my life for me. I did it pretty successfully for some years before I ever heard of Richard Stoddard Aldrich."

We were now launched on the "high old row" of which she was to remind me several times in later years. It was worthy of the name. Gertrude blazed at me for attempting to dominate her. She accused me of surliness; of being a dog in a manger ever since I had come home. According to her, my behavior in Chicago and lately had been a revelation to her—an unpleasant one.

If she spoke of revelations, I retorted—and I found myself shouting—what did she think her conduct had revealed to me?

She chose to take this as an accusation of unfaithfulness. How dared I make such a charge against her, she demanded?

"I didn't!" I shouted.

"You most certainly did." She followed this by pointing out that she had not once questioned me about the women I must have met in England. Well, then, why shouldn't she make friends of men she had met in the service?

"No man likes finding that his wife is an indiscriminate flirt." With a gesture of total defiance Gertrude pulled off her hat and threw it at my face. I ducked, and the hat sailed past me, to land behind the sofa.

Her anger had now risen beyond flood-water mark. I thought for a moment she was going to attack me with her bare hands. I caught them both and gripped them tight while she struggled to free herself.

"Northfield . . . Northfield . . . NORTHFIELD . . ." I commanded.

It was so long since either of us had used our code word that it was several seconds before its significance pierced Gertrude's rage. Then suddenly I felt her go limp. I gathered her into my arms.

In the peace after the storm we arranged to get out of New York that same afternoon, leaving our worries and differences behind us, and go up to the Cape.

We let ourselves out of the apartment without another thought of Gertrude's hat.

Years later, on Easter Sunday, Gertrude and I were walking along Fifth Avenue with her newly acquired West Highland terrier, Angus, when we met Mrs. Jenkins similarly engaged with her Trixie.

While the dogs rubbed noses we exchanged compliments.

"Why, Jenkie," Gertrude exclaimed with genuine admiration, "how smart you look! And what a sweet hat!"

"I'm not surprised you like it, Miss Lawrence," Mrs. Jenkins observed.

"You aren't?" Gertrude asked, apparently puzzled.

"Well, that's the best of a really good hat when you get one," Mrs. Jenkins said blandly, favoring me with a wink. "It never dates."

SUGGESTIONS FOR STUDY

1. With what special difficulties did Mr. and Mrs. A have to contend? According to Aldrich, what was the reason this couple overcame their conflicts?

2. Which sort of marriage would you prefer, a completely peaceful one or one containing quarrels, heated, even violent? Explain the reasons for your choice.

3. What is the effect of jealousy upon marriage?

4. In the big quarrel over Gertrude's correspondence with R—, with whom did you sympathize? Why? Do you think this quarrel could have been as violent as it was if husband and wife had not been deeply in love? Explain.

5. What is your opinion of using a "code word" such as "Northfield" to stop arguments? What are the characteristics of a good code word for such a purpose?

6. Write a composition in which you describe some family quarrel you may have witnessed or taken part in. Be sure to give clearly the issues at stake, the arguments used on both sides, and the outcome of the quarrel.

7. Make a list of new ideas about love and marriage which you have discovered (though maybe not accepted) by reading the three selections in this section.

Adult Life

What is meant by adult life is not easy to define. Maturity involves the individual's mental, emotional, spiritual growth; it relates to the ripening of his power to make commonsense judgments: it includes all the richness the individual has absorbed from family background, schooling, real-life experiences, the exposures to books, television, music, art, science. To the biographee's adult life the biographer will usually devote the greater percentage of pages. It is from this period in the person's life that frequently come the honors, the services (Shakespeare's soldier and justice), the contributions that have made the individual "inspire" a biography.

This section, "Adult Life," introduces to you four eminent adults: a world renowned medical missionary, an easy-going thinker, a great musician, and a lexicographer (maker of dictionaries). You will see them in moments of mature wisdom—and also in moments of weakness. From reading these portions of their lives you may gain both new understanding of the meaning of adult life and also inspiration to resolve that your own life will be truly adult.

Albert Schweitzer Decides

HERMANN HAGEDORN

At the age of twenty-nine, Albert Schweitzer was already an accomplished musician, an author-authority on Bach, a competent teacher, and a promising theologian. Quite a record for a young adult! And, in the estimate of his friends and colleagues, he was destined for an even more brilliant future.

But, being truly adult, Dr. Schweitzer formulated his own notions of success and of what constitutes happiness and the good life. To him there was a higher calling. A spiritual hand had been laid upon him, inspiring him with a divine passion to do much more with his life. To alter the course of his adult life by going to Africa as a medical missionary was not an easy decision to make; and Schweitzer, like other great men, was misunderstood by his associates.

In his biography of Albert Schweitzer, *Prophet in the Wilderness,* Hermann Hagedorn tells of that fateful year when Dr. Schweitzer obeyed the promptings of his heart. As you read this selection, bear in mind that even though few of us have the gift of greatness that was Schweitzer's, nevertheless many of us may, in the course of our own lives, be confronted with the same decision that Schweitzer faced and handled so heroically.

SCHWEITZER'S STUDENT YEARS passed like a summer vacation. He was happy, and sufficiently objective in his happiness to know it. Happiness! What had he told himself about it? You had to pay for it? You had to give something to those who had never had it?

He thrust the idea from his mind. Why shouldn't he enjoy, why shouldn't he drink deep? After all, it was no vulgar rapture he pursued. What loftier passion was there than the pursuit of beauty and truth?

"You must pay," said the Voice in his heart.

"Pay? How?"

"In service, to those who have not known happiness, to those who are starving, in body or soul, to those who are writhing in pain. You, who are not starving, you who do not know what pain is, you, laden down with blessings, owe a debt."

"Is not scholarship service? Thought? The pursuit of truth? The sweeping away of ignorance and conventional conceptions? Is not art service?"

"The fortunate of mankind, the greatly blest, are called to more immediate service."

"What kind?"

"The service of the heart and of the hand. The simple, unheroic act, the persistent, day-in-day-out giving of yourself to people who cannot possibly compensate you for what you give."

"All this?"

"Is it too much?"

"No. It is not too much for what I have had, for what today I possess."

In the parsonage at Gunsbach, one bright Whitsunday [1] morning, Albert Schweitzer lay in bed listening to the birds singing in the first warmth of the new year. Such a morning! The apple trees, white with bloom, the lilacs shouting with scent, the young green almost covering the windows of the church that lifted its tender spire up from the warm Alsatian valley. Who would not, at twenty-one, feel the heart throb with delicious joy and remember other delights, experienced through the long, rich years?

The rapture of living lifted him clear out of himself so that the Voice he had fled from and sought to silence spoke as it had never before spoken.

He did not now protest. But dimly he recognized how much he was being asked to give up. A career, recognition, success, fame. . . . Into his consciousness leapt words that were familiar yet obscure: "He that loseth his life shall save it." He had never known before what they meant. He did not really know now, but he knew they applied.

[1] *Whitsunday:* the seventh Sunday after Easter; Pentecost.

"You must pay."

Yes, but how *did* one pay for such benefactions, so freely given? How . . . had . . . Jesus . . . paid?

A carpenter's shop till he was thirty. His skill with tools; the hills of Judea, the meadows, the lake, sunrises, sunsets and the young moon; his mother, his brothers and sisters, his friends. All these, wholly to enjoy . . . until he was thirty; then God, and Man, for as long a time as might be granted him.

Thirty. That meant nine years. You could do much in nine years. And what then? What would be expected of him at the end of the nine years?

What matter? He would know when the time came. To remember was the main thing. To remember. Never to let the resolution fail, the irrational fire be quenched. The rest was in God's hands.

[Nine years passed in study and thought, friendship, writing, music and Bach, theology and preaching, philosophy, and— through it all—the continuing resolve he had made to give up his life to service at the end of the time.]

Nine years. . . . The ninth was almost spent. Albert Schweitzer was less than three months under thirty and, though his resolve was as sharp and clear as ever, he had no idea what form the "direct service to mankind" to which he had committed himself, should take.

One day on his desk in the theological college he picked up a green–covered magazine which proved to be a report of the Paris Missionary Society. Had it not sent out the devoted Casalis whose letters his father had read from the pulpit in Gunsbach when he was a boy? He laid the magazine aside unopened; but that evening, returning to his desk, his eye was caught by the title of one of the articles. He read, and became absorbed. The President of the Society, a fellow-Alsatian, was pointing out how starved for workers the French Congo was. The picture he drew of savages tortured by superstition and pain came to life for Schweitzer in a blaze of revelation.

He closed the magazine and quietly began his evening's work.

His search was over. He knew at last what his "direct service" should be.

January 15, 1905. The nine years were ended. Under a northern window in his study, the daughter of an old friend was painting his portrait. Countess d'Erlach has been gravely ill and the doctor hoped that the palette and brushes might hasten her recovery. Intent on her work, she did not dream of the thoughts racing through the mind of her model on his thirtieth birthday. Schweitzer was thinking of his resolution, of Africa, and of the man in the parable who, "desiring to build a tower, first counts the cost whether he have wherewith to complete it." What were the essentials? Health, for one, and he had it abundantly. Sound nerves, energy, practical sense, toughness, prudence. He had them all. As for personal wants, he had none that the jungle could not satisfy. Had he the temperament to bear possible failure? Here too the answer was affirmative. There was one thing more. Had he any thought of heroism? If he had, the undertaking was wrong. Only a man who had no thought of heroism, he told himself, but only a sense of obligation, undertaken with sober enthusiasm, was capable of becoming the kind of "spiritual adventurer" the world needed.

He must go as a medical missionary, if he went at all. To talk about the religion of love was not enough. He must practice it. The need in the Congo, moreover, was obviously not for another teacher or preacher, but for a doctor. The Congo's immediate tragedy was neither ignorance nor spiritual vacuity, but pain. How long would it take to become a physician, a surgeon? Six years, perhaps seven? Well, he could face it.

The Countess skilfully put a stroke here, another stroke there. The likeness was extraordinary. But she never guessed that the imagination behind the deep, dark eyes she had painted so well was in French Equatorial Africa.

Schweitzer did not immediately tell his family and friends of his decision to put aside the achievement and the promise of his career as a scholar, teacher, preacher and musician, and become a medical missionary. "I am by nature very uncommunicative as to everything which concerns my personal life," he explained in a private letter, forty years later. "I inherited this (together with writer's cramp) from my mother." He hated to talk of what was nearest his heart. He hated even more the implication of self-righteousness involved in the announcement of so drastic a determination. So he said nothing, only quietly cleared the road for the beginning of his medical studies.

If he had had any worldly ambition in him, he might have been tempted, in the months that followed, to weaken on his youthful resolution. The Devil took him up a mountain from which he could see all Europe and the continents beyond. His revolutionary volume on Bach, demonstrating that he was not merely a transcendent geometrician of music but a supreme tone-painter, acutely sensitive to every mood of the natural world, had made him somewhat of a personage in Paris. He was the leading spirit of a small group and was invited to be its organist. Brilliant *salons* opened their doors to him. He was asked to give lectures on the giants of German literature and philosophy. Across France's southern border, the Orfeo Catala of Barcelona engaged him to play the organ for its periodical Bach concerts. Europe was taking note of one of its coming young men.

In Paris, on a chilly day in October, 1905, nine months after the Countess had completed his portrait, Schweitzer dropped in a mailbox a half-dozen letters telling his family and closest friends of his decision to go to Africa as a medical missionary. The news was a bombshell in Paris as well as in Gunsbach and Strasbourg.

Schweitzer could deal with the dismay of his father and mother, for he could count on their trust not only in his motives but in his judgment. They feared that he was going off on an adventure which would be too difficult for him and in which he would fail because he would be trying to live a life other than that for which he seemed destined by the nature of his gifts. They did not pretend to understand, but they recognized that there must be a very deep reason behind the revolutionary decision of this levelheaded son of theirs, and supported him with their faith. They knew, moreover, that there was no budging him.

His colleagues at the University and his other friends were less trusting, reproaching him, above all, for failing to take them into his confidence in advance. In vain he confronted his theological associates with St. Paul's boast that he had not "conferred with flesh and blood" in setting his own course. St. Paul, they implied, was irrelevant. The point was, had he, Albert Schweitzer, gone crazy? *Umsatteln*—to shift from one career to another—was to most Germans of that generation the sign of an instability of judgment and purpose as reprehensible as wanton divorce. And to do it, when he was more than halfway up the ladder! So to forget himself and the dignity of the position he had won! So to wreck at the outset what promised to be a great career!

The waste of it!

The waste! Wasn't that what Judas had said when Magdalene had poured the expensive ointment over Jesus' feet? [2]

"Why should you, with the intellectual world at your feet, bury yourself alive in the most neglected corner of the earth?" Did not the Gospels have something to say about buried talents?

Yes, Schweitzer said, but they had something to say also of Dives and Lazarus and something quite definite about losing your life in order to gain it.

"You are serving mankind where you are, doing something for which your whole background and education have fitted you. Is not scholarship service? Is not teaching service? Is not preaching service?"

Of course. But such service was too easy. It was not really service unless the giving hurt.

"The Negro of Central Africa isn't your job. The white man of the western world *is*. Other men can work among the Africans, men without your gifts for scholarship and art."

True. But not enough were doing it.

His friends called him a sentimentalist. "The nations who live in the bosom of nature are never so ill as we are, and do not feel pain so much."

He wondered.

"You are casting pearls before swine. Christianity is something too high for primitive man."

[2] See John 12:1–8.

To that argument he had no answer. Was it possible that it was true?

"Give lectures for the benefit of your savages, if you must," a distinguished woman adjured him. "You can help them much more that way than by going to Africa yourself."

He quoted Goethe to her, "In the beginning was the deed"— *Im Anfang war die Tat.*

She shrugged her shoulders. "That's out-of-date. Nowadays, propaganda is the mother of action."

Most painful to Schweitzer were his encounters with men and women who professed to be—and in most areas of their lives were —Christians. He knew that they had read the New Testament and were familiar with its stories of lives turned radically from their courses in answer to the call of Christian love. Surely they must understand what to human reasoning seemed irrational, that there were times when every human plan, every human ambition, must yield to the command of Jesus? It was torture to him to open his heart to the point of declaring the depth of the impulsion that had moved him to his decision; and all he received in return was incredulity, the charge of conceit, and suspicion of his motives. What was really behind all this nonsense: Was he disappointed in the public recognition that had come to him? Had he been crossed in love?

The idea of his going to Africa was bad enough. But to go as a doctor! If he must go, why not as a regular missionary? He had his degree in theology, he had been ordained as a minister, he enjoyed teaching and preaching. Why, in God's name, then, go as a doctor and study for years in a field completely removed from any which even his versatile mind had touched?

Once again Goethe came to his support, Goethe who makes the characters in which he has most nearly depicted himself—Faust and Wilhelm Meister—end their days, one as an engineer redeeming land from the sea, the other as a surgeon—in order that they may find wholeness and redemption in selfless action.

He tried to make his friends see that Christian practice was more important than Christian eloquence, and failed. For weeks, well-meaning colleagues battered him with arguments and probed his heart for hidden motives. He felt grateful to those who merely thought him a little off his head, and treated him with friendly mockery.

Twenty years later a French writer in *Le Menestrel* suggested possibly the chief reason for the opposition Schweitzer encountered: really to accept the conceptions motivating Schweitzer obligated a man either to go and do likewise or in humility to face the fact that he himself did not possess the love and courage required.

SUGGESTIONS FOR STUDY

1. In Dr. Schweitzer's mind what were the requirements for happiness? What can you add? What was his "Voice in the heart"?

2. What did Schweitzer consider to be the qualifications necessary for work in the Congo mission field? How many of these qualifications do you lack?

3. How does a "spiritual adventurer" differ from an ordinary adventurer?

4. Why did Schweitzer's colleagues reproach him? How did Schweitzer answer their reproaches?

5. Schweitzer had no argument against the idea that Christianity is something too high for primitive men. What arguments might he have used?

6. Schweitzer's friends were suspicious of his motives for entering upon this new career. State the three motives that the friends of Schweitzer attributed to him for entering upon his new career in Africa. According to the French writer in *Le Menestrel*, what was the real reason the friends of Schweitzer opposed his decision to go to Africa?

7. What inspiration did Schweitzer find in the writings of Goethe?

8. As you think along with Albert Schweitzer when he faces up to his important decision, how can you tell that it is an adult making the decision rather than an adolescent?

9. Give examples from this selection which show that the Bible can be quoted to support both sides of an argument. Recall Antonio's remarks in Shakespeare's *The Merchant of Venice*, Act I, Scene III: "The devil can cite Scripture for his purpose."

10. Ask other members of your class to think of persons within their acquaintance who re-ordered their lives after reaching age thirty

—perhaps changing professions. How successful were these persons? What persons in your acquaintance have changed vocations too often; that is, tried too many things and spread themselves too thin? What kind of schooling best prepares you for life, if at the time you are in school, you have no definite notion of what your calling is to be?

11. At the present time how much do you feel the world as a whole has gained by Schweitzer's work in Africa, or lost by the work he gave up in Europe?

12. State how Albert Schweitzer is a superb example of the statement that he who would save his life must lose it.

Thoreau at Walden

VAN WYCK BROOKS

The total life span of Henry Thoreau consisted of only forty-four years. Without seeking adventure on icy mountains or tramping about the world, Thoreau found adventure and maturity by living intensively and reflectively in the immediate area around Concord, Massachusetts. He felt that man-made towns, government, laws often intruded upon man's making the most of his individuality. And nature he loved keenly and deeply. Today, when *things* seem to count for much, it is a real mental tonic to expose ourselves to the grown-up *ideas* of this "very stubborn and opinionated young man."

Van Wyck Brooks has written a much-honored book called *The Flowering of New England, 1815–1865*, one volume in his studies of American literature. The selection "Thoreau at Walden" (in effect a biographical essay written in a graceful narrative style) is a chapter from this book. Let Mr. Brooks introduce you to this alert observer, quiet rebel, and endearing naturalist.

HENRY THOREAU had built a hut at Walden. In March, 1845, he borrowed Alcott's axe—which he took pains to return with a sharper edge—and cut down some tall, arrowy pines for the timbers, studs, and rafters. For the boards he bought a shanty from one of the Irish laborers on the railroad. The hut was ten feet by fifteen, shingled and plastered, with a garret and closet, a trap-door below, a brick fireplace, windows at the sides and a door facing the cove. The cost, all told, was $28.12—less than the annual rent of a student's room in Cambridge. There was a bean-field, close by, with a patch of potatoes, corn, peas, and turnips. Thoreau seldom indulged in beans. He exchanged his crop for rice in the village. Rice was the proper diet for one who loved so well the writings of the Oriental sages.

From the book THE FLOWERING OF NEW ENGLAND by Van Wyck Brooks. Copyright 1936, 1952 by Van Wyck Brooks. Reprinted by permission of E. P. Dutton & Co., Inc.

He had long cherished the notion of a forest-life. There was nothing new in his own adventure, and he could not understand why his friends thought it was so peculiar. Some of them spoke as if he had gone to the woods in order to starve or freeze. Emerson had bought land on both sides of the pond, intending to build a summerhouse, and Henry had carried out the project. . . . Henry felt at home in his woodland dwelling. It made him think of some of those mountain-houses he had seen on his inland excursions, high-placed, airy, fragrant, with a fresh, auroral atmosphere about them. It was quiet, clean and cool, fit to entertain a traveling god. For company, birds flitted through his chamber, red squirrels raced over the roof, chickadees perched on the armfuls of wood he carried. There were moles living in the cellar. He had occasional visits from a hare. . . .

There was nothing about his "experiment," as his friends liked to call it, to arouse such curiosity and contempt. It was a common-sensible undertaking, and only a slight departure from Henry's usual mode of living. His average weekly outlay, for necessaries he could not supply himself, was twenty-seven cents. A few days at manual labor, building a boat or a fence, planting, grafting, or surveying—six weeks of work out of the year, when he had grown extravagant and had to have a microscope—gave him an ample surplus. Why should anyone live by the sweat of his brow and bore his fellowmen by talking about it? Why should not everyone live with an ample margin?—as anyone could do, provided he followed the path of simplification, logically and ruthlessly enough. The mass of men led lives of quiet desperation. Why, if not to maintain a "standard of living" that every law of the universe opposed? Did they not know that the wisest had always lived, with respect to comforts and luxuries, a life more simple and meagre than the poor? . . .

Henry believed, and wished to prove, that the more one simplified one's life the less complex the laws of life would seem. Why all this pother about possessions? He liked to think of the ancient Mexicans, who burned all their goods every fifty years. . . . This was the kind of reform that Henry thought was worth considering. He meant to have his furniture, actual and symbolic, as simple as an Indian's or an Arab's. There were three bits of limestone on his table. They had to be dusted every day, while the furniture of his mind was still undusted. Out of the window, quick! If he had had the wealth of Croesus,[1] Henry's mode of living would not have been different. Space, air, time, a few tools, a notebook, a pen, a copy of Homer, what could he wish more than these? A bath in the pond at sunrise, a little sweeping and cleaning, then a bath for the intellect, perhaps in the *Bhagavad-Gita,*[2] the pure water of Walden mingling in his mind with the sacred water of the Ganges. The day was his, for any wild adventure.

Sometimes, on a summer morning, he would sit for hours in his sunny doorway, amid the pines and hickories and sumachs, in undisturbed solitude and stillness. The birds flitted noiselessly about him. He could feel himself growing like the corn. What did he care for worldly interests? It was his vocation to discover God. . . .

His life here seemed to flow in its proper channels. It followed its own fresh currents, and he felt himself lurking in clear thought as the trout lurked under the leafy banks. Not so much as a bubble rose to the surface. At sunset, he jumped into his boat and paddled to the middle of the pond. There he played on his flute, while the charmed perch hovered about the stern, and the moon traveled over the floor of the pond, strewn with the wrecks of the forest. The wildest imagination could not conceive the manner of life he was living, for the Concord nights were as strange as Arabian nights. He struck the side of the boat with his paddle, filling the woods with a circle of sound. What a pleasant mission it would be to go about the country in search of echoes!

What could he say to a man who feared the woods, who shuddered at their solitude and darkness? What salvation was there for such a man? Did he not know that God was mysterious and silent? Henry could never have wearied of the woods, as long as he could visit a nighthawk on her nest.

Round and round the pond, Henry followed the footpath worn by the feet of Indian hunters, old as the race of men in Massachu-

---

[1] *Croesus:* a rich Asian king of the sixth century, B.C.
[2] *Bhagavad-Gita:* the supreme devotional scripture of India.

setts. The critics and poets were always complaining that there
were no American relics, no ruins to remind one of the past. Yet
the wind could hardly blow away the surface anywhere, exposing
the spotless sand, but one found the fragments of some Indian pot
or the little chips of flint left by some early native arrow-maker.
When winter came, and the scent of the gale wafted over the
naked ground, Henry tramped through the snow a dozen miles to
keep an appointment with a beech tree, or a yellow birch perhaps,
or some old acquaintance among the pines. He ranged like a grey
moose, winding his way through the shrub-oak patches, bending
the twigs aside, guiding himself by the sun, over hills and plains
and valleys, resting in the clear grassy spaces. He liked the wholesome color of the shrub-oak leaves, well-tanned, seasoned by the
sun, the color of the cow and the deer, silvery-downy underneath,
over the bleached and russet fields.

He loved the shrub-oak, with its scanty raiment, rising above
the snow, lowly whispering to him. It was one of his own cousins,
rigid as iron, clean as the atmosphere. It loved the earth, which
it over-spread. The squirrel and the rabbit knew it well, and Henry
could understand why the deermouse had its hole in the snow by
the shrub-oak's stem. Winter was his own chosen season. When,
for variety in his walks, he had only a rustling oak-leaf or the
faint metallic cheep of a tree-sparrow, his life felt wholesome and
sweet as the kernel of a nut. Alone in the distant woods or fields,
in the modest pastures tracked by rabbits, on a bleak and, to most,
a cheerless day, when a villager would be thinking of his fire, he
felt himself grandly related to earth and Heaven. Cold and solitude were his dearest friends. Better a single shrub-oak leaf at
the end of a wintry glade, rustling a welcome at his approach, than
a ship-load of decorations from the kings of the earth. By poverty
—if one chose to use the word—monotony, and simplicity, he felt
crystallized, as water and vapor are crystallized by cold.

All praise to winter, then, was Henry's feeling. Let others have
their sultry luxuries. How full of creative genius was the air in
which these snow-crystals were generated. He could hardly have
marveled more if real stars had fallen and lodged on his coat.
What a world to live in, where myriads of these little discs, so

beautiful to the most prying eye, were whirled down on every traveler's coat, on the restless squirrel's fur and on the far-stretching fields and forests, the wooded dells and mountaintops—these glorious spangles, the sweepings of Heaven's floor. He watched the men cutting the ice on the pond. Some of this ice, stowed in the holds of ships, was going over to India; and many a seeker of Brahma in Calcutta was destined to drink from his own Walden well.

If winter drove one indoors, all the better. It compelled one to try new fields and resources. Days of merry snowstorms and cheerful winter evenings by the fire. Evenings for books of natural history, Audubon, for one. It was pleasant to read about the Florida Keys, the flowering magnolia, the warm spice-breezes, while the wind beat the snow against one's window.

These were the days for writing, days to speak like a man in a waking moment to others in their waking moments. For Henry was hard at work. He had begun to write a book, the *Week on the Concord and Merrimac Rivers*, the story of the journey with his brother, never to be forgotten, when they had doubled so many capes and run before the wind and brought back news of far-away men.

He did not propose to crowd his day with work, even if the book had to be written. A writer, he thought, should saunter to his task surrounded by a halo of ease and leisure, and the labor of his hands should remove from his style all trace of sentimentality and palaver. One did not dance idly at one's writing when one had wood to cut and cord. As the strokes rang cheerily through the wood, so the stroke of the pen should ring on the reader's ear. Was the voyage an old story, eight or nine years old, and only a week at that? It represented a lifetime's memories. No boy who had grown up on the Mississippi recalled those floating enchantments, the riverboats, and the fabulous rivermen, with more of a thrill than Henry felt, remembering the canal-boats of his childhood.

Henry was not by nature a hermit. He might have frequented the barrooms, he thought, if he had had any business that called him thither. Almost every day he walked to the village, to trade his beans for rice, to get a boot repaired, to collect the news of the family. Sometimes he returned late at night, with a bag of rye or Indian meal, sailing back under the moon to his harbor in the woods. It was only that he was wary of gossip. He did not wish to lumber his mind with the rubbish that most men seemed to rejoice in; the details, for example, of some case in court.

One day he was arrested in the village for refusing to pay his poll-tax. He felt as Alcott felt. The government supported slavery, the government was backing the Mexican War; well, he would not support the government. He did not wish to trace the course of his dollar until it bought a man, or bought a gun to shoot a Mexican. He spent the night in jail—a fruitful night. It inspired his essay on *Civil Disobedience*. He wished to establish a principle, that one man locked up in jail for refusing to countenance slavery would be the end of slavery, or, to express it on a broader basis, "If the alternative is to keep all just men in prison, or give up war and slavery, the State will not hesitate which to choose." A foolish notion, many people thought. But some of them changed their minds, in later years, when one of Henry's Hindu readers, Gandhi, acting on the principle, disturbed the British Empire for several months. The next morning, Henry, released from jail, gathered some of the boys and girls for a huckleberry party, on a hill, from where the State was nowhere to be seen.

He never fastened his door at Walden, though sometimes, in his absence, he had unwelcome visitors. How did Mrs. X happen to know that his sheets were not as clean as hers? But nothing was ever stolen, except his copy of Homer. One had to keep one's eye on bookish people.

Once Henry left his house for a fortnight's excursion. He had cousins in Bangor, Maine, one of them in the lumber trade, a good excuse to visit the northern woods. He wished to study the Indians in their forest wilderness, and he wished to climb Mount Katahdin. He never traveled without prayer and fasting, for he did not wish to dissipate his mind.

Later, another friend, an Englishman, invited him for a visit in England. Henry said no. If Europe was much in his mind, and became more and more to him, Concord might become less and less; and what sort of bargain would that be? He did not wish his life to lose its homely savor. If the fields and streams and woods that he loved so well, and the simple occupations of his townsmen, ever ceased to interest and surprise him, what culture or wealth could ever make up for the loss? He did not wish to go to Europe, nor did he wish to go—like the farmers—west. What could he think of this foolish American habit, going east or west to a "better land," without lifting an honest finger to till and redeem one's own New England soil? As for the rush to California, it was a disgrace to humankind—digging gold, the merest lottery, a kind of toil, if it deserved the name, in no sense beneficial to the world. A startling development, this, of the ethics of trade and all the modes of getting a living. It filled Henry with a cold scorn. Were not all the essentials of life to be found in Concord, ten times found if one properly valued them?—which a man could only do if he stood his ground. Henry had something to say to the men in the covered wagons, who were running away from something besides the rocks. If the men in the covered wagons had no ears for Henry, he would be glad to wait for a few generations. The great-great-grandsons of the covered wagons would be ready to listen to him.

SUGGESTIONS FOR STUDY

1. Give the specific facts about the hut Thoreau built at Walden Pond.
2. What did Thoreau think his "vocation" to be? To what conclusions about this vocation did he come?
3. What kind of books did Thoreau read?
4. For what reason was Thoreau willing to go to jail? Do you think that such behavior was more effective in Thoreau's day than today? Why or why not?
5. What impression of Thoreau's personality do you get from this selection? Make a list of qualities which, in your opinion, best characterize a mature person. How does Thoreau measure up to your standard?
6. Is thinking work? Is it hard work? Explain. What do you think would happen if many people acted and thought like Thoreau?
7. For the ambitious student: Obtain a copy of the essay, "Civil Disobedience." What principles does Thoreau set forth? What is your reaction to these?

Two Parties for Toscanini

SAMUEL CHOTZINOFF

Arturo Toscanini, the world-renowned orchestra conductor, possessed a singleminded devotion to his work which was the admiration of all. But, like most geniuses, he could on occasion display a childishness which his associates found very difficult to cope with. This short sketch from *Toscanini: An Intimate Portrait*, by Samuel Chotzinoff (himself a well-known pianist and music critic), shows our great man behaving at his childish worst and then atoning in the grand manner which made all around him his slaves.

THE SPELL that Toscanini cast on everyone around him during those years [World War II] was powerful and unflagging. Whether grave or gay, vengeful or beneficent, he magnetized alike players, page boys, servants, executives, friends, and even his family. They trembled at his frown and basked in his smile. At NBC his every wish was attended to in the spirit of a favor conferred by him. To be allowed to remove his sopping garments was like assisting at a rite. To sit next to him in a motor car or at table, to have him address one as *"caro,"* [1] to attend a concert or a play with him, to entertain him—all these became memorable events. No one stopped to examine and analyze or question his strange and unprecedented power. He ruled over our hearts and minds. His judgments were accepted like articles of faith. We took to our hearts the people he liked and looked askance at those he dropped. We loved the music he loved, became skeptical about the music he despised, and accepted without question the music that he, having summarily cast out, as summarily restored to favor. When with him we talked about him. We never tired of hearing him talk about himself; when away from him we never ceased

Reprinted by permission of Samuel Chotzinoff.
[1] *Caro:* dear (Italian).

recalling his words, looks, gestures, opinions. When he telephoned to one of us, we hastily apprised one another, through a telephone relay, of the happy occurrence. And indeed it was thrilling to lift up the receiver and hear one's name pronounced *sotto voce*,[2] hoarsely, vibrating with the fast tremolo so characteristic of the Maestro's speech.

We spent much of our leisure time in thinking up ways to amuse him. At the end of one season we planned to surprise him with a great party at the Sarnoffs', which was to be in the form of an old-fashioned vaudeville show put on and performed by his friends. The enterprise was of considerable magnitude, and brought with it great anxieties, for the participants were amateurs like myself, and the professionals among us assumed roles quite outside their specialties. Marc Connelly, the playwright, staged the show and acted in one of the sketches; Walter Toscanini, the Maestro's son, danced a Russian Hopak, while Efrem Zimbalist, in Russian peasant costume, played the harmonica. An acrobatic number enlisted the clumsy gymnastics of six amateurs, all dressed in tights and spangles; while I, in white tie and tails that swept the floor, sang Victor Herbert's "Ah, Sweet Mystery of Life" and led the grand finale. Rehearsals went on for weeks, and a professional tumbler was hired to coach the gymnasts in their routine.

All this was kept secret from the Maestro. On the day of the show Mrs. Toscanini told him only that they were to dine that evening at the Sarnoffs! When they arrived at the house, they found themselves in a press of people all in evening dress. The raucous noise of a jazz band smote the Maestro's ears. He thought they had mistaken the house. But his wife assured him they hadn't, and piloted him into a great solarium on the top floor, which had been fitted up to look like a Broadway night club, with small tables, a dance floor, and a thick velvet rope barring the entrance. At the rope stood Mr. Royal, dressed as a headwaiter and made unrecognizable by a strange wig. He consulted a sheet of paper in his hand, asked the by-now-bewildered Maestro his name, and, on being told, commanded him to spell it. This the Maestro did, and the "headwaiter," glancing up and down his paper, said that

[2] *sotto voce:* under the breath (Italian).

no reservation had been made in any such name. The Maestro, utterly at a loss, was about to turn tail when Mr. Royal, fearing the joke had gone too far, removed the rope, passed them through, and showed them to a table in the very first row. The Maestro glared about him, sat down, dropped his head on his chest, covered his eyes with his hand, and remained so for the rest of the evening. The guests, about eighty in number, surrounded him, but the Maestro's ostentatious unhappiness put a damper on everybody, and more particularly on the cast, who were appalled at the prospect of displaying their amateur talents before the grim, unseeing, hostile guest of honor. Some of the actors, having taken a peep at the Maestro through the wings, burst into tears and vowed not to go on. But the feelings of the other guests had to be considered, and at a hurried meeting of the cast backstage it was decided to proceed with the show. So the show went on, unseen by the Maestro, and only nervously observed by the guests, whose attention shifted alternately from the stage to the brooding conductor. The injustice and the unfairness of the Maestro's behavior had their effect on those who had worked so hard to amuse him. A certain bravado now animated the cast as it went through its paces. The acrobats leaped higher than they had at rehearsals. Walter Toscanini executed his Russian dance with a gusto that subsequently laid him up with an injured leg for weeks; Marcia Davenport, attempting a split during a can-can number, landed on the floor with such force as to be obliged to wear a cast for her injured back for months; and I, with the aid of a concealed microphone in the lapel of my tailcoat, advanced boldly to the Toscanini table and roared "Ah, Sweet Mystery of Life" straight into the Maestro's frozen face.

There was supper and dancing after the show. Still the Maestro sat unmoving, his hand over his eyes. Fair ladies came and sat beside him and attempted to flirt. Mrs. Sarnoff brought him food especially cooked to his taste. It was all to no avail. Mrs. Toscanini, apologetic and embarrassed, attempted to explain that her husband had been upset by the noise and the lights, and that he did not like surprises on principle. At one in the morning, with tears in her eyes, she begged her husband to go home. "I will stay to the bitter end," he muttered gloomily, in the voice of one condemned. So he stayed on, prolonging the pall he had cast over the party, while the jazz orchestra blared away and the people ate and danced halfheartedly and finally melted away. Mr. and Mrs. Toscanini were among the last to go, leaving the indignant cast to express their resentment openly and take what comfort they might in recalling the polite expressions of sympathy from the rest of the audience.

This unfortunate episode had, however, a pleasant sequel. For, having indulged his spleen to the full, the Maestro began to regret the pain he had caused. Some time later he conveyed his repentance obliquely by suggesting that if we ever gave another show, he would like to be a participant. This unexpected offer instantly obliterated whatever resentment we still felt. We hastily made plans for another show with the Maestro as star. We concocted a series of comedy turns and sketches, and recruited a cast of celebrated artists. The presence of Toscanini and a half-dozen popular soloists gave us an excuse for presenting the entertainment as a benefit for the Chatham Square Music School, a non-profit school for talented young musicians on New York's lower East Side. Even so, we failed to grasp fully the drawing-power of a cast that included Toscanini, Heifetz, Horowitz, Tibbett, Milstein, Adolph Busch, Alfred Wallenstein, and the late Emanuel Feuermann.

Although we could have sold out Madison Square Garden, we rented the tiny Chanin Theater, seating two hundred persons. We had printed and mailed out invitations to purchase tickets at fifteen dollars apiece, but the price also included a midnight supper and dance with liquor and food. For a time our ticket sale was negligible. On investigation we learned that most of those to whom we mailed invitations refused to believe that the cast of characters for a revue entitled *Say Ah!* could possibly include some of the greatest musical artists in the world. Believing themselves the victims of a hoax, they had thrown the invitations into their wastepaper baskets. But two or three days before the night of the performance, word got around that Toscanini, Heifetz, Horowitz, Feuermann, *et al,*[3] were actually rehearsing for *Say Ah!* We sold

[3] *et al.:* See footnote, page 194.

all the tickets in one afternoon, disappointing many persons who telephoned too late.

The Maestro's "number" in *Say Ah!* was called "Toscanini and his Children's Orchestra." It was a take-off on a "Youth Orchestra" then recently organized by Leopold Stokowski. The Maestro's "Children's Orchestra" consisted of some thirty instrumentalists, with Heifetz as concertmaster. They were to appear in short pants and white blouses, and the Maestro was to wear a long, old-fashioned Prince Albert coat, with a bandanna handkerchief sticking out of a rear pocket, an exaggerated starched collar, and a large four-in-hand. The music he selected included short popular pieces such as "*Loin du Bal*," "Tritsch-tratsch Polka," "Skaters' Waltz," and Mozart's farcical "A Musical Joke."

A dress rehearsal was called for very late in the evening of the night before the performance. Out of deference to the Maestro, we asked him to rehearse his number first, though it came last on the program. This mark of respect almost resulted in the abandonment of the show. For the Maestro rehearsed his little pieces as painstakingly and arduously as if they had been exalted works of Beethoven. If the members of the orchestra had thoughts of enjoying themselves in the preparation of light "hotel" music like "*Loin du Bal*," they were quickly disabused. For three hours Toscanini and the little band of noted instrumentalists labored to perfect the small pieces until they sounded like miracles of orchestral balance. As we of the non-musical cast listened, we were struck by the inferior quality of our own poor amateur dramatic efforts. Some of us flatly announced that we would withdraw. Mr. Herbert Graf, our stage director, observed sadly that we could not possibly appear on a program with Toscanini and his remarkable players, and he suggested that the Maestro enlarge his portion of the program to a full evening's entertainment. We all agreed, with the exception of one amateur dancer who was to have been the star in a burlesque of a ballet to the music of Debussy's "Afternoon of a Faun." Made unhappy by the decision to abandon everything in the show but the Toscanini "number," this fledgling Nijinsky fled to a dressing-room, where I discovered him lying on the floor dressed in his faun's costume, alternately sobbing and drinking from a bottle of whisky he had thoughtfully provided for himself. I informed the Maestro of our decision as he took his place in the first row of the theater to watch the rehearsal of the rest of the show. He expressed great surprise, but declared that he would reserve judgment until he had an opportunity to see for himself. By then it was one a.m. I hurriedly rounded up the actors. Nervous and shaken, we went through our numbers while the Maestro watched us intently through his pince-nez,[4] which he held lengthwise in front of him. After the final number I leaned over the stage and with sinking heart asked him what he thought. "Wonderful!" he said gravely. I brought the glad news to my dejected and perspiring colleagues, and we spent several hours celebrating.

The next evening I arrived early at the theater. Only the Maestro was backstage, dressed in the Prince Albert (he had spent half a day at Brooks Brothers being fitted) and nervously pacing up and down. Soon the rest of the cast arrived and were crowded into the few little dressing-rooms the tiny theater afforded. Half-dressed actors kept rushing in and out of the corridor, jostling the Maestro, who, having dressed at home, did not rate a dressing-room. He got in everybody's way, but there was no place else for him to go. As his was the last number on the program, he would have been in ample time had he arrived at ten instead of seven. When reminded of this, he said it was his habit to arrive at a performance ahead of the audience.

The show was a stunning success. A sketch in which Heifetz (as a barefoot, tatterdemalion Tennessee hillbilly), Horowitz (as a Dostoyevsky-ish piano student), Tibbett (as a vainglorious singer), and Feuermann (as a Tyrolese cellist) applied for admission to the Chatham Square Music School brought down the house. Heifetz played a Virginia reel on an inexpensive violin, which I, in the character of the school's director, broke irately over his head. Horowitz, looking like a character out of Gorky's *The Lower Depths*, kept mumbling idiotically: "I play the piano" when asked what he would play. Mr. Tibbett, clad in white ties and tails, came out to sing the Prologue from *Pagliacci*, which he did seriously and beautifully. But at a certain point his trousers began

4 *pince-nez* (păns'nā): eyeglasses clipped to the nose by a spring.

almost imperceptibly to slip down. At the final high G, delivered with clarion force and tonal beauty, they fell to the floor as the stage quickly blacked out. The house rocked with laughter. Rachmaninoff, sitting in the balcony, seemed to resent the planned accident at the Prologue's climax, and he left the theater, presumably in displeasure.

Another sketch warmly greeted was "The Maestro Comes to Dinner," which spoofed the terror inspired by the Maestro's acceptance of a dinner engagement. Wanda Horowitz, Toscanini's daughter, assumed the role of her father and looked startingly like him in get-up and bearing—so much so that many in the audience thought that the Maestro was playing himself. In the skit the hostess discovers, a moment before the arrival of her distinguished guest, that the cook has put too much salt in the *polenta*.[5] Unwilling to face the Maestro's wrath, the family decides to commit suicide in a body. The host draws a revolver and shoots everyone in the room. Each one dies resignedly. But Mrs. Heifetz, the mother of the violinist, injected an impromptu line as she expired: "Good-by, Jascha," she gasped, "I know *you* will understand!"

The climax of the evening came at the end with Toscanini and his Children's Orchestra. Never had light music been played with such brilliance, verve, beauty, tonal balance, and general perfection! In a certain crescendo-decrescendo passage in Mozart's "A Musical Joke," Toscanini made the men of the orchestra rise slowly to their feet and then sink slowly back. The audience stood up and cheered. And the Maestro, loath, as usual, to take curtain calls alone, made his "children" rise innumerable times as he stepped down from the podium and took his place among them. After the show, artists and audience repaired to a large adjoining room for supper and dancing to the music of a jazz band. Our joy at the success of the show was slightly tempered with regret that the Chatham Square School benefited only to the extent of $2,200 instead of the great sum the presence of such stars should have netted.

[5] *polenta:* a thick porridge (Italian).

SUGGESTIONS FOR STUDY

1. Contrast the plans and programs of the two parties held for Toscanini. What do you think about Toscanini's behavior at the first party? How would you describe the nature of Toscanini's party spirit at the second one?

2. The biographer speaks of "the injustice and the unfairness of the Maestro's behavior." Why did this behavior not turn people against Toscanini?

3. Exchange opinions on whether or not an unpredictable temperament is a necessary element of genius.

4. How many of the musical compositions mentioned do you know? Find out whether or not Toscanini, as a conductor, made any recordings of these. Bring to class and play two recordings of the same musical composition, one conducted by Toscanini, the other by someone else. See if you can detect any of Toscanini's personality traits in the way the music is conducted.

5. Toscanini's start as a musical conductor is unusual and dramatic. Some member of the class should look up the details and report them to the class.

Dr. Johnson Goes to Dinner

JAMES BOSWELL

Boswell's *The Life of Samuel Johnson* is among the greatest biographies ever written and is certainly the most famous in the English language.

The brief selection which follows not only will introduce you to this great book but also will give you a glimpse of another great man who was a mixture of childishness and maturity. Aren't we all?

I AM NOW to record a very curious incident in Dr. Johnson's life, which fell under my own observation, and which I am persuaded will, with the liberal-minded, be much to his credit.

My desire of being acquainted with celebrated men of every description, had made me, much about the same time, obtain an introduction to Dr. Samuel Johnson and to John Wilkes, Esq.[1] Two men more different could perhaps not be selected out of all mankind. They had even attacked one another with some asperity in their writings; yet I lived in habits of friendship with both. I could fully relish the excellence of each; for I have ever delighted in that intellectual chemistry, which can separate good qualities from evil in the same person. . . .

My worthy booksellers and friends, Messieurs Dilly in the Poultry, at whose hospitable and well-covered table I have seen a greater number of literary men than at any other, except that of Sir Joshua Reynolds,[2] had invited me to meet Mr. Wilkes and some more gentlemen, on Wednesday, May 15. "Pray (said I,) let us have Dr. Johnson."—"What! With Mr. Wilkes? not for the world, (said Mr. Edward Dilly;) Dr. Johnson would never forgive me." —"Come, (said I,) if you'll let me negotiate for you, I will be answerable that all shall go well." DILLY. "Nay, if you will take it

---

[1] *John Wilkes:* English political agitator.
[2] *Sir Joshua Reynolds:* famous English portrait painter.

upon you, I am sure I shall be very happy to see them both here."
Notwithstanding the high veneration which I entertained for Dr.
Johnson, I was sensible that he was sometimes a little actuated by
the spirit of contradiction, and by means of that I hoped I should
gain my point. I was persuaded that if I had come upon him with
a direct proposal, "Sir, will you dine in company with Jack
Wilkes?" he would have flown into a passion, and would probably
have answered, "Dine with Jack Wilkes, Sir! I'd as soon dine with
Jack Ketch." [3] I therefore, while we were sitting quietly by ourselves at his house in an evening, took occasion to open my plan
thus:—"Mr. Dilly, Sir, sends his respectful compliments to you,
and would be happy if you would do him the honour to dine with
him on Wednesday next along with me, as I must soon go to
Scotland." JOHNSON. "Sir, I am obliged to Mr. Dilly. I will wait
upon him—" BOSWELL. "Provided, Sir, I suppose, that the company
which he is to have, is agreeable to you." JOHNSON. "What do you
mean, Sir? What do you take me for? Do you think I am so ignorant of the world, as to imagine that I am to prescribe to a gentleman what company he is to have at his table?" BOSWELL. "I beg
your pardon, Sir, for wishing to prevent you from meeting people
whom you might not like. Perhaps he may have some of what he
calls his patriotic friends with him." JOHNSON. "Well, Sir, and what
then? What care *I* for his *patriotic friends*? Poh!" BOSWELL. "I
should not be surprized to find Jack Wilkes there." JOHNSON. "And
if Jack Wilkes *should* be there, what is that to *me*, Sir? My dear
friend, let us have no more of this. I am sorry to be angry with
you; but really it is treating me strangely to talk to me as if I could
not meet any company whatever, occasionally." BOSWELL. "Pray,
forgive me, Sir: I meant well. But you shall meet whoever comes,
for me." Thus I secured him, and told Dilly that he would find him
very well pleased to be one of his guests on the day appointed.

Upon the much expected Wednesday, I called on him about
half an hour before dinner, as I often did when we were to dine
out together, to see that he was ready in time, and to accompany
him. I found him putting his books in order, and as they were
generally very old ones, clouds of dust were flying around him.

[3] *Jack Ketch:* the hangman.

He had on a pair of large gloves such as hedgers use. His present appearance put me in mind of my uncle, Dr. Boswell's description of him, "A robust genius, born to grapple with whole libraries." He was covered with dust, and making no preparation for going abroad. "How is this, Sir? (said I). Don't you recollect that you are to dine at Mr. Dilly's?" JOHNSON. "Sir, I did not think of going to Dilly's: it went out of my head. I have ordered dinner at home with Mrs. Williams." BOSWELL. "But, my dear Sir, you know you were engaged to Mr. Dilly, and I told him so. He will expect you, and will be much disappointed if you don't come." JOHNSON. "You must talk to Mrs. Williams about this."

Here was a sad dilemma. I feared that what I was so confident I had secured, would yet be frustrated. He had accustomed himself to show Mrs. Williams such a degree of humane attention, as frequently imposed some restraint upon him; and I knew that if she should be obstinate, he would not stir. I hastened down stairs to the blind lady's room, and told her I was in great uneasiness, for Dr. Johnson had engaged to me to dine this day at Mr. Dilly's, but that he had told me he had forgotten his engagement, and had ordered dinner at home. "Yes, Sir, (said she, pretty peevishly,) Dr. Johnson is to dine at home."—"Madam, (said I,) his respect for you is such, that I know he will not leave you, unless you absolutely desire it. But as you have so much of his company, I hope you will be good enough to forego it for a day: as Mr. Dilly is a very worthy man, has frequently had agreeable parties at his house for Dr. Johnson, and will be vexed if the Doctor neglects him to-day. And then, Madam, be pleased to consider my situation; I carried the message, and I assured Mr. Dilly that Dr. Johnson was to come; and no doubt he has made a dinner, and invited a company, and boasted of the honour he expected to have. I shall be quite disgraced if the Doctor is not there." She gradually softened to my solicitations, which were certainly as earnest as most entreaties to ladies upon any occasion, and was graciously pleased to empower me to tell Dr. Johnson, "That all things considered, she thought he should certainly go." I flew back to him, still in dust, and careless of what should be the event, "indifferent in his choice to go or stay;" but as soon as I had announced to him Mrs.

Williams's consent, he roared [to his Negro servant,] "Frank, a clean shirt," and was very soon drest. When I had him fairly seated in a hackney-coach with me, I exulted as much as a fortune-hunter who has got an heiress into a post-chaise with him to set out for Gretna-Green.[4]

When we entered Mr. Dilly's drawing-room, he found himself in the midst of a company he did not know. I kept myself snug and silent, watching how he would conduct himself. I observed him whispering to Mr. Dilly, "Who is that gentleman, sir?"—"Mr. Arthur Lee."—JOHNSON. "Too, too, too," (under his breath,) which was one of his habitual mutterings. Mr. Arthur Lee could not but be very obnoxious to Johnson, for he was not only a *patriot*, but an *American*. He was afterwards minister from the United States at the court of Madrid. "And who is the gentleman in lace?"—"Mr. Wilkes, Sir." This information confounded him still more; he had some difficulty to restrain himself, and taking up a book, sat down upon a window-seat and read, or at least kept his eye upon it intently for some time, till he composed himself. His feelings, I dare say, were awkward enough. But he no doubt recollected his having rated me for supposing that he could be at all disconcerted by any company, and he, therefore, resolutely set himself to behave quite as an easy man of the world, who could adapt himself at once to the disposition and manners of those whom he might chance to meet.

The cheering sound of "Dinner is upon the table," dissolved his reverie, and we *all* sat down without any symptom of ill humor. There were present, beside Mr. Wilkes, and Mr. Arthur Lee, who was an old companion of mine when he studied physick at Edinburgh, Mr. (now Sir John) Miller, Dr. Lettsom, and Mr. Slater, the druggist. Mr. Wilkes placed himself next to Dr. Johnson, and behaved to him with so much attention and politeness, that he gained upon him insensibly. No man ate more heartily than Johnson, or loved better what was nice and delicate. Mr. Wilkes was very assiduous in helping him to some fine veal. "Pray give me leave, Sir;—It is better here—A little of the brown—Some fat,

[4] *Gretna-Green:* a village in Southern Scotland, the scene of many runaway marriages.

Sir—A little of the stuffing—Some gravy—Let me have the pleasure of giving you some butter—Allow me to recommend a squeeze of this orange;—or the lemon, perhaps, may have more zest."— "Sir, Sir, I am obliged to you, Sir," cried Johnson, bowing, and turning his head to him with a look for some time of "surly virtue," but, in a short while, of complacency.

SUGGESTIONS FOR STUDY

1. What impressions of Johnson's maturity or lack of maturity have you obtained from this selection?

2. What opinion of Wilkes did Johnson have? How did Boswell manage to get Wilkes and Johnson together? What did you learn from this selection about the use of tact and diplomacy in gaining an objective?

3. In giving a dinner party what importance do you attach to the guest list? What is your opinion of friends who, invited to a dinner or a party, ask you about your guest list?

4. What evidence is given that might lead you to conclude that Johnson was not sympathetic toward Americans? Let some ambitious student check this biography or others to see whether or not Johnson had this attitude, and why.

5. Before moving on to the last section of this book, give some thoughtful consideration to this matter of maturity. Make a list of characteristics which you could call mature and also a list of those which indicate immaturity. Check the qualities in both lists which you think apply to you.

The Close of Life

To the reader of biography, there are a number of reasons why the subject of death is of interest. For one thing, the way a person faces death is often a clue to his total personality. If a person faces death courageously and triumphantly, the chances are that he has lived a courageous and triumphant life. In biography the author, having already presented the entire life of his subject, is enabled to present his death in its proper proportion as it relates to the person's total life.

Biographies also include the effect of the person's death upon his friends, family, and others who care about him. Confronted with the death of their friend, many people reveal the impact the life of the deceased had upon them. When the biographer tells us their reactions, our knowledge and appreciation of the person's life is significantly enhanced.

And finally, death, as viewed by most people, is not the end of life. Many of us do not agree with Shakespeare that the sixth and seventh ages of man are "second childishness and mere oblivion." The human personality survives death, and in ways which can be represented only symbolically, lives on. Biography is, in a sense, an integral part of this living beyond the grave since the biographer, by recording for future generations the life of a great man or woman, has made it possible for that person to live on in the hearts and minds of the readers.

A Last Letter

The name of Tom Dooley, the "jungle doctor" of Laos, is enrolled in the hearts of all the human family as a self-sacrificing, humane, and devout servant of God. Dr. Dooley will be remembered along with Father Damien, David Livingstone, and the countless others whose mission in life it was to use their minds and wills in the never-ending fight to relieve physical suffering in those areas of the world where they felt they were most needed.

Dr. Dooley's career was cut short in 1961 by his untimely death from cancer at the age of thirty-four. It remains now for Tom Dooley's biographers to uncover for us what deep inward personal convictions caused him to lead such an exemplary life. In the preparation of the biographies, no doubt letters such as this one, written just prior to his death, will be an invaluable aid. The letter is addressed to The Rev. Theodore M. Hesburgh, President of Notre Dame University in South Bend, Indiana.

Hong Kong
December 2, 1960

Dear Father Hesburgh:

They've got me down. Flat on the back . . . with plaster, sand bags, and hot water bottles. It took the last three instruments to do it, however.

I've contrived a way of pumping the bed up a bit, so that, with a long reach, I can get to my typewriter . . . my mind . . . my brain . . . my fingers.

Two things prompt this note to you, sir. The first is that whenever my cancer acts up . . . and it is certainly "acting up" now . . . I turn inward a bit. Less do I think of my hospitals around the world, or of 94 doctors, fund raising, and the like.

Reprinted by permission of The Reverend Theodore M. Hesburgh, C.S.C.

More do I think of one Divine Doctor, and my own personal fund of grace. Is it enough?

It has become pretty definite that the cancer has spread to the lumbar vertebrae, accounting for all the back problems over the last two months. I have monstrous phantoms . . . as all men do. But I try to exorcise them with all the fury of the middle ages. And inside and outside the wind blows.

But when the time comes, like now, then the storm around me does not matter. The winds within me do not matter. Nothing human or earthly can touch me.

A wilder storm of peace gathers in my heart. What seems unpossessable I can possess. What seems unfathomable, I fathom. What is unutterable, I can utter. Because I can pray. I can communicate. How do people endure anything on earth if they cannot have God?

I realize that external symbols that surround one when he prays are not important. The stark wooden cross on an altar of boxes in Haiphong [1] with a tortured priest . . . the same magnificence of the Sacred Heart Bernini altar [2] . . . they are essentially the same. Both are symbols. It is the something else that counts.

But just now . . . and just so many times, how I long for the Grotto.[3] Away from the Grotto, Dooley just prays. But at the Grotto, especially now when there must be snow everywhere and the lake is ice glass and that triangular fountain on the left is frozen solid and all the priests are bundled in their too large, too long old black coats and the students wear snow boots. . . . If I could go to the Grotto now, then I think I could sing inside.

I could be full of faith and poetry and loveliness, and know more beauty, tenderness, and compassion. This is soggy sentimentalism, I know. Cold prayers from a hospital bed are just as pleasing to God as more youthful prayers from a grotto on the lid of night.

But it's telling a mother in labor, "It's okay, millions have endured the labor pains and survived happy. . . . You will, too." It's

[1] *Haiphong:* a town in North Viet-Nam.
[2] *Bernini altar:* an altar by the famous artist Bernini in the Sacred Heart church on the Notre Dame campus.
[3] *Grotto:* a replica, on the Notre Dame campus, of the famous Catholic shrine at Lourdes, France.

consoling. . . . but doesn't lessen the pain. Accordingly, knowing prayers from here are just as good as from the Grotto doesn't lessen my gnawing, yearning passion to be there.

I don't mean to ramble. Yes, I do.

The second reason I write to you just now is that I have in front of me the *Notre Dame Alumnus* of September, 1960.

And herein is a story. This is a Chinese hospital run by a Chinese division of the Sisters of Charity (I think). Though my doctors are British, the hospital is as Chinese as shark's fin soup. Every orderly, corpsman, nurse, and nun knows of my work in Asia, and each has taken it upon himself to personally "give" to the man they feel has given to their Asia. As a consequence, I'm a bit smothered in tender, loving care.

With a triumphant smile this morning one of the nuns brought me some American magazines (which are limp with age and which I must hold horizontal above my head to read). An old *National Geographic*, two older *Times,* and that unfortunate edition of *Life* [4] . . . and with these, a copy of the *Notre Dame Alumnus.* How did it ever get here?

So, Father Hesburgh, Notre Dame is twice on my mind . . . and always in my heart. That grotto is the rock to which my life is anchored.

Do the students ever appreciate what they have, while they have it? I know I never did. Spent most of my time being angry at the clergy . . . 10 p.m. bed check, absurd for a 19-year-old veteran, etc., etc., etc.

Won't take any more of your time; did just want to communicate for a moment, and again offer my thanks to my beloved Notre Dame.

Though I lack a certain buoyancy in my bones just now, I lack none in my spirit. I must return to the States very soon, and I hope to sneak into that grotto . . . before the snow has melted.

My best wishes to the students, regards to the faculty, and respects to you.

Very sincerely,
Tom Dooley

[4] edition of *Life:* an edition of *Life* which contained an article which Dr. Dooley considered uncomplimentary.

SUGGESTIONS FOR STUDY

1. While he was in pain, of what value to Tom Dooley were religious symbols?

2. Dr. Dooley expressed one regret about his attitude during his school days at Notre Dame. What is it? How can you arrange your life in such a way as not to have to express the same regret later on?

3. What is a grotto? What was the difference between the way Dooley prayed inside the grotto and the way he prayed outside of it? He says: "That grotto is the rock to which my life is anchored." In your own experiences so far, what places are there which have a special meaning for you? What places which you have not yet visited have some special religious significance for you? What places are there in the world which you would care to visit if you knew you were soon going to die?

4. Why were the hospital personnel anxious to smother Tom Dooley with "tender loving care"?

5. Some young people have as their aim in life to make a great deal of money. What do you think was Tom Dooley's real aim or goal in life?

6. Remembering that Father Hesburgh is a priest of the Roman Catholic Church, as well as the president of a famous university, what do you think were his thoughts and feeling at the time he received this letter from an alumnus of his school?

7. Write a letter expressing your appreciation of the contribution made to your life by some person or some institution.

The Death of Gandhi

VINCENT SHEEAN

In 1948 Mahatma Gandhi, the great Hindu religious and political leader, was assassinated as he was entering a prayer-ground in New Delhi, India, to hold a prayer-meeting. In the group waiting for the leader was Vincent Sheean, the well-known American journalist, who was rapidly becoming a convert to Gandhi's principles.

In the following account of Gandhi's assassination from *Lead Kindly Light,* Vincent Sheean relates the details of the assassination and shows us his own attitude and emotions upon witnessing the death of a respected and beloved friend. You will find related here some extremely unusual things, difficult for you and me to comprehend, but worth our serious thought and consideration.

I GOT A TAXI and went out to Birla House in time for the prayer-meeting. This time I was alone. I stationed my taxi under a tree opposite the gate of Birla House and walked down the drive to the prayer-ground. It was not yet five o'clock and people were still streaming in on foot, in cars and with tongas. As I came on to the prayer-ground at the end of the garden I ran into Bob Stimson, the Delhi correspondent of the B.B.C. We fell into talk and I told him about the journey to Amritsar and what had taken place there. It was unusual to see any representatives of the press at the prayer-meeting; Bob explained that he had submitted some questions to the Mahatma for the B.B.C. and thought he might as well stay for the prayers since he was on the premises. He looked at his watch and said: "Well, this is strange. Gandhi's late. He's practically never late."

We both looked at our watches again. It was 5:12 by my watch when Bob said: "There he is." We stood near the corner of the wall, on the side of the garden where he was coming, and watched the evening light fall on his shining dark-brown head. He did not walk under the arbor this evening but across the grass, in the open lawn on the other side of the flower beds. (There was the arbored walk, and a strip of lawn, and a long strip of flower bed, and then the open lawn.) It was one of those shining Delhi evenings, not at all warm but alight with the promise of spring. I felt well and happy and grateful to be here. Bob and I stood idly talking, I do not remember about what, and watching the Mahatma advance toward us over the grass, leaning lightly on two of "the girls," with two or three other members of his "family" (family or followers) behind them. I read afterward that he had sandals on his feet but I did not see them. To me it looked as if he walked barefoot on the grass. It was not a warm evening, and he was wrapped in home-spun shawls. He passed by us on the other side and turned to ascend the four or five brick steps which led to the terrace or prayer-ground.

Here, as usual, there was a clump of people, some of whom were standing and some of whom had gone on their knees or bent low before him. Bob and I turned to watch—we were perhaps ten feet away from the steps—but the clump of people cut off our view of the Mahatma now; he was so small. Then I heard four small, dull, dark explosions. "What's that?" I said to Bob in sudden hor-ror. "I don't know," he said. I remember that he grew pale in an instant. "Not the Mahatma!" I said, and then I knew.

What followed must be told just as it happened (*to me—me*) or there is no truth in it.

Inside my own head there occurred a wavelike disturbance which I can only compare to a storm at sea—wind and wave surg-ing tremendously back and forth. I remember all this distinctly; I do not believe that I lost consciousness even for a moment, al-though there may have been an instant or two of half-conscious-ness. I recoiled upon the brick wall and leaned against it, bent almost in two. I felt the consciousness of the Mahatma leave me then—I know of no other way of expressing this: he left me. The storm inside my head continued for some little time—minutes, perhaps; I have no way of reckoning. Then I was aware of two things at once, a burning and stinging in the fingers of my right hand and a similar burning and stinging in my eyes. In the eyes it was tears, although of some more acid mixture than I had known, and on my fingers I did not know for a while what it was, because I put them in my mouth (like a child) to ease the burning. In the wildness and confusion of that moment a young Indian—unknown to me—came to where I was doubled up against the wall and said: "Is he dead? Is he dead?" The young Indian had staring eyes and was as filled with horror as I was, I suppose, although I do not know why he asked me such a question. "I don't know," I said, taking my fingers out of my mouth to do so.

Then I looked at my fingers. On the third and fourth fingers of my right hand blisters had appeared. They were facing each other, on the sides of those fingers which touch. The blister on the third finger was rather large and was already filled with water. The blister on the fourth or little finger was smaller. They had not been there before I heard the shots.

The storm returned inside my head, but briefly, very briefly. I sat on the edge of the wall and looked at my fingers and then put them back into my mouth: they burned far worse than is usual with blisters. What was this?

Then flooding into my memory came the visions in Vermont the summer before, the dreams since, the many, many dreams in which I had endeavored to interpose myself, my arm, my leg, or my body between the inevitable murderer and Mahatma Gandhi. How could such things be? That was the question that streamed through my head incessantly. *How can such things be?* was the exact form in which it appeared, and came back again and again through the next hour and a half (or indeed at decreasing intervals for two or three days).

Now, of course, I know that the blisters were a psychosomatic phenomenon which, although curious and interesting, present no great element of novelty to science. For me, however, at that moment, they were an overwhelming evidence of connection with this dreadful deed—of my failure, at least, to die for the Mahatma, the last best hope of earth. An unspeakable misery consumed me.

It was during this time, apparently, that many things happened: a whole external series of events took place in my immediate neighborhood—a few yards away—and I was unaware of them. A doctor was found; the police took charge; the body of the Mahatma was carried away; the crowd melted, perhaps urged to do so by the police. I saw none of this. The last I saw of the Mahatma he was advancing over the grass in the evening light, approaching the steps. When I finally took my fingers out of my mouth and stood up, dry-eyed, there were police and soldiers and not many people, and there was Bob Stimson. He was rather breathless; he had gone somewhere to telephone to the B.B.C. He came with me down the steps to the lawn, where we walked up and down beside the flower-bed for a while. The room with the glass doors and windows, by the rose garden at the end of the arbor, had a crowd of people around it. Many were weeping. The police were endeavoring to make them leave. Bob could not tell me anything except that the Mahatma had been taken inside that room. (On the following day he told me that he had seen him carried away, and that the *khadi* which he wore was heavily stained with blood.)

Presently Bob had to go and I was left alone in the garden. Almost everybody else vanished too; I think the police cleared the place several times. Why they did not put me out I do not know. (Since then I have thought that perhaps Mr. Nehru, who must have been there by then, told them to ignore me—it would consort with his great and subtle kindness.) I walked up and down beside the flower-bed, which I now observed to be filled with petunias of the same kind and colors as those which I had lately seen stretching beside the fountains and streams in front of the Taj Mahal. At this point I was numb with horror and went through these motions meaninglessly, only the surface of mind and body engaged. Underneath there was a deadness, a kind of suspended animation.

A young American came there and spoke to me. I took him to be a representative of the United Press. He said that he was not; that he was from the American Embassy and had never been to the prayer-meeting before; he had just arrived in India from China. He went away, and after a while he came back again. This time I thought he was from the Associated Press (confusing him, each time, with young Americans whom I actually had met). He told me again that he was from the embassy. I took in nothing that he said to me, but later on I learned that it was this young man who, at the moment of the assassination, actually captured the assassin and held him for the Indian police, and after turning the assassin over, searched the crowd for a doctor. When I knew this in the following week it gave me a sort of tribal pride to think that although I had been paralyzed and helpless, there was one of my breed who had been useful.

The garden now was almost empty and the sun was going down behind the prayer-ground. There were two more people who came and spoke to me. One was a young Indian—perhaps the same one who had spoken to me on the prayer-ground—who was weeping bitterly. He said: "He will recover, won't he? He will recover?" I said these words exactly: "If he still has consciousness he may recover. He has great resources. But if he has lost consciousness he cannot recover. There is nothing the consciousness can do against a bullet." (I believed that his consciousness had gone because it had left me, but I did not want to say so to the woe-stricken young man.) Another Indian, much older, but also weeping bitterly, said: "This means some great disaster for the world, does it not?" I said: "I am afraid that you may be right."

Then they, too, went, as did the police, and the garden was absolutely empty except for me. This was the state of things for about an hour. Why I remained (and why I was allowed to remain) I do not know. I had some vague idea that perhaps Mr. Nehru would pass by and I could ask him if it was true or not. But this could not have been the real reason; it was what is called unconscious behavior. (Actually Nehru was on the other side of the house some of the time, speaking to the vast crowd that had assembled outside the walls; and part of the time he was in the room with the glass doors and windows, where the Mahatma lay, a few feet away from me.) I wandered between the rose garden and the petunia beds. With one part of my mind I was noticing these flowers and the neat little wooden labels that Mr. Birla's gardeners had stuck into the ground beside the roses. One yellowish rose was called "Lord Lonsdale," I remember, and even then (so peculiar is the human brain) I wondered why.

But most of the time I was prey to an unexampled misery. At times it submerged me so utterly that I lost all but the faintest surface consciousness of my surroundings. There was a small summer-house or perhaps family temple beyond the rose garden, a few feet beyond the glass room where the Mahatma lay. When I could no longer stand up or walk I had recourse to the steps of this small, closed house, leaning or sitting on the edge of them, more often than not bent in two. Words went through my head in two ways—two forms of what the behaviorists so naively call "talking with concealed musculature." One was the ordinary way of words pronounced, words sounding in the inner ear. The other was precisely like ticker tape—words visible in the mind but unheard. Most of them were from Shakespeare or the Bible, and were undoubtedly thrown up by the unconscious memory, but with an agonizing suddenness and an effect of unbearable truth each time. One was quite incongruous, from Macbeth: *She should have died hereafter; there would have been a time for such a word.* (Incongruous, that is, for the pronoun *she*, but otherwise quite applicable.) Another was: *I cried to him from the depths and he answered me.* Another was: *Father, why hast thou forsaken me?* These last two appeared both verbally and visually in my mind many times, shaking my whole being each time.

I was helped out of this traumatic condition by the appearance of Bob Neville's wife and sister on the other side of the garden wall. His sister called: "Jimmy! Jimmy!" and I looked for the source of the sound. The wall of the garden was in baroque style with decorative circles. Through one of these I saw Bob's sister and wife, neither of whom spoke further; by their mere presence and their look I knew that they had felt something about my unfathomable unhappiness and wanted to help me. I therefore tried, with some success, the operation we call "pulling ourselves together"—I stood straight, breathed deep, dried my eyes and tried walking up and down beside the house, that is, on the side between the house and the garden wall. Here, in due course, Edgar Snow appeared. He was as shaken, I suppose, as everybody else in Delhi must have been on that day. I said to him: "I've lost my only *guru*.[1] I'll never learn anything now." He told me about Nehru's speech to the great crowd outside the walls.

[1] *guru:* a religious teacher (India).

We walked around the garden once, and even up to the prayer-ground, where Ed showed me the place where the Mahatma fell. The prayer-ground was empty, except for a soldier standing guard over that spot and the cartridge-shells which lay there at his feet.

Swirling and dense and immeasurable, like all Indian crowds, the great mass of people surrounded the house outside the garden walls. It was very difficult to get through and out, but when we succeeded in doing so we found my taxi where I had left it two hours before, under the tree. I had, of course, forgotten it. It took us back to the city.

The Mahatma was cremated on the following day (Saturday, January 31, 1948) on the immense plain beside the river Jumna outside of Delhi in the presence of a vast multitude. There followed the thirteen days of mourning prescribed for orthodox Hindus of his particular caste. On the thirteenth day, which was February 12, 1948, his ashes were distributed to the seven sacred rivers of India.

SUGGESTIONS FOR STUDY

1. How does the author explain the blisters on his fingers? His dreams in Vermont? His feeling of the consciousness of the Mahatma leaving him? (Explain *psychosomatic*.) What is your explanation of these phenomena?

2. What is meant by "talking with concealed musculature"?

3. What events showed the position held by Gandhi in Sheean's heart? In the hearts of the people? What are some of the things said about Gandhi at the time of the assassination?

4. What did Bob Stimson's action immediately after the assassination tell you about him?

5. Let some member of the class report on Gandhi's life and teachings. What recent events in America show indications of Gandhi's influence?

6. Write a brief account of what happened to you upon the death of some relative, or friend, or national figure. Tell it "just as it happened (*to you—you*) or there will be no truth in it."

A Mighty Heart

CATHERINE DRINKER BOWEN

To Chief Justice Oliver Wendell Holmes, Jr., was granted a long life. When ninety, he submitted his resignation as a Justice of the United States Supreme Court. He knew that he did not have much longer to live, but death to him was a part of life and living. He was almost ninety-four when he died. Catherine Drinker Bowen, an expert in fictionalized biography, has wonderfully presented, in this selection from *Yankee from Olympus*, the quiet drama of a great man dying greatly.

SILENCE, RESIGNATION. To sit in one's library in the morning and read eulogies of oneself, receive admiring visitors. . . . Was there any praise, were there any crowns in heaven or earth to take the place of the work a man loved and had relinquished? In all his life, Holmes had never been without a job. At night the papers on his desk, the Year Book with the marker at the page—these had been for him the bridge between night and morning. The very act of waking each day had been exciting, with the battle waiting. "Bugler, blow the charge! I am ready. . . ."

And now the bugler blew his charge no more. The battle was over, the challenger was still. Holmes felt tired, exhausted. When he tried to write his friends about his resignation, it was hard even to hold the pen.

Anxiously the household watched him. For the past ten years Dr. Adams, the family physician, had said the Judge would die if he stopped work. Holmes, indeed, had said it himself. Now the prophecy seemed in danger of fulfillment.

But it was not fulfilled. For Holmes, fate had not reserved this particular defeat—to die of heartbreak because he was no longer

useful. Three years of life remained, and they were not to be unhappy years. Once more Holmes rallied, once more his spirit
reasserted itself.

It was to Pollock [1] he gave testimony. It was "wonderful and
incredible to have no duties"; he could not have believed how
much he would like it. There was so much to learn! His secretary
read aloud by the hour while Holmes played solitaire or sat listening. Often he seemed to doze, but if the secretary stopped reading,
Holmes sat forward instantly. "What?" he would say. "What,
Sonny?" And he would begin instantly to discuss the book. Just
before they went to Beverly Farms, Holmes wrote to Pollock that
he must surely be getting cultivated—his secretary calculated they
had read 4,500,000 words! Spengler and John Dewey, Salter and
Belloc and McDougall and C. D. Broad—"sweetened," Holmes
said, by rereading all of Sherlock Holmes. He couldn't agree with
Parrington and Beard that the American Constitution represented
a triumph of the money power over democratic individualism. Be-
littling arguments always have a force of their own. "But you and
I," Holmes added to Pollock, "believe that high-mindedness is not
impossible to man."

Frankfurter came, one day, with the manuscript of a book about
Brandeis, a companion volume to the one he had got out about
Holmes. Would the Judge write an introduction? Very gladly,
Holmes said. He had known Brandeis—how long? Why, it was
half a century! Ever since the '70s when Brandeis emerged from
the Law School. . . . "In moments of discouragement that we all
pass through," Holmes wrote, "Brandeis always has had the happy
word that lifts one's heart. It came from knowledge, experience,
courage and the high way in which he has always taken life.
Whenever he left my house I was likely to say to my wife, 'There
goes a really good man.'"

Beverly that summer was beautiful. Fanny's rose garden
bloomed riotously and his own patch of wild flowers seemed
lovelier than ever. Old friends came out from Boston, bringing
their grandchildren. Holmes enjoyed these young people. There
was singular and striking beauty now to Holmes's face, a quality

[1] *Pollock:* a writer on law.

almost luminous. Sitting on the porch he discussed life with Betsy Warder, aged sixteen. "I won't refrain from talking about anything because you're too young," Holmes told her, "if you won't because I'm too old."

In the fall when he returned to Washington, Frankfurter sent down a new secretary as usual. It would do the young men good, he said, to be with Holmes even if he was no longer on the Court. Holmes protested, but he was very glad to have a man in the house to talk to. The secretary, arriving in October, watched the Judge with amazement, particularly at breakfast. Why, the old man attacked his breakfast like a cavalry officer in the field! Porridge—a heaping plateful with thick cream, lots of sugar. Fruit, broiled fish, muffins, marmalade, coffee. After breakfast the Judge announced he was going to loaf all day. "Ninety-two has outlived duty," he said with what seemed a vast satisfaction. Half an hour later he was calling for the secretary to read to him. "Let's have a little self-improvement, Sonny."

Beyond all other traits, this perpetual thirst to learn surprised both young and old. Franklin D. Roosevelt, a few days after his inauguration in 1933, came round to call. He found Holmes in his library, reading Plato. The question rose irresistibly. "Why do you read Plato, Mr. Justice?"

"To improve my mind, Mr. President," Holmes replied.

It was true. *The rule of joy and the law of duty seem to me all one.* Years ago, Holmes had said it, and time had not disproved it. To the beholder there was something enormously reassuring in this spectacle of a man so old and so wise, who still desired to learn.

The morning the President called, Frankfurter was there, and Harold Laski. Three days earlier—March 5—Roosevelt had closed the banks, laid an embargo on gold and called a special session of Congress for March ninth. March ninth was tomorrow. Tomorrow the President, standing before Congress would present his plan for the national emergency.

Rising when his visit was ended, Roosevelt paused at the door, turned earnestly to Holmes and addressed him as the greatest living American. "You have lived through half our country's history; you have seen its great men. This is a dark hour. Justice Holmes, what is your advice to me?"

Holmes looked at him. "You are in a war, Mr. President," he said. "I was in a war, too. And in a war there is only one rule: Form your battalions and fight."

The seasons rolled by . . . Spring and summer. . . . Beverly, with Fanny's delphinium still blue and tall by the gate. Washington again, with the Justices coming round to call. Brandeis and Cardozo, Stone with a new etching for Holmes to pass upon. Frankfurter, bounding up the long stairs to the library, his arms full of new books, talk bubbling on his tongue.

One day—it was the twenty-third of February, 1935—Holmes came down the steps in the early afternoon with his secretary and got in the car to go for a drive. It was a bitter day, windy, with a threat of snow. Next morning Holmes had a cold. "You shouldn't have let him go out," Mary Donnellan told the secretary. "Mrs. Holmes wouldn't have let him, on such a day." The household gathered round reproachfully. "Why don't you call the doctor, Mr. Rowe? Mrs. Holmes would have called the doctor."

The Judge went to bed, sneezing, and the sneeze turned to a cough, to something worse. Holmes was ninety-three, and he had pneumonia. By the first of March, the city knew that he was mortally ill.

Holmes knew it too, and was not dismayed. "Why should I fear death?" he had remarked to his secretary a few weeks earlier. "I have seen him often. When he comes he will seem like an old friend." Holmes had loved life. . . . "If the good Lord should tell me I had only five minutes to live, I would say to Him, 'All right, Lord, but I'm sorry you can't make it ten.'" He had loved life and he had believed in it. . . . *"If I were dying my last words would be: Have faith and pursue the unknown end."*

Now he was dying—and he said nothing half so dramatic. He lay quietly, joking with the nurses. What was the use of all this trouble—coaxing an old man to eat, giving him stimulants? "Lot of damn nonsense," Holmes grumbled, moving his long legs under the covers. Life was—what had he called it, in that speech at Harvard? "Life is action and passions." People said death was a rest from labors. It wasn't a rest—it was an obliteration, a passing of bone into dust, of one set of chemicals into another set of chemicals. And that was right too. Very right and proper.

He had had his share. Six years ago, half of life had died, with Fanny [his wife]. But even half of life had been good. *To have done what lay in you to do, to say that you have lived, and be ready for the end* . . . Oliver Wendell Holmes waited quietly in his bed.

March 2, 3, 4 . . . Across the street in an office building, newspapers held the death watch. Was the Justice going to live until his ninety-fourth birthday? Photographers hung round the front door, taking pictures of Chief Justice Hughes, of Brandeis, and Mrs. Roosevelt. Taxi drivers, cruising by, called out to the policemen stationed at the door. "How is he? How is the Judge?"

On the fifth of March, late in the afternoon, newspapermen saw an ambulance stop outside the door. An oxygen tent was carried in. Holmes, opening his eyes, watched the huge, unwieldy contraption wheeled to the bed, saw them lift the tent above his face. He made a movement. "Lot of damn foolery," he said clearly.

People were kind; they went to enormous trouble to give an old man a few more breaths. . . . His father hadn't died this way, boxed under a tent with a glass window. His father had died sitting in the library at home. The book had fallen from his hand. . . . How red the sky had been, above the Charles River! . . . *"What is it for me, Wendell—King's Chapel? Very well, that is all I want to know."*

Very well . . . very well. . . . *It is well.* . . . There was something his mother used to read to him and Ned and Amelia, on Sundays, from the Bible . . . "And they asked, 'Is it well with thee? Is it well with the child?' And she answered, *'It is well.'* " . . .

At two in the morning the doctors knew the end was near. They took the oxygen tubes away. Holmes lay with his eyes closed, breathing quietly. Outside, in the March garden, wet branches creaked and from the alley came the sound of wheels. As the doctors watched, Holmes died, taking his departure so quietly it was hard to tell when he was gone.

Mark Howe, the signs of grief plain on his face, went downstairs, opened the front door. From across the street a dozen newsmen rushed at him, notebooks in hand. They listened, then raced for the telephone. Justice Oliver Wendell Holmes was dead.

The funeral was held at All Souls Church—the old, white-pillared building that stands at the head of Sixteenth and Harvard Streets. A wet wind blew across the square. People stood on the curb, watching the Justices at the church steps. The bell tolled. . . . That was Brandeis, they said, going up the steps; the Justices were to be pallbearers. Those six men waiting beside them had been Holmes's secretaries. The service wouldn't be long; this was a Unitarian Church. Afterward the army would carry the Judge to Arlington.

"And Moses chose from among the people able men, such as feared God, men of truth, hating unjust gains, and set them over the people to judge them at all seasons. . . ."

The minister's voice was slow. . . . Outside, mounted police-men turned traffic away from the church. . . . "At the grave of a hero"—the minister was reading from Holmes's own words now —"at the grave of a hero we end, not with sorrow at the inevitable loss, but with the contagion of his courage; and with a kind of desperate joy we go back to the fight."

The President and Justices waited beside Holmes's grave. The procession came in sight, winding down the hill past Lee's house. Soldiers lifted the coffin, covered with the American flag, bore it across wet turf. Eight infantrymen raised their rifles and fired . . . a volley for each wound. . . .

Ball's Bluff . . . Antietam . . . Fredericksburg.

A soldier, standing a little apart, raised his bugle and blew taps.

OLIVER WENDELL HOLMES
Captain and Brevet Colonel
20th Massachusetts Volunteer Infantry, Civil War
Justice Supreme Court of the United States
March 1841   March 1935

From the floor of Congress, from the White House, from the Inns of Court in London, scholars and statesmen gave tribute, and for a few days the people mourned. But Holmes's real fame was to come slowly; the growth of his influence was to be as measured, as deep and sure, as the forces that had shaped him. Time, events, history itself, would prove his dissents. One by one they became law . . . *Hammer v. Dagenhart.* Child labor can be regulated by Congress . . . *Lochner v. New York.* The liberty of the citizen to do as he pleases does not mean he can force other men to work twelve hours a day . . . *Coppage v. Kansas . . . Truax v. Corrigan,* and in Massachusetts, *Vegelahn v. Guntner* and *Plant v. Woods.* "I think the strike a lawful instrument in the universal struggle for life."

Free speech, like truth itself, cannot be achieved by statute. But the Bill of Rights was still worth fighting for. *Abrams v. the United States . . . Gitlow v. the People of New York . . . United States v. Rosika Schwimmer.* . . . "Free thought—not free thought for those who agree with us but freedom for the thought that we hate."

There was indeed a great contagion in this courage—a courage not born with Holmes but handed down with all the accumulated force, the deep spiritual persuasion, of the generations behind him. Abiel Holmes and Abiel's father, Captain David. Great-grandmother Hewet, teaching herself to read Vergil in a log cabin. Sally Wendell and Sally's father the Judge. Abiel's eldest son, small and light-minded but as fierce, when his heart was roused, as any patriot of them all. . . . "Ay, tear her tattered ensign down" . . . "I am too much in earnest for either humility or vanity, but I do entreat those who hold the keys of life and death to listen. . . ."

Men called the doctor's son the Great Dissenter. The title was misleading. *To want something fiercely and want it all the time—* this is not dissent but affirmation. The things Holmes wanted were great things, never to be realized. How can man realize the infinite? *Have faith and pursue the unknown end.*

"Whether a man accepts from Fortune her spade and will look downward and dig, or from Aspiration her axe and cord, and will scale the ice, the one and only success which it is his to command is to bring to his work a mighty heart."

SUGGESTIONS FOR STUDY

1. What is a eulogy? In what respect do you consider this chapter a eulogy?

2. What statement had the family physician made about Justice Holmes? How much truth do you feel there is in the doctor's statement?

3. What is meant by Holmes's comment: "But you and I believe that high-mindedness is not impossible to man"?

4. How did Justice Holmes show a "perpetual thirst to learn"? What are other ways of showing this desire to learn?

5. After his resignation, how was Holmes still useful to his friends? How did these friends contribute to the last years of his life?

6. Explain what is meant by Holmes's words to the sixteen-year-old: "I won't refrain from talking about anything because you're too young if you won't because I'm too old"?

7. What about Holmes amazed the secretary? Why was it amazing to him?

8. Holmes stood very high in his profession. How have his court decisions influenced our thinking? What admirable qualities do these decisions illustrate? In this selection what other admirable qualities in the man are made clear to you?

9. This selection is from a fictionalized biography. In this case to what real advantages do you feel the biographer has employed this method? What abuses of it, if any, do you note? Cite some sentences which to you are obviously fictionalized accounts of what happened?

10. State as clearly as you can and in your own words Holmes's attitude toward death. How does his attitude differ from yours? What factors in Holmes's life do you feel might be responsible for such an attitude as his?

11. Write a theme in which you state by specific examples how Part Two of this book has enlarged your conception of a rich, abundant life.

Further Reading in Biography

Antin, Mary	*The Promised Land*
Baker, Rachel	*The First Woman Doctor*
Bartholomew, Carol	*My Heart Has Seventeen Rooms*
Bell, Margaret E.	*Touched with Fire*
Bok, Edward	*The Americanization of Edward Bok*
Brickhill, Paul	*Reach for the Sky*
Buchan, John	*Pilgrim's Way*
Coolidge, Olivia	*Winston Churchill and the Story of Two World Wars*
Daugherty, James	*William Blake*
Jenkins, Elizabeth	*Elizabeth, the Great*
Eaton, Jeanette	*David Livingstone, Foe of Darkness*
Huxley, Elspeth	*The Flame Trees of Thika: Memories of an African Childhood*
Kane, Harnett	*Miracle in the Mountains*
Manchester, William	*A Rockefeller Family Portrait*
Mehta, Ved	*Face to Face*
Randall, Ruth P.	*Mary: a Biography of the Girl Who Married Abraham Lincoln*
Robinson, Mabel L.	*Runner of the Mountain Tops*
Roos, Ann	*Man of Molokai*
Shaw, Wilbur	*Gentlemen, Start Your Engines*
Simons, David	*Man High*
Sterne, Emma Gelders	*Mary McLeod Bethune*

Tharp, Louise Hall	*Until Victory*
Vining, Elizabeth Gray	*Friend of Life*
Wise, Winifred E.	*Rebel in Petticoats*
Woodham-Smith, Cecil	*Florence Nightingale*

Glossary

---

abhorred   regarded with horror.
absolution   forgiveness; a setting free from guilt.
acidly   in a biting manner.
actuated   moved to act.
ad lib   to add lines not in the script.
adjured   earnestly appealed.
admonishing   warning kindly.
aerialist   performer on a high-flying trapeze.
affirmation   a positive statement; assertion of belief
affluent   abundant.
albeit   although.
allay   to put to rest; to relieve.
alloy   mixture with other attitudes, or elements.
amalgam   a combination of qualities.
amassing   gathering together in a bunch.
ambiguous   doubtful; uncertain; understood in more than one way.
amiable   kindhearted and goodnatured.
anachronistic   inconsistent in point of time with the surroundings.
analyst   one who analyzes.
anemic   lacking healthy or sufficient blood; hence, pale or weak.
animated   made lively and full of spirit.
anon   soon (or a *time* soon).
antagonizing   opposing; coming in conflict with.
anticlerical   opposed to the clergy or church hierarchy.
apathetic   without feeling; lacking any real concern.
apprised   informed; notified.
ardently   eagerly.
arid   dry and barren.
arrogance   self-centered snobbishness.
arrogant   self-centered and snobbish.
asceticism   discipline achieved through self-denial and following a
   high ideal.
askance   sideways; thus, with distrust.
asperity   roughness or sharpness of temper.
aspiration   an inner drive causing one to seek higher and better things.

assiduous   continuous and careful in attention to duty.
assimilate   to incorporate or to absorb.
atavistic   referring to a reversal to a distant and primitive trait.
austerity   plainness, without anything fancy.

bailiwick   proper place of action; home area.
bait   to torment.
behaviorists   school of psychology holding that psychological theories
   should regard only observable data and should neglect the mind
   and consciousness.
bellicose   warlike.
benefactions   charitable donations.
benefactress   one who gives help or financial assistance.
betimes   early.
billeted   assigned to lodgings.
blandly   gently.
bombastic   using more and larger words than necessary to convey
   clear meaning.
boorish   unmannerly.
bristled   took on an aggressive manner.
brusque   abrupt.

calligraphy   penmanship.
candor   open honesty; frankness.
cantor   a choir director, as Bach was by profession.
capacious   roomy; full of meaning.
capitulate   surrender to the enemy or opponent.
caste   class of society, rigidly observed in India.
Caucasian   member of the white race.
chafe   fret.
cheeky   impudent.
circumspect   discreet and cautious.
cloying   filling or feeding beyond satisfaction, thus going so far as to
   cause disgust.
cohorts   companions in a battle or struggle.
collaboration   working jointly on an intellectual project.
colloquy   conversation.
commissary   a store which supplies equipment or provisions.
compendium   a summary of the main points of a science.
compositor   typesetter.
compost   fertilizer.
concavity   curved indentation.
concession   agreement to give in on a point of an argument.
conciliatory   in a manner to win over; causing to agree.
confabulation   easy-going conversation.

confidante a woman to whom secrets are entrusted (masculine form: confidant).

conjecture guessing.

conjury magic.

connivance passive cooperation.

consort wife or husband.

constituency the voters in a given district.

constituents members of a district represented.

consummate highest; finest; best.

contagion communication of an influence to other hearts and minds.

contemporaries people of the same age, or of the same general time in history.

conventional growing out of tradition or custom.

coquetry flirtatious behavior.

cordon a line or circle of persons around a place.

cordwainer shoemaker.

cortege procession.

countenance facial composure.

courtiers those in attendance at a royal court.

cul-de-sac blind alley; way having no outlet.

currying dressing or combing the coat of a horse.

decorum observance of accepted standards.

decree nisi a legal document granting a divorce, provided some cause for its not being granted does not appear within a certain time after the issuance of the document.

deference courteous regard for another's wishes.

denunciation the pointing out of something or someone as evil.

depreciated declined in value.

deprivations losses; absence of necessities.

derelict unable to assume any responsibility.

despicable worthy of hatred.

desultory jumping from one thing to another.

devoid empty.

diatribes bitter and prolonged discussions.

didoes silly carryings-on.

disabused set right; undeceived.

disinterested not influenced by regard to personal advantage.

disparage to lower verbally in rank; to depreciate.

dissenter one who, through strong principle, takes frequent exception to the popular view.

dissipate to scatter and waste away.

dissociated became disconnected from.

dissolution breaking up.

divest take clothing off.

docilely   with obedience.
dogma   beliefs, especially long-held and conservative beliefs.
dudgeon   ill humor.
durst   dared.

emaciated   lean, very thin from loss of flesh.
embargo   a stoppage by the government.
enhance   to make greater.
equine   pertaining to horses.
eradicate   weed out; pull out by the roots.
essential   ideally perfect and complete.
estranges   keeps at a distance; takes away from.
eulogies   orations of high praise.
evoked   brought forth.
excoriation   stripping the skin off; hence, severe censure.
exorcise   to drive away an evil by use of a holy name.
extraneous   external; outside.
extroverted   having interests centered on external actions and objects;
    interested in others.
exuberant   overflowing; plentiful.

façade   the face or front of anything.
fastidiously   with excessive care.
feline   catlike.
feminist   one who believes in and works for women's rights.
fete   to honor.
flageolet   a flute-like musical instrument.
foppery   foolishness; the folly of seeming too good.
forage   suitable for animal food.
franchise   positive right or privilege; a being empowered to act.
freethinker   one who forms independent decisions.
friable   easily broken up or pulverized, said of soil.
furlough   leave of absence.

galvanized   excited; stimulated.
gerrymanders   patchwork or strung-out political districts; acts of so
    districting areas as to give one party unfair advantage.
ghetto   area of a city to which Jews were restricted traditionally.
grandiloquent   using fancy speech in speaking or writing.
gratuitously   without being called for by circumstances; offered extra.

harrow   to pulverize and smooth the soil; also a farm implement used
    to do that work.
harrowing   vexing, tormenting; extremely distressing.
haze   to taunt or tease.

hostling   caring for horses.
hypothetical   assumed without a proof.

idyll   pleasing interlude of natural charm and simplicity.
illiterate   ignorant or uneducated.
imbued   becoming impressed or penetrated with an idea.
impending   quickly approaching; near.
imperious   commanding; strong with authority.
imperturbably   in a manner not marked by being upset or concerned; serenely.
impetuous   hasty or impulsive in feeling or in action.
implacable   not to be put aside.
implication   an idea implied, or expressed indirectly; something strongly suggested.
implicitly   without question; with complete faith.
import   significance; importance.
impotent   helpless; lacking power.
improvised   off hand; hastily put together.
impulsion   a sudden inclination to act; an impulse.
incendiary   tending to flame up; fiery.
incited   urged on into action.
incompatible   not capable of being together, because of contradictions.
incompetent   unable to handle one's own affairs or responsibilities.
incongruous   having inconsistent qualities; not fitting the circumstances.
incorrigible   incapable of correction or improvement.
incredible   extraordinary; improbable to believe.
incredulity   act of withholding belief; the finding something too much for belief.
indecorum   lack of proper behavior.
indignant   angry because of unjust treatment.
individualism   individual personality considered as the center of power and freedom.
indolence   state of being indisposed to labor.
indomitable   of great endurance; unconquerable.
inebriated   intoxicated with liquor.
ineffaceable   indelible; difficult to erase.
ineradicable   incapable of being erased.
inevitable   unavoidable.
innovations   introductions of new things; new ways of doing things.
inordinate   not kept within reasonable bounds.
insurrection   a rising up against the legal authority in a given area.
interlude   an intervening space or event.
interpose   to place between.

intuitively   naturally, without being told or taught.
irrational   not based on reason; unreasonable.
irrelevant   not connected in importance with the matter at hand.
irrepressible   uncontrollable.
irritant   that which irritates.

khadi   garment of homespun cotton cloth made in India.
kine   cattle.

laconic   concise; saying much in few words.
laving   flowing against; rubbing together, as in washing.
legato   smooth and connected.
legerdemain   sleight of hand; magic.
lithe   pliant and easily bent.
lorry   delivery van; truck.
luminous   shining and full of light.

maledictions   curses; opposite of benedictions.
malodorous   foul smelling.
marathon   a long-distance contest, or an endurance contest.
marauding   roving to raid or to plunder.
mawkish   sickly sentimental.
maxim   a general truth expressed in a few words.
minutiae   small, precise details.
misalliance   an improper or erroneous combination.
musculature   the muscle arrangement, as of the vocal cords, considered as going through the actions of its function.
myriad   of great number.
mystic   of or pertaining to a spiritual experience.

naively   with unaffected simplicity.
nil   nothing.
nirvana   the dying out in the heart of passion, hatred, and delusion. (Buddhism.)
non-committal   characterized by one's refusing to commit himself.
nonpareil   a size of type.
norm   standard pattern.
nostalgia   sentimental longing to return to those things which are past.

obdurate   unyielding and hardhearted.
objective   showing the ability to view events in an impersonal and unbiased manner.
obliquely   inclined to one side; subtly.
obliterated   wiped out; erased.

obliteration an erasing; a blotting out.
obnoxious objectionable; causing great dislike.
obsessed influenced by a fixed idea, to an unreasonable degree.
obstinate holding tightly to a certain opinion or course of action; stubborn.
ominous foretelling something of a bad or evil nature.
opulent-looking wealthy-looking.
oracles persons given to uttering authoritative or wise decisions.
orthodox proper; conservative; expected because generally accepted.
ostentatious showy; overly pretentious.

palatable agreeable to the taste; pleasing.
palaver idle and profuse talk.
pantomime a scene acted out without any speaking.
paradox contradiction.
paradoxically in a contradictory way.
paranoia type of insanity in which the patient thinks that all people are against him.
paraphernalia equipment or apparatus.
parody an imitation done for comic effect.
patron a sponsor.
patter rapid dialogue containing jokes.
perfunctory mechanical and indifferent.
petrification a becoming stonelike with fear or awe.
philanthropic generous; given to helping mankind.
platitudes commonplace statements of obvious and well-known truths.
post-chaise a type of closed carriage, seating from two to four persons.
potential possibility of becoming something greater or finer.
pother fuss and worry.
pragmatism a belief in facts and realities, as opposed to theories.
precarious exposed to hazards; uncertain.
precipitate to hasten; to urge onward.
precipitately hastily.
preoccupied having the attention occupied beforehand.
predecessors ones that came before.
pretext that which is assumed to hide the true reason for an attitude or an action.
privations being without those things which are necessary.
prodigious great in degree or quantity.
prodigy an extraordinary person.
psychoses mental diseases. (singular: psychosis.)
psychosomatic pertaining to bodily disorders induced by one's own mind or imagination.
pyrotechnic resembling fireworks; of the nature of an outburst.

raiment   clothing.
rallied   revived; recovered strength.
raucous   disagreeably hoarse.
reaction   tendency to move in a different direction, as in political thinking one may tend to return to an older order of society.
reasserted   asserted again; reaffirmed.
receptivity   openness to experience and willingness to receive it.
recipient   receiver.
reciprocal   shared by both sides; mutual.
recouped   gained back.
recourse   other way to turn for help.
refurbish   brighten up; make like new again.
relinquished   given up; abandoned.
repercussions   results; reactions to something; echoes.
reprehensible   worthy of blame or reproof.
reprieve   pardon.
reprisals   acts of revenge or retaliation.
reproach   to blame.
repudiated   denied; opposed as false.
reserve   self-restraint.
resonant   ringing and resounding.
revelation   the revealing or uncovering of something new and marvelous.
reverberating   resounding; continuing for a while in force.
reverberations   echoes; continued rumblings.
rhetoric   the art of expressing oneself well in speech or writing.
rigor   strict adherence to a severe program.
rout   complete victory, with the enemy in rapid retreat.

salable   capable of being sold.
salons   receptions in fashionable French homes, or the rooms in which they were held.
salutary   healthful; having or promoting a beneficial outcome.
salve   improve; heal.
sanction   approval.
savor   a distinctive quality, taste, or flavor.
schizophrenics   insane persons who have lost mental contact with their environment.
sedative   calming.
semantics   the science of word meanings.
shrouds   vertical cables, from rail to mast, in a sailing vessel.
Sicilians   inhabitants of Sicily, an island south of Italy; also their descendants.
skeptical   doubtful.
sloos   swamps.

smooch   a farm implement used to crush the soil.
solarium   a sun-room.
solicitations   pleas for acceptance.
soliciting   trying to obtain by asking for.
solicitude   excessive sympathy.
sophistry   deceptively subtle reasoning.
sortie   an attack by besieged troops against the besiegers.
spontaneous   arising from natural feeling without hesitation.
stark   entire; absolute.
strumpets   low women.
subtle   difficult to detect; not obvious.
successively   one after another, without a gap between.
summarily   without delay or formality.
summation   the total accumulation.
superfluous   more than what is necessary; surplus.
supplicating   requesting with humble earnestness.
surliness   rudeness; ill-natured behavior.
surtout   a long, close-fitting overcoat.
swale   a small marshy meadow.

tactically   as a part of one's tactics or plan.
tantalum   a hard, acid-resisting metallic element.
tenacity   holding power; tight-gripping strength; persistence.
tenets   beliefs.
titillating   tickling; causing to laugh.
tongas   light, two-wheeled vehicles. (India.)
transcended   rose above and beyond.
transcendent   going beyond what is presented in one's experience.
transition   passage from one stage or state to another.
transports   fits of delight.
traumatic   pertaining to the condition resulting from a wound, injury, or shock.
tremolo   the rapid repeating of a tone without obvious breaks; quick vibration.
tribunals   courts.
truculent   fierce and savage.

unassertive   not willing to push oneself forward.
unerringly   without mistake; correctly.
unmetaphorical   real; actual.
unprecedented   being without former example.
unscrupulous   without principles.

vacuity   emptiness; void.
valid   well-grounded in fact.

vehemently   with strong feeling; very eager to convince.
veneration   respect combined with awe.
versatile   capable of performing a variety of things.
visceral   internal; proceeding from within.
vitriolic   bitterly uncomplimentary and critical.

woodeny   stiff; with little expression.